& UNIX Integration Guide

About the Authors . . .

Steve Burnett is a technical writer and systems administrator whose interests for the last several years have focused around heterogeneous system integration and modular documentation. A member of USENIX and SAGE, he holds a Master's degree in technical communication from North Carolina State University. Steve was a co-author of Osborn's *Windows NT & UNIX Integration Guide,* and has contributed to other books, including Que's *Using Linux*; *Client/Server Programming With RPC and DCE*; *Using Netscape 2*; *Using Netscape 3*; and *Netscape Starter Kits*. Steve enjoys spending time with his wonderful wife Merrie, listening to music, supporting the conservation efforts of the Duke University Primate Center, and making music on Chapman Stick and theremin. He can be reached at **burnett@pobox.com** if you have corrections, questions, or comments about this book.

David Gunter is an information technology consultant and author based in Cary, North Carolina. In addition to software development, he has been involved with supporting and managing diverse systems and networks for more than 10 years. David has a master's degree in Computer Science from the University of Tennessee. He has worked as both a lead and contributing author on several computer books, including the best-selling *Special Edition Using Linux* series. His other publication credits include Que's *Using Linux*, First, Second, and Third Editions; *Using the Internet*, Third Edition; *Netscape Starter Kit*; *Using Netscape 3*; *Using Netscape 2*; *Client/Server Programming with RPC and DCE*; *Using UNIX*, Second Edition; and *Using Turbo C++ 4.5*. When not writing, consulting, researching, or surfing the Net, David spends as much time as possible with his wonderful wife, their dog, and their two cats.

Lola Gunter is a technical consultant in Cary, North Carolina. She has worked in web and multimedia software development as a computer consultant and as a manager of technical documentation. Her publication credits include the Que titles *Using Linux*, Third Edition; *Using Multimedia ToolBook 3.0*; and *Client/Server Programming with RPC and DCE*. She has a bachelor's degree in computer science from the University of North Carolina at Asheville. In addition to the web and the Internet, her interests include working with stained glass, roughhousing with her German shepherd, and traveling.

WINDOWS 2000 & UNIX Integration Guide

STEVE **BURNETT**
DAVID **GUNTER**
LOLA **GUNTER**

Osborne/**McGraw-Hill**

Berkeley New York St. Louis San Francisco
Auckland Bogotá Hamburg London Madrid
Mexico City Milan Montreal New Delhi Panama City
Paris São Paulo Singapore Sydney
Tokyo Toronto

Osborne/**McGraw-Hill**
2600 Tenth Street
Berkeley, California 94710
U.S.A.

For information on translations or book distributors outside the U.S.A., or to arrange bulk purchase discounts for sales promotions, premiums, or fund-raisers, please contact Osborne/**McGraw-Hill** at the above address.

Windows 2000 & UNIX Integration Guide

1234567890 AGM AGM 019876543210

Book: 0-07-212165-3
CD: 0-07-212166-1
parts of
ISBN 0-07-212167-X

Publisher
Brandon A. Nordin
Associate Publisher, Editor-in-Chief
Scott Rogers
Acquisitions Editor
Megg Bonar
Acquisitions Coordinator
Stephane Thomas
Technical Editor
Mike McClune
Copy Editor
Robert Campbell
Proofreader
Stefany Otis
Indexer
Valerie Perry
Computer Designers
Elizabeth Jang
Lauren McCarthy
Dick Schwartz
Illustrators
Robert Hansen
Michael Mueller
Beth Young
Series Design
Peter Hancik
Cover Design
Will Voss

This book was composed with Corel VENTURA™ Publisher.

To Merrie: Thanks again. I love you.
—-Steve

AT A GLANCE

CONTENTS

ACKNOWLEDGMENTS

First, I'd like to thank David and Lola Gunter, who authored two-thirds of the first edition between them. This second edition would have been more difficult to complete and poorer in quality without the foundation of their excellent original material from the first edition. Next, I'd like to thank Megg Bonar, Stephane Thomas, and Wendy Rinaldi of Osborne, who collectively provided great assistance in coordinating this project. A very special thanks as well to Osborne's fantastic Production crew for their work on the layout and illustration—and my gratitude to anyone else at Osborne who worked on this book project, whether or not we ever corresponded. Mike McCune's work as technical editor was also helpful. I can't leave out the amazing-as-usual work of my agent, David Fugate, in coordinating everyone smoothly. Jack Tackett's contribution to this edition also deserves mention.

Leland Wallace and Jacob Frelinger made numerous constructive comments and suggestions during the writing of this book. Jay Cuthrell and Brandon Reinhart each provided a much-needed emergency source of screenshots when my test platform destabilized again. Gary Tyreman of Hummingbird Communications also offered excellent and appreciated advice on short notice, as did James Clark. Dr. Thomas Martini provided the means for me to finish an important part of this project. Thanks to my great co-workers at webslingerZ; with their help, I had the flexibility to respond to the project's schedule. Finally and most importantly, my wife Merrie remained tolerant and supportive when the schedule interrupted our plans on several occasions.

CHAPTER 1

The Roles of UNIX and Windows in the Modern Network

Microsoft holds the lion's share of the PC operating system market, and is rapidly making inroads into the high-end workstation market, the traditional bastion of UNIX. For this reason, there is an increasing need to integrate Microsoft Windows systems with UNIX systems in a heterogeneous environment. Traditionally, administering Windows systems has required very different sets of skills from those required to administer UNIX systems, with each camp unaware of the services and software available to the other. This book is a guide to help each side of the UNIX/NT environment understand the other.

INTEGRATING WINDOWS AND UNIX

In this book, we'll discuss Windows and UNIX integration issues and present "real world" solutions to common problems. In addition, we'll cover a sampling of both commercial and freeware products that can be used to implement integration solutions.

The book deals with more than just the boundary where UNIX and Windows meet. Some sections discuss equivalent tools on UNIX and Windows platforms, such as sendmail on UNIX and Exchange on Windows. Other sections address how to share resources or file system services between UNIX and Windows. We present real problems and issues that you are likely to encounter.

Every environment is different. You might have a Windows network and decide you want to add a UNIX server to handle mail, news, and Internet access for performance or security reasons. You might have a mixed environment of UNIX and Windows workstations to meet the varying demands of your users for system performance or software tools. Or, you might primarily be running a Microsoft shop that is just getting into UNIX development and integration. Regardless, there are lots of issues where Windows and UNIX come together.

Who Is This Book For?

If you are an intermediate or advanced system or network professional who is responsible for creating and managing a mixed network of UNIX and Windows systems, this book is for you. It's intended for people who work as administrators with either UNIX or Windows, have user-level knowledge of the other platform, and find themselves needing to integrate the two. This includes the UNIX system administrator who now needs to include Windows workstations in the company network, as well as the Windows administrator who needs to add UNIX workstations to his or her Windows network.

Since we're targeting both types of system administrators, you may see some rudimentary material in some of the chapters. Remember that there are different levels of administrators with different backgrounds. So, if some information is a bit basic for you, just skip over it and head on to the good stuff!

What Is This Book About?

In this book, we'll explore issues you're likely to encounter when integrating UNIX and Windows. We'll discuss a variety of topics that are critical in successfully managing an integrated network. These include issues you might encounter on either platform, and some that are unique to either Windows or UNIX. We'll cover Windows-specific issues, UNIX-specific issues, and integration solutions where we can.

Think of this book as a toolkit containing products, components, and techniques, plus the information you need to help you make Windows and UNIX work together in an office environment. In addition to the information within these pages, the book includes a CD-ROM containing shareware, freeware, and commercial demo products designed to assist with UNIX/Windows integration, tools, and a selection of useful FAQs. Specific topics that we cover include:

- **Windows file services on UNIX** Discussion of the types of file services and browsing capabilities supported by Windows. This discussion emphasizes the Samba product for providing Windows file services via UNIX. It includes sections for installing, configuring, and troubleshooting Samba. (See Chapter 2.)
- **UNIX file services on Windows** Introduction to the types of file services supported by UNIX. This includes discussion of the NFS filesharing protocol, with emphasis on providing UNIX file services via Windows, as well as discussion of both commercial and freeware NFS products, and how to use them to provide UNIX file services from Windows computers. (See Chapter 3.)
- **Backups in a mixed environment** Introduction to the various file system types, backup strategies, and tools that are applicable in an integrated network. This includes discussion of commercial tools such as Legato Networker. (See Chapter 4.)
- **Mail services with SMTP** Introduction to electronic mail. This includes discussion of UNIX sendmail architecture and configuration, discussion of basic Windows Exchange configuration, and UNIX-to-Exchange mailbox migration. (See Chapter 5.)
- **Mixed printing environments** Discussion of the various printing environments in Windows and UNIX. This covers integration issues and techniques, implications for user clients, and commercial solutions, such as Network Instruments' NIPrint, an lpr and lpd client for Windows. (See Chapter 6.)
- **Networking Windows and UNIX** Introduction to problems and protocols that you may encounter when networking Windows and UNIX. Discussion includes the Windows Internet Name System (WINS); dynamic TCP/IP configuration using DHCP, including advantages and disadvantages; and specific protocol information, including NetBT. (See Chapter 7.)

- **Scripting Windows** Discussion of the command-line functions in Windows 2000 and its built-in scripting capabilities, as well as other scripting languages including Perl, Python, and Tcl/Tk. (See Chapter 8.)
- **DNS configuration** Discussion of the Domain Name System: its purpose and its function. Configuration information includes examples for both Windows and UNIX. (See Chapter 9.)
- **Remote Access Service** Introduction to Remote Access Service (RAS). Learn here about configuration and management, setting up remote dialing, using RAS for Internet access, and routing IP via Windows. Discussion of the PPTP protocol also appears here. (See Chapter 10.)
- **Microsoft Internet Information Server** Introduction to the Microsoft IIS server. Installation and configuration comments and advice for IIS under Windows are included. (See Chapter 11.)
- **UNIX Web servers** Introduction to UNIX-based web servers. Installation and configuration information is included for Apache under UNIX. (See Chapter 12.)
- **Other Internet servers** Discussion of Internet services such as Usenet news and the web. Platform-specific implementation details are provided for protocols and servers including NNTP, FTP, and HTTP. (See Chapter 13.)
- **Linux** The phenomenon of the Linux operating system, its history, and its rapid expansion into the business world, as well as specific advice for integrating Linux with Windows. (See Chapter 14.)
- **Desktop applications** Introduction to cross-platform desktop applications. See this topic for discussion of X Window-based applications and UNIX utilities for Windows, such as Hummingbird's eXceed; Windows emulators and mirroring software on UNIX hardware; and other GUI solutions such as Citrix WinFrame. (See Chapter 15.)
- **System and network management** General system management advice. Look here for descriptions of Windows 2000 Server's built-in tools, as well as protocols (SNMP, MIBs, JMAPI, WBEM), the Network Computer (NC) and its implications, and web-based interfaces and Java-based management trends in systems and network management tools. (See Chapter 16.)
- **Common Desktop Environment (CDE)** Frequently asked questions about the Common Desktop Environment, a standard desktop interface for UNIX that provides services to end users, systems administrators, and application developers. (This section of the book is reprinted from the website **http://www.laxmi.net/cde.htm**, with permission from authors Aditya Talwar and Vivek Arora. See Appendix A.)
- **Server Message Block (SMB)** Instructions for using the Server Message Block protocol to share printers and other system resources between Windows-based and Linux-based environments. (These instructions are reprinted with permission of the author, David Wood, whom you can reach at **dwood@plugged.net.au**. See Appendix B.)

- **sendmail** Frequently asked questions about sendmail, an Internet mail platform for electronic communications, applications, and services. (This section of the book is reprinted from the website **http://sendmail.org/**, with permission from the Sendmail Consortium. See Appendix C.)

What This Book Is Not About...

Integration encompasses a great many topics. Alas, this book doesn't cover them all. Although we do cover a great deal of material, there's plenty more to know. Here is a series of topics that this book *does not* address. If you need these questions answered, you'll want to look elsewhere:

- Developing cross-platform software for UNIX and Windows
- Porting UNIX software to Windows or vice-versa
- Setting up a UNIX or Windows network from scratch

DUELING OPERATING SYSTEMS?

UNIX and Windows grew up in different ways and, as a result, have played different roles in the modern office network. Whereas UNIX primarily came from the minicomputer and engineering realm, Windows has a history rooted in the personal computer world.

These two operating systems have very different histories and legacies. You will find that many system administrators are extremely opinionated about one system or the other. Windows administrators will complain that UNIX is old, is outdated, and has cryptic commands. UNIX administrators complain that Windows is unreliable, doesn't scale well, and is a Microsoft product. The amusing thing is that both sides are at least partially correct.

The History of UNIX

UNIX was developed in the late 1960s. Since that time, it has evolved into the predominant enterprise operating system, providing a reliable and stable multitasking, multiprocessing, and multiuser environment.

One of the reasons for UNIX's current popularity among workstation vendors is its portability. It has a layered architecture and is written in a relatively architecture-neutral language. These features, and relatively cheap source-code availability, have made UNIX an excellent choice for many vendors looking for a fast way to get an operating system on their new hardware.

The History of Windows

Microsoft began shipping Windows NT in 1993. Prior to that, Microsoft and IBM were jointly developing OS/2. Microsoft believed, however, that OS/2 would not have long to live if it couldn't keep up with new hardware, and so began its own project independent of IBM to produce a more portable version of OS/2 that could be moved quickly between different hardware platforms. This was the NT, or *New Technology*, project. The NT project became Windows NT as Microsoft abandoned the OS/2 effort.

Early releases of Windows NT were buggy. With Windows NT 4.0, however, Microsoft began to make headway into traditional UNIX territory, and the company has continued to attempt to improve scalability and reliability, as well as add features and capabilities found in the server market. Microsoft has set out to develop an integrated solution for businesses that includes file and print services, communication services, applications, and intranet and Internet services.

Windows provides a wide selection of features typically found in workstation or mainframe operating systems, including:

- A robust file system
- Multiprotocol networking
- Distributed file system support
- Distributed system management
- Access control list-based security

UNIX Networking

UNIX grew up in the engineering world. Because of its speed, power, and flexibility, it has been the operating system of choice for businesses that need to move mission-critical applications from mainframes. Because most commercial versions of UNIX are produced by companies that also sell workstation hardware, UNIX has traditionally found its place in the high-performance computing market. Table 1-1 lists some of the traditional roles that UNIX has filled in the business arena.

Windows Networking

Unlike UNIX, Windows 2000 grew out of the IBM personal computer platform. Windows' goal in life is to be Microsoft's workstation-quality operating system. Unlike UNIX, Microsoft Windows 2000 has its roots in the personal computing arena, with much more emphasis on graphical user interfaces and desktop applications. Microsoft is expanding the role of Windows into arenas typically associated with servers. It's important to note here that the Windows 2000 family has evolved from what was originally intended to be Windows NT 5, and thus has no association with the Windows 95 or 98 operating system.

The Windows 2000 family consists of four different products:

- Windows 2000 Professional
- Windows 2000 Server
- Windows 2000 Advanced Server
- Windows 2000 Datacenter Server

Role	Description
Heavy-duty I/O	Applications that require high I/O bandwidth, such as databases, commonly use a UNIX implementation platform. Most versions of UNIX run on custom hardware and are capable of offering higher-performance I/O bandwidth.
Multitasking server	UNIX is a multitasking operating system designed to make it easy to work with multiple processes.
Web server	UNIX has long been the de facto operating system for Internet applications, including web servers. Today UNIX is still the most popular platform for the Internet *and* the web.
SMTP server	Electronic mail via SMTP has commonly resided on UNIX systems. Many organizations use UNIX as their primary mail server because of its power and reliability.
News server	As with web servers, Usenet news is commonly implemented via NNTP servers running on UNIX platforms.
File server	Given large amounts of disk space, UNIX servers can make very effective file servers for both application and user directories.
Database server	Large-scale, heavy-duty commercial databases are very common in the UNIX world. Commercial products such as Oracle, Sybase, and Informix all operate under multiple versions of UNIX.
CPU-intensive applications	Desktop UNIX workstations are commonly used in engineering and design, because they provide the optimum platform for CPU-intensive applications such as CAD and CAM.

Table 1-1. Traditional Roles of UNIX Servers

Windows 2000 Professional is intended as the successor to Windows NT 4 Workstation, the general use workstation operating system. The members of the Windows 2000 Server trio are all intended to act as servers, but with increasing degrees of scalability, as well as support for increased amounts of memory, failover, and other features.

NOTE: Microsoft provides a more detailed overview of the Windows 2000 platform family on the web at **http://www.microsoft.com/windows2000/guide/platform/overview/default.asp**.

In today's network, you might find Windows 2000 providing SQL Server database support, or providing electronic mail or file services via Exchange. Other common uses for Windows 2000 servers are as file, application, and print servers for PC desktop workstations running some Windows variant. Microsoft is making inroads to the web server market with its Internet Information Server, but UNIX still dominates in this area.

More and more companies are adopting Windows 2000 for both server and client platforms, but they do have concerns. Many information systems managers are concerned with Windows' scalability and robustness. Others are hesitant to wholeheartedly adopt "the Microsoft way": The difficulties and lack of information that hinder integration of non-Microsoft systems and services with existing systems often mean a transition to, rather than a coexistence with, Windows.

Advantages and Disadvantages of Integration

Nowadays, distinctions between the two operating systems are starting to blur as Windows begins to mature as a product. Mixed environments are becoming increasingly common. Through integration, businesses can leverage the operating system strengths that best suit their needs. For example, a UNIX server might provide your Internet backbone—serving as the web server platform and providing a news and e-mail gateway. Some people might run Windows 95, 98, NT, or 2000 workstations within a Windows network. UNIX users in the same network might use applications like Microsoft Word or Microsoft Project (located on a Windows NT or 2000 server) on their workstations by running Citrix's WinDD and sharing files exported via NFS from a Windows workstation or via Samba. Neither operating system is the perfect solution for all situations. You need to carefully evaluate which operating system, or combination of services from different operating systems, will serve you better.

SUMMARY

So where do you go from here? UNIX and Windows both seem to be facts of life in today's office network. Although they evolved from very different backgrounds, both operating systems overlap in the services that they now provide.

Your goal, as a system administrator, is to implement effective strategies for maximizing your computing resources. If you are running a mixed network with both Windows and UNIX systems, the chances are that you will want to develop some type of interoperability—and that you are much more familiar with one of these two operating systems than you are with the other.

In this book, we attempt to present ideas and solutions to help you succeed at integrating your Windows and UNIX environments. Here we will address some of the most common problems and concerns that you may encounter—and we'll give you the workable solutions you need.

CHAPTER 2

NT File Services on UNIX

UNIX and Windows NT have taken different routes as they have become common operating systems in today's computing environment. Now, however, it is somewhat normal for a UNIX system administrator to be handed a few NT workstations to manage, or for an NT/PC support group to be charged with designing networks and supporting UNIX workstations.

Faced with such a mixed environment, the creative systems administrator will look for ways to get Windows NT and UNIX working together to maximize system resources and user productivity. One way to accomplish this is to provide cross-platform file services and print services from your servers.

CROSS-PLATFORM SERVICES TO THE RESCUE

Cross-platform file services maximize the usefulness of your file servers by allowing connections between clients that run different operating systems. Similarly, cross-platform print services allow the maximum number of users to access your printers, even if not all of those users work in the same operating environment.

In this chapter, we will look at the issue of cross-platform file services—specifically, providing Windows NT-accessible file services from a UNIX platform. We will look at some of the issues involved with mixing different file systems, review the common network protocols involved, and explore some of the tools that are available to facilitate UNIX-to-NT file system services.

NOTE: In case you are wondering, cross-platform file services work both ways. In addition to UNIX providing file services for Windows NT, an NT server can be used to provide UNIX-accessible file services as well. (Chapter 3 will give you more information about UNIX file services on Windows NT servers.)

INTRODUCTION TO SMB

Let's assume, for the sake of this chapter, that you have a group of UNIX servers that provide file services and application services for desktop UNIX workstations. Then, out of the blue, you find yourself having to support Microsoft clients as well. The reasons why don't particularly matter. In fact, no one probably consulted you at all before installing Windows NT; they just expect you to make it work!

In this situation, an effective solution could be to make your UNIX systems act as servers for the NT systems. In order to do this, you first need to make the two systems communicate. To make them communicate, you need to know a little about SMB.

SMB is an abbreviation for the *Server Message Block* protocol, which is the standard protocol that Windows NT uses for sharing file and print services. It was designed as a protocol for sharing files, printers, and ports between computers. It also supports sharing of communications elements, such as mail slots and named pipes. It was first developed by Microsoft and Intel as the Open-NET File Sharing Protocol, which was released in 1987.

SMB operates in a request-response fashion, wherein the client sends requests, contained in Server Message Blocks (SMBs), to the server. The server receives these SMBs, interprets them, and sends a response back to the client. Whenever a computer shares a resource over the network via SMB, it becomes a server in this scenario. When a computer attaches to a shared resource, it becomes a client. In Windows 2000, it is possible to act as both a server and a client simultaneously. SMB communication takes place by means of the NetBIOS interface, which can operate over a variety of protocols, and although Windows 2000 no longer requires NetBIOS, it can be added for legacy support.

NOTE: In a mixed NT and UNIX environment, the most common use of NetBIOS is called NetBIOS over TCP/IP, also known as NetBT. (For more information on NetBIOS and NetBT, see Chapter 7.)

Once a client connects to a server and is authenticated, the client can proceed to send commands to the server to open files, read and write files, close files, delete files, search directories, and execute other file and directory commands. These commands are encapsulated in specially formatted SMBs. There are different formats of SMBs to handle the different commands available. In addition, the SMB protocol has evolved into different protocol variants.

The SMB protocol provides two levels of security in its security models. The first security model supported by SMB is *share-level security.* Under the share-level security model, shared resources, known as *shares,* can be assigned a password. Knowing the password will grant a user access to the share. The second type of SMB security is known as *user-level security.* With user-level security, access protections are applied to individual files, and access rights are determined on a per-user basis. A user must be authenticated by the share server and assigned a numeric user ID. This user ID is then compared to the access protections assigned to each file.

CIFS—COMMON INTERNET FILE SYSTEM

Microsoft, the original developer of SMB, is busy cranking out a new and improved file and print sharing protocol. The *Common Internet File System* (CIFS) is designed to be a viable alternative to Sun's WebNFS protocol and to support file and printer sharing over the World Wide Web.

CIFS has several advantages over SMB, with support for TCP/IP and DNS being among the most visible. Under CIFS, server names are actually DNS names, complete with host and domain components. This change moves CIFS away from the limited NetBIOS name structure, where no domain information is available, thus getting rid of the need for WINS servers. CIFS also supports such developments as Unicode filenames for internationalization, as well as the extended file attributes found in most modern file systems.

CIFS has not yet been widely adopted. Microsoft has offered it to the Internet Engineering Task Force as a draft standard, and many vendors have pledged support for this protocol. Currently, however, the two sides of the UNIX-to-NT file-sharing coin remain SMB and NFS.

INTRODUCTION TO SAMBA

In order to provide NT-native file system support and print sharing from a UNIX file server to NT workstations, you must find a way to convince UNIX to provide SMB protocol support. One of the easiest ways to provide file and print sharing is with the Samba package. Samba, developed in Australia by Andrew Tridgell, is an SMB server package that runs under UNIX. Using Samba, UNIX systems can create shares that can be used by Windows-based computers. Samba also provides tools that allow UNIX users to attach to shares from Windows computers, and to transfer files.

NOTE: In addition to running on UNIX servers, Samba also runs under VMS, NetWare, and OS/2.

Samba runs on many different varieties of UNIX. Currently, Samba is available for the following operating systems:

- SunOS
- Solaris 2.2 and above
- Linux, with and without shadow passwords
- SVR4
- ULTRIX
- OSF/1 (Compaq DEC Alpha only)
- OSF/1 with NIS and Fast Crypt (DEC Alpha only)
- OSF/1 V2.0 Enhanced Security (DEC Alpha only)
- AIX
- BSDI
- NetBSD
- Sequent
- HP-UX
- SGI, including IRIX 4.*x.x* and IRIX 5.*x.x*
- FreeBSD
- NeXT 3.2 and above
- NeXT OS 2.*x*
- NeXT OS 3.0
- ISC SVR3V4 in POSIX mode
- ISC SVR3V4 in iBCS2 mode
- A/UX 3.0

- SCO with shadow passwords
- SCO with shadow passwords, without YP
- SCO with TCB passwords
- SCO 3.2v2 (ODT 1.1) with TCP passwords
- Intergraph
- DGUX
- Apollo Domain/OS sr10.3 (BSD4.3)

With this many operating systems supported, chances are that a version is available for your particular type of UNIX. Samba is freely available under the terms of the GNU Public License and can be downloaded from the primary Samba website at **http://samba.anu.edu.au/samba/**. This site is an excellent source for Samba-related information, documentation, and mailing lists, as well.

Before you dismiss Samba as yet another free software solution and head off in search of "real" software, consider how many people are using Samba. The Samba website has a survey that lists many of the Samba installations around the world. For example, Bank of America has about 1,200 Samba hosts, providing services to 15,000 clients!

COMPILING AND INSTALLING SAMBA

The first step in setting up a Samba server is to download the Samba software. Fire up your favorite web browser and head down under to the closest Samba mirror site, listed at the main Samba website, located at **http://samba.anu.edu.au/samba/**. From here, you will find links to the source distribution, as well as to the various binary distributions. Samba is available in precompiled binary format for a variety of UNIX systems. However, most system administrators will probably prefer to download the source distribution and custom-build Samba to meet their needs. This way, you know that no one did strange things to your code, and you have the source on hand if you need to make modifications, patches, or enhancements.

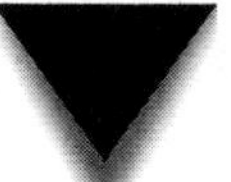

TIP: If you use Red Hat Linux or a system that uses the Red Hat Package Manager (RPM) , such as Caldera's OpenLinux, then you can install the source package and compile from there. You can also simply install the RPM if you trust the package.

Put the source distribution in its own directory on your system, preferably wherever you keep source distributions for other packages, and extract it from the archive file that you downloaded. Once you have unarchived the distribution, you should see a directory named something like samba-1.9.16p11. Change into this directory and you're ready to start building the distribution.

NOTE: For detailed instructions on how to install Samba, consult the file INSTALL.TXT that comes with the Samba distribution.

Editing the Makefile

The first step in building the distribution is to configure the file that controls the build process, known as the *Makefile*. Change directory to the source directory, make a backup copy of this file, and then edit the original with your favorite UNIX text editor.

At the top of the Makefile, you will see some configuration lines like these:

```
# The directories to put things in. If you use multiple
# architectures or share the samba binaries across NFS then
# you will probably want to change this layout.
BASEDIR = /usr/local/samba
BINDIR = $(BASEDIR)/bin
SBINDIR = $(BASEDIR)/bin
LIBDIR = $(BASEDIR)/lib
VARDIR = $(BASEDIR)/var
```

The information in these lines determines where Samba is installed. By default, Samba is installed in the /usr/local/samba directory. If you need it to be installed somewhere else, change the value of the BASEDIR variable. For example, if you wanted to install Samba in /usr/local/utils/samba instead, you would edit BASEDIR to be

```
BASEDIR = /usr/local/utils/samba
```

NOTE: Lines starting with the # character in the Makefile are comments; they are ignored during the build process.

In addition to the line changing the base directory where Samba is installed, several additional lines allow you to change where specific files are installed. Simply read through the first page or so of the Makefile to find the appropriate entries. The comments are very helpful.

Once you have decided where to install Samba, you need to configure the Makefile so that it compiles for your particular version of UNIX. As you scroll down through the Makefile, you will see sections for several different operating systems, all commented out, similar to these:

```
# This is for SUNOS 4. Use the SUNOS5 entry for Solaris 2.
# Note that you cannot use Sun's "cc" compiler
# as it's not an Ansi-C compiler. Get gcc or acc.
# Note that if you have adjunct passwords you may need the GETPWANAM
# or PWDAUTH option. There have been reports that using
# PWDAUTH may crash your pwdauthd server so GETPWANAM is preferable
# (and probably faster)
```

```
# contributed by Andrew.Tridgell@anu.edu.au
# FLAGSM = -DSUNOS4
# LIBSM =
# AWK = nawk

# Use this for Linux with shadow passwords
# contributed by Andrew.Tridgell@anu.edu.au
# add -DLINUX_BIGCRYPT if you have shadow passwords
# but don't have the
# right libraries and includes
# FLAGSM = -DLINUX -DSHADOW_PWD
# LIBSM = -lshadow

# Use this for Linux without shadow passwords
# contributed by Andrew.Tridgell@anu.edu.au
# AXPROC defines DEC Alpha Processor
# FLAGSM = -DLINUX -DAXPROC
# FLAGSM = -DLINUX
# LIBSM =

# Use this for Linux with shadow passwords and quota
# contributed by xeno@mix.hive.no
# Tested on the 1.3.57 kernel and ext2fs filesystem.
# Notes:
# /usr/include/sys/quota.h must be a symlink to
# /usr/include/linux/quota.h
# The directory quota here must be a symlink to your quota package.
# I just do 'ln -sf /usr/src/quota-1.50 quota' in this directory to
# get it to work.
# FLAGSM = -O3 -m486 -DLINUX -DSHADOW_PWD -DQUOTAS
# LIBSM = -lshadow

# This is for SUNOS5.4 and later (also known as Solaris 2.4 and
# later)
# contributed by Andrew.Tridgell@anu.edu.au
# FLAGSM = -DSUNOS5 -DSHADOW_PWD -DNETGROUP
# LIBSM = -lsocket -lnsl
# AWK = nawk
```

This is only a sample of the configuration entries in the Samba Makefile. There is an entry for each operating system that Samba supports. To configure the Samba installation for your particular version of UNIX, find the appropriate section and uncomment the configuration flags. For example, if we were installing on a Linux system without shadow passwords running on an Intel processor, we would modify the comments in the following section of the Makefile:

```
# Use this for Linux without shadow passwords
# contributed by Andrew.Tridgell@anu.edu.au
# AXPROC defines DEC Alpha Processor
# FLAGSM = -DLINUX -DAXPROC
FLAGSM = -DLINUX
LIBSM =
```

Similarly, if we were installing on a Sun running Solaris 2.4 or later, we would use the following section instead:

```
# This is for SUNOS5.4 and later (also known as Solaris 2.4 and
# later)
# contributed by Andrew.Tridgell@anu.edu.au
FLAGSM = -DSUNOS5 -DSHADOW_PWD -DNETGROUP
LIBSM = -lsocket -lnsl
AWK = nawk
```

CAUTION: Make sure that you only enable one operating system section of the Makefile, as Samba will not build correctly if multiple sections are uncommented. If you do uncomment multiple sections, and Samba manages to build, it may behave unpredictably.

Building Samba

After you have modified the Makefile so that you can build Samba for your particular version of UNIX, simply issue the make command at the UNIX prompt to build the Samba distribution. You will see a lot of messages produced by the compiler during the build process. If you have trouble with the build, or you just want to keep a record of the build messages for reference, you can capture the output to a file with the command

```
# make | tee /usr/local/samba/buildlog.txt
```

After Samba compiles and links, you can install Samba by issuing the make install command. You need to be logged in as root in order to issue install Samba. The make install command copies the various pieces of the Samba distribution to their proper locations in your file system, and it installs the Samba man (short for manual) pages in the appropriate directories.

NOTE: If you are a bit paranoid about running install scripts blindly, rest assured that most versions of UNIX allow you to see what the make install command will do before actually doing it. If your version of make supports the –n option, you can type **make –n install.** This will cause make to go through the steps of the installation process and print out what it is doing, without actually doing anything.

At this point you should have a basic Samba configuration installed. The next step in the process is to configure Samba for your particular environment.

CONFIGURING SAMBA

Before you can use Samba as an NT file service provider, you have to configure it properly. When you configure Samba, you set its operational parameters, create entries for the directories that you want to share, and make network printers available. Samba configuration also enables you to establish user access permissions for shares.

Virtually all parts of the Samba configuration process are managed by a central configuration file called smb.conf. If you chose to install Samba in its default location, the file should be located in the /usr/local/samba/lib directory. The file is in ASCII format and is editable by your favorite UNIX text editor.

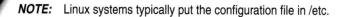

NOTE: Linux systems typically put the configuration file in /etc.

The syntax of the smb.conf file is pretty straightforward. The file is broken into sections, with the section names in square brackets. Within each section, parameters are set by statements in a *name = value* format. The easiest way to get familiar with the Samba configuration file is to work through the details of one. The following listing shows a sample smb.conf file:

```
[global]
   printing = bsd
   printcap name = /etc/printcap
   load printers = yes
   guest account = pcguest
;  This next option sets a separate log file for each client. Remove
;  it if you want a combined log file.
   log file = /usr/local/samba/log.%m
;  You will need a world readable lock directory
;  and "share modes=yes"
;  if you want to support the file sharing modes for multiple users
;  of the same files
;  lock directory = /usr/local/samba/var/locks
;  share modes = yes

[homes]
   comment = Home Directories
   browseable = no
   read only = no
   create mode = 0750
```

```
[printers]
   comment = All Printers
   browseable = no
   printable = yes
   public = no
   writable = no
   create mode = 0700

; you might also want this one, notice that it is
; read only so as not to give
; people without an account write access.
;
; [tmp]
;   comment = Temporary file space
;   path = /tmp
;   read only = yes
;   public = yes
;
; Other examples.
;
; A private printer, usable only by fred. Spool data
; will be placed in fred's
; home directory. Note that fred must have
; write access to the spool directory,
; wherever it is.
[fredsprn]
   comment = Fred's Printer
   valid users = fred
   path = /homes/fred
   printer = freds_printer
   public = no
   writable = no
   printable = yes
;
; A private directory, usable only by fred.
; Note that fred requires write
; access to the directory.
[fredsdir]
   comment = Fred's Service
   path = /usr/somewhere/private
   valid users = fred
   public = no
   writable = yes
   printable = no
;
```

```
; A publicly accessible directory, but read only,
; except for people in the staff group
[public]
   comment = Public Stuff
   path = /usr/somewhere/public
   public = yes
   writable = no
   printable = no
   write list = @staff
;
; a service which has a different directory for each
; machine that connects this allows you to tailor configurations
; to incoming machines. You could also use the %u option to
; tailor it by username. The %m gets replaced with the machine
; name that is connecting.
[pchome]
  comment = PC Directories
  path = /usr/pc/%m
  public = no
  writable = yes
;
;
; A publicly accessible directory, read/write to all users.
; Note that all files created in the directory by users will
; be owned by the default user, so any user with access can
; delete any other user's files. Obviously this
; directory must be writable by the default user. Another user
; could of course be specified, in which case all files would be
; owned by that user instead.
[public]
   path = /usr/somewhere/else/public
   public = yes
   only guest = yes
   writable = yes
   printable = no
;
;
; The following two entries demonstrate how to share a
; directory so that two users can place files there that
; will be owned by the specific users. In this setup, the
; directory should be writable by both users and should have
; the sticky bit set on it to prevent abuse. Obviously this
; could be extended to as many users as required.
[myshare]
   comment = Mary's and Fred's stuff
```

```
   path = /usr/somewhere/shared
   valid users = mary fred
   public = no
   writable = yes
   printable = no
   create mask = 0765
```

Special Sections

In addition to the custom sections that control access to shares, the smb.conf file has three special sections, [global], [homes], and [printers]. Let's look at these first.

Global Section

The [global] section is used to configure parameters that apply to the server as a whole, and to provide defaults for other sections. Take a look at the [global] section from the previous sample configuration file:

```
[global]
   printing = bsd
   printcap name = /etc/printcap
   load printers = yes
   guest account = pcguest
;  This next option sets a separate log file for each client. Remove
;  it if you want a combined log file.
   log file = /usr/local/samba/log.%m
```

The first entry tells Samba what type of printing subsystem is available on your UNIX system. Different versions of UNIX handle printing differently. The second line lets Samba know where the printer characteristics are defined. The load printers = yes line tells Samba to go ahead and load all the printers in the printcap file so that they are available for browsing. The next line specifies a username for a guest account entry. This username is used to authenticate guests for services that allow guest users to connect. On some systems, this can be set to the username nobody; however, on other systems, the nobody user will not be able to print. This username typically shows up in the password file as a valid, nonprivileged user that is not able to log in. The last line in the [global] section sets access logging with a log file for each client that connects. The %m parameter in the log filename will be replaced with the client name, so that there will be a separate log file for each client.

Homes Section

The [homes] section allows clients to connect to a user's home directory, without having a specific entry for the directory in the smb.conf file. When a service request is made, the rest of the smb.conf file is searched to find the specific service that was requested. If the service is not found, and the [homes] section is present, the password file is searched to find the home directory for the user. Samba then makes the user's home directory available as a share by cloning the [homes] section entry. Here is a sample [homes] entry:

```
[homes]
   comment = Home Directories
   browseable = no
   read only = no
   create mode = 0750
```

The comment field is used by a client attempting to see what shares are available on this server. The next parameter controls whether Samba will display home directories in the network browse list. The read only parameter controls whether a user will be able to create and change files in their home directory. The create mode parameter sets the file permissions for a user's home directory. In this case, permission is set to read/write/execute for the user, and read/execute for group access.

NOTE: UNIX file permissions can be represented in octal format as well as alphabetic format. (For more information on permissions, see the man page for the UNIX chmod command.)

Printers Section

The [printers] section is used in a manner similar to the [homes] section. If the [printers] section is present, a user can connect to any printer defined in the UNIX host's /etc/printcap file, even if the printer does not have a service entry in the smb.conf file. Take a look at the [printers] section from the previous sample configuration file:

```
[printers]
   comment = All Printers
   browseable = no
   printable = yes
   public = no
   writable = no
   create mode = 0700
```

Some of these parameters will look familiar from the other two special sections we have just discussed. The comment, browsable, and create mode parameters are the same as you've just seen. The printable parameter simply tells Samba that this is a printer resource that you can print to. Setting the public parameter to "no" disables guest access and prevents unauthorized users from printing to printers on your system. The writable parameter is set to "no" because this is a printer resource, not a file system resource.

If you have problems with the stair step effect, such as this:

```
This is line one.
                 This is line two.
                                  This is line three.
```

Then make sure you have load printers=yes in your [printers] section. This should be all you need to make sure no weirdness is associated with the lpr command.

Here's an example [printers] section just for reference:

```
# NOTE: If you have a BSD-style print system there is no need to
# specifically define each individual printer
[printers]
   comment = All Printers
   path = /var/spool/samba
   browseable = no
# Set public = yes to allow user 'guest account' to print
   guest ok = no
   writable = no
   printable = yes
```

The other thing to check is whether there is a way to configure your Windows machine to send CR/LF instead of just LF. You also might look at /var/spool/lpd/lpl/printfilter and see if you see any mention of stair stepping.

Sharing File Systems

Once you've set up your system defaults for general operation, home directories, and printing, you can move on to setting up shared directories. Configuring a share with Samba is very easy: simply add a new section for the share you want to create, and fill in the parameters. There are many different parameter options that you can provide when creating shares, depending on how you wish to limit access, browsing, permissions, and so on.

NOTE: For a complete list of all the parameters allowed in the smb.conf file, see the man page for smb.conf.

Let's look at a couple of examples of creating a share. In the first example, we are going to create a shared directory that is only accessible by one user.

```
[testshare]
   comment = A Sample Test Share
   path = /usr/local/private
   valid users = skippy
   browseable = yes
   public = no
   writable = yes
   printable = no
```

You've seen a lot of these parameters before, from reading about the special sections in the Samba configuration file, so we won't bore you to death going over them again. The two new lines that are particularly interesting are the path = /usr/local/private line and the valid users = skippy line. The path parameter tells Samba which directory to make available as a network share; in this case, it is the /usr/local/private directory. The valid users parameter is used to restrict access to a particular user on the system.

Let's look at one more share definition, for completeness.

```
[public]
   comment = Public Stuff
   path = /usr/local/public
   public = yes
   writable = no
   printable = no
   write list = @staff
```

This particular share definition creates a share named "public" that is designed to be readable by anyone, with only users in the staff group having write access. When you set the public parameter to yes, Samba allows guest access to this account, with no write access. However, the write list parameter allows you to create a list of users who can write to this directory, overriding the writable parameter.

In the case of this share, the list of users who can write to this directory is set to @staff. The @ symbol tells Samba to interpret the name that follows as a UNIX group name, defined in the /etc/group file. Alternatively, you can list usernames separated by commas in this type of list. You can also mix usernames and group names, as long as the group names are preceded by the @ symbol.

NOTE: If you need to restrict access to certain shares, either for read or write access, consider creating UNIX groups and giving those groups access with the read list and write list Samba parameters.

USER AUTHENTICATION WITH SAMBA

In order to access resources that have been shared with Samba, users need to be authenticated. User authentication allows Samba to restrict access to shares and to control read and write permissions for files and directories. Currently, Samba supports three different mechanisms for authenticating user access to shares, all of which are controlled by the security keyword in the smb.conf file.

Share Security

The share security option tells Samba to restrict access according to share permissions. This is the oldest security model available in Samba and provides the least security.

User Security

The user security option tells Samba to use username validation for access to network shares. When a user attempts to connect to a share on a Samba server, Samba attempts to validate the user's username and password in the local password file. If the user is validated, the user is granted or denied access to the share according to its share permissions. This option is very useful if your PC-based accounts have the same usernames as your UNIX-based accounts.

In order to use the user security option, you must create accounts on your UNIX system for all of your PC users that will be connecting to Samba shares. Some system administrators may be reluctant to do this, as it can greatly increase the number of user entries in the system password file and thus make password file management more difficult.

Server Security

Fortunately, there is a solution to the problem of having to provide UNIX usernames for all your PC-based users. Samba now allows you to redirect all user authentication requests to a separate SMB server. This SMB server does not have to be another UNIX system running Samba; it can be any SMB server capable of authenticating users, such as a Windows NT computer. So, by electing to use the server security model, you can centralize all your PC usernames and passwords on an NT system and use that system for Samba authentication!

In order to set up server-based security, add two lines such as the following to the [global] section of the smb.conf file.

```
security=server
password server = NTSRV1
```

The first line, security=server, tells Samba to use the server security model. The second line tells Samba which computer will act as the authentication server. You must specify the NetBIOS name for the authentication server, not its DNS name. Chances are that you will have to edit your /etc/hosts file and add an entry for the authentication server's NetBIOS name.

CAUTION: By using server authentication, you are trusting another server to accurately verify all users and authenticate them for you. Never rely on a password server that you do not trust completely!

The remote authentication server will authenticate all usernames and passwords automatically. If authentication should fail, Samba will resort to the user security model as a fallback mechanism.

PRINTING WITH SAMBA

Not only does Samba enable you to share file systems with clients, it lets you share printers as well. When a PC-based client prints to a Samba server, the server receives the request, translates it, and passes it on to the UNIX printing system. Samba does not do the actual printing; it merely acts as the middleman.

Printing to UNIX Printers

Providing a printer configuration with Samba is very similar to sharing a file system. In fact, there are a couple of ways to do it. The easiest way to set up SMB printing is to create the [printers] special section of the smb.conf file and use it in conjunction with your UNIX /etc/printcap file. Remember from earlier in this chapter that the [printers] section provides defaults for all printers in the /etc/printcap file. If you add the directive load printers = yes to this section, Samba will load your /etc/printcap file and apply all the defaults to the printers it finds there.

In order to print correctly, Samba needs to know what kind of printing subsystem your variety of UNIX supports. Samba supports several different printing subsystems. If your version of UNIX uses the lpr command, you should set printing = bsd in the [global] section of smb.conf. Similarly, if your UNIX uses the lp command, you should set printing = sysv. HP-UX and AIX have their own print settings, hpux and aix, respectively.

Samba uses the printing subsystem specified in the smb.conf file to determine what default commands to use for printing and print management. Usually, Samba makes reasonable guesses for the default commands. However, if you want total control, you can adjust the print commands directly within the Samba configuration file. Several options allow you to provide new commands for Samba to use. Three of the most common commands to customize are listed in Table 2-1.

Samba Directive	Example	Purpose
print command	print command = lpr -r –P%p %s	Samba uses this directive as the actual command for printing a file. The %p macro is automatically replaced with the name of the printer, and the %s macro is replaced with the name of the spool file to be printed.
lpq command	lpq command = lpq –P%p	This directive is used to query the printing subsystem and return a list of jobs in a given printer. The %p macro is replaced with the name of the printer.
lprm command	lprm command = lprm –Pp %j	Samba uses this directive to remove a job from a print spool. The %j macro is replaced by the job number returned by the lpq command.

Table 2-1. Common Print Command Customizations for Samba

In addition to making available all the printers in the /etc/printcap file via the [printers] section of your Samba configuration file, Samba also supports exporting individual printers as shared network printers. This is accomplished in much the same way as exporting individual shared file systems. By sharing individual printers instead of using the system default printers, you can prevent users from seeing all the printers on your system, restrict access to certain subsets of printers, and provide a finer level of control over each printer.

To create a new shared printer, simply create a section for it in the Samba configuration file. Let's look at an example:

```
[graphicprt]
  comment = Graphics Staff Printer
  valid users = @graphics
  path = /var/spool/graphicsprt
  printer = graphics_prt001
  public = no
  writable = no
  printable = yes
```

We want to create a new printer share for use by staff in the graphics group. This configuration entry creates a new share with the SMB share name graphicprt. By using the valid users = @graphics directive, we ensure that only people in the graphics group have access to the printer. The path directive is used to direct print jobs to the appropriate spool directory, and the printer directive gives the name of the printer so that Samba can find it in /etc/printcap. In addition, we've set the public = no directive to prevent guest users from printing to this printer.

That's all there is to it. As you can see, it is very simple to create and share a new printer definition with Samba. You can, of course, customize more details for individual printers by adding the appropriate configuration directives. For a complete list of the customization directives supported by Samba, see the man page for the smb.conf file.

Printing to PC Printers

Now that you've seen how easy it is to create new print shares via Samba, you're probably ready for something a bit more difficult. You're probably wondering if you can use Samba to print to PC-based printers in addition to sharing UNIX-based printers. Well, you can, but it's not a particularly easy task. Before attempting to use PC-based printers, you should have some familiarity with configuring UNIX-based printers and editing the /etc/printcap file.

The first step to sharing a PC-based printer is to create an entry for that printer in the UNIX system's /etc/printcap file. Here is an example printcap entry for a Hewlett-Packard DeskJet 870Cse printer:

```
dj870:\
     :cm= DeskJet 870Cse:\
```

```
    :sd=/var/spool/lpd/dj870:\
    :af=/var/spool/lpd/dj870/acct:\
    :if=/usr/local/etc/smbprint:\
    :mx=0:\
    :lp=/dev/null:
```

This format looks horribly cryptic, but that is just the way the /etc/printcap file works. One line in this entry that is particularly interesting is this line,

```
:if=/usr/local/etc/smbprint:\
```

which tells the printing system to use the file /usr/local/etc/smbprint as an input filter. This file is a shell script that actually calls the appropriate Samba program to print to the PC computer.

NOTE: If you are one of the UNIX gurus among us, you may have noticed an accounting file line in the /etc/printcap entry, specifically, :af=/var/spool/lpd/dj870/acct:\. This line must be present for printing to work. The smbprint script uses the accounting file entry to determine the path to a special configuration file.

The detailed syntax of the printcap file is beyond the scope of this chapter. For more information on the inner workings of the printcap file, see the man page for printcap.

Next, you need to provide Samba with some configuration information for this printer. You'll do this in the following directory,

/var/spool/lpd/*printname*

where *printname* is the name of the actual printer (in this case, dj870). Use your favorite UNIX text editor to create a file named .config. This file should contain three lines that give the NetBIOS name of the PC with the printer attached, the name of the printer share, and the password required to connect to the shared printer. So, continuing on with our example, the file /var/spool/lpd/dj870/.config might contain the following lines:

```
server=GRAPHSRV
service=HPDJ_870CSE
password=""
```

These entries tell Samba that the NetBIOS name of the PC server is GRAPHSRV, and that the server is sharing its printer with the share name HPDJ_870CSE. No password is required to connect to this print service.

So you see, you can get Samba to print to a PC-based print share, but it is just a bit more complicated than printing to a UNIX-based share. If you want to see the ugly details of how this all works, take a look at the smbprint shell script that comes with the Samba distribution. This script handles the fine points of printing to PC-based shares and has some detailed examples.

RUNNING SAMBA

Wow! We're almost there. After all that configuration, you are finally ready to fire up Samba and get to work. However, before you actually start Samba, you should verify that your configuration file is correct and free of errors. Samba provides the testparm program to do this for you. If testparm confirms that your configuration file will work, you can go ahead and start up Samba.

The actual Samba server consists of two UNIX daemons, smbd and nmbd. The smbd process is the daemon that provides SMB file and print service sharing. The nmbd daemon is a support process that provides NetBIOS name server support. In fact, nmbd can provide most of the features and flexibility of a WINS server on Windows NT.

When starting the Samba daemons, you must decide whether to start them as daemons at boot time or to have them automatically started from inetd. Don't try to do both—bad things can happen to Samba if you do. Starting the Samba processes as daemons will cause them to run continuously, which takes up a little CPU time and process space. However, if run directly as daemons, the Samba processes will respond slightly faster to service requests. Starting the Samba processes from inetd will ensure that they only start when a request is sent; however, they will be slower to respond to connections, since the processes will have to be created each time a connection request comes in.

Starting Samba as a Daemon

To start the Samba processes as a daemon, simply give the following two commands as root:

```
/usr/local/samba/bin/smbd -D
/usr/local/samba/bin/nmbd -D
```

Using the –D flag causes Samba to start as a daemon that will continue to run after the creating process is terminated. This is not the default behavior. You must use the –D flag if you want to run the processes as daemons.

In order to have the Samba processes start automatically, simply include the two preceding commands in your local startup script.

Starting Samba from inetd

The inetd process is a UNIX daemon that is charged with automatically starting other processes as requests come in for them. Since the inetd daemon starts other processes automatically, processes do not need to be running continuously, consuming CPU time and memory. The Samba processes can be started via inetd if necessary, but this can make Samba seem slower, as the processes will have to be started for every service request.

NOTE: The syntax of the inetd configuration files is different on different varieties of UNIX. Consult the man page for inetd.conf for the exact syntax required by your platform.

To enable Samba via inetd, first edit the /etc/services file with your favorite UNIX text editor. Look for entries for TCP port 139 and UDP port 137. If none are found, add the following lines to your /etc/services file:

```
netbios-ns      137/udp
netbios-ssn     139/tcp
```

If you find service entries on UDP port 137 and TCP port 139, make a note of the service names. You will need them for the next step.

Next, you need to add entries into the inetd.conf file, so that inetd will be able to start the Samba processes. A typical set of entries would look like this:

```
netbios-ssn stream tcp nowait root /usr/local/samba/bin/smbd smbd
netbios-ns dgram udp wait root /usr/local/samba/bin/nmbd nmbd
```

REMEMBER: The syntax of inetd.conf can vary. Check the man pages to be sure you're using the correct format for your situation.

If you found entries for UDP port 137 and TCP port 139 when you checked the /etc/services file earlier, compare the service names to the service names in the first column of these two inetd.conf entries. The service names must match exactly. Some versions of UNIX use different capitalization or use underscores instead of hyphens in the service names. If the service names on your system are different, change these inetd.conf entries to match.

At this point, you can simply restart the inetd process so that it will re-read its configuration file. Many versions of UNIX allow you to do kill –HUP on the process ID of inetd, to cause it to re-read its configuration file without having to stop and start the inetd process.

Using smbclient

Not only can Samba make UNIX directories and printers available as network shares to Windows computers via SMB, but you can also use Samba to access shared directories on other Windows computers as well. Samba provides a client program, appropriately named smbclient, that enables you to attach to other network shares.

The smbclient program provides a line mode interface similar to FTP that allows you to transfer files with a network share on another SMB server. It does not allow you to mount an SMB share as a local UNIX directory. You can also use smbclient to list the available shares on another server as well.

Although smbclient accepts several command line options, most users use the program either to query a server to find out what shares are available, or to connect to a server to transfer files. In order to list the shares available on a particular SMB server, use the –L option with smbclient, as in the following example:

```
smbclient -L -I ntsrv.mydomain.com
```

The second set of arguments, –I ntsrv.mydomain.com, specifies the DNS host name or IP address of the server. Since UNIX, by default, doesn't know anything about NetBIOS names, the –I argument allows you to give the DNS name of the server instead. Without the –I argument, smbclient will treat the server name as a NetBIOS name and will attempt to resolve it via the standard NetBIOS name resolution process.

NOTE: For more information on how NetBIOS names are resolved, see Chapter 7.

The second common use for smbclient is to connect to a network share and exchange files. Let's assume that you want to connect to the service \\NTSRV\PUBLIC as the user smith. Using smbclient, the command would be

```
smbclient '\\NTSRV\PUBLIC' -I ntsrv.mydomain.com -U smith
```

Samba may prompt you for a password if one is required to connect to the service. Note that the NetBIOS name for the server and the share are enclosed in single quotes. This is to keep the UNIX shell from trying to translate the \ characters.

Once you have connected to a share, smbclient provides commands that are very similar to FTP. For example, you have get, put, cd, and dir available. For a complete list of commands, you can simply type **help** at the command prompt.

Using smbmount

Although smbclient provides an FTP-like interface, Samba also allows UNIX systems to mount Samba shares as file systems using the smbmount command. This program is an interface to the SMB file system, smbfs. smbfs is a file system that understands the SMB protocol.

NOTE: See **http://samba.anu.edu.au/samba/** for this collection of programs, which makes mounting a SMB share as easy as mounting any other network file system. The site also contains lots more information on SMB and NetBIOS over TCP/IP. There you will also find explanations for such concepts as NetBIOS names and sharing.

The smbmount program has the following command line,

smbmount *servicename mount_point* [*options*]

where *servicename* is the SMB designation, and follows the conventions for the smbclient program. The *mount_point* parameter designates a UNIX directory that becomes the entry point for the NT file system you are mounting. This directory should have the appropriate file permissions. (See the man entry for the smbmount command if you'd like further information on its various options.)

USING SHARITY

Samba is by no means the only SMB server for UNIX, although it is one of the most popular. Another very popular alternative is the commercial product Sharity from Objective Development. Sharity is a software package that runs on UNIX machines and enables you to mount shares exported by Windows (2000, NT, 95, 98, and so on), OS/2, Samba, AppleShare IP, and others in your file system just as you can with smbmount. Unlike smbmount, Sharity supports browsing (as does the Windows Network Neighborhood), and has a GUI for dialogs and for configuration.

Sharity supports the following platforms: Linux, Solaris, SunOS, HP-UX, SGI/IRIX, BSDI, NetBSD, FreeBSD, OpenBSD, NEXTSTEP 3.*x*, OPENSTEP/Mach 4.*x* (i386, m68k, PA-RISC, Sun), AIX, OSF/1 (DEC-UNIX), Mac OS X(Server), and SCO Unixware.

Although Sharity is a commercial product, you can download a demo version for testing, and Objective Development does provide source code. For more information see their website at **http://www.obdev.at/Products/Sharity.html**.

THE TOTALNET ADVANCED SERVER

Yet another very popular alternative to Samba is the commercial product TotalNET Advanced Server (TAS), developed by Syntax, Inc. As one indication of the product's popularity, Sun Microsystems has announced that it is shipping its new Netra™ NFS 150 Version 1.1 servers with a fully functional TAS server installed. You can learn more about TotalNET Advanced Server from the Syntax, Inc., site, **http://www.syntax.com**.

TAS is a robust client/server solution aimed at integrating dissimilar operating systems. It provides SMB-based connectivity to a variety of SMB clients, including Windows NT, LAN Manager, LAN Server, and DEC Pathworks. In addition to the SMB client connectivity, TAS goes a couple of steps further by providing NetWare connectivity via the IPX/SPX protocol suite, and Macintosh connectivity using AppleTalk. Each of these three areas—SMB, NetWare, and Macintosh—is referred to as a *realm* by TAS.

The TotalNET Advanced Server consists of several components. Administrative tasks are handled through a user-friendly HTML interface called TotalAdmin. The TotalAdmin interface allows system administrators to manage the TAS configuration from a standard web browser. By incorporating a web browser management scheme, TotalAdmin provides a consistent interface for changing servers, service names, and passwords; viewing error logs; sharing new resources; and modifying security parameters. Since TotalAdmin is web browser–based, administrators can easily manage TAS remotely from any computer equipped with a web browser.

TAS also includes a component known as the *Enterprise Name Server*, which maintains a database of the NetBIOS names and machine addresses used by all computers in the network. This database is automatically updated with NetBIOS names and addresses.

TAS is a robust application server that makes it easier to connect UNIX and NT systems via SMB. Syntax has just released TAS version 5.4.1, which has a variety of features, including

- **Support for unmodified clients** There is no need to modify client operating system installations in order to have them work with TAS.
- **Scalability** TAS is based on a multithreaded architecture that scales well to provide support for large numbers of clients.
- **Username mapping** TAS provides username mapping via a set of mapping files. These mapping files are used to map usernames from PCs to UNIX systems transparently.
- **Unified filename mapping** TAS supports long filenames in all three supported realms, and will map filenames as readably as possible, subject to the operating system limitations on particular clients.
- **Security** TAS supports three different methods for authenticating users: proxy authentication, encrypted passwords, and clear text.
- **Browsing** TAS supports Microsoft's browsing standards, and can participate in network browsing.
- **Print services** TAS provides access to print devices, whether they are attached to the TAS server, function as network printers or are attached to network servers. TAS is also capable of providing print redirection to remote TAS servers and other SMB servers.

TAS Security

TAS is designed to have a flexible security policy that can be configured to suit the needs of the system administrator. Under TAS, user passwords can be transmitted either as clear text or in encrypted form.

Clear text password transmission is less secure, but offers the most flexibility. Clear text passwords are managed with native UNIX tools such as the passwd program and may be stored in any supported UNIX authentication database, including NIS, NIS+, DCE, and the /etc/passwd file.

Encrypted passwords offer a higher level of security than clear text passwords. Encrypted user passwords are stored in a special TAS password file. The client encrypts a password with a one-way encryption algorithm and sends the password to the TAS server. The TAS server then validates the password against the TAS database. Using the encrypted password scheme requires you to use the tnpasswd utility program, supplied with TAS, for managing user passwords.

TAS also supports proxy authentication, similar to that found in Samba. With proxy authentication, another server, known as the *proxy server,* is used to authenticate user passwords. Since password authentication is delegated to another server, system administrators rely on the native security measures available on the proxy server. With proxy authentication, TAS has no impact on the password storage or management. When enabling proxy authentication for NetBIOS clients, you must assure that the proxy server understands the SMB protocol. Under NetWare, the proxy server must be a NetWare server. Proxy authentication is not supported for Macintosh clients running AppleTalk.

Managing Usernames with TAS

Different operating systems support different standards for usernames. Under most versions of UNIX, usernames are limited to eight characters in length. However, under Windows NT, usernames can be up to 32 characters in length. In order for a user to access UNIX services when being authenticated directly by TAS on UNIX, the user's PC username must match their UNIX username.

This issue creates problems when system administrators have already devised a naming convention and would normally have to change all PC usernames to match the more restrictive UNIX usernames. Fortunately, TAS provides a username mapping function.

Username mapping in TAS allows the system administrator to establish a mapping database that translates the PC username into a UNIX username. This mapping is performed on the server's side of the network conversation and is transparent to the user. In order to simplify management of the username mapping database, username mapping is managed via TAS's TotalAdmin web-based interface.

SUMMARY

One of the best ways to maximize a diverse UNIX and Windows NT environment is to implement file and printer sharing. This allows you to maximize your resources, both in terms of file servers and by making network printers available to users.

In this chapter, we've looked at a couple of ways to implement file and print sharing. The Server Message Block, or SMB, protocol is commonly used by Microsoft Windows 2000/NT and Windows 95/98 as a file-sharing mechanism. We introduced the SMB protocol and discussed how Microsoft uses it for file services. We also introduced the Common Internet File System (CIFS) as an up-and-coming protocol designed to support file and print sharing over the World Wide Web.

Next, we examined three different ways of implementing Windows-compatible file services on UNIX. The first, Samba, is a freely available SMB server implementation that runs under UNIX and provides the capability to create custom file shares. Samba can also be used to share home directories and UNIX printers. With a little creativity, Samba can be used to allow UNIX users to print to PC-based printers as well. Samba is very widely implemented, with some sites having thousands of servers and clients.

Next we discussed another program for file and printer sharing called Sharity. Sharity is a software package that runs on UNIX machines; enables you to mount shares exported by Windows OS/2, Samba, AppleShare IP, and others in your file system.

The third implementation that we examined is a commercial product from Syntax, Inc. Known as TotalNET Advanced Server, or TAS, this product provides SMB services from UNIX as well. In addition to providing SMB services, TAS also facilitates file and print sharing with NetWare- and AppleTalk-based computers.

As you can see, some very viable solutions are available that provide NT file and print services from UNIX. In the next chapter, we'll look at the reverse side of the coin—namely, how to provide UNIX-accessible file services from NT systems by using the NFS protocol.

CHAPTER 3

UNIX File Services in Windows

Information is critical in business. People need access to many types of information—spreadsheets, reports, business modes, schedules, and so forth—and to the applications that manipulate that information. One of the biggest challenges in distributed, heterogeneous networks is giving users access to the files and applications they need, wherever those files exist on the network. The Network File System (NFS) allows UNIX and Windows users to easily access files on either platform.

WHAT IS NFS?

The Network File System (NFS) was one of the most important technologies to emerge from the Ethernet-TCP/IP-UNIX environment of the 1980s. It was announced in 1984, and has since become the de facto standard for distributed file services in multivendor internetwork environments. In a nutshell, NFS hides underlying details about where files are physically stored. It allows files that are physically located elsewhere to appear as if they are part of a local file system. NFS is both a standard specification and a set of software products that enable file access across a network.

NFS primarily utilizes two different protocol mechanisms: the External Data Representation (XDR) protocol, which operates at the Presentation layer, and remote procedure calls (RPCs), which operates at the Session layer. These two protocols are the foundation for all NFS interaction. RPC provides the basis for message exchanges between clients and servers. The XDR protocol provides data translation between different types of computers and operating systems.

From a user's perspective, NFS is transparent. Depending on how NFS has been set up, users may be able to log onto any workstation in their network and see their files. Files that are physically under a different operating system are just as easily accessed as those under the operating system they're using.

From a system administrator's standpoint, NFS is a distributed file system. An NFS server has one or more file systems that are mounted by NFS clients. To NFS clients, remote disks look like local disks. This also means that many different NFS client computers, centralizing file utilization, can access files on an NFS server.

Although NFS provides a mechanism to share files, it doesn't provide the capability to run applications across platforms. For example, if you're a UNIX user and have a Windows directory mounted through NFS, you can change directories to what looks like a fairly normal UNIX directory. However, if there are Windows programs in that directory—say, Microsoft Word or Intuit Quicken—you won't be able to run them. To do that, you need desktop application emulator software like Tektronix's WinDD or Sun's WABI.

A BRIEF HISTORY OF NFS

NFS was originally developed by Sun Microsystems, Inc., in the mid-1980s, to simplify the sharing of files between different types of computers. Sun published the specifications and created a UNIX implementation, which they now also license to other developers.

NOTE: Companies that currently license and resell NFS include IBM, NEC, Pyramid Technology, Compaq, Hewlett-Packard, Fujitsu, NCR, and Silicon Graphics, to name but a few.

Since its initial development, NFS has grown to support global, scalable, high-performance file sharing in environments consisting of UNIX workstations and servers, minicomputers, mainframes, and PCs. Today, NFS is the de facto standard for distributed file access, and NFS implementations are usually bundled with UNIX operating systems. Because the specifications are in the public domain, many different hardware and software vendors have implemented NFS on a variety of hardware platforms.

A TECHNICAL OVERVIEW

NFS is both scalable and flexible. It supports small and large networks, as well as a wide range of hardware and operating systems. It can effectively support small networks of fewer than 10 clients or large networks of more than 25,000 clients, physically scattered over the globe.

NFS is built on the RPC protocol and imposes a client/server relationship on the computers that use it. This means that NFS software is installed on the NFS server and on each NFS client. An NFS server is a host that owns one or more file systems and makes them available on a network. NFS clients then mount file systems from one or more servers. In addition, NFS provides file-locking services, which control multiple accesses to the same file.

In an NFS environment, a Windows system can act as either an NFS client or an NFS server. By accessing an NFS client of a UNIX NFS server, Windows users could access remote UNIX NFS servers as if they were local file systems. By accessing a Windows NFS server with UNIX clients, UNIX users could access remote Windows file systems.

FILE PERMISSIONS

Preserving file permissions is one of the key functions that NFS software performs when transferring files between NT and UNIX. Maintaining continuity can be tricky, however, because the NT File System (NTFS) under Windows NT and 2000 supports a higher degree of access control than is possible under UNIX.

Windows Permissions

Windows 2000 supports three file systems: FAT, FAT32, and NTFS. Just to add confusion, Windows NT NTFS is not quite the same as the Windows 2000 NTFS. In Windows 2000, the NTFS file system is the preferred system type, and is required for:

- Active Directory (and the use of Domains within Active Directory)
- File encryption using the Encrypted File System feature of Windows 2000

- Remote Storage. (What used to be named Tape Backup in the Administrative Tools folder will only back up NTFS.)
- Disk quotas for users
- Services for Macintosh, and
- Other services

Under Windows NTFS, each file and each directory are owned by one account. The owner of this account is the only one who has the right to access, modify, and secure it from outside access. By default, the owner is the user who created the resource.

NOTE: An exception to this is a user who is in the Administrator group. In this case, all users who are in the Administrator group co-own any resource created by any group member.

In addition to permissions, each file and directory has at least one access control list (ACL) entry that defines a user's or group's access to a file or directory. By using multiple ACLs, you have a great deal of control over who has access to what.

Windows User Permissions

The owner of a file or directory can grant a user any of the levels of access listed in Table 3-1.

Table 3-2 shows directory permissions required for each level of access.

Level of Access	Actions Permitted
No Access	None. User cannot view or access the file or directory by any means.
List	Viewing the contents of the directory (User cannot read the files in the directory, or modify them in any way.)
Read	Viewing and reading files Executing programs (User cannot modify files.)
Add	Saving new files to the directory (User cannot view or read the files in the directory.)
Add and Read	Viewing and reading files Executing programs Saving new files (User cannot modify existing files.)

Table 3-1. Levels of User Access in Windows

Level of Access	Actions Permitted
Change	Viewing and reading files Executing programs Saving new files Modifying and deleting existing files Changing file attributes Deleting the directory
Full Control	Viewing and reading files Saving new files Modifying and deleting existing files Changing permissions Taking ownership away from the current owner
Special Access	Owner or any user granted P permission can custom-build an access control entry for an ACL.

Table 3-1. Levels of User Access in Windows *(continued)*

Level of Access	Read (r)	Execute (x)	Write (w)	Delete (d)	Change Permissions (p)	Take Ownership (o)
No Access						
List	√	√				
Read	√	√				
Add	√	√				
Add and Read	√	√	√	√		
Change	√	√	√	√		
Full Control	√	√	√	√	√	√
Special Access (any combination)	√	√	√	√	√	√

Table 3-2. Windows NTFS Directory Permissions

Table 3-3 lists file permissions required for each level of access.

Windows 2000 Group Permissions

Windows 2000 contains two types of groups—local groups and built-in groups. *Local groups* are used to assign rights and permissions to a local system and resources. They are user-defined, and are used to assign permissions to files and directories. *Built-in groups* are designed for system management. They are predefined, and preassigned specific rights aimed at system management. Both types of groups can contain local users, domain users, and global groups. From trusted domains, each type of group can also contain users and global groups.

UNIX Permissions

In UNIX, there are three categories of access permissions: user, group, and other (also known as world) for files and directories. Each category is set to individually enable or disable read (r), write (w), and execute (x) privileges. UNIX systems also store a numeric owner (UID) and group (GID) identifier for each file or directory. Together, access permissions and identifiers determine a user's access to a file or directory.

NOTE: UNIX permissions also determine the file type. For example, even if a file is really executable, it cannot be run unless the execute (x) flag has been set.

Table 3-4 lists the levels of access that the owner of a file or directory can grant to herself (owner), her group (group), or everyone else (other or world).

Level of Access	Read (r)	Execute (x)	Write (w)	Delete (d)	Change Permissions (p)	Take Ownership (o)
No Access						
Read	√	√				
Add and Read	√	√				
Change	√	√	√	√		
Full Control	√	√	√	√	√	√
Special Access (any combination)	√	√	√	√	√	√

Table 3-3. Windows NTFS File Permissions

Level of Access	Actions Permitted
Read	Reading files Viewing the contents of the directory
Write	Modify and deleting existing files and directories Creating new files and directories
Execute	Using *cd* to move to the directory Executing files

Table 3-4. Levels of Access in UNIX

Owners typically have rwx (read, write, and execute) access, whereas group and world access are typically more limited. Typically, members of the same group have read and write (but not execute) permissions, and everyone else has read-only permission. However, file owners can change these permissions any way they want to.

UNIX File Permissions

User permissions define access for a file's owner. Each user should have a different UID. When a user saves a file in NFS, the UNIX system automatically saves the UID in the file's directory entry, similar to a directory entry for a file under the NTFS or FAT file system. Each user who accesses the file with the same UID receives the owner's access permissions.

UNIX Group Permissions

Group permissions define access for all users who belong to a group. A user may be a member of several groups; however, only one group is active at a time. Each group has a unique GID. As in the case of user permissions, when a user saves a file in NFS, the UNIX system saves the GID of the user's current group in the file's directory entry. Each user who accesses the file with the same GID receives the group's access permissions.

File Mapping

When you transfer files between UNIX and Windows using NFS, file permissions must be mapped to equivalents on each system. The first step is to authenticate the user's identity. NFS software attempts to translate the user login ID to an equivalent login ID on the other system. If NFS can't translate the login ID, the next step is to use a translation table. If there isn't a translation, the NFS software can either assign an ID or end the connection.

NOTE: Windows NFS products, such as Hummingbird Communication's NFS Maestro and NetManage's Chameleon™ NFS/X, handle mapping in roughly the same way.

For example, when a Windows user accesses a UNIX file system via NFS, the authentication process may use a special daemon on the UNIX system that attempts to translate the Windows login ID to a UNIX account name. If the daemon can't translate the login ID, the NFS product uses a UID/GID translation table instead. If no translation is available, the NFS software can either assign an ID or end the connection.

NOTE: Most Windows NFS products maintain a translation table. It usually must be set up before using the NFS software.

When a UNIX user creates a file under NTFS, the NFS software often uses the NTFS Special Access permission flags rather than standard NTFS access types (Add, Full Control, and so on). This allows NFS to assign the appropriate access to files. For example, under UNIX, write permission also implies delete. Depending on the Windows NFS product you choose, the software may set Special Access flags for both write and delete.

The owner, group, and other UNIX access permissions directly map to three Windows ACL entries for a file on NTFS. These correlations are as follows:

UNIX Permission	Windows ACL
Owner	User permissions
Group	Group permissions
Other (or world)	Group Everyone permissions

File mapping is handled differently among the various Windows NFS products. As you look at different Windows NFS products, there are a few questions you may want to consider:

- How does the software handle special file and directory permissions in place of the NTFS default permissions?
- How does the software handle SID (system ID) mappings between Windows users and groups and UIDs and GIDs on their UNIX counterparts?
- How does the software handle naming differences between UNIX and Windows?

NFS FILE-NAMING ISSUES

One problem that you may run into when integrating UNIX and Windows file systems with NFS is the way the two platforms handle alphabetic case in filenames. UNIX file systems are completely case sensitive. This means that the files TEST, test, and Test can all exist in the same directory. These names refer to three different and distinct files.

Windows, by contrast, preserves filename case but does not recognize differences in case. Thus, if you stored a file with the name TEST, it would be written to disk as TEST.

However, you could refer to the file in a program as test, and Windows would open the file TEST. The Windows insensitivity to case in a filename prevents you from having multiple files with the same name, differing only by case, in the same directory. In fact, some Windows programs will change the case of the filename when they save the file to disk.

Since UNIX is case sensitive, and Windows is not, problems can occur when you are trying to access files via NFS. UNIX clients will attempt to map the filename exactly as you typed it, so you must get the case correct. Windows clients going to UNIX servers may or may not change the case of the filename before sending it to the UNIX system as a request. Different Windows NFS programs handle filename case differently.

NFS IN UNIX

Since we're looking at using NFS as a means of sharing file systems between UNIX and Windows, let's start off by exploring how NFS works in the UNIX environment. Because NFS is the de facto method of sharing file systems under UNIX, virtually all UNIX systems are already capable of functioning as either NFS clients or NFS servers. Sometimes a single UNIX system will perform both client and server roles.

A word of caution is warranted here, however. It is easy to design bad NFS configurations that are difficult to administer and impossible to secure from outside intrusion. Since the goal of NFS is to mount file systems transparently to the user, it is very tempting for the system administrator to export and mount things all over the place. You should design your NFS setup carefully, taking the time to decide which machines will be servers, which will be clients, and exactly what the role of each machine will be.

A complex, organic NFS configuration can be a nightmare to administer. In addition, your users will want things to stay the same as much as possible. When setting up an NFS environment, you should take care to make files available in the same directory structures as much as possible in order to minimize the impact on your users. Your users will thank you for it, or rather, they won't hassle you because things suddenly stop working.

Exporting File Systems

Virtually all versions of UNIX use a text configuration file for specifying the file systems that will be made available via NFS. In most cases, this file is named /etc/exports. Most versions of UNIX are set up to automatically become an NFS server if they have file systems configured for export. So when a UNIX system boots, it typically looks for the /etc/exports file and becomes an NFS server if it finds it.

NOTE: Under Sun Solaris, some of the filenames and commands are different from those listed here. These files and commands are given as examples only, although they work on a wide variety of UNIX systems.

The /etc/exports file lists the file systems that a UNIX system makes available via NFS. In addition to listing the file systems, it also contains access permissions and restrictions for those file systems. NFS does not advertise its exported file systems the way some other operating systems do. Instead, it maintains a list of currently exported file systems, which it uses to respond to mount requests from NFS clients.

Most UNIX file systems or subdirectories can be exported via NFS, with a couple of exceptions. Only local file systems can be exported; you cannot export a remote file system via NFS. Also, if you try to export a subdirectory or a parent directory of a file system that is already exported, the file system that you are trying to export must be on a different physical partition or device. Thus, if /usr/local is exported via NFS, you cannot export /usr/local/bin unless it exists on a different partition or device.

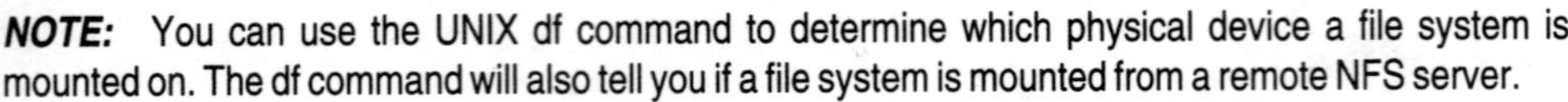

NOTE: You can use the UNIX df command to determine which physical device a file system is mounted on. The df command will also tell you if a file system is mounted from a remote NFS server.

Exporting file systems via NFS is actually a two-step process. First, you must create the appropriate entries in the /etc/exports file. Then you must tell UNIX to actually make the file systems available. The syntax of the /etc/exports file is not very complicated. Let's look at an example:

```
# A sample /etc/exports file
/projects  -access=fa:dumas,rw=fa:dumas  /usr/local/bin -ro,anon=nobody
/home/biff  -access=wks03,rw=wks03
/home/security_hole
```

Here you can see that each line lists a file system to be exported plus the options, if any, for that file system.

Table 3-5 lists some of the most commonly used options in the /etc/exports file.

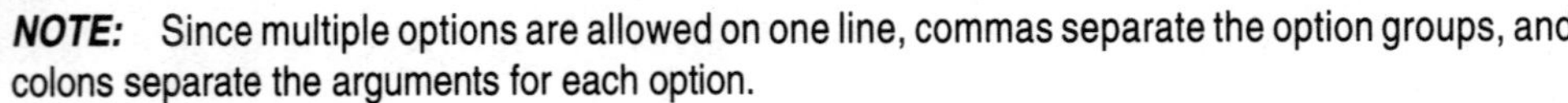

NOTE: Since multiple options are allowed on one line, commas separate the option groups, and colons separate the arguments for each option.

Looking back at our sample code, you can see that we are exporting four file systems. The first line,

```
/projects   -access=fa:dumas,rw=fa:dumas
```

makes the file system named /projects available. Its access restrictions limit all access to workstations fa and dumas. Only these two workstations can write to the file system.

The second export line,

```
/usr/local/bin    -ro,anon=nobody
```

makes the /usr/local/bin directory available. Its options limit its use to read-only, and map any anonymous users to the nobody UID. Since no hosts are listed in an access list, all hosts on the Internet can mount this file system, although the mount will be read-only.

Option	Function
–access=*host*:*host*: ...	Allows mount access only to the hosts in the access list. No other hosts will be able to mount this file system.
–anon=*uid*	Maps anonymous users (i.e., users who do not appear in the server's password database) to the specified user ID. This option is used to restrict access from anonymous users. Most systems set the anonymous user to be the system user nobody.
–ro	Makes a file system read-only, which prevents others from writing to it.
–rw=*host*:*host*: ...	Grants read/write access to the specified hosts. No other hosts will be able to write to the file system. If no host name is specified, all hosts will be given write access to this file system.
–root=*host*:*host*: ...	Allows the root user on a particular file system to be treated as root on this exported file system. Use with caution.

Table 3-5. Common Export Options for the /etc/exports File

The third entry in the /etc/exports example file,

```
/home/biff        -access=wks03,rw=wks03
```

is very similar to the first entry. The /home/biff directory is exported with access and read/write privileges granted only to host wks03.

The fourth line in our sample file,

```
/home/security_hole
```

has no access options; it makes the directory /home/security_hole available to everyone.

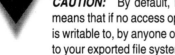

CAUTION: By default, NFS will grant read/write access and impose no access restrictions. This means that if no access options are specified, the directory /home/security_hole can be mounted, and is writable to, by anyone on the Internet. This is a bad arrangement! You should always control access to your exported file systems, especially read/write access. By comparison, the /usr/local/bin directory is mountable by anyone but is read-only. If your site uses the Network Information Service (NIS), you can set up netgroups of workstations to limit access to file systems via NFS.

Once you have entered your file systems into the /etc/exports file, you need to make them available via NFS. Many systems use the exportfs command to do this. Other UNIX variants use the nfsd daemon to export file systems directly. For the purposes of our example, we will assume that you are using the exportfs command.

NOTE: In Solaris, the command for exporting file systems is called "share," and it has a slightly different syntax.

The exportfs command can be used to export all file systems in the /etc/exports file, export only a selected file system, or re-export all the file systems. To export all unexported file systems, simply enter this command:

```
# exportfs
```

If you want to re-export all the file systems in your /etc/exports file, use the –a option, as shown here:

```
# exportfs -a
```

This causes the nfsd daemon to re-export all file systems, including the ones already exported.

Mounting File Systems

Now that you have exported your file systems from your NFS server, you need to mount them at your NFS clients. Since this is the UNIX section of the chapter, let's spend a couple of minutes talking about how to mount these exported file systems to a UNIX client. Keep in mind that the NFS server that has exported these file systems could be either a UNIX or Windows system. For the purposes of mounting the file systems, it doesn't make any real difference.

Under UNIX, there are two basic ways to mount an NFS file system. For long-term mounts that you want to remount every time your system boots, you can place an entry in the default file systems file, typically called /etc/fstab. When your UNIX system boots, the mount command will read this file and will then attempt to mount every file system in the file. Here are a couple of lines from a generic /etc/fstab file that show how you would list NFS file systems for automatic mount.

REMEMBER: The syntax of this configuration file will differ slightly among versions of UNIX.

```
server:/home/marcus       /home/marcus     nfs   rw,hard    0 0
zippy:/pub                /pub             nfs   rw,hard    0 0
```

The first entry on each line (server:/home/marcus in this example) lists the name of the NFS server, followed by a colon, then by the name of the exported file system. The second entry here, /home/marcus, tells the mount command where we want the file system mounted locally. The third entry here, nfs, tells mount to treat this as an NFS file system. The fourth entry, rw,hard, is a list of mount options that tells mount to make the file system read/write and to hard-mount it. The last entries, 0 0, are numbers used by the UNIX fsck utility that automatically checks file systems. In general, NFS mounts should always have this entry set to 0 0.

The second way to mount exported NFS file systems is to mount them directly with the mount command. For example, to mount the first file system entry in the previous example, we would give this command:

```
# mount -t nfs -o rw,hard server:/home/marcus /home/marcus
```

You can see that most of the information from the /etc/fstab line is used in the mount command. The –t nfs option tells mount that this is an NFS file system. The –o rw,hard option tells mount to mount the file system read/write and hard. The next two things on the line are the server and file system, and the destination mount point, respectively. If you use the mount command, the new file system will remain mounted until you either unmount it or reboot the system. If you reboot the system, the new file system will not be remounted unless you place an appropriate entry in the /etc/fstab file.

Hard Mounts vs. Soft Mounts

You may be wondering about the hard mount option from the previous section. NFS can mount file systems in one of two ways, known as *hard mounts* and *soft mounts.*

In a hard mount, NFS treats the file system like a local device. If the NFS server goes down, or the network link between the server and client becomes unavailable, any processes that try to access the NFS resource will hang, as the NFS client tries repeatedly to access the resource. This is known as *process blocking.* It looks to the client as though a local disk has dropped offline. When the server's exported file system becomes available again, NFS will allow the blocked processes to resume operation, thus guaranteeing the integrity of data written to the hard-mounted file system.

Using a soft mount changes the behavior slightly. With a soft mount, the NFS access to the remote file system will eventually fail, and the process will continue automatically. While this will prevent processes from hanging, it does not guarantee that data will be written correctly to file systems that are soft-mounted. You should not use a soft mount on any file system that you are writing data to. Also, soft mounts may hang if the connection fails.

WINDOWS SERVICES FOR UNIX

The Windows Services for UNIX (SFU) Add-On Pack for Windows 2000 Server includes both server and client for NFS, in addition to a UNIX command shell, support for the UNIX Network Information Services (NIS) directory service, and a number of UNIX utilities. When installed on either Windows 2000 Professional or Windows 2000 Server, the NFS support permits mapping of an exported file system from a UNIX server just as if it was a native Windows share, using either the UNIX server:/export format or the Windows \\server\share format.

The default file access permissions for the Windows NFS client are read, write, and execute for the user (owner) of the file, but they are restricted to read and execute for the owner's group and all other users. Filename mappings can preserve case or automatically convert to either all lowercase or all uppercase. Optional existing filename matching can be set to ignore the case. For a mixed environment, where users will be accessing files from both Windows and UNIX, configure filename mapping so that it automatically converts to lowercase, but configure filename matching to ignore case. The NFS Server can be installed only on a Windows Server, but it allows sharing via NFS to NFS clients on any platform.

HUMMINGBIRD NFS MAESTRO

One of the disadvantages of using NFS as a file-sharing system in Windows is that you need to install NFS servers and clients on your Windows systems. Fortunately, several third-party Windows-compatible packages are available to choose from, in addition to the NFS server and client available from Microsoft as part of the Windows Services for UNIX Add-On Pack. The first NFS package that we'll examine is NFS Maestro, available for Windows NT from Hummingbird Communications, Ltd. (As of this writing, Hummingbird hasn't released a version for Windows 2000.)

NFS Maestro is an NFS server and client implementation, designed to run under Windows NT. Since NFS Maestro is only the NFS server portion, you will need an NFS client in order to mount NFS-exported NFS partitions on an NT machine. UNIX systems typically have native NFS clients. NFS Maestro provides both an NFS server and an NFS client for Windows NT that operate as NT services. These services operate at the Ring 0 level of the operating system, as a kernel mode implementation. Users of NFS Maestro can make available any standard disk or CD-ROM that is locally attached. NFS Maestro also supports the NIS directory service as well.

Installation

One of the nice things about NFS Maestro is its ease of installation. Simply run the setup program from the NFS Maestro installation media, and select the destination directory. NFS Maestro tells you when installation is complete. That's all there is to the installation phase!

Configuration

Configuring NFS Maestro is fairly simple as well. NFS Maestro, like UNIX, uses a list of exported file systems, located in a file named EXPORTS. The EXPORTS file must be located in the NFS Maestro install directory.

When NFS Maestro is first installed, a skeleton EXPORTS file is created, which does not contain any valid file systems. NFS Maestro will attempt to automatically start, and it will generate an error indicating a bad or missing EXPORTS file. In order to add file systems to the EXPORTS file, you must first stop NFS Maestro.

To stop the NFS Maestro service, open the Control Panel and select Services. Highlight the service named HCLNFSServer, and click the Stop button. Once the NFS server service has been stopped, you can edit the EXPORTS file and add your file systems to export.

The EXPORTS file for NFS Maestro uses a syntax that is very similar to the common UNIX syntax and is documented very well in the skeleton EXPORTS file. The following is the skeleton EXPORTS file from NFS Maestro, with one valid file system added at the end:

```
#Entries in this file are formatted as either of:
#
#       Resource [ host1 [ host2 ... hostn ] ]
#
#       Resource [  Option[,Option...] ]
#

#Note that spaces are important in this file. Export entries are
# defined as follows:
#
#
#       Resource     Print Queue name or pathname of the directory
#                       (e.g., c:\usr\home)
#                       (UNIX- type entries are  also valid, e.g.,
#                               /usr/home=c:\usr\home.)
#
#       host?           Client's machine name (e.g., PC-1)
#

#      Option  Specifies optional characteristics for the directory
#              being exported. More than one option can be entered
#              by separating them with commas. The first option
#              must be preceded with a dash (-). The default
#              export parameters are access for everyone and
#              read-write permission for everyone.
#         Choose from the following options:
#
#       ro
#              Exports the directory to all users with read only
#permission. If not specified, the directory is exported
#with read write permission.
#
#       rw=Client1[:Client2:Client3...]
#              Exports the directory with read write permission to
#the machines specified by the Client parameter. All other users
#have read only permission.
```

```
#
#       access = Client1[:Client2:Client3...]
#               Restricts access to client(s) listed. Can be used in
# combination with read-write option to further define permissions.

#
#       root = Client1[:Client2:Client3...]
#               Allows user root access from the client(s) listed.
#
#       There should be only one line for each resource exported.
#The first entry for a resource will take precedence over
#any other entries for the same resource.
#
# To export your entire C: drive to some clients read-only, some
# clients read-write and allow root access from some hosts, the
#following would be used.

#
#/c ro,access=host1,host2,rw=host3,host4,root=host3
#
# host1 and host2 has read-only access
# host3 and host4 has read/write access
# root on host3 has root permission
# host5 can't access the drive
#
#
#below are the file systems that We are testing with
#Comment:  I don't think we should export directories that don't

# exist.
#       could we not check for this and not export them.
c:\public -ro,access=marcus
```

Once you have entered your file systems into the EXPORTS file, you can restart the HCLNFSServer service from Services in Control Panel.

Security

While Windows supports three different types of file system, only the NTFS system provides security and access control at both the file and directory levels. By exporting NTFS file systems, you gain the ability to control file system access according to the native permissions and access control lists set on the exported NTFS file system. Since NFS Maestro runs as an NT service, it preserves NTFS file permissions on exported NTFS file systems.

If you export a file system that is FAT-based, you will have no user-level or individual control for file accesses. You will only be able to say which workstations are allowed to access the file system, and if they are read-only or read/write.

Name Mapping

In order to access an exported NFS file system, a user must be authenticated. UNIX and NT NFS clients automatically authenticate their users locally by having them log into the system. If NFS Maestro is used as a stand-alone server, the user attempting to access an NFS resource must have a valid NT username. If the user has a valid username, the username is compared to an internal list to find the mapping between usernames and UIDs. Some systems, such as UNIX, have static UIDs that are always assigned to a specific user. On other systems, such as PC-based clients, the users do not have static UIDs. NFS Maestro allows the system administrator to build a list of username-to-UID mappings with the Control Panel for Name Mappings (see Figure 3-1), which is installed with NFS Maestro.

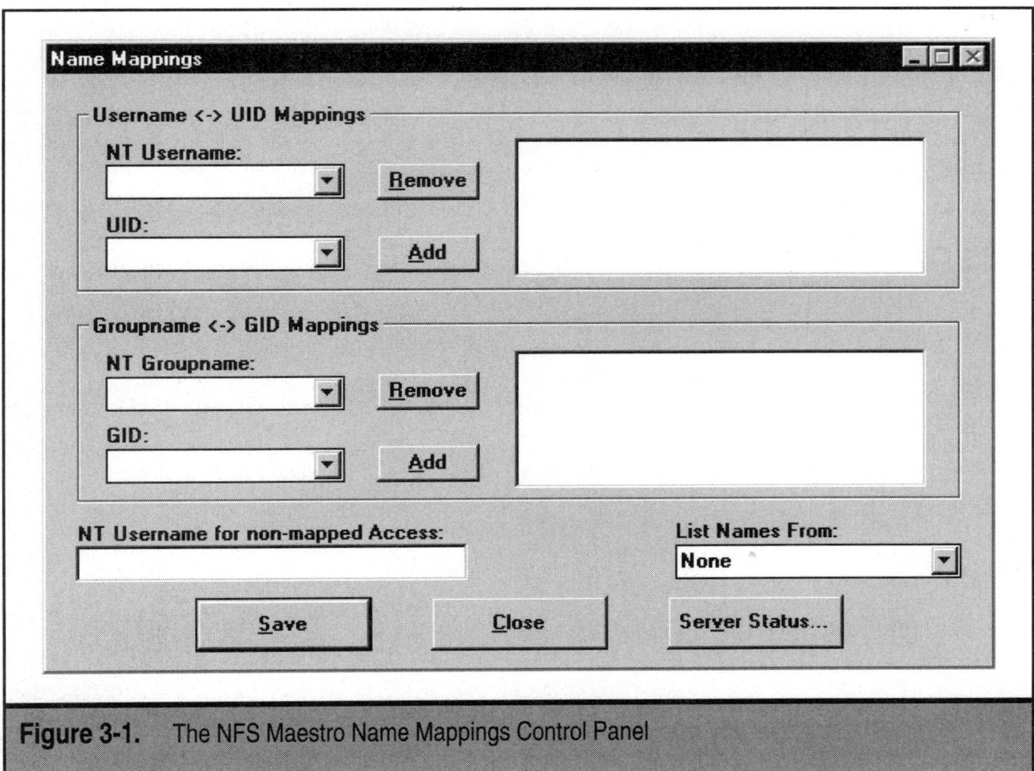

Figure 3-1. The NFS Maestro Name Mappings Control Panel

NETMANAGE NFS

Another commercial NFS implementation is available from NetManage. As a component of its Chameleon/UNIXLink 97 package, NetManage's NFS implementation, called InterDrive, provides robust NFS client and server software. This new release supports long filenames for more descriptive naming, as well as the capability to refer to file systems via Windows NT UNC names. The UNIXLink 97 package also integrates NFS file access into the Windows Explorer interface, making it easy to access remote drives and directories.

THE SOSSNT SERVER

Those of you looking for an inexpensive NFS solution shouldn't feel left out. The SOSSNT server, an acronym for Son of Stan's Server for NT, is an NT port of the PC-based SOSS NFS server. The software is freely available under the terms of the GNU Public License.

Running the RUNSOSS.BAT file located in the SOSSNT executables directory starts SOSSNT. SOSSNT uses an exports file named EXPORT.US to export NFS file systems. In addition, SOSSNT provides support for NTFS security and for mapping UNIX and NT user IDs and group IDs.

Although SOSSNT is not the most feature-rich NFS server available, it is free, and it comes with full source code. It is fairly easy to install and configure. One significant downside, however, is that SOSSNT does not run as a native NT service, but rather as a batch file. This requires that the batch file be started every time the NT server is rebooted. SOSSNT can be downloaded from the web at **http://www.loa.espci.fr/winnt/sossnt4/ sossnt4.htm**.

SUMMARY

In the UNIX world, NFS is the de facto standard for sharing file systems. When integrated with a Windows environment, it can provide a viable means of sharing file systems between UNIX and Windows. In this chapter, we've looked at what NFS does, and we've explored its history—including some technical aspects of NFS and how it manages file system permissions. We also examined the effects of alphabetic case in filenames when you are exporting NFS file systems.

A computer using NFS can function as either an NFS server or an NFS client. UNIX typically provides NFS capability as a native component of the operating system, and Windows no longer requires that you purchase third-party add-on products. Here we examined how to configure UNIX as either an NFS server or an NFS client, and we looked at some commercial and free solutions for Windows.

Properly thought out and implemented, NFS can provide the link that you need to share file systems between your UNIX and Windows systems. It does have limitations, including file case mapping, UID and GID mapping, and the requirement that you install software on every Windows computer. However, if you have a computing environment with a large number of UNIX systems, NFS could be the solution you are looking for.

CHAPTER 4

Backing Up Data in a Multiplatform Environment

What's the most valuable element of a computer network? Many people would probably answer, "the computers." They'd be wrong: It's the *data* contained in the computers that's most important, whether that data is your personal cookbook on your home computer, your doctoral thesis in progress on your laptop, or the new software product that two hundred people at your company have spent six months' time producing. Backing up the data on a computer is much like having auto insurance. All kinds of problems can happen to your car: the engine can fail (your hard disk can die), someone can crash into your car (crack your network), or you can wreck your own car (forget the administrator password or delete files unintentionally). Backups are a safety precaution and a fact of life. All sorts of things can go wrong and damage or completely erase your data. Hardware can fail, software can malfunction, and users can accidentally delete files.

With your company's future riding on the integrity of its data, backups are a part of system administration that no administrator can ignore. When you add the issue of supporting multiple operating systems, such as UNIX and Windows, to the mix, things get even more complicated. In this chapter, we will explore some of the things you need to consider when performing backups in a multiplatform environment.

BACKUPS ARE ESSENTIAL

There can be any number of reasons why your computer data could become lost or damaged. Regardless of the reason, the users of your computer systems expect to be able to retrieve their programs should they become lost or accidentally deleted. The very survival of your company may ride on your having the ability to restore files from backup. Clearly, you need to have a comprehensive backup plan that adequately protects your software and data.

Not only do you need to simply do backups, you need to decide on a whole range of issues. For example, you will need to decide on the backup schedule, the type of media and backup device to use, which file systems to back up, what kind of offsite storage, if any, you will use, and what kind of documentation you will have for your backup process. Depending on the size of your computing environment, you may have some cost issues as well. For example, do you need a robotic tape changer? Do you need to do backups at 2:00 A.M. to minimize user down time? If you need to do backups in the middle of the night, will you have to pay an operator to come in and monitor the backup process?

Just when you think you've thought of all the problems, the issue of cross-platform backups rears its ugly head. If you have a mixed UNIX and Windows shop, which you probably do or you wouldn't be reading this book, you get a whole new set of problems. Do you try to integrate backups of both systems into one common set of backup software? If so, how? If not, how are you going to manage two sets of backups? Do you buy a commercial product, or "roll your own"?

So you see, backups are an essential part of managing any computing environment. However, having a good backup strategy requires some careful planning and attention to detail. Let's look at some solutions to these problems and explore some different backup options for different platforms.

SCHEDULING BACKUPS

How often do you need to back up your data? Well, that depends to a large degree on your specific computing needs and how quickly you need to have data restored. In an ideal world, you would like to be able to restore any deleted file at any time. Of course, keeping your backed-up data completely current may not be a realistic goal—but you should be able to restore any file to a previous state that is within a few hours to a day old.

When you perform backups, you usually have at least a couple of options for the type of backup that you do. *Full backups,* sometimes called *image backups,* duplicate every file on the system. By comparison, *incremental backups* (also called *differential backups*), duplicate only those files that have changed since the last backup session.

Some systems support different types of incremental backups. For example, you may choose to duplicate only those files that have changed since the last incremental backup, or you may wish to duplicate every file that has changed since the last full backup. On most UNIX systems, the dump program allows you to make incremental backups at a variety of levels. This allows you to schedule different degrees of backup for different days. For example, if you are using different backup levels, a Level 2 incremental will back up anything that has changed since the last Level 0, Level 1, or Level 2 backup. A Level 1 incremental backup will back up any files that have changed since the last Level 0 or Level 1 backup.

NOTE: In your computing environment, you probably have certain files and file systems that are more critical than others. Your backup policies should reflect these differences. Your operating system software probably doesn't change very often, for example, so it can be backed up with less frequency than your databases.

Let's look at some sample backup schedules. If you have a very time-sensitive computing environment, you might find it necessary to back up all your data every day. This would mean a daily full backup. While this schedule gives you the most security, it is also the most time consuming. You will have to ensure that you have adequate down time every day to perform the backup, as well as adequate bandwidth on your backup devices to handle the volume of data.

Another option is to perform a full backup once a week—every Saturday night, for example—and then perform incremental backups every other day of the week. When you restore files from this type of backup arrangement, you start by restoring from the full backup, then restore from the most recent backup backward to the least recent. This way, you are not copying over files that have already been restored. By using the one full backup and daily incremental schedule, your data is protected, even though you might have to go to several tapes to completely restore your system.

If you find yourself without enough resources to perform backups as often as you'd like to, you may need to use a schedule that has multiple levels of backups. Such a schedule might have a full backup once a month, Level 1 incremental backups once per week, and Level 2 backups on the other days. By doing a full backup only once each month, you limit your maximum backup device use to the shortest time possible. As Level 1 backups will take less space than a full backup, but more space than a Level 2 backup, backup resources are minimized here as well. The disadvantages are that it can take significantly longer to restore files, and you might find yourself in a bind if one of your Level 1 tapes or your full backup tape develops a defect.

OFFSITE STORAGE

Whenever you develop and implement a backup plan, you should include provisions for storing at least some of your backup media offsite. In the event that fire, flood, or some other natural disaster damages your offices, offsite backups could save your company from financial disaster.

Ideally, you could store all your backup media in an offsite location. However, if you have a large amount of data that is backed up on a regular basis, this might be prohibitive due to the amount of backup media. Also, if all your backups are in an offsite location, it becomes very inconvenient to easily restore files. After all, you really don't want to hop in your car, drive to an offsite storage facility, find the right tape, drive back to work, restore a file, and take the tape back to offsite storage every time someone deletes a file by accident!

As with all things backup-related, offsite storage decisions are a balancing act between safety and security on the one hand, and cost and inconvenience on the other. Many sites choose to store only full backups offsite. If your site performs a full backup weekly, with daily incremental backups, you might opt to keep one week's work of backups onsite, but move the files from the rest of your backup rotation to an offsite location.

If you have multiple sites that are backed up regularly, each site should have a designated offsite storage location. To minimize cost, you could use a different company location as the offsite storage facility. For example, the Denver branch could send its offsite tapes to the San Francisco office, the San Francisco office could send its offsite tapes to the Atlanta office, and the Atlanta office could send its offsite tapes to the Denver office. This type of plan minimizes cost, but since the offsite backups are not physically close to the office to which they belong, they are not immediately accessible. If Denver had a sudden need for its offsite backup tape from San Francisco, it would have to be sent by courier.

What are your alternatives to using another branch office for offsite storage? There are companies that will provide secure, fireproof, offsite data storage for a fee. If you have a small company, a very cheap, secure, and effective solution is to rent a safe deposit box or two at a local bank.

DOCUMENTATION

It seems that all system administrators have a mixed love/hate relationship with system documentation. On the one hand, they love having accurate documentation that reflects the current system configuration, all modifications to hardware and software, and all current policies and procedures. On the other hand, many system administrators are already doing enough work for three or four people—and writing and updating process and configuration documentation just never seems to make it to the top of the To Do list.

Now that we have admitted that documentation is rarely one of a system administrator's favorite tasks, we have to tell you that you need to document. When you devise a backup strategy for your operation, you should make sure that the backup process is fully documented. By "fully documented," we mean that you need to document not only the actual backup process, but also all the critical information associated with backups.

Your documentation for the current backup process should include lists of the file systems or disks that are backed up, which computers they are located on, and the exact backup schedule for each disk or file system. This backup schedule needs to include dates and times of backups, plus what backup levels are performed when. In addition, you need to specify the tools used for the backup, as well as the exact procedures for performing both backups and restores, the details of your tape rotation plan, and the details of your offsite storage arrangements.

This document is always a work in progress. As you make changes to your computing environment, you must make changes to the documentation. Make sure that you keep your process documentation up to date so that it accurately reflects your current procedures. Also, make sure that other members of your staff, as well as your managers, know where your documentation is so that things will run smoothly if you're sick or otherwise unavailable.

UNIX BACKUPS

Before we start discussing the specifics of backing up UNIX systems, we need to look at how UNIX handles disks and partitions. UNIX attempts to make virtually everything look to the user like a file or directory. The UNIX file system is constructed like an inverted tree, with a single root directory at the top. Directories descend from this root directory, each of which contains other files and directories. A pathname in UNIX is a list of directories separated by / characters.

If a pathname is complete, it will start with a / character, indicating that the path starts at the root directory. Some sample pathnames might look like /usr/local/bin/perl and /usr/local/lib. In the first example, /usr/local/bin/perl, the leading / character indicates that the path starts at the root directory. The components usr, local, and bin are the subdirectories in the path. So usr is a subdirectory of the root directory, local is a subdirectory of the usr directory, and bin is a subdirectory of local. The last entry in the path, perl, is the name of a file in the /usr/local/bin directory. In the second example, /usr/local/lib, usr is a subdirectory of the root directory, and local is a subdirectory of usr. The last element, lib, is a subdirectory of local. Notice that the syntax for directory names and filenames in a path statement is identical in UNIX. You can't just look at the pathname and know if it refers to a directory or a file. If you aren't that familiar with UNIX, you can get confused fairly easily here.

Did you notice that we did not refer to specific disks or disk partitions anywhere in the path statement? What disk and partition is /usr/local/bin/perl located on? You can't tell from the file's path. UNIX tries to hide this information from the user, in order to make the file system look like one big logical tree structure.

In reality, different disks and partitions really make up the file system tree. UNIX mounts a specific disk and partition to a particular directory name in the file system tree. So, as you change directories down through the directory tree, you can actually switch to directories that are physically located on different disks.

UNIX automatically mounts these disk partitions into the directory tree at boot time, according to the instructions in the configuration file. This file will be called /etc/fstab, /etc/vfstab, or something similar (depending on your version of UNIX). This file, written in typically cryptic UNIX syntax, contains a list of disks and partitions to mount, along with the names of the directories where each should be mounted.

By now you probably want to know what all this has to do with backups under UNIX. Well, it is important for a couple of reasons. First of all, depending on the way you do your backups, you might need to know which disk and partition a directory structure is located on before you can back it up. Second, if you have a catastrophic system failure and you need to restore from backup completely, you definitely will want to know how your disk partitions are laid out, and which file systems correspond to which disks and partitions.

REMEMBER: It is a very good idea to keep up-to-date copies of all your disk partition maps, as well as your file system mount configuration file, /etc/fstab. This information will be critical if you need to perform a complete restore! Also, this information should be replicated offsite in case of catastrophes.

UNIX provides several different utilities that can be used for system backups. These utilities differ in their sophistication. Some are useful for quickly archiving files, while others can manage more detailed backup strategies. We will look at three utilities that are the most commonly used for backups. You will likely find at least two of these utilities on any UNIX system that you encounter. In addition to these native UNIX utilities, there are several third-party software packages for performing backups. A bit later in the chapter, we will look at a couple of these that can handle multiple platforms.

Using tar for Backups

One of the easier UNIX utilities that can be used to perform backups is the tar program. With its name coming from the words "tape archive," you can guess that tar was developed to archive files and directories onto tape. In reality, you can use tar to back up to almost any backup device, including other disk partitions.

Another common use of tar is to create an archive file, commonly called a *tar file.* A tar file allows you to make a copy of a group of programs, or an entire directory tree, and store it in a single file.

NOTE: Much installable UNIX software that you download from the web is in tar file format.

Using tar for backups has both advantages and disadvantages. As for its advantages, tar is relatively easy to use, once you master its syntax. It is also widely available on virtually every UNIX platform. Tar files can typically be read by any UNIX system's version of tar. In addition, tar has been around a long time and is very reliable.

However, tar has some significant disadvantages that may rule it out completely for your backups. Different UNIX operating systems have different versions of tar. Some of these versions limit the length of the filename that can be backed up. This can prevent you from being able to back up a very deep directory tree, as the total length of the file pathnames can exceed the capability of your version of tar. Also, some versions of tar are incapable of making backups that span multiple tapes. Special UNIX files, such as device files located in the /dev directory, cannot be backed up with tar. Finally, tar doesn't know anything about a file's backup history, so it has no way to support incremental backups. If you want to perform incremental backups with tar, you will need to write some shell scripts to manage the details of incremental backups yourself.

If you look at the man (short for manual) page for tar, its syntax looks pretty complicated. The tar utility has a lot of options, many of which you will probably never use. By mastering only a few options, you can use tar pretty effectively. Table 4-1 shows some of the most common options for the tar command.

Option	Description
c	Creates a tar archive or tar file.
t	Prints the table of contents for a tar archive.
x	Extracts a file from a tar archive and restores it to disk.
v	Verbose output. Gives a detailed description of what tar is doing.
p	Preserves ownership, group, and permission information when restoring files.
f *filename*	Tells tar to operate on the tar archive named *filename.* The *filename* argument can either be an actual filename or a device name.

Table 4-1. Commonly Used Options for the tar Command

These options will get you through most of the situations that you will encounter when using tar. In addition to these frequently used options, some versions of tar support the z option, which tells tar that the output file is to be compressed. Some versions also support the M option, which tells tar to create the output on multiple volumes.

Doing Backups with tar

Okay, let's look at how we actually can use tar to back up files and directories. In this first example, we are going to back up a user's directory to a tar file.

```
tar cvf /tmp/smith.tar /home/smith
```

The c option tells tar that we are creating a tar archive. The v option tells tar to be verbose in its output. The f /tmp/smith.tar option tells tar that the tar archive being created is going to be named smith.tar.

Now what if, instead of making a tar archive file, we want to back up Mr. Smith's directory to a tape? We can use the exact same syntax, except you will need to change the tar archive filename to be the name of the tape device. Let's say you have a tape device on your UNIX system, and the tape drive is named /dev/rmt3. In order to back up Mr. Smith's home directory to the tape drive, we change the command to

```
tar cvf /dev/rmt3 /home/smith
```

NOTE: Physical device names are different under virtually every vendor's version of UNIX. We will use the /dev/rmt3 format in our examples, but be aware that the device names associated with your UNIX system may well be very different.

Restoring from Backups

Restoring files from a tar archive is very similar to backing them up. Let's say, for example, that you have just downloaded a nifty new UNIX utility, and you want to extract the tar archive. For the purposes of this example, let's assume that you've downloaded the file to the /tmp directory and named it newstuff.tar, and you want to expand the archive into the /usr/local/src directory. You would then use the command

```
tar xvf /tmp/newstuff.tar /usr/local/src
```

As you can see, the command to expand the tar file looks almost identical to the command used to create the archive in the first place.

REMEMBER: Before restoring files from an archive, it is usually a good idea to look at the table of contents for the archive just to make sure that everything is where you think it is. To look at the table of contents for a tar archive, use the command tar tvf *filename*, where *filename* is the name of the archive file.

Directories in Archive Files

When you are creating a tar archive, either directly to a backup device or to an archive file, tar allows you to specify which files can go into that archive. Since you can either give a list of files, possibly with a wildcard, or you can give a directory name, how your tar file is structured depends on the way you specify the files.

If you choose to create a tar file giving the name of a directory, tar will add the directory entry to the tar file first, then recursively descend into the directory, adding the files and directories that it encounters. The net result of this is that when you extract the files from the tar file, tar will recreate the top directory entry first.

On the other hand, if you simply give a list of files, tar will add them to the archive without creating a directory entry at the top. When you extract the files from the archive, you will end up with a bunch of files in your current directory.

It is usually preferable to use a directory name as the top-level entry in a tar archive, if possible. This way, when the tar file is expanded, the only thing that will be created in the target directory is a new directory entry. All the files from the tar archive will be expanded in this new directory.

Let's look at an example to help clarify this a bit. Assume that you have written a new piece of UNIX utility software that you want to turn into a tar file and put out on the Net for everyone to use. You have all the source code for your new utility software in a directory called niftyutil. With all the source and header files for your utility software, the niftyutil directory contains somewhere over 100 files. How do you make the tar file?

Your first option is to change directory to the niftyutil directory and create the tar file there. For example, you could type

```
$ cd niftyutil
$ tar cvf ../niftyutil.tar *
```

The first command changes directory to the niftyutil directory, and the second command creates the tar file. The tar file is created one directory level up, with the name niftyutil.tar.

What happens when a user downloads this software to his /usr/local/src directory, and then expands it? Well, the unlucky user gets over 100 files in his /usr/local/src directory! Why? Because when you created the tar file, you did not add a directory entry as the first item.

NOTE: If you look carefully at this example, you will see that we create the tar file up one directory. We can't create it in the current directory because we have used a wildcard to tell tar to add all files in the directory to the tar file. If we create the tar file in the same directory, tar will try to add the tar file to the tar file, and it will probably get very confused!

Instead of changing into the niftyutil directory as we did in the previous example, you could create the tar file as follows:

```
$ tar cvf niftyutil.tar niftyutil
```

Using the tar command this way adds the niftyutil directory as the first entry in the tar file. So, when a user expands this version of the tar file, only the niftyutil directory will be created in the target directory.

Using cpio for Backups

The next step up from tar is the cpio utility. The name "cpio" comes from "copy archives in and out." Like tar, cpio creates archive files; however, it overcomes some of the limitations of tar. With cpio, you can back up special files such as device files, and cpio has a bit more intelligence when it encounters bad blocks or bad sectors while restoring files.

However, cpio still has some disadvantages. The program still has length limitations on pathnames (though the length limitations are longer than those required by tar), and some users find its syntax to be cryptic. As with tar, cpio does not provide intrinsic support for incremental backups.

You'll find that cpio is a bit strange in the way that it processes filenames and creates archives. You see, cpio reads the names of the files to archive from the standard input stream and writes the result of the archive to the standard output stream. This means that you will virtually always see the output of some command that generates a list of files redirected as input to cpio. Also, you will virtually always see the output of a cpio command redirected into another file. We'll see an example of this in just a moment.

As with tar, cpio has a lot of command options, but you can usually get by with only a few. Table 4-2 lists some of the most common command options for cpio.

Okay, let's look at how to create cpio archive files. Logically, the process is very similar to using tar. As with tar, cpio allows you to either use a filename or a device name as the output. In our first example, we're going to revisit Mr. Smith's home directory from a few examples ago. If we want to create a cpio archive of Mr. Smith's directory, we could do it as follows:

```
# cd /home
# ls -R smith | cpio -o > smithdir.cpio
```

We do a recursive listing of the smith directory and pipe the output of the ls command to cpio. The cpio command uses the –o option to create an output file and redirects the output file into the file smithdir.cpio. We could have used other commands, such as find or cat, to generate the list of filenames to archive.

REMEMBER: Just as with tar, it is a good idea to use a directory name as the first entry in the cpio output file. Also, make sure to create the cpio output file in a different directory than the one you will be archiving.

Option	Function
i	Reads in a cpio file from the standard input. Copy in mode.
o	Creates an output cpio file from the standard input. Copy out mode.
b	Causes cpio to read and write with a block size of 5,120 bytes per record. This option is used to cause data to be written more efficiently to tape.
v	Verbose mode. Tells cpio to give verbose output about what it is doing.
d	Creates directories as needed.

Table 4-2. Commonly Used Options for the cpio Command

Now that we have archived Mr. Smith's home directory, let's restore it to a new location, /home/visitors/smith. We do this as follows:

```
# cd /home
# mkdir visitors
# cd visitors
# cat /home/smithdir.cpio | cpio -id
```

Notice that we use the cat command to send the cpio file into cpio via the standard input. The –i option tells cpio that we are sending it a cpio file. The –d option tells cpio to create any subdirectories as needed.

Using dump for Backups

The most powerful backup utilities that are native to most versions of UNIX are the dump and restore commands. The dump command provides real backups (including all special and device files), handles multiple volumes, provides support for incremental backups, and does not have a filename path length limitation.

In order to support incremental backups, dump writes information to a special file, typically called /etc/dumpdates. The /etc/dumpdates file contains information about which file systems have been backed up, when they were backed up, and which level of dump was performed.

When you use dump to perform a backup of your system, especially a Level 0 or Level 1 backup, the file systems need to be in an inactive state. This prevents changes from being made to files as they are being backed up. If a file system is actively having changes made as it is being backed up, dump may not record an accurate copy of some files, and they may be impossible to restore.

You have a couple of options here. The safest way to guarantee that there is no file system activity is to bring the system down to single-user mode. Once it is in single-user mode, only the system administrator can log in, and no cron jobs are started automatically. However, UNIX requires operator intervention in order to bring the system to single-user mode, do backups, and then bring the system back up to multiuser mode. Your other option is to perform backups at a period of very low system use, typically in the middle of the night or on weekends. When scheduling backups for the middle of the night, take care not to run backups during a time when cron might be starting other jobs that will modify the file system. Even if there are no interactive users on your system, having the accounting program write to the file system during a Level 0 dump can completely corrupt the dump so that it cannot be restored!

As with the other backup and archive utilities, there are several commonly used options for the dump command. Table 4-3 lists the most common options for dump.

As with all UNIX utilities, the version of dump for your system may have different options. Check the system documentation for your particular flavor of UNIX if you need more in-depth information on dump's parameters.

Unlike tar and cpio, dump usually operates at the disk-partition level. Therefore, you need to know which disk partitions and file systems you have, and where they are mounted in your file system tree. This way, all your backups correspond directly to a

Option	Description
0-9	The dump level. A dump level of 0 backs up everything. A dump level of 1 backs up everything that has changed since the last Level 0 dump. A dump level of 2 backs up everything that has changed since the last Level 1 or Level 0 dump, whichever is more recent. Dump levels 3 through 9 work the same way.
u	Causes dump to update the dump record file, typically /etc/dumpdates. Most versions of dump do not update this file automatically; you must explicitly tell it to do so.
s	The size of the backup tape in feet.
d	The density of the backup tape in bytes per inch.
f	The filename to dump to. This filename is typically a system device name, such as the tape drive /dev/rmt3.
v	Verifies the integrity of the backup against the original files.

Table 4-3. Common Options for the dump Command

specific disk partition. This makes it a lot easier to rebuild a disk after it has had a complete crash. Alternatively, you can specify a directory name to back up instead.

Let's look at an example of the dump command. Assume that you want to back up your /home file system, and /home is located on disk partition /dev/sda4. To perform a Level 0 dump of /dev/sda3, to a tape that is 1,600 feet long at 1,200 bytes per inch, and store the dump on tape drive /dev/rmt0, you would use the command

```
dump 0usdf 1600 1200 /dev/rmt0 /dev/sda3
```

This does look pretty cryptic, but you can figure it out easily. The 0 indicates a Level 0 dump. The u tells dump to update the dump record file. The next three options, s, d, and f, specify the tape size, density, and dump device, respectively. Notice that all three of these options take parameters. The dump command allows you to group the options and then follow them, by the parameters, in the correct order. So, we see sdf grouped together, with 1600 being the parameter for the s option, 1200 being the parameter for the d option, and /dev/rmt0 being the parameter for the f option.

REMEMBER: It is very important that the parameters for the options be listed in the same sequence as the options that they correspond to.

Most versions of UNIX support a variant of the dump command that allows you to do dumps over the network. This allows you to back up computers that do not have backup devices directly attached to them. This variant of dump is typically called rdump, with the corresponding variant of restore, called rrestore.

WINDOWS BACKUPS

In the Windows arena, you will typically run into the following file system types:

- **FAT** Used by DOS, the FAT (File Allocation Table) file system is supported by almost every operating system in existence, including Linux.
- **FAT32** Used by Windows 98 and up, the FAT32 file system allows for larger volumes.
- **NTFS** Introduced in Windows NT, NTFS provides for a finely granular set of permissions and on-the-fly compression.
- **NTFS5** Windows 2000's version of NTFS is called NTFS5. Similar to the Windows NT version of NTFS, NTFS5 adds support for built-in encryption, enhanced ACLs (Access Control Lists), and other features. NTFS5 is not compatible with the Windows NT NTFS. However, Windows 2000 can operate in a mixed mode, with both types of file systems. Additionally, Service Pack 5 for Windows NT included facilities to allow Windows NT to work with NTFS5 file systems.

NOTE: If you wish to use Services for Macintosh or Active Directory, you must be using NTFS.

While still supporting the DOS FAT file system, Windows also provides the NTFS file system as a native mode option. Under Windows 2000, file systems are structured with a particular disk or disk partition as the top-level component, as opposed to the root directory in a UNIX environment. One consequence of this is that you can have several logical drives in a Windows environment, each with complete and different file systems, whereas UNIX generally provides a single logical file system that attempts to conceal the hardware details as much as possible.

Working with Windows 2000 Remote Storage

Like UNIX, Windows 2000 ships with a backup utility. While not extremely full-featured, this backup utility is adequate for general use. Windows 2000 provides a tape backup utility that, while it does not have all the features of a more robust third-party backup solution, is at least guaranteed to be available for all installations of Windows 2000 Server. Named Remote Storage, the utility is started from the Administrative Tools group under Programs in the Start menu, as shown in Figure 4-1. (Alternatively, you can double-click

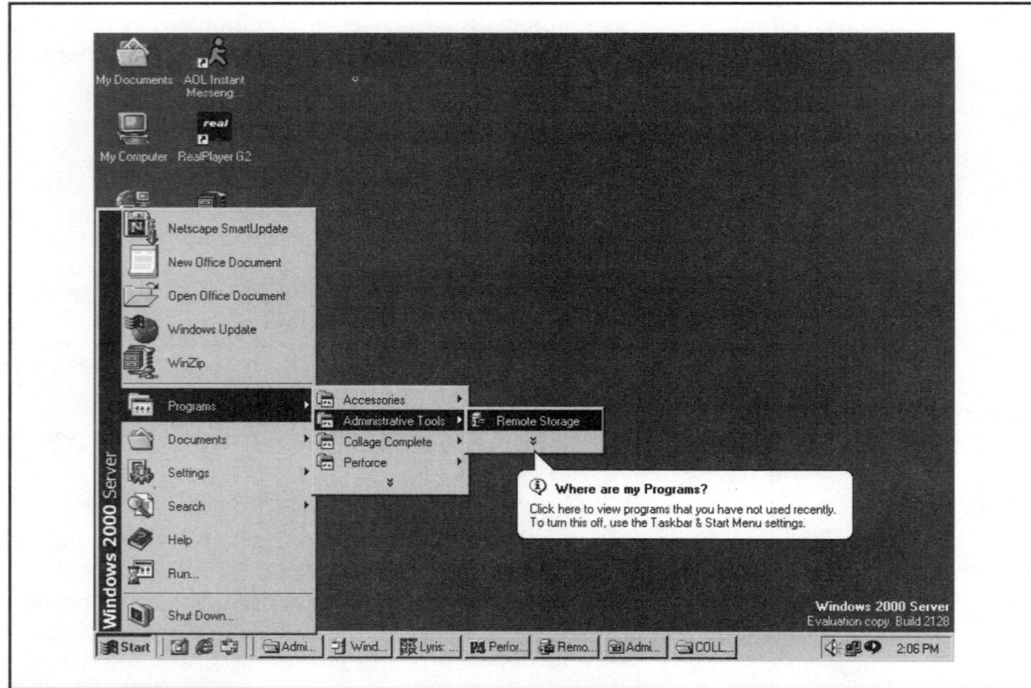

Figure 4-1. The Remote Storage Utility startup path

the My Computer icon on the Windows desktop, then double-click the Control Panels Folder, then open the Administrative Tools folder, and double-click on the Remote Storage icon.)

NOTE: Windows Remote Access is not installed by default in Windows 2000 Server Setup; you will have to select it during the operating system install process.

When you first start Remote Storage, its main screen is displayed, as shown in Figure 4-2. As you can see, two windows are visible. One window lists all the drives available for backup, including any shared folders on other computers that you have mapped as network drives. The other window shows the current tape drive status.

Basically, the file selection mechanism in Remote Storage is very similar to the Windows Explorer interface; simply browse through the directories and select the ones that you want to back up.

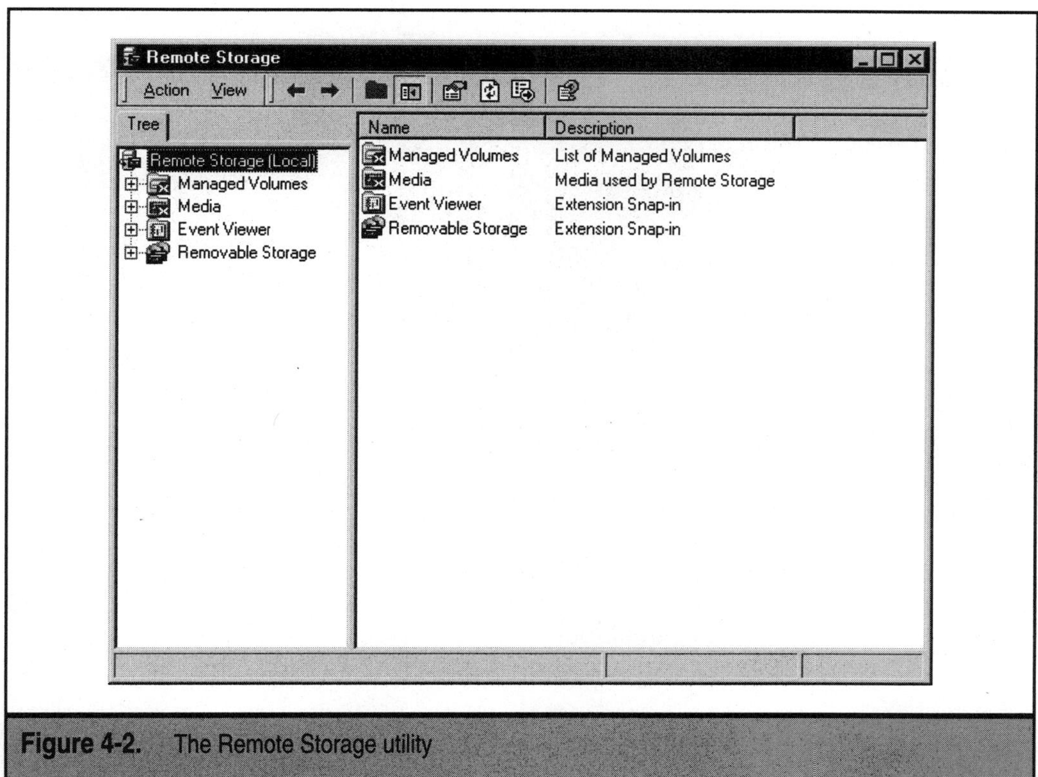

Figure 4-2. The Remote Storage utility

NOTE: Regardless of which files you select, Remote Storage will only back up the files that you have access to. Windows file permissions and share permissions are still in effect.

Limitations of Windows Remote Storage

Remote Storage is bundled as a component of the Windows 2000 operating system, but it is not as full-featured or robust as other commercial tools. Remote Storage has some serious limitations that may cause you to look for another commercial tool, depending on your needs:

- **No support for any type of remote or client/server operation** Remote Storage must be run from a computer with an attached tape drive and cannot be managed remotely. There is no way for a backup server to poll clients over the network and back them up. This means that in order to back up drives on a remote computer, you must share them so that they are accessible from a Windows computer with an attached tape drive. This may be undesirable, or not even possible, depending on how your network is set up.
- **Limited tape drive support** Remote Storage is designed to work only with SCSI 4mm, 8mm, and DLT tape drives. At this time, there is no way to use another type of medium, such as optical, WORM, or Iomega Jaz disks. Nor does Remote Storage support backups to another disk partition.
- **Inflexible file system support** Remote storage supports only the NTFS file system.
- **Inability to perform mirror backups** Remote Storage is designed as a file backup utility; it cannot perform mirror backups. (A *mirror backup* creates a disk image identical to the disk being backed up.)
- **No facility for scheduling unattended backups** If you want to run scheduled, unattended backups at a later time with Remote Storage, you must write a batch file that uses the ntbackup command. When run from a batch file, the ntbackup command does not support backing up individual files; only directories can be backed up. To schedule a backup at a particular time, use the at command.

NOTE: To use the at command, you must have the Scheduler service running.

As you can see, there are some serious limitations to the Remote Storage program. However, if you are in a small computing environment with only a few servers and clients, it can be a very easy-to-use solution.

CROSS-PLATFORM ISSUES

As you have seen, tools are available for performing backups under both UNIX and Windows, although both have their limitations. When it comes time to address backup issues in a multiplatform environment, the situation becomes even more challenging. None of the native backup tools represent a truly effective solution. UNIX and Windows have different types of file systems with very different structures, as well as different permission mechanisms. They also have different commonly used ways of exporting or sharing file systems.

The backup solution that you choose for your network depends, to a large degree, on your network environment itself. What are your primary operating systems? Are you primarily a UNIX shop with a few Windows clients? Or are you a large Windows shop that uses Windows for file and application servers, with only a few UNIX workstations? In the first case, you might want to consider a cross-platform backup system that uses one of your UNIX servers as your primary backup server. In the second case, you might want to use a Windows system as your primary backup server. If you choose to use a commercial client/server solution, you will need to know which packages support which operating systems as clients and servers.

Backing Up Exported File Systems

One way to back up file systems in a multiplatform environment is to export the file system, via some server protocol, and have a backup server attach to it and back it up. To export a file system, the client essentially becomes a file server for a brief period of time.

The client, depending on the type of system being used as the backup server, would make its file systems available to the server via a protocol such as NFS or Microsoft Networking (NetBT). The server then attaches to the exported file system, either by mounting it (if the server is part of a UNIX system) or mapping it to a network drive (if the server is part of a Windows system). The server then proceeds with the backup, detaching itself from the exported file system at the appropriate time.

This sounds quite simple, but in reality, performing backups using exported file systems in a multiplatform environment can be very difficult. Here are four points to consider:

- The NTFS file system has an extensive file permission structure that includes Access Control Lists (ACLs). If you are using a Windows-based NFS server to export file systems to a UNIX system for backup, file permissions and ACLs may not be retained correctly if the file system is restored. Different implementations of NFS for Windows NT handle ACLs in different ways.
- The NFS (Network File System), unlike Windows, does not convert a filename to uppercase when searching for a file. Windows preserves filename case when writing the file to disk, but when you retrieve the file, it treats TheFile.txt,

THEFILE.TXT, and thefile.txt as the same file. Under UNIX, these would be three different files, since UNIX completely implements case-sensitive directory and filenames.

- Support for transparently attaching to SMB-shared file systems, such as with Microsoft Networking or Samba, is very limited. On the UNIX side, many SMB clients such as Samba operate within the context of a command-line program, which is unsuitable for backups. On the Windows side, most UNIX systems do not support SMB shares without third-party software. Even then, the areas to be shared are usually required to be special directories set aside for that purpose.
- If none of the preceding reasons stops you from trying to do backups with exported file systems, consider that you must actually export or share these file systems in order to back them up. Depending on your environment, this can pose a great security risk. Are your network and NFS setup secure enough that, when you share the root partition of your primary server, you can guarantee that no one can break in and steal your passwords and configuration files? How secure will your Registry be when you share your Windows boot drive?

If you can work around all these issues involved with cross-platform file system sharing, it can be an inexpensive solution. However, the intelligent system administrator should be prepared for problems.

Client/Server Backup Systems

In order to solve the multiplatform backup problem, several companies have developed backup software that runs in a client/server mode. One primary computer, typically the server with the backup device attached, serves as the backup server. This computer will have a special server package installed that sets backup times, parameters, and computers and file systems to back up.

Each client that is to be backed up will run a special client program. Depending on the operating system, the client software can be run as a background process in UNIX, a Windows service, or a foreground interactive program. At certain predetermined times, the server polls the client computers and initiates a backup over the network.

Since the client sends the data directly to the server without relying on an intermediate process, client/server backup circumvents the problems associated with using exported or shared file systems as a backup source. There is no need for the server to mount the shared file systems from the client. All that the server and client need is a clear network communications path between them.

Commercial Multiplatform Tools

Okay, you've decided that you really do need to install a commercial, cross-platform, network backup tool. What are your options? There are several companies that produce this type of product, although they will support different types of clients and servers. Backup tools from different manufacturers will have different limitations as well. The following sections give some examples of popular multiplatform backup software packages, and point out where you can go for more information.

Legato Networker

Networker is a high-powered, very effective, enterprise-wide tool for distributed systems backup. It operates effectively as a client/server solution in networks with multiple operating systems. As of this writing, Networker supports Windows NT, NetWare, and a variety of UNIX systems, including Solaris. In addition, Networker provides support for a wide variety of backup devices, including robotic tape changers. It also provides an easy-to-use graphical interface that greatly simplifies backup and restore procedures. Finally, Networker also includes a bare-metal disaster recovery option, restoring all data, application, and operating system files, including user settings and preferences. For more information on Legato Networker, see Legato's website at **http://www.legato.com**.

Cheyenne ARCserve

Cheyenne Software produces ARCserve, another top-quality tool for distributed backup. The ARCserve server is available for Windows, UNIX, and NetWare, with client software available for a wide variety of platforms, including Windows NT, multiple types of UNIX, Windows 95/98, OS/2, NetWare, and Macintosh. ARCserve also provides backup and restore modules for databases such as Oracle, Sybase, and Informix, and workgroup applications such as Lotus Notes. Many types of backup utilities are supported, including various tape libraries and tape RAIDs, optical libraries, and Storage Area Networks (SANs). For more information about Cheyenne's ARCserve line of products, see the storage management section of their website at **http://www.cai.com/arcserveit/**.

VERITAS Backup Exec

VERITAS purchased Seagate Software in 1998–9 and acquired a leading supplier of third-party backup and storage management tools. VERITAS was selected by Microsoft to provide three of the four storage components embedded in Windows 2000: NTbackup, Removable Storage Services (RSS), Logical Disk Manager (LDM), and WinINSTALL Limited Edition. VERITAS Backup Exec (originally Arcada Backup Exec) is a 32-bit native backup solution designed to operate on Windows platforms; it provides extensive client support for a wide range of operating systems, including support for SAN solutions and a huge array of media and strategies. The quality of the documentation is also high. As another useful point to consider, Microsoft itself recently standardized on the use of VERITAS Backup Exec Network Storage Executive (NSE). If you need a Windows-oriented backup solution with cross-platform support, you should look at VERITAS. For more information on VERITAS' range of backup and data management and availability solutions, you can check out their website at **http://www.veritas.com**.

HIBACK

HIBACK from HICOMP provides yet another multiplatform backup tool. In addition to providing clients for a large number of operating systems, HIBACK's server component HIBARS also runs on Windows and most UNIX systems, as well as Linux. HIBACK supports a wide array of media and is also designed to support databases. HIBACK provides demo versions of some of their products, available for download from their website at **http://www.hicomp.com/**.

Retrospect

While originally based in the Apple Macintosh environment, Dantz's Retrospect provides an excellent Windows backup solution, with strong support for mixed Macintosh and Windows (including Windows 2000) environments across networks, and good performance. For more information, see the Dantz website at **http://www.dantz.com/**.

PerfectBACKUP+

Merlinsoft's PerfectBACKUP+ is a primarily Linux-based backup solution that supports several flavors of UNIX, and NetWare, in a free version. As of this writing, the latest version (6.1) is primarily Linux-oriented, but the company will be providing Macintosh and Windows clients. For more information, see Merlinsoft's website at **http://www.merlinsoftech.com/**.

SUMMARY

Multiplatform backups are a difficult task, no matter what your computing environment looks like. In this chapter, we examined the different backup utilities available under UNIX and Windows, and we looked at how to establish a secure, reliable backup schedule. We then looked at the problems surrounding multiplatform backups and explored solutions. We discussed the details of client/server backup tools and examined the issues surrounding backing up exported and shared file systems. Finally, we discussed some commercially available products that can help solve some of the problems that you will encounter when doing multiplatform backups.

Backups are an essential component of systems management. At some point, a disk drive will fail, a server will crash, or a user will delete crucial files. Only if you've established a consistent, thorough backup plan will you be able to recover the data. The very survival of your company, and your job, may depend upon having a good backup policy in place. However, while vital, a backup plan is only part of a fully developed disaster recovery plan, which is beyond the scope of this chapter.

CHAPTER 5

Mail Services with SMTP

Electronic mail was one of the earliest capabilities to evolve when computer networks were first being developed. As networks have grown, so have many different standards and formats for file transfer, electronic mail, and other functions. Over time, numerous general formats for cross-networked communication have evolved. One of these is *Simple Mail Transfer Protocol*, or SMTP. In addition to a more standardized format for electronic mail messages, techniques were needed that could route mail between the different networks. One almost ubiquitous answer to the problem of mail routing is found in Eric Allman's sendmail. Of course, sendmail has not been the only answer to electronic mail transfer.

This chapter will first discuss some of the general issues of electronic mail across multiple heterogeneous networks and the Internet in general. Concepts and definitions will be presented, along with the mail standards as defined in the RFCs (Requests for Comment) that sendmail and other applications have tried to address, and several of the protocols defined for use in electronic messaging. The next section of this chapter will cover sendmail: the UNIX-based subsystem in widest use on the Internet. The final section of this chapter will discuss Microsoft's Exchange Server for Windows NT as a mail and groupware tool.

ELECTRONIC MAIL: AN OVERVIEW

This section will present a broad overview of electronic messaging. The first part will discuss some of the general concepts of electronic mail, including two basic kinds of mail software and where sendmail belongs in the division. The next part of this section will focus on RFCs (Requests for Comment), where the protocols used to communicate within and across networks are defined. The last part of this section explains some of the protocols used to define electronic messages.

History and General Concepts

IBM's PROFS was one of the first widely used office mail systems. Mainframe-based, PROFS had features similar to modern e-mail systems such as Exchange and Notes: strong administration and management tools, security customization, and scheduling capabilities. PROFS and other messaging systems of the time shared several similarities: Whether mainframe or UNIX-based, they were text-based and host-based centralized messaging systems.

As personal computers grew in acceptance and spread through corporations, people started to take advantage of the shift in computing power from the glass-wall mainframe system to the more distributed desktop systems. An early application of personal computer LANs was file sharing, using a central file server and a shared, universally accessible network drive. Messaging systems were one of the first areas to take advantage of the new power on users' desktops, and so host-based messaging shifted (in some cases) to LAN-based messaging.

Shared-File Messaging

LAN-based messaging, also called shared-file messaging, is exemplified by such products as cc:Mail. In shared-file messaging, the desktop client has all the power and all the control. Clients send messages to a mailbox, which is simply a server directory, and poll the server to retrieve mail from their specified mailbox directory. The server is passive and only stores messages; it does no processing or sorting and has no provisions to set rules to control message flow. Shared-file messaging provided the following gains over host-based messaging:

- Added attachments to text-only messages
- Allowed lower-cost servers
- Provided a simplified setup
- Improved performance for some actions

However, shared-file messaging systems introduced new problems. Because each user needed full access to the file system, including others' mailboxes, security was an issue. Also, since each client polls a mail server to see if there's new mail, network traffic went up. While server or workstation performance may be a bottleneck at times, network bandwidth is, more often than not, the limiting factor.

Client/Server Messaging

Client/server messaging systems broke up the tasks of message processing between the desktop workstations and the servers. By using a push model for messages, mail clients no longer clog the network by constantly polling for new messages. Client/server messaging has also improved shared-file messaging by enhancing security so that users have a more difficult time reading others' mail. Finally, with a more intelligent server, sorting and processing of messages can occur before messages are transferred across the network to a client.

Mail User Agents and Mail Transport Agents

Three major concepts of electronic mail transport an administrator should know about are the *mail user agent* (MUA), the *mail transport agent* (MTA), and the *mail delivery agent* (MDA). An MUA is the user interface—the software with which the user reads mail, organizes mail into directories or folders, and sends mail. People prefer different features in MUAs, and not all MUAs are available on all platforms. Many MUAs can coexist on the same machine. For example, a UNIX workstation may have installed and usable, by anyone logged in, the following MUAs: mailx, elm, pine, mailtool (if Solaris is running), and dtmail (if the Common Desktop Environment is present). A given user can use any resident MUA to write and address mail. Other MUAs are included in multipurpose software, such as the mail capabilities built into Lotus Notes and Netscape Mail. MUAs are more commonly referred to as e-mail clients.

The sendmail program, however, is a mail *transport* agent. MTAs aren't used to write a mail message; they're used to route the mail from one MUA on a machine to another MTA. Thus, sendmail is not intended as a user interface routine but is used only to deliver preformatted messages. Mail routing can occur either locally or from another machine or network. In a local mail transfer, where both the sender and destination have accounts on the same machine, the MTA is responsible for transporting mail from itself to a local MDA, and in the process possibly transforming protocols, addresses, and routing the mail. For example, a message created on a UUCP network will require some transformation before a person on a TCP/IP network can receive that message. The MTA acts as a gateway, a mechanism for getting a message from one network to another network that uses different protocols. In the vast majority of cases, there will be only a single MTA on a given machine.

Although sendmail handles SMTP mail transfer between MTAs directly, sendmail relies on mail delivery agents (MDAs) to handle local delivery from the sendmail queue to a queue used by an MUA. Two common MDAs that sendmail is often configured to use are /bin/mail and procmail. While /bin/mail is almost universally available on UNIX systems, procmail is also widely available and is both faster and much more capable than the standard /bin/mail, providing strong capabilities for advance sorting and processing of mail. The relationships among these three components of electronic mail are shown in Figure 5-1.

An analogy for the MUA/MTA/MDA relationship is that an MUA does what a person does when that person wants to send a letter in the physical world—she writes a letter, wraps it in an envelope, puts an address and stamp on it, and then delivers the letter to a post office. MTAs are like the post office, accepting the letter and examining the address, reformatting the address if necessary, and routing the letter either to a mailbox in the same post office (if the letter is local), or to another post office (for a remote destination). An MDA is the postal worker who delivers the mail from the post office to your location. In the case of a gateway, as was just mentioned, the analogy could be extended. An MTA

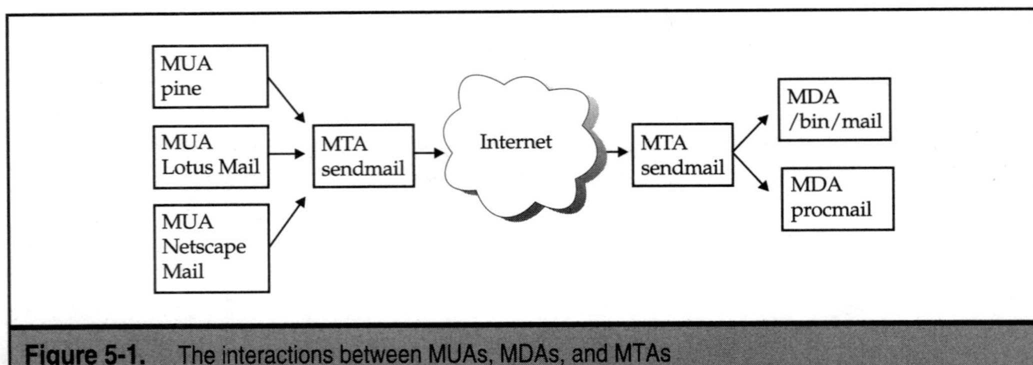

Figure 5-1. The interactions between MUAs, MDAs, and MTAs

that receives a letter for a destination in another country has to transfer that message to another MTA that knows how to deliver letters in the destination country.

RFCs

A Request for Comment (RFC) is a formal description of protocol formats used on the Internet. These protocols are also adhered to by many non-Internet systems. The Internet Engineering Task Force (IETF) issues the Requests for Comment (RFCs). The RFCs are identified and referred to by number for brevity—it's easier to refer to RFC822 than "Standard for the Format of ARPA Internet Text Messages." There are over two thousand RFCs as of this writing, some made obsolete by later RFCs. To find a given RFC, look for the IETF on the World Wide Web at **http://www.ietf.org/**.

Many of the RFCs set standards for mail exchange, and sendmail and other MTAs address the needs and definitions of many of these protocols. However, attempting to describe in detail all of the RFCs relevant to mail transport and formatting could take years. This section will confine its scope to presenting the reference number, the title, and a short definition of some of the RFCs most important to mail transfer over the Internet.

In chronological (and thus numeric) order, the RFCs relevant to sendmail are presented in Table 5-1.

Number	Title	Comments
RFC819	Domain Naming Convention for Internet User Applications	
RFC821	Simple Mail Transfer Protocol	Defines SMTP.
RFC822	Standard for the Format of ARPA Internet Text Messages	Defines the format (headers, body, and how to separate the two) for Internet text mail messages.
RFC976	UUCP Mail Interchange Format Standard	Defines the UNIX-to-UNIX Copy Protocol (UUCP) format of mail messages between two UNIX systems.
RFC1123	Requirements for Internet Hosts—Application and Support	Extends and updates RFC822, mostly by clarifying ambiguous issues in the original document.

Table 5-1. The Requests for Comment Associated with sendmail

Number	Title	Comments
RFC1327	Mapping between X.400(1988) / ISO 10021 and RFC822	Updates RFC822.
RFC1521 RFC1522	MIME (Multipurpose Internet Mail Extensions) Parts One and Two	Provides another extension to the mail format defined in RFC822 by defining Multipurpose Internet Mail Extensions (MIME), which, among other things, allows insertion of binary files such as graphics and sound into mail messages. These two are now obsolete due to RFC2045–2049.
RFC1651	SMTP Service Extensions	Introduces ESTMP (Extended Simple Mail Transfer Protocol).
RFC1652	SMTP Service Extension for 8-bit MIME Transport	
RFC1653	MTP Service Extension for Message Size Declaration	
RFC1869	SMTP Service Extensions	Makes RFC1651 obsolete.
RFC1870	SMTP Service Extension for Message Size Declaration	Makes RFC1653 obsolete.
RFC1891	SMTP Service Extension for Delivery Status Notifications	
RFC1892	The Multipart/Report Content Type for the Reporting of Mail System Administrative Messages	
RFC1893	Enhanced Mail System Status Codes	
RFC1894	An Extensible Message Format for Delivery Status Notifications	
RFC2045–2049	MIME (Multipurpose Internet Mail Extensions) Part One through Five	Makes RFC1521 and RFC1522 obsolete.

Table 5-1. The Requests for Comment Associated with sendmail *(continued)*

Protocols

The sendmail program uses the Simple Mail Transfer Protocol (SMTP) to move messages between two mail servers. Acting only as a server-to-server protocol, SMTP requires another protocol, such as POP3, to collect and process messages locally and deliver the messages to a particular user. SMTP is the communications protocol used most commonly in UNIX-based networks for mail over TCP/IP (Transmission Control Protocol/Internet Protocol) links. Unlike the UUCP (UNIX-to-UNIX Copy Program) protocol, which has to have a map of all machines between the sender and the destination, TCP/IP allows one system on a network to talk directly to another by passing packets of information back and forth between the two. Protocols used over the Internet are also presented in a format called Request for Comment (RFC), issued by the Internet Engineering Task Force. For example, the SMTP protocol just mentioned is defined in RFC821, appropriately titled "Simple Mail Transfer Protocol." This section will present some of the relevant protocols.

SMTP and ESMTP

SMTP is a TCP-based client/server protocol, originally defined in the IETF's RFC821. SMTP is complex in details, but it is fundamentally simple. After a reliable connection is established, the mail client (MUA) initiates a brief handshaking sequence with the mail server (MTA). The client then sends one or more messages to the MTA for delivery. Before each message is sent, the mail client sends a list of the message's local recipients and the sender's address. In an obvious paper mail parallel, this information is referred to as the message's *envelope*.

The handshaking sequence and message content exchange takes place in a formal language made up of four-character commands and three-digit reply codes. For example, an ESMTP mail exchange log might look like this:

```
$ /usr/sbin/sendmail -v phil@testbox.org < message
phil@testbox.org...Connecting to blackbox.testbox.org. via smtp...
220 blackbox.testbox.org ESMTP Sendmail 8.8.5/8.8.5/; Sat, 18 Feb

1998 17:32:24 -0700
>>> EHLO malkuth.hesod.org
250 blackbox.testbox.org Hello richard@malkuth.hesod.org
[168.9.100.13], pleased to meet you
>>> MAIL From:<richard@malkuth.hesod.org>
250 <richard@malkuth.hesod.org>... Sender ok
>>> RCPT To:<phil@testbox.org>
250 Recipient ok
>>> DATA
354 Enter mail, end with "." on a line by itself
>>> .
250 WAA11745 Message accepted for delivery
phil@testbox.org... Sent (WAA11745 Message accepted for delivery)
```

```
Closing connection to blackbox.testbox.org.
>>> QUIT
221 blackbox.testbox.org closing connection
```

A framework for additional features in electronic mail is called the *Extended Simple Mail Transport Protocol* (ESMTP). ESMTP is a mechanism by which extensions to traditional SMTP can be negotiated between the client and the server. The mechanism as described in RFC1651 is open-ended; two of the possible extensions have been defined in RFC1652 and RFC1653.

RFC1652 defines 8-bit MIME transport, which allows users to send 8-bit data in mail messages without having to use base64 format, quoted-printable format, or another encoding method. Furthermore, this is accomplished without the breakage that can result from sending 8-bit data to an RFC821-compliant SMTP server that doesn't know what to do with the incoming components.

Message size declaration, as defined in RFC1653, offers a graceful way for servers to limit the size of messages they are prepared to accept. With RFC821 SMTP, the only possibility is for the server to discard the message after it has been sent in its entirety (after the message has crossed the network onto the server). There is no way for the mail client to be told that the size of the message is the reason it has been discarded.

Other extensions possible with ESMTP include requesting a delivery status notification on outgoing messages so that senders can be notified when messages arrive at their destination, and negotiating encryption between secure mail servers to ensure more secure e-mail.

Mail Message Format

SMTP defined how to transfer a mail message across the Internet but did not define how to recognize a mail message. RFC822 defines the format of Internet electronic mail messages. The format is simple, as befits a standard:

- A header containing various required and optional message attributes
- A blank line
- The message contents

In the following sample message, the header fields predominate:

```
Return-Path: phil@testbox.org
Received: from blackbox.testbox.org (blackbox.testbox.org
[168.9.100.10]) by malkuth.hesod.org (8.8.5/8.8.5) with ESMTP id
WAA01322 for <robert@hesod.org>; Sat, 18 Feb 1998 18:17:06 -0500
Received: from beta.testbox.org (beta.testbox.org [207.266.47.2]) by
blackbox.testbox.org (8.8.5/8.8.5) with SMTP id WAA13732 for
         <robert@hesod.org>; Sat, 18 Feb 1998 18:22:06 -0500
Message-Id: <199802180506.WAA13732@blackbox.testbox.org>
X-Sender: pete@blackbox.testbox.org
```

```
X-Mailer: Macintosh Eudora Lite Version 2.1.2
Mime-Version: 1.0
Content-Type: text/plain; charset="us-ascii"
Date: Sat, 18 Feb 1998 18:22:08 -0500
To: robert@hesod.org
From: Phil Wylie <phil@testbox.org>
Subject: Test message
This is a test message.
Phil
```

The blank line after the Subject line divides the header from the message body that follows. Any subsequent blank line is part of the message body and has no structural significance. Most header fields (such as Subject) are brief and have a fairly obvious meaning, while some others (such as Received ...) are lengthy and not readily understood. For a good explanation of the many standard and less-standard header fields, see Chapter 35 of *Sendmail, Second Edition* by Bryan Costales and Eric Allman (O'Reilly and Associates, 1997).

Each header line consists of a keyword-value pair that defines a single characteristic for that message. A required characteristic of a mail message is the recipient of the message, as specified by the keyword To:, one or more spaces or tab characters, and then the recipient's mailing address. In our test message, the line looks like this:

```
To: robert@hesod.org
```

POP and IMAP

POP (*Post Office Protocol*) and IMAP (*Internet Message Access Protocol*) are both Internet-based message protocols. Of the two, POP is the older protocol. IMAP was designed to include POP capabilities and adds support for offline, online, and disconnected modes of remote mailbox access. POP and IMAP are both defined in IETF RFCs; POP3 is defined in RFC1939, and IMAP4 is defined in RFC1730.

POP was designed to support *offline* mail processing. In the offline paradigm, mail is delivered to a mail server, and a user operates a mail client program that connects to the server and downloads all of the pending mail to the user's local machine. All mail processing of those messages is local to the mail client machine. Offline mode functions as a store-and-forward service, intended to move mail when requested from the mail server or drop point to a single destination mail client machine, usually a personal computer. Once the mail has been delivered to the mail client, the messages are then deleted from the mail server.

IMAP can also do offline mail processing, but IMAP's main functionality lies in online and disconnected modes of operation. In online mode, mail is also delivered to a mail server, but the mail client does not download all of the mail at once and then delete it from the server. In a client/server style, the client can ask the server for only the headers of messages, or the bodies of selected messages, or to search for messages meeting certain criteria. Messages in the mail repository on the server can be marked with various status flags, such as read or deleted, and they stay in the server repository until they are explicitly removed by the user's actions, which may not occur until a later session. Essentially, IMAP is designed to permit manipulation of remote mailboxes as if they were local to the user. Depending on the mail client's implementation of IMAP and the mail behavior defined by the mail administrator, users can either save messages directly onto the client machine or save them on the server, as they desire.

Offline as well as online mailers allow access to new incoming messages on the mail server from a variety of different mail clients. However, offline and online modes suit different requirements and styles of use. Offline mode is best suited for users who use a single client machine routinely, but offline mode is ill-suited for the users who wish to access their recent messages or stored-message folders from different machines at different times. Using offline mode is equivalent to downloading mail and then deleting the mail from the server, so using offline mail access from different computers at different times causes mail to become scattered across different desktops. This is not entirely true if you are working in a distributed environment, such as the OSF's DCE (Distributed Computing Environment), and are using a common network file system. Such a file system may impede network performance and file locking, depending on the implementation. In such cases, the access mode is more online than offline; it only appears offline to you. However, when used via dial-up, offline access does minimize connection time, as well as consumption of server resources.

The differences between online and offline access modes can be summarized in a few sentences. Offline mode is user-initiated retrieval to a single client machine with the following characteristics:

- Minimal use of connection time
- Minimal use of server resources

Online mode has these characteristics:

- Interactive access to multiple mailboxes from multiple clients
- Ability to use different computers at different times
- Ability to use dataless client machines
- Platform-independent access to multiple mailboxes
- Possibility of concurrent access to shared mailboxes

The ability to access one's incoming and message archive folders from different computers, at different times, may be unimportant to those who always use the same desktop to access their mail. However, remote access is a significant advantage for those who use multiple computers.

POP and IMAP do share several common characteristics:

- Both can support offline operation.
- Mail needs to be delivered to a shared, always operational mail server.

- New mail is accessible from a variety of client platform types, and from anywhere on the network.
- Both are defined by Internet RFCs as open protocols.
- Clients are available for multiple platforms, both freeware and commercial.
- Protocols deal only with accessing mail; both POP and IMAP rely on SMTP to send mail.

POP's primary advantage is that it is a simpler protocol than IMAP; this makes it easier to implement. IMAP has several advantages over POP: IMAP can manipulate persistent message status flags, and it can store messages in addition to fetching them so that you can append a message from an incoming message folder to an archive folder. IMAP can access and manage multiple mailboxes on the same server, or on different servers, at the same time. IMAP's ability to allow concurrent updates and access to shared mailboxes is useful if multiple individuals are processing messages coming into a common inbox—a change made by one is presented to other active mail clients in real time.

IMAP is also suitable for accessing non-mail format data such as Usenet postings or documents. Finally, IMAP can also operate in offline mode for minimum connection time and/or server impact. Consider a low-bandwidth connection, typically a dial-up connection. If a message arrives with a several-megabyte video file attached to a one-line text message that reads, "Take a look at this demo," POP will send the entire message. Using an IMAP client allows you to just transfer the header or body of the text without the attached video file, letting you decide if you want to wait for the video to download.

X.400

X.400 is an older mail standard supported by several MTAs. It is a non-IETF standard, having been originally defined by the International Telecommunications Union (ITU) and the International Standards Organization (ISO). The X.400 standards are published jointly by ISO and ITU.

X.400 and Internet mail have several things in common:

- Both are primarily hierarchical, with administrators at a higher level assigning names at the level below.
- Both use a restricted character set for naming.
- Both can be separated into components that are important to the mail network.
- Both claim to be globally unique addressing schemes.
- Neither maps cleanly into the other.

Contrast the following two strings:

```
G=Allan; S=Meyers; O=testbox; OU=mailserver; PRMD=admin; ADMD=admin; C=org
```

and

```
Allan.Meyers@mailserver.testbox.org
```

There are several apparent differences:

- The second line is shorter.
- The first line has labels for pieces of the address.
- One element (admin) occurs twice in the first, but not at all in the second.
- The order of the elements mailserver and testbox is reversed.
- Typing the first requires more keystrokes to be used.

There are also differences that aren't apparent at first, but that become clearer when you compare the underlying technology of X.400 with that of Internet mail. While Internet mailers route as a unit on **mailserver.testbox.org**, ADMDs and PRMDs often expect to route on the C,ADMD,PRMD triplet only; ADMDs route primarily on the C,ADMD portion. The **mailserver.testbox.org** portion is resolvable from a unique root using DNS from any node on the Internet. There is no process executable in real time that determines whether PRMD=admin; ADMD=admin; C=org is a valid triplet from any X.400 node. The details involved in attempting to map an Internet e-mail address to an X.400 address format can be found in the IETF's RFC1327.

NOTE: RFC1506 acts as a tutorial on RFC1327. RFC1494, RFC1495, and RFC1496 specify how mappings work between X.400 and Internet mail when MIME is considered.

X.500

In order to send a message, you must define the following:

- The content of the message
- The sender (you)
- The recipient

Two of these components are addresses. If you do not know a person's address, you need a way to find it. Directory services attempt to assist people in finding the address of a recipient (hopefully the user knows what his own address is). X.500 was one attempt to define a global directory service, and LDAP (Lightweight Directory Access Protocol) tried to make X.500 easier to implement (that's why the word "lightweight" was included in the protocol's name). This section will discuss the concepts and structure of X.500 and LDAP.

A directory service depends on a namespace—a method of referencing and retrieving a group of related information, such as a person's name, organization, physical address, and e-mail address. In X.500, the namespace is hierarchical and explicitly defined, requiring a somewhat complicated management strategy. X.500's naming model defines the structure of the entries in the namespace, but it does not specify the presentation format of that information to the user. Each entry in a X.500 DIT (Directory

Information Tree) is a collection of attributes. Much as the RFC822 mail message header definitions, each attribute is defined as containing a type element and a corresponding value attribute element.

The X.500 standard defines several object classes for directories, with the capacity for locally defined extensions. The basic object classes include such categories as alias, country, locality, organization, and person (name). Objects are defined by their attributes. There are approximately forty basic attribute types, including Common Name (CN), Organization Name (ON), Street Address (SA), and country (C).

Users access a directory through a DUA (*directory user agent*). A DUA transfers the directory request to a DSA (*directory system agent*) through DAP (*directory access protocol*). A directory is composed of at least one DSA. Multiple DSAs may share directory information between themselves. If they cannot share information (usually for business or security-related reasons), a DSA may refer the DUA's request to a specific DSA.

X.500 is an application-level protocol using the OSI stack to communicate over the network, which can require a great deal of processing overhead. LDAP, as defined in RFC1777, was created to allow access to X.500 without the same overhead as a full X.500 DAP implementation. The basic model of LDAP is a client using the TCP/IP protocol, interacting with a single LDAP server. That LDAP server uses OSI protocols to communicate with other X.500 servers on behalf of the client.

LDAP—Lightweight Directory Access Protocol

Like X.500, LDAP bases its directory model on entries, where the distinguished name is used to precisely refer to an address. But where X.500 uses a structured approach to the data, LDAP uses a simpler string-based approach for representing directory entries, described in RFC1779. LDAP initially supported only simple authentication (use of a clear text password) and Kerberos 4 for security purposes. Under the pressure of the massive growth of commerce over the Internet, LDAP has evolved from a lightweight gateway to an X.500 directory, and then to a more robust, middleweight stand-alone directory service. Netscape Corporation has been driving efforts to integrate web access to LDAP, for example, as defined in the LDAP URL section of RFC1959. Netscape was also involved in extending LDAP to use the SSL (Secure Sockets Layer) protocol, which would add user authentication, data encryption, and data integrity protection, and would also support access control lists and define a format for directory interchange.

At the time of this writing, directory interchange is a contentious topic: IBM, Novell, Oracle, and Lotus Development cofounded the Directory Interoperability Forum with the intention of assisting development of directory-based applications founded on existing open standards such as Lightweight Directory Access Protocol (LDAP), and new standards such as the proposed Lightweight Directory Update Protocol (LDUP) to allow LDAP systems to replicate and update data across servers. However, replication is a sticking point in the discussion; replication requires a high degree of parallelism in directory data structure and product architecture between any two given servers. Microsoft is hesitant to share that level of trust with a wide variety of systems and is recommending data sharing through synchronization. Microsoft has published the specification for the synchronization protocol for use with Active Directory. Through the use of Active Directory Connectors, based on a set of APIs called DirSynch, ADCs act as gateways between Active Directory and data in other directories. ADCs have been announced to link Microsoft's Active Directory with both Novell's NDS and Microsoft's Exchange Server 5.5, with more expected.

At the end of 1999, a directory to the XML (Extensible Markup Language) interface proposal was presented to the Organization for the Advancement of Structured Information Standards (OASIS), the World Wide Web Consortium, and BizTalk. The DSML (Directory Services Markup Language) 1.0 specification, which allowed directories to share information with each other as well as with web applications and services, was submitted to standards bodies by a group of six vendors (Bowstreet Software, IBM, Microsoft, Novell, Oracle, and the Sun-Netscape Alliance). DSML can be described as an extension to LDAP, allowing a more dynamic exchange of information. While directories are chiefly used for maintaining information on users and controlling access and security, the DSML proposal uses XML to let directories also store and share metadata on web applications and business processes. It will be interesting to see the progress of this proposal.

Cisco has a partnership with Microsoft to develop a Windows-based Cisco Networking Service for Active Directory, as well as a UNIX version of Active Directory. In mid-1999, however, possibly due to the long wait for Windows 2000, Cisco adopted Netscape Directory Server to manage access to its e-commerce website. At the time, Netscape Directory Server was the only LDAP solution that natively supported the standards-based security and data exchange capabilities in LDAPv3. At this time, Cisco is unlikely to release the efforts of the partnership until sometime after Microsoft freezes the development of Active Directory. Cisco has also announced plans to add support for Novell's NDS to its IOS (Internet Operating System) at first via LDAP, and later through the DEN (Directory-Enabled Networking) standard.

In a related note, SAP AG and Baan are providing Active Directory enabling to their management software platform clients. Oblix Inc. recently announced it would release a version of its Corporate Services Architecture directory browsing software for Active Directory as well as Novell's NDS.

Microsoft's Active Directory is the third directory service to natively support the LDAPv3 standard (the first two being Netscape Directory Server, and Novell's Novell Directory Service as of Version 8). Novell's NDS ships for Netware, Solaris, Windows NT, and AIX, as well as the OS/390 system. Netscape Directory Server is also widely cross-platform, being available for Windows and several flavors of UNIX. Oracle's Oracle Internet Directory, Innosoft's PowerDirectory, and IBM's SecureWay Directory are also available.

The next major move in the industry will be in the area of metadirectory services. To illustrate why, in most companies, directory information such as user identities is spread across a variety of repositories, including multiple directories, databases, and applications. A directory spanning the enterprise would be a good place for collecting, keeping, collating, and managing that data, but such a task is immense. A metadirectory provides the management tools necessary to aggregate that data into a manageable whole. In July 1999, Microsoft purchased Zoomit, makers of the widely used Via Server metadirectory application, used to tie disparate network, system, and application directories into a single repository. Over time, it is expected that Active Directory will add capabilities approaching that of a metadirectory; until then, if you are running Windows 2000 and Active Directory, Zoomit's metadirectory is likely to be a strong contender for your needs.

SENDMAIL

This section will discuss sendmail, one of the most widely used—and almost as widely reviled—subsystems in all of UNIX. The installation, configuration, and maintenance of sendmail have long been recognized as nightmarish procedures. According to a University of Illinois study, however, sendmail is used nonetheless by nearly 80 percent of all ISPs and by a majority of Fortune 100 businesses.

In general, this assessment is largely true; sendmail is difficult to configure, and can be approached in much the same way that novices approach UNIX. At one point, one person complained in a Usenet newsgroup (**comp.unix.admin**) that UNIX made it easy to shoot himself in the foot. Another person replied that if UNIX prevented the first person (a comparative novice) from doing something stupid, it would also prevent the second person (a comparative expert) from doing something clever. In response to charges that sendmail administration is complicated, Eric Allman, the creator of sendmail, said, "Configuring sendmail is complex because the world is complex." Thus, sendmail administration follows the guideline set by Spider Man: "With great power comes great responsibility." The good news about sendmail is that it can do just about anything you can think of. The bad news about sendmail is that it can do just about anything you can think of. Telling it how to do what you want it to can be a chore.

On the positive side, although sendmail is difficult to work with, recent versions have improved the task of sendmail configuration and administration substantially. The addition of a large set of m4 macros, and using intelligible names for options in addition to the single-character switches in the configuration file, has made sendmail configuration an easier task than previously. The sendmail program is also a mature product. While flaws are still found, sendmail is used in enterprise networks for mail delivery across a wide set of networks and in high-volume environments.

History of sendmail

In order to understand why sendmail is what it is, you should know some of what happened, and how sendmail grew to fit a particular role. This section will provide a short overview of how sendmail came to be.

In the late 1970s, Eric Allman was studying and working at the University of California at Berkeley. The predecessor to sendmail, called delivermail, was released in 1979 and addressed the problem of transferring mail between the three current networks on campus: ARPANET, which was using NCP (Network Control Protocol); a UUCP mail system; and an internal network called BerkNet.

The following year, ARPANET started to convert from NCP to TCP (Transmission Control Protocol). Previously, mail was delivered using FTP (File Transfer Protocol), but then SMTP (Simple Mail Transfer Protocol) was developed to handle the new mail requirements for the possible growth of the network by several orders of magnitude.

In response to these changes in the networks, Allman adopted an inclusive approach to formats of electronic mail messages. If a message didn't match the formats, sendmail attempted to make the message's format fit, rather than immediately rejecting the message. Allman also chose to limit the functional goal of sendmail to routing mail, rather than write an end-user mail tool such as elm or pine. The first public release of sendmail was released with the 4.1c version of BSD (Berkeley Software Distribution) UNIX. Like most UNIX software, sendmail is available in raw uncompiled form, with users expected to compile their own versions before installation.

Meanwhile, others were extending sendmail's capabilities. In the late 1980s, a Swedish developer, Lennart Lovstrand, created a significantly enhanced version of sendmail, dubbed IDA sendmail. IDA sendmail development was eventually taken over by Neil Rickert and Paul Pomes of Illinois, who continued to extend and improve the program. At about the same time, Paul Vixie started work on a variant of sendmail that he dubbed KJ (King James) sendmail. In addition to these freeware efforts, several additional versions of sendmail were developed by commercial vendors, including Sun Microsystems and Hewlett-Packard, who saw the need for features that weren't available in the existing versions. The result of all this parallel development was the existence of several versions of sendmail—with varying feature sets and incompatible configuration files.

To address this chaos, Allman began a major rewrite of sendmail in the mid-1990s. He made significant improvements, incorporated many of the features available in the earlier, conflicting versions, and improved security. To this day, Allman continues to update and improve sendmail, adding new features as the need for them is recognized, and eliminating security flaws as they are discovered. A future, long-term goal of Allman's is a completely rewritten version of sendmail, aimed at meeting additional future needs. In March 1999, Eric Allman founded Sendmail, Inc. (**http://www.sendmail.com**), which sells Sendmail Pro, a shrink-wrapped edition modeled after the open-source version of the program. Sendmail Pro has been thoroughly tested on several different platforms, and includes such extra features as a web-based administrative interface. Sendmail, Inc., also continues to fund development of the open-source freeware adaptation of sendmail, and provides forums at **http://www.sendmail.net** where freeware users can share information. Enhancements planned for the next major freeware edition (Version 8.10) include SMTP authentication, IPv6 support, and various performance improvements, such as the use of multiple queues and buffered file I/O to avoid creating temporary files on disk. A mail filter API to improve spam control and virus protection will probably be deferred to Version 8.11.

Architecture

This section will not address detailed issues of installing sendmail. In general, compilation and installation of the sendmail distribution is often uncomplicated. The source package includes make-description files tailored for many different systems, as well as a build script that chooses the correct one for the local environment. (See the section "Pointers and Further Information" later in this chapter for information about finding sendmail on the Internet.) Occasionally you will need to make some minor changes to the closest make-description file to match the specific local system. Of course, be sure to read the README files before proceeding with compiling sendmail from the source.

See sendmail Run

The sendmail program itself typically runs on UNIX systems as a *daemon* in order to listen for incoming mail. A daemon is a UNIX system program that runs in the background without a controlling terminal window. When run as a daemon, sendmail will fork (unless instructed not to on startup) and run in the background, listening on socket 25 for incoming SMTP connections. The command to run sendmail as a daemon on a Berkeley UNIX–based system might look something like this:

```
/usr/lib/sendmail -bd -q30m
```

This command is often included as part of the startup commands executed when the UNIX system boots. Here is a sample of a command, taken from a startup script named sendmail.init on a Linux system, found in the /etc/rc.d/init.d directory:

```
# Start daemons.
echo -n "Starting sendmail: "
daemon sendmail -bd -q1h
echo
touch /var/lock/subsys/sendmail
;;
```

You can see the –bd command switch that launches sendmail as a daemon and the –q1h switch that instructs it to check the queue once per hour. In contrast, the sample command preceding this has the –q switch instructing sendmail to check the queue every thirty minutes.

NOTE: Several of the sendmail commands with specific options have aliases. (These are not to be confused with mailing-address aliases.) For example, another name for the sendmail –bd command is smtpd.

The first action sendmail takes when started is to read the /etc/sendmail.cf configuration file. The sendmail.cf and dependent configuration files are presented in the next section.

Configuration: the sendmail.cf File

One reason sendmail is considered to be extremely powerful is the full access provided to the underlying configuration files. As mail messages are funneled through sendmail's configuration files, sendmail performs all message routing functions, including parsing, forwarding, delivering, returning, and queuing. This section describes the major configuration options available within sendmail.

The sendmail.cf file is the core of sendmail. A complex configuration file read only once at run time, sendmail.cf contains three important types of information:

- Options such as operational control switches, mailer definitions, and the locations of other sendmail sub-configuration files
- Macros for use in rulesets
- Rulesets for rewriting addresses on incoming and outgoing messages

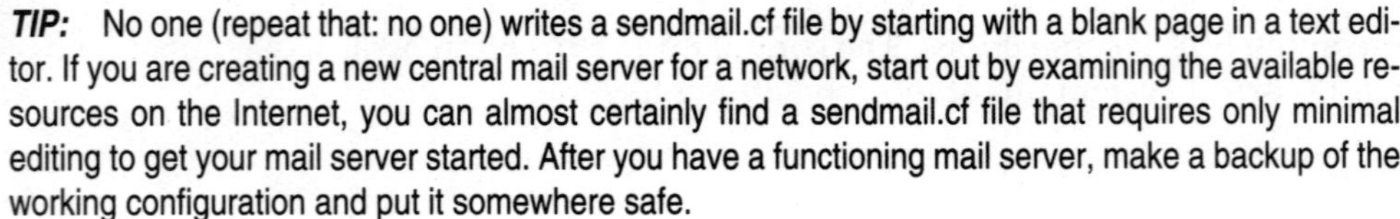

TIP: No one (repeat that: no one) writes a sendmail.cf file by starting with a blank page in a text editor. If you are creating a new central mail server for a network, start out by examining the available resources on the Internet, you can almost certainly find a sendmail.cf file that requires only minimal editing to get your mail server started. After you have a functioning mail server, make a backup of the working configuration and put it somewhere safe.

For those people who don't want to write a sendmail.cf file from a blank page but can't seem to find a template that fits their needs, Version 8 of sendmail added the use of m4, which is a macro preprocessor that is used to generate sendmail.cf files containing the features you select. A sendmail m4 creation file typically should be given a .mc (macro configuration) file suffix, but this is not required for the process to work. Many sample .mc scripts are supplied with the standard sendmail distributions.

For example, a minimum .mc file for a Solaris workstation (without appropriate comments) might look something like this:

```
OSTYPE(solaris2)dnl
MAILER(local)dnl
```

These two lines are the only two required macros in a .mc file. You are likely to want more features, but this file, named smallest_solaris.mc, can be run with the following command (assuming that you are in the /usr/lib/sendmail/cf/cf directory, which is where the standard sendmail distribution places m4 files):

```
m4 ../m4/cf.m4 smallest_solaris.mc > sendmail.cf
```

The m4 calls the m4 preprocessor, the ../m4/cf.m4 identifies m4's default configuration file, smallest_solaris.mc is the two-line macro configuration file, and the output is placed in the sendmail.cf file. Now that you have used m4 to generate a sendmail.cf file containing exactly the features you requested, you will still need to customize the sendmail.cf file for use at your site. Using m4 for sendmail.cf generation, however, is fast and accurate. In addition to the many m4 macros that ship with the sendmail distribution, you can also write your own as you feel necessary, and include them for use.

For a quick jumpstart on sendmail configuration, there is a World Wide Web form interface to the m4 configuration tool for Version 8 of sendmail at **http://www.completeis.com/sendmail/sendmail.cgi**. Specify your desired options on the form, and a sendmail.cf file reflecting your choices will be returned. If nothing else, you'll get a look at the complexity of a sendmail.cf file.

FILE LOCATIONS The sendmail.cf file is the first file that sendmail reads on startup, and it contains the locations of all other subconfiguration files used by sendmail. These files and their default locations are listed in Table 5-2.

These are only the default locations of the files. Since their locations are defined within sendmail.cf, you can set them to whatever names and directory paths you like.

OPTIONS There are far too many options in sendmail to list them all. The syntax for options comes in two types: cryptic and less cryptic. In the cryptic version of option syntax, the O (capital o, not zero) command starts an option command in the sendmail.cf file. To illustrate, here are two sample commands from a sendmail.cf file:

```
OA/etc/aliases

O AliasFile=/etc/aliases
```

Both of these commands accomplish the same thing: They tell sendmail to look in /etc/aliases for the aliases file. Notice the syntax change: The single character version (OA) does not contain a space between the O and the letter signifying which option is being set, while the name version (O AliasFile) must contain a space between the O command and the name of the option. Like all other sendmail commands, the O must be in the left-most position on the line, which is also column 1.

This restriction prevents misinterpretation of commands, such as this next line, which can also be found in a sendmail.cf file:

```
DMMOON
```

Filename and Location	Description
/etc/aliases	ASCII text list of defined aliases to names
/etc/aliases.db	Database of aliases complied from /etc/aliases
/etc/sendmail.hf	Help file
/var/log/sendmail.st	Collected statistics
/var/spool/mqueue/*	Temporary files for mail queue
/var/run/sendmail.pid	Process ID of the daemon

Table 5-2. Default Locations and Descriptions of the sendmail Configuration Files

This command defines (D) a macro (M) to have the value (MOON), so you can use $M in the rewriting rules instead of typing MOON. Without the restriction that commands are identified by the left-hand column, the O in MOON might be interpreted as a command.

The preceding examples illustrate the form of the option command for use within a configuration file. However, options can be defined either in an m4 macro file or on the command line. The command line versions of the preceding options would be preceded by a hyphen and either a lowercase o, to indicate a single-character option command, or an uppercase O, to indicate a named option command, like so:

```
-oA/etc/aliases
```

and

```
-O AliasFile=/etc/aliases
```

or

```
-OAliasFile=/etc/aliases
```

NOTE: Some UNIX vendors ship sendmail with the operating system but do not necessarily ship the latest version. In most cases (as with Release 8 of sendmail), the vendor-supplied version will include a precompiled binary and a predefined sendmail.cf file, but little else of the full sendmail package. The default setup is usually designed for a desktop workstation from which all mail is forwarded to a central mail exchanger; however, this configuration is generally unsuitable for use as a central mail exchanger. If the default doesn't meet your needs, sendmail's large installation base will prove invaluable: There is probably a sample configuration file in existence that will require only minor modifications before it works for you.

Rulesets

The sendmail program uses rules to rewrite addresses on incoming and outgoing mail. These rules are the center of sendmail's capability, as well as its complexity. The sendmail rewriting rules constitute a specialized text-oriented programming language, designed to perform two core tasks:

- ▼ Examining each recipient's address to determine which of one or several MDAs should be used to send messages to (or nearer to) their destinations
- ▲ Transforming addresses in both the envelope and the message headers to facilitate deliveries and replies

By generalizing the tasks to use rewriting rules, instead of coding the tasks directly, Allman made sendmail flexible enough to be adapted and extended as mail protocols were updated, replaced, or added. Adding a rule to transform an address is easier for most people than hacking the source code, which is what would be required if Allman hadn't designed rulesets.

Rewriting rules are organized into *rulesets.* A ruleset is a subroutine or module consisting of a sequence of rules. When an address is passed to a ruleset, the subroutine passes the address to each of its rules in order. If the matching clause matches the investigated address, the rule is applied, the address is transformed, and the result is passed to the next rule. If the address does not match the current rule, the address is not transformed and the next rule in the set is tried.

RULESET SYNTAX Rulesets are identified by numbers: Each new ruleset begins with an S in the left-hand column, followed by its identifying number. Each rule in the set follows. Rules begin with the letter R, and are not numbered. The ruleset is terminated when a non-R command is encountered. Here is an example:

```
######################################
###    Ruleset 0 -- Parse Address   ###
######################################
S0
R$*             $: $>98 $1          handle local hacks
```

Rule syntax is cryptic, but fairly simple. Each rule has a left-hand side and a right-hand side. A comment portion is optional. The two sides and the optional comment are separated by tabs (not spaces). The left-hand side is compared to the address as a pattern. If the pattern matches the left-hand side, the address is transformed by the rule's right-hand side and is passed on to the next rule.

In sendmail.cf, an octothorp (#) begins a comment line. Empty lines are ignored. The S0 defines the beginning of Ruleset 0. The R on the next line defines the beginning of a rule. The $* accepts every address that is passed to it, and the $: $>98 $1 passes the address to Ruleset 98 for further processing. The phrase "handle local hacks" is a comment. Since rules are tab-delimited, the comment portion does not require a comment marker (#) at its beginning.

THE MAIN RULESETS There are several standard rulesets. These rulesets can appear in any order in sendmail.cf; when sendmail reads the configuration file, it sorts the rules appropriately. A ruleset that is not present when expected does not cause an error when the configuration file is read. Instead, it is treated as if it were present but contained no rules.

The main rulesets have the following functions:

- Ruleset 0 resolves an MDA by reading the address.
- Ruleset 1 processes the sender's address.
- Ruleset 2 processes the recipient's address.
- Ruleset 3 preprocesses all addresses.
- Ruleset 4 postprocesses all addresses.
- Ruleset 5 rewrites unaliased local users.

ALIASES An *alias* is a convenient abbreviation for one or more full mailing addresses. Although an alias may be merely a nickname for a longer address you don't want to type every time, such as "fred" for "frederick.smith@somecompany.com," an alias can also be the name of a list of several recipients. Many MUAs maintain their own alias lists, but these alias lists are normally in formats that aren't sharable with other MUAs. For example, if you typically use Sun's mail tool on a Solaris platform, its alias file will not be available to Netscape Mail when you write a letter with that tool. In contrast, the many possible alias lists contained in aliases maintained in sendmail's alias file will be recognized and expanded when a message is processed by sendmail, regardless of the MUA used to create that message. The sendmail program allows for multiple alias files, up to 12 (and that number is also configurable).

Survival Tips

Administration of sendmail is, as previously mentioned, highly complex. Just as you should look to others who have successfully built mail servers, and their sendmail.cf files in particular, you should also listen to other advice they might have. This section presents some of the more important tips on working with sendmail.

Debugging Mode

The sendmail –d command-line switch starts sendmail in debugging mode. Debugging mode can produce a great deal of output, too detailed to go into specifics in this book. To see the debugging mode in operation, enter the following command in a UNIX terminal window:

sendmail -d *your_local_name* < /dev/null

This command will mail a message of /dev/null (nothing) to yourself and display the resulting actions as sendmail processes the message. The output will typically be several screens worth of information. For a more concise example of debugging, enter the following command, using the –d0.1 command-line switch to return a minimum of information:

sendmail -d0.1 -bp

The response should resemble the following:

```
Version 8.8.5
Compiled with: LOG MATCHGECOS MIME7TO8 MIME8TO7 NAMED_BIND NETINET
 NETUNIX NEWDB QUEUE SCANF SMTP USERDB
============ SYSTEM IDENTITY (after readcf) ============
      (short domain name) $w = homebase
  (canonical domain name) $j = homebase.testbox.org
         (subdomain name) $m = testbox.org
              (node name) $k = homebase.testbox.org
========================================================
Mail queue is empty
```

You can see useful information in this response, all of which would have been included in the first example (but buried with the other details of a general debugging output). This command shows the following:

- **Line 1: Version number of sendmail running** This will help you determine whether you need to apply the latest security patch.
- **Lines 2 and 3: Compiled options** These lines tell you which options were selected when sendmail was compiled.
- **Lines 4 through 9: System identity** These lines explain how sendmail processed the host name.
- **Line 10: Mail queue status** This tells you whether the mail queue for the user (you) running the command is empty or full. This line is the minimal response when using the mail queue –bp command-line switch.

The options available in debugging mode are many and varied; sendmail can be instructed to return only the types of information you want. For example, if you want to watch the daemon in operation, you need to include the –d99.100 command-line switch as part of the selected debugging options. Otherwise, the daemon will not include its own output.

Rule-Testing Mode

Use of the –bt command-line switch with the sendmail command runs sendmail in rule-testing mode. The rule-testing mode allows you to test the result of changes you've made to the sendmail configuration files. Enter this command in a UNIX terminal window:

```
sendmail -bt
```

You should see a response similar to this next listing:

```
ADDRESS TEST MODE (ruleset 3 NOT automatically invoked)
Enter <ruleset> <address>
>
```

You should notice that the prompt is now >, indicating you are in sendmail's interactive rule-testing mode. Enter a ruleset number as a starting point for address processing and an address for testing. For example, entering

```
> 3 testuser@testbox.org
```

returns the following response:

```
rewrite: ruleset   3   input: testuser @ testbox . org
rewrite: ruleset  96   input: testuser < @ testbox . org >
rewrite: ruleset  96 returns: testuser < @ testbox . org >
rewrite: ruleset   3 returns: testuser < @ testbox . org >
```

You can see that the address is broken into pieces in ruleset 3, passed to ruleset 96, and then back to ruleset 3.

NOTE: Running sendmail in rule-testing mode starts a new sendmail process, which reads the sendmail.cf file after you've made changes. At this point, a sendmail daemon running on the same system won't have noticed the changes to the configuration file, and it won't notice the new rules until the daemon is stopped and restarted. Of course, you should always have a copy of the working sendmail.cf file safely stored elsewhere while you are editing the configuration file.

Even without your editing the configuration file, the –bt switch is an excellent way to learn the workings of sendmail on a current system. As the –bt switch doesn't change any of sendmail's configuration, using –bt can serve as a self-paced tutorial to a functioning sendmail configuration.

Restart the Daemon After Editing Configuration

The sendmail program only reads the sendmail.cf file once on startup. Whenever you change the sendmail.cf file, you must restart sendmail in order to have the sendmail daemon reread the sendmail.cf. This advice sounds almost as basic as asking, "Is the system still plugged in?" It can, however, be forgotten after too long a session spent staring at sendmail.cf rulesets in a text editor.

Rebuild the Aliases Database

Also, if you add aliases to the /etc/alias file, remember to rebuild the aliases.db alias database by running sendmail with the –bi command-line flag. Another name for the sendmail –bi command is newaliases.

CAUTION: sendmail may take several minutes to rebuild a large aliases database, and mail delivery will be suspended while the aliases database is rebuilding.

Keep Backups

Similarly basic advice: Always keep a version of the old (as in working) sendmail.cf file, especially when changing the active version. Returning to a working configuration (by copying the old file back into place, and then killing and restarting the sendmail daemon) takes only a minute or two, and you can debug what went wrong with the edited file at your leisure.

Upgrade sendmail Quickly

Often, the latest version of any given software package is distrusted, on the theory that while old bugs were fixed or new features added, another bug was introduced. Therefore, a general rule of thumb is to wait a while after a new version of software appears, and let some other person's network meltdown. However, sendmail is an exception to this general rule. New versions of sendmail are sometimes released because a flaw has been found that "allows non-local users to issue arbitrary commands as root." The sendmail program is a rare case in the software world where early adoption is a good idea. Keep up with sendmail upgrades, or acknowledge that you are probably leaving an exploitable security breach. As should be your usual practice, remember to copy the old working version of sendmail and configuration files elsewhere for fast restoration if a problem occurs during the upgrade. The problem of security flaws in older versions of sendmail is exacerbated by the fact that some UNIX vendors ship sendmail with the operating system, but do not necessarily ship the latest version. Solaris 2.5.1, for example, included sendmail Version 8.7, when Version 8.8 had been available for months. Given the security flaws in earlier versions, if a system is accessible from the Internet, either upgrade or remove the older sendmail from that system.

Look Elsewhere to Solve the Problem

Finally, sendmail is not always the source of the problem. The sendmail program uses the Domain Name System (DNS) to help it deliver mail to remote users. Proper handling of mail requires that both sendmail and DNS be accurately configured. For example, sendmail queries the local DNS daemon to find any recorded Mail Exchange MX records for the recipient's domain. If no MX records are listed for a domain, sendmail will query DNS for CNAME (Canonical Name) or A (Address) records to determine a possible mail exchanger. If your local DNS server configuration contains an erroneous MX record, even a correctly configured sendmail daemon may never see incoming messages. Remote MTAs (other sendmails on remote mail servers, for example) may never see mail intended for users in their domains because the local DNS directs the messages incorrectly.

Pointers and Further Information

As this chapter has repeatedly stressed, sendmail administration is not for everyone. If you are interested in or required to deal with sendmail, there are some excellent resources for further information.

Seek Help

The first reference to examine is Bryan Costales and Eric Allman's book *Sendmail, Second Edition,* mentioned earlier in this chapter. This book, at over a thousand pages, is the definitive reference on the topic of sendmail and should be considered mandatory if you are working with sendmail at all. Nicknamed the "bat book," because the cover illustration features a fruit bat (the rumor that the illustration is of a vampire bat is a minor myth), *Sendmail, Second Edition* covers sendmail through Version 8.8. Other books exist that address sendmail issues, but this book is the one resource you must have.

The Sendmail Consortium maintains a website devoted to being a resource for the freeware version of sendmail at **http://www.sendmail.org**. From this website, you can find the FTP source to use in compiling sendmail for your system, as well as several other resources. The README files distributed with the source code, of course, contain much specific information and should be read before proceeding with compiling and installing sendmail on a system. In addition to this, an active set of message boards and discussion groups at **http://www.sendmail.net** is sponsored entirely by Sendmail, Inc., as part of its support for the Open Source sendmail community. The Usenet newsgroup **comp.mail.sendmail** is a high-volume newsgroup devoted to sendmail administration. An extensive FAQ (frequently asked questions) file on sendmail is edited and maintained by Brad Knowles, with monthly updates. The **comp.mail.sendmail** FAQ can be found on the Internet at **http://www.sendmail.org/faq/**. As is usual with Usenet newsgroups, new readers of a newsgroup are requested to please read the FAQ files compiled from the newsgroup, then read the newsgroup before posting a question that's been answered weekly for the last two years. This newsgroup is an excellent resource for the latest news or configuration advice.

Finally, procmail was mentioned earlier as a powerful replacement for the standard mail delivery agents because of its preprocessing capabilities. The latest version of procmail, along with FAQs, can be found at **http://www.procmail.org**.

CERT and CIAC Advisories

The U.S. Department of Energy's Computer Incident Advisory Capability (CIAC) was established in 1989 to provide computer security services to employees and contractors of the United States Department of Energy. The CIAC manages mailing lists for the following two electronic publications:

- ▼ **CIAC-Bulletin** CIAC Information Bulletins and Advisory Notices containing important, time-critical computer security information
- ▲ **CIAC-Notes** A periodic collection of less urgent computer security information

To subscribe to one of these lists, send mail to **majordomo@tholia.llnl.gov**. In the BODY (not subject) of the message type (either or both):

```
subscribe ciac-bulletin

subscribe ciac-notes
```

Why are these mailing lists described in a chapter about sendmail? Because sendmail has been the source of several security violations for UNIX-based systems over the years. If a security flaw is discovered in sendmail, a fix or patch will likely be rapidly developed, and severe sendmail security flaws will be the focus of a CIAC Bulletin or Advisory.

Other Mail Transport Agents

The sendmail program's cryptic commands and confusing configuration have caused some people to renounce sendmail altogether. However, these people still need an MTA. This section discusses a few of the alternatives to sendmail available for the UNIX world, such as Qmail and ZMailer.

Qmail

Qmail, written by Dan Bernstein of Australia, is intended as a complete replacement for the entire sendmail subsystem on UNIX hosts that operate as mail servers. Bernstein's goals in writing Qmail included security, simplicity, reliability, and efficiency. Since security was considered paramount, Bernstein designed Qmail to minimize the use of setuid and root, which have been areas of attack in sendmail, along with a five-way trust partitioning that provides multiple security checks.

A significant strength of Qmail is its support for mailing lists. Qmail makes it very easy for local users to set up their own mailing lists via a generalizable forwarding mechanism. An additional module allows simplified management of subscription requests for mailing lists. Since Qmail tracks mail messages until it reaches a "finally delivered to" address, Qmail examines the result and compares the destination to the originator, preventing endless mail-forwarding loops.

Qmail is also simplified in comparison to other MTAs. Qmail's forwarding mechanism, which allows users individual mailing list control, substitutes for other MTAs' separate mechanisms for forwarding, mailing lists, and aliasing. This reduces Qmail's overall size, which reduces the lines of code that need to be bug-checked, and also reduces the load on the mail server.

Qmail is designed to be a feature-rich replacement for sendmail. Qmail supports RFC821 and RFC822, RFC974, RFC1123, RFC1651, RFC1652, RFC1854, and RFC1939 (for POP3 services), as well as a long list of features. A wrapper for Qmail allows it to masquerade as sendmail to MUAs, so the thousands of users of the (for example) pine MUA don't have to change their configuration when sendmail is replaced by Qmail.

For reliability, Qmail was designed with a straight-paper-path philosophy that was intended to ensure that a message, once accepted into the system, will never be lost. Qmail supports a user mailbox design called maildir, in addition to the older mbox format. The maildir user format is designed to survive if the mail server crashes during delivery. The maildir format is also designed to work well for mail delivery under NFS (Network File System) networks.

When one speaks with administrators using Qmail, efficiency is a word that continues to come up in the conversation. Partially as a result of Qmail's simplicity, several reported instances exist of networks switching to Qmail on a smaller fileserver than was used for sendmail, and seeing improved mail handling throughput.

On the other hand, there are some possible concerns when comparing Qmail to sendmail, which , however clunky, can do almost everything asked of it. At least one administrator out there has likely faced and solved a problem using sendmail, similar to the one confronting you right now, or the one you'll eventually face. Qmail users haven't had enough time yet to solve the world's problems. Although Qmail is simple to administer, the simplicity may limit the product's flexibility. Finally, sendmail has been in constant use worldwide since 1979, whereas Qmail didn't achieve 1.0 release status unitl January 1997. With these caveats in mind, Qmail may still be a strong contender as a replacement for sendmail at some sites, especially if a mail server is serving many high-volume mailing lists. Qmail's design specifications and its supporters are enough evidence that it is worth exploring the option of testing Qmail for use as your network's MTA. You can find a list of Qmail mirror sites at **http://www.qmail.org/**.

ZMailer

ZMailer is intended for gateways, mail servers, or other large site environments that have extreme demands on the capabilities of the mailer. ZMailer was intended to handle some of the higher-volume mail server requirements where sendmail begins to have difficulty. As with every MTA since (and including) sendmail, security was a primary goal. Like sendmail, ZMailer was designed to have a high amount of flexibility, with extensive configuration options and a generalized database interface. The database interface allows ZMailer to draw routing information from

- Sorted files
- Unsorted files
- dbm, ndbm, and gdbm databases
- nis (yellow pages)
- DNS through a BIND resolver (Berkeley Internet Name Domain, a widely popular implementation of DNS)

ZMailer supports the MIME facilities for message transport, as initially defined in RFC1521 and RFC1522. ZMailer also provides a mail-to-Usenet-news gateway and has support for mailing lists. ZMailer is supplied with a default configuration file that is designed to work for most sites. This configuration file is likely to require at least some customization to work for your site. More information on ZMailer is available from **http://www.zmailer.org/** or through the Usenet newsgroup **comp.mail.zmail**.

Sendmail for Windows NT

MetaInfo, Inc., had initially ported a then-current release of sendmail (Version 8.8) to Windows NT, and added a graphical user interface (GUI) for managing the configuration files. In 1999, Sendmail, Inc., purchased the Windows NT port from MetaInfo; they have since updated the application. As of this writing, Sendmail for NT Version 3.0 is based on the latest open-source sendmail Version 8.9.3.

As with several vendor-shipped versions of UNIX sendmail, Sendmail for Windows NT ships with a preconfigured sendmail.cf file that is intended to address the needs of many networks. Since Sendmail for Windows NT is a port of the sendmail source code, MetaInfo claims that the sendmail configuration and data files are transferable between UNIX and NT mail servers. Since distributed and remote management is an important issue, Sendmail for Windows NT also includes a web-based administration and configuration tool.

Supported Protocols

As a port of UNIX sendmail, Sendmail for Windows NT is an SMTP-compliant MTA. Like Qmail, this product includes integration of POP3 account administration as defined in RFC1939, as well as full support of MIME attachments. Sendmail for Windows NT also supports the finger protocol as described in RFC1288, which allows remote clients to discover basic information about users on the local system.

NOTE: Windows 2000 includes the finger command if the TCP/IP protocol has been installed. As a separate comment, many administrators will disable the finger service on a given server to improve security.

Installation

Installation is a straightforward process. Like most Windows programs, Sendmail for Windows NT uses an Installation Wizard to aid setup. During the installation, the wizard checks system requirements, folder permissions, and current domain information, as well as initializing the system Registry. The Registry is updated with several new values in the HKEY_LOCAL_MACHINE hive, in the directory \Software\MetaInfo\Sendmail\Parameters.

Configuration

There are two ways of configuring Sendmail for Windows NT:

- Configuring sendmail either through manual editing of the configuration files, or through a web-based Administrator tool
- Configuring sendmail to operate as an application under Windows NT

NOTE: Manual editing of the configuration files was covered in the "Architecture" section of this chapter.

Web Administrator is a form-based application that allows the use of a web browser such as Netscape Navigator or Microsoft Internet Explorer to edit the sendmail configuration files, including sendmail.cf, sendmail.cw, and the aliases files. Since Sendmail for Windows NT is a port of UNIX sendmail, administrators who are already experienced with UNIX sendmail may prefer to edit the files directly, as they have done previously. One detail that provides evidence of the UNIX port is that filenames in the sendmail.cf file must use / (forward slash—the UNIX syntax), rather than \ (backslash—the Windows and DOS syntax) as the directory separator character.

By default, the Web Administrator tool uses port 5000 instead of the standard HTTP (Hypertext Transfer Protocol) port of 80. You can access a nonstandard port for a protocol by specifying the port after the machine name. For example, you can launch Web Administrator by starting your preferred web browser and entering the following URL,

http://*mailserver*:5000

where *mailserver* is the name of the Windows NT machine on which sendmail is installed.

On the Config Security page of the Sendmail Control Panel, you can configure the Web Administrator to allow access only from networks or machines that you specify. You can also change the Web Administrator's port address to some value other than 5000. Once you make these changes, you must restart your web service before the change can take effect.

CAUTION: Using the Web Administrator for configuration essentially precludes any future manual editing. For example, in all of the subconfiguration files that the Web Adminstrator alters (i.e., every file listed in Table 5-2 except sendmail.cf), all comments will be stripped out. The absence of comments might make returning to a manual editing strategy very difficult, whether sendmail remains on Windows NT or you move the mail server back to a UNIX workstation.

MICROSOFT EXCHANGE SERVER

Microsoft Exchange 2000 Server is a Windows 2000–based product offering a wide array of message and data capabilities. Some of these capabilities include several features designed to improve group information sharing and work flow, customizable extensions through MAPI, support for a wide variety of protocols, and tight integration with the operating system. First, this section will examine some of Exchange Server's features, then its components and architecture. The next section will discuss the close integration between Exchange 2000 Server and Windows 2000, followed by some strategic advice to consider when planning an Exchange Server implementation. The last section will provide two tools designed to aid migration of UNIX mailboxes to Windows Exchange sites.

Overview of Features

Administration of Exchange 2000 Server is conducted primarily through an Administrator graphical user interface. The Administrator GUI resembles the Windows File Manager and allows you to select any object within the Exchange hierarchy and view its properties. Exchange Server is designed to allow backing up of messaging stores without shutting down the mail server, a feature that has become more important as electronic mail becomes critical to operations. Multiple routes between sites can be defined so that when one path goes down, a secondary path is available immediately.

Forms

Forms allow you to define workflow of electronic documents through your organization. Using the Forms Designer, you can create many of the common documents used in your organization online and place the information in a database-accessible format without having to scan or rekey the data. Does anyone remember when a promise of business computing was a paperless office? While almost all of us are still waiting for that promise to be fulfilled, electronic forms are a step closer toward reducing the clutter of paper on most computer professionals' desks.

The Forms Designer is actually a simplified version of a Visual Basic programming environment. Although you can use the Forms Designer without any knowledge of Visual Basic, experienced Visual Basic developers can apply their knowledge to create extremely robust forms. A form is a (usually small) Visual Basic application.

NOTE: Using forms in an organization requires the use of Exchange clients that are capable of supporting Visual Basic. As of this writing, the Macintosh Exchange client cannot use forms, because Visual Basic has not been ported to the Macintosh OS.

MAPI

The Messaging Application Programming Interface (MAPI) is a group of functions allowing integration of add-ons into the Exchange environment. The MAPI functions can be called by C, C++, or Visual Basic programs, through an OLE-messaging component, to directly manipulate Exchange objects. The Microsoft Exchange mail client and Microsoft Outlook are both built on MAPI. The MAPI specification is easily available, and many third-party developers have released products intended to work with and extend Exchange. Some of these third-party extensions to the Exchange environment include fax, logon, and message retrieval capabilities, as well as security enhancements, such as the integration of PGP public-key cryptography into the Exchange mail client.

Protocols

Exchange 2000 Server supports ESMTP, allowing many of the features mentioned in the second half of the "SMTP and ESMTP" section of this chapter, such as delivery status notification and server-defined maximum size limits on incoming messages.

Exchange 2000 Server includes full support for Lightweight Directory Access Protocol (LDAP) built into both its clients and the server. Microsoft intends that its Active Directory support LDAP3 and work with X.500, using subsets of the Directory Access Protocol and Directory Systems Protocol components of X.500. Exchange 2000 Server can also be configured to act as a POP3 server, if this is your preference.

Webmail

The web browser–client feature of Microsoft Exchange 2000 Server allows you to read your Exchange mail and view folders, both public and private, over the World Wide Web via HTTP (Hypertext Transfer Protocol). Here are the requirements for the client-end web browser:

- Frames
- Java
- JavaScript

The current versions of both Netscape Navigator and Microsoft Internet Explorer meet these requirements.

REMEMBER: To use the webmail feature, Java and JavaScript must be enabled, as well as present, in the browser. Some corporations require users of Java-equipped browsers to turn off Java, considering it a security violation.

In addition to a browser, as described previously, and the URL for the Exchange 2000 Server, you will need the username for the Exchange mailbox in order to read your mail. You will not need a login name to view public folders, documents, files, and newsgroups designated as world-accessible.

NNTP

Network News Transfer Protocol, as defined in RFC977, is a simple text-based protocol similar to SMTP that allows the following:

- Reading of news articles by clients from a server
- Posting of news articles from clients to servers
- Transfer of news messages between servers

RFC1036 defined the format of news messages similar to the format defined for mail messages in RFC822, but with the addition of a few header formats required for news usage that were not necessary for mail transfer (such as the newsgroup header).

Exchange treats Usenet newsgroups as public folders: Newsgroups served through the Exchange Server are placed in public folders. Administrators can control access to the public folders on an action (read/write/delete) level for each user or group of users. This newsgroup-public folder relationship is bidirectional: Any public folder can be published as a newsgroup via NNTP to any newsreader application that can reach that particular Exchange Server.

Components and Architecture

Exchange Server consists of four major components:

- System Attendant
- Message Transfer Agent
- Information Store
- Directory Service

as well as some optional components. All of these interact to provide Exchange's set of services. This section will present descriptions of these four components and their interactions.

Core Exchange Server Components

The System Attendant is the central intelligence for an Exchange server. Acting as a maintenance service, the System Attendant monitors connections between Exchange servers, and also collects other information about each Exchange server for use by monitoring tools. The System Attendant is responsible for creating destination addresses for new mail recipients, and it is also responsible for compiling routing tables, verifying directory replication, and logging information about mail messages for tracking purposes.

The Message Transfer Agent acts just as sendmail does in the UNIX world. The Exchange MTA maps addresses, routes messages, and (where necessary) provides message format conversion to the destination system's format standard, if known. The MTA also replicates the Directory Service between Exchange servers in a site.

The Information Store is a server-based storage facility, holding all data received by an Exchange server. The Information Store is composed of these two separate databases:

- **Private** Stores messages in all users' mailboxes. Users can store messages in personal folders on their local workstations; however, by default, Exchange stores messages on the server.
- **Public** Stores all the public folders.

The Information Store enables administrators to set maximum size limits and access permissions on every mailbox or public folder it contains. The Directory Service contains information on every defined Exchange user, mailbox, and distribution list for that Exchange site. In addition, Exchange can also incorporate organizational information as part of the address: A person's entry in the Exchange Server's Global Address Book can include that person's manager as well as their staff. Having such information as part of that person's address properties simplifies the process of getting messages sent to the correct group of people. The Directory Store also holds the routing tables compiled by the System Attendant. This mass of information is shared between every Exchange server on the site.

Optional Exchange Server Components

One of the optional Exchange components is the Key Management Server, which provides the ability to digitally sign and encrypt messages. Within this chapter, a discussion of the Key Management Server is found in the "Exchange Server Security Extensions" section. Other optional components of Exchange include several connectors. A connector links a Microsoft Exchange server with other servers. For example, a site connector links an Exchange Server into another Exchange server to form a multiserver Exchange site. For linking to non-Exchange mail servers, Microsoft provides connectors for X.400, Microsoft Mail, Lotus cc:Mail, and SMTP, as well as to a PROFS gateway.

Exchange and Windows Integration

Exchange is closely integrated with Windows 2000 in several areas. This section will discuss the logical layout of sites and domains, and close with some of the integrated security features.

Sites and Domains

Exchange architecture relies on the central concepts of sites and organizations. An *organization* is the top level of the Exchange installation. Within an organization, there may be many sites. A *site* consists of one or more Exchange servers with a reliable, high-speed connection between the servers. Windows domain boundaries do not necessarily have any relationship to Exchange site boundaries: All Exchange servers in a site must have a reliable network connection to all other site members, but they may reside in other trusted Windows domains. More about the relationship of sites and domains is presented in the "Planning a Microsoft Exchange Implementation" section of this chapter.

Exchange Security

Microsoft Exchange is tightly integrated with Windows 2000. One of the areas in which this integration is pronounced is in security. Exchange uses several of the security capabilities within Windows. This section provides a brief overview of Windows security and then discusses some of the advanced security specific to Exchange, such as key management.

WINDOWS SECURITY Windows security relies on four concepts:

- Authentication
- Domain architecture
- Account type
- Access controls

In order to gain access to Windows system resources, every user, process, or service must log into the system. Authentication is the process of requesting a username and password from every user, process, or service, and verifying the match of the two. Once the identity (the username) and validation (the password) are confirmed as matching, Windows assigns that user, process, or service the appropriate security context. The security context defines the access allowed to that identity. Microsoft Exchange uses Windows' authentication process—once a user logs in, the operating system determines if that user is allowed to access Exchange.

A Windows domain is one or more Windows 2000 (or NT) Server or servers using the same security scheme and user account registry set. Within a domain, there are three kinds of servers: Primary Domain Controllers (PDCs), Backup Domain Controllers (BDCs), and Stand-Alone Servers.

Every domain must have at least one PDC. PDCs replicate the security database to all BDCs. A PDC must have Windows NT Server reinstalled to change to a BDC or a Stand-Alone Server.

BDCs maintain a backup of the security database for the domain, and provide load balancing by answering authentication requests if the PDC is busy. A BDC can be promoted to a PDC, but it must have Windows NT Server reinstalled to change to a Stand-Alone Server.

Stand-Alone Servers have no responsibilities for authenticating logins. It is recommended that servers dedicated as Exchange servers, as SQL servers, or for other client/server applications be configured as Stand-Alone Servers. Stand-Alone Servers cannot be converted to either PDCs or BDCs. A Windows NT Server must be reinstalled in order to change the role of a Stand-Alone Server within the domain.

With a single login, a user can access every Windows NT server and all attached resources within that domain. Two domains can have

- No trust relationship
- A one-way trust relationship, where a user in Domain A can access any resource in Domain B, but a user in Domain B cannot reach any resource in Domain A
- A two-way trust relationship, where all users in both domains can reach all resources in both domains

---

NOTE: Trust relationships are actually always one-way; a two-way trust relationship actually consists of two one-way trust relationships, but the two are separate issues.

In Windows NT 4.0, trust relationships were not transitive; in other words, if Domain A and Domain B trusted each other, and Domain B and Domain C trusted each other, Domain A did not necessarily trust Domain C.

Trust relationships are defined from within both domains by means of a password chosen for the occasion. They are severable from either side.

NOTE: Don't bother remembering the trust password. About fifteen minutes after defining the trust relationship, Windows changes the password to something else—and doesn't reveal it. Thereafter, it changes the password approximately once a week.

There are two main kinds of Windows accounts: *user accounts* and *service accounts.* User accounts can be assigned to a Microsoft Exchange mailbox, either singly or multiply. A user must be defined in the same domain that the Exchange server is a member of, or in a domain trusted by the Exchange server's domain. When Windows Server starts, several services launch and log into the system automatically.

Windows provides access controls by defining each user or service as having specific permissions to access network resources. The following are the network resources for which Windows provides access controls:

- **Mailbox** Each mailbox can have one or more user accounts set as the user public folder. The owner of a public folder can allow mailboxes, distribution lists, and other public folders the rights to read, create, edit, or delete the public folder's contents.
- **Directory** Directory permissions are set as part of the user's account database, allowing actions within those directories.
- **Group** Windows NT has local groups and global groups. Grouping together accounts with similar needs means that less time needs to be spent on administration. Local groups can contain users (both from the same or from trusted domains) and global groups, but they cannot contain other local groups.

EXCHANGE SERVER SECURITY EXTENSIONS Microsoft Exchange Server provides additional security features beyond those in Windows. An optional component of Exchange Server, the Key Management Server provides for digital signatures and encryption of messages through the use of public-key cryptography. Both CAST and DES encryption algorithms are supported.

NOTE: Only one Exchange Server can be used as a Key Management Server. Having multiple advanced security databases can lead to errors in authentication as well as encryption.

Planning a Microsoft Exchange Implementation

Advance planning is important to reduce unexpected costs. Microsoft has defined a planning strategy for implementing Exchange in many situations. Although this is a very general set of guidelines, many of these steps will be applicable to many situations. Admittedly, several of these steps may look like common sense to you, but unfortunately, common sense isn't always common.

1. Assess the users' needs.

   What do the users need to be able to do? Are they heavy users of electronic mail? (In Microsoft's original implementation of Exchange, they discovered their employees averaged 38 messages per person per day.) If users are expecting to make strong use of Exchange's public folders for sharing information, you may want to define some Exchange servers specifically as public folder servers, allowing mail service to be isolated from the shared folders when backups must be performed.

2. Identify your company's geographic spread.

   The company's geographical profile can assist in answering several questions, such as what connectors are best suited to link parts of your organization. Since network costs tend to closely parallel the geographic spread of a company, your company's geographic distribution may provide a visual key to connection speeds between sites.

3. Choose a naming strategy.

   What naming scheme will you use for your organization, sites, servers, mailboxes, distribution lists, public folders, and custom recipients? Good naming strategies allow simple addition and identification of sites, servers, gateways, connectors, users, and all other required objects. Exchange Server uses three levels in its directory-naming scheme. The first level, Organization, is equivalent to the X.500 Organization [O] and the X.400 PRMD address element. The second level, Site Name, is equivalent to the X.500 Organizational Unit [OU] and the X.400 Organization address element. The third level of Exchange objects are X.500 Common Names.

4. Assess the network.

   Network topology should be a major factor in planning an Exchange installation. In addition to examining the cable type, connection bandwidth, network traffic patterns, and reliability of the connections between portions of the network, in this planning phase, you also consider the protocols and operating systems in use on the network.

5. Choose or discover a Windows NT domain topology.

   Since Exchange Server relies on Windows NT security to authenticate users and permit Microsoft Exchange Server services, you will need to carefully understand the existing NT domain model for the organization. If you're just beginning to implement Windows NT in your organization, congratulations! You have a chance to do it right! A domain is a group of servers that share common security policy and user account databases. Changing a domain structure once it is implemented is extremely difficult. Site boundaries depend on the domain structure in place, and sites spanning domain boundaries require the domains to trust each other. Allowing a trust relationship between two Windows NT domains may be prohibited at OSI Layer 8—the company politics layer.

6. Determine the number of sites and site boundaries.

   Based on the information you gathered in the preceding steps, what is the appropriate number of sites, and the appropriate size for each site, in your organization? Here are some additional points to consider:

   - All Microsoft Exchange Server computers within a site must be able to communicate through synchronous RPCs (remote procedure calls).
   - Windows NT security must be set up in a way that allows the Microsoft Exchange Servers within a site to authenticate each other.
   - Permanent connections must exist between Exchange Server computers in a site.

7. Link your sites.

   Microsoft Exchange provides several connectors for linking sites together. The site connector, for example, uses RPCs for communications and provides load balancing and fault tolerance between servers, but at the expense of increased network traffic (the default setting for synchronizing between two connected Exchange servers is five minutes). The RAS dial-up connector is limited to the speed of the modems involved, but it can be defined as a backup connector in case someone with a backhoe accidentally cuts the physical cable your site connector travels over. Exchange also provides an X.400 connector, an Internet Mail Service connector for SMTP mail servers, and Microsoft Mail and Lotus cc:Mail connectors.

8. Plan your sites.

   Each site will have at least one server, but how many? Will different Exchange servers be tasked to perform separate functions? Who will administer the servers in the organization?

9. Plan the servers on each site.

   This step identifies the hardware and software requirements of each server.

10. Plan connections to other systems.

    Exchange Server includes a wide array of gateways for use with SMTP mail systems, Microsoft Mail and Lotus cc:Mail, and several others. The information you discovered in steps 1 and 4 should be useful here.

11. Validate and optimize the system design.

    In simple English, go back, look at the requirements, examine the anticipated load, and then review (for example) the domain models and see if an alternate plan meets the requirements better.

12. Execute the plan.

    At this point, you identify what you need to do to implement the design you created in the previous 11 steps. What hardware do you need to order and when, what happens to users' current mailboxes, how will implementing the plan affect current network support, and so on.

UNIX Mail–to–Exchange Migration Tools

As an example of how to migrate a UNIX-format mailbox into Microsoft Exchange, here is a Perl script that can remail entire mailboxes. When run by a sendmail-trusted entity such as root, the script should deliver the mail without rewriting the From: lines. Admittedly, this only avoids the "manually" part of "without manually resending each message." The script either edits or inserts a Subject: header line to indicate the folder from which the message came.

```
#!/usr/local/bin/perl5
$debug=0;
usage() if ($#ARGV < 1);
$smopen = 0;
$user = shift @ARGV;
foreach (@ARGV) {
        forwardmail( $user, $_ );
}
# End of Main Program --------------------------------------------------
sub forwardmail {
        local($user, $folder) = @_;
        local($smopen, $needsubj);
        #
        # open the old mailbox and pipe the messages found within through
        # 'sendmail' for delivery.
        #
        if ( open(MBOX, "$folder") ) {
                $smopen = 0;
                while (<MBOX>) {
                        if (/^From (\S+)\s/) {
                                $from = $1;
                                close(SENDMAIL) if ($smopen);
                                printf "From: $from\n";
                                open(SENDMAIL, "| /usr/lib/sendmail
                                  -f${from} $user");
                                $smopen = 1;
                                $needsubj = 1;
                        } else {
                                if (/^Subject: /) {
                                     s/^Subject: /Subject: [fwd: $folder] /;
                                        print;
                                        $needsubj = 0;
```

```
                                } elsif ((/^$/) && ($needsubj)) {
                                        print SENDMAIL "Subject: [fwd:
                                          $folder] (no subject)\n";
                                        $needsubj = 0;
                                }
                                print(SENDMAIL);
                        }
                }
                close(SENDMAIL) if ($smopen && (! $debug));
        }
        $smopen = 0;
close(MBOX);
}
sub usage { die "usage: pkgfolders user_name folder [...]\n"; }
```

As an alternative to Exchange as a mail client, there is HP OpenMail. HP OpenMail supports all the functions of the Exchange client, including calendars, public folders, and address books. Available for HP-UX and several other UNIXes, as well as Linux, HP OpenMail can be used as a drop-in replacement for Exchange on a UNIX or Linux platform. For more information, see the OpenMail website at **http://www.ice.hp.com/cyc/om/00/index.html**.

MAILING LIST MANAGERS

E-mail is one of the dominant uses of the Internet, so dominant it has been called the real killer app of the Internet. Although e-mail is most often in the form of personal mail from one person to another, sometimes it's easier to send the same message to more than one person. So if you write a message to the same group of people over and over, you might want to set up a mailing list. A *mailing list* is a list of e-mail addresses hidden behind a single address. Some mailing lists can be set up so that only one person can send mail to everyone on the list, or so that everyone can write to the list. A list can also be configured to be moderated, so that all messages to the list are sent to a list administrator for approval before being sent out to everyone. An excellent overview of mailing lists and their configurations is *Managing Mailing Lists* by Alan Schwartz (O'Reilly and Associates, Inc., 1998).

This section will present three UNIX-only mailing list managers (majordomo, smartlist, and mailman), and will then discuss two other mailing list managers that are primarily used in the Windows environment, but that have also been ported to some versions of UNIX.

Majordomo

Majordomo is one of the most common mailing list programs on the Internet, and especially on UNIX systems. Once the mailing list is created with majordomo, the list can be maintained entirely through e-mail without needing to log in directly to the mail server. To illustrate, this section will take you step-by-step through how to create a mailing list with majordomo on a Linux system. These instructions will be similar if you are using most UNIX systems as well, but you're advised to check for differences before beginning.

What You'll Need

Before you can create a mailing list with majordomo, you will need the following:

- A UNIX system that you have administrator (root) access to
- sendmail or another mail transport agent
- Perl, since majordomo is a Perl script

Majordomo's website, including an elaborate FAQ and documentation, is at **http://www.greatcircle.com/majordomo**. To begin, go to the website, then download and install majordomo (you'll need to be able to log in as root to do this). Once you have majordomo installed, here's how to make a mailing list named "daubentonia."

1. Log in.
2. Change to the root account by entering

    su root

    followed by the root password (unless you are already root).
3. To move to the /etc/ directory, enter

    cd /etc/
4. To edit the aliases file, enter

    vi aliases
5. Write a block that looks like this:

    # my daubentonia
    daubentonia: "|/usr/local/majordomo/wrapper resend -l daubentonia daubentonia-list"
    daubentonia-list: :include:/usr/local/majordomo/lists/daubentonia
    owner-daubentonia: *your_username*
    daubentonia-owner: *your_username*
    daubentonia-approval: *your_username*
    daubentonia-request: "|/usr/local/majordomo/wrapper request-answer daubentonia"
6. When you're done, remember to save your work and exit vi:

    Esc :wq
7. To compile the aliases, enter this command:

    newaliases

You should see a reply that looks like this:

```
/etc/aliases: 5 aliases, longest 22 bytes, 325 bytes total
/etc/aliases.majordomo: 32 aliases, longest 44 bytes, 1932 bytes total
```

8. Enter

    cd /usr/local/majordomo/lists

9. To create a new file that will contain the e-mail addresses of the subscribers, enter

    vi daubentonia

   to create a new file that will contain the e-mail addresses of the subscribers. Type in your e-mail address, then save and quit vi.

10. Enter

    chown majordom daubentonia

    to change the file's ownership from root to majordom.

11. Enter

    chgrp daemon daubentonia

    to change the file's group membership from root to daemon.

12. Enter

    exit

    to get out of root.

13. In your mail program, send mail to the listname. In this example, it's **daubentonia@*your_server_name_goes_here*.com**.

    Majordomo will create a configuration file in /usr/local/majordomo/lists named daubentonia.config.

14. Customize the config settings. The following are some suggested changes to the default settings for a new list:

    - From

        admin_passwd = daubentonia.admin

      to

        admin_passwd = *whatever_you_want*

    - From

        description =

to

description = A mailing list for daubentonia discussion

- From

  mungedomain = no

  to

  mungedomain = yes

- From:

  reply_to =

  to

  reply_to = daubentonia-list

- From

  subject_prefix =

  to

  subject_prefix = [DAUBENTONIA]

Majordomo is one of the primary mailing list managers for the UNIX platform, but what's available for Windows platform users? There are two major mailing list managers on the Windows platform: Lyris, and Lsoft's LISTSERV.

SmartList

If you have a UNIX system and are running procmail already (mentioned in "Seek Help" earlier in this chapter and available at **http://www.procmail.org/**), procmail is the core of a mailing list manager called SmartList. If you're already using procmail, adding SmartList may be a good option. SmartList offers almost all the standard features of a mailing list, and it includes the capability of a web administrator interface (built as a CGI for the web server, in Perl). For further information, see the Smartlist FAQ at **http://www.hartzler.net/smartlist/SmartList-FAQ.html**.

Mailman

Mailman is a UNIX-only mailing list manager built on the Python scripting language. Mailman provides the general features of most mailing list managers such as moderation, subscribe/unsubscribe, and mail-to-Usenet gatewaying and archiving, but it is very strongly oriented toward the web. Each mailing list in Mailman is automatically set up with a web page, providing information on the list, and subscribing and unsubscribing are conducted from the web in general. Mailman is in active development, and not all desired features are fully implemented as of yet; for example, you can edit the archive template via the web, but it isn't used when creating the archive files.

Mailman requires a UNIX system and the Python scripting language. For more information on Python, visit the main Python website at **http://www.python.org/**. For further information on Mailman, see the Mailman website at **http://www.list.org/**.

Lyris

The Lyris mailing list manager is available for Windows (Windows 95 and up) as well as Solaris, and as of this writing, a port of the application to Linux is in a public beta stage. To install Lyris, you will need your system to have the following characteristics (regardless of the operating system):

- A web browser
- A web server
- A full-time dedicated Internet connection (128K minimum) with static IP address with forward and reverse resolvable DNS.

One of the best things about Lyris is its price: A fully usable version, only limited to a maximum of two hundred users per individual list (but with no restriction on the number of lists that can be created), is downloadable and free. Other than that limitation, there is no difference in the Lyris package between the free version and the unlimited use version; to expand the list limit, you can purchase a registration code from Lyris and enter it, unlocking the limit with no need to install a new version. The design of Lyris places an emphasis on scalability and reliability.

Lyris can be found on the World Wide Web at **http://www.lyris.com**. An extensive demo of the web interface can be found at **http://www.lyris.com/demo**. Lyris can also be custom-configured using the Perl scripting language, and several useful Perl scripts have been contributed by various users and are downloadable from the Lyris website at **http://www.lyris.com/down/scripts.html**.

L-Soft's LISTSERV

L-Soft's LISTSERV was first available in 1986, and given its widespread use and longevity, it is stable, fast, and excellent for many users. LISTSERV has been ported to Windows 95/98 and Windows NT, several varieties of UNIX, and VMS.

L-Soft produces two products: LISTSERV and LSMTP.

- **LISTSERV** L-Soft's mailing list manager is optimized for speed and reliability, with a high degree of database integration. LISTSERV has a web-administrative front-end, several levels of security, and many options for configuration. LISTSERV also provides database integration for targeted mass-market mailings.
- **LSMTP** Designed for maximum throughput of messages, LSMTP is designed to serve very large e-mail lists faster and more efficiently than a sendmail-equipped system of similar power could. L-Soft claims LSMTP can handle

delivering three to four hundred thousand messages per hour on a reasonable Pentium II-based system, while a small Alphaserver can handle one million messages per hour. L-Soft also states even fast UNIX workstations using sendmail can barely handle delivering fifteen to twenty thousand messages per hour.

For more information, visit L-Soft's website at **http://www.lsoft.com**.

Outsourcing a Mailing List

Administering a mailing list can be easy or hard. Various mailing list managers provide varying degrees of user-friendliness, delegation, and automation, but they all require an amount of control over system resources and autonomy that a given group might not have available. If this is true in your organization, outsourcing your mailing list might be the best option. Outsourcing can be a good option for a short-term informal working group, or for a geographically distributed team. Two firms on the web that manage mailing lists, offering file libraries for binaries and archiving of the messages for later reference, can be found at **http://www.onelist.com** and **http://www.egroups.com** respectively.

CAUTION: Outsourcing your mailing list may or may not be a good idea, depending on the image you wish to project of your firm. If the only information resource for your product is an externally operated mailing list, the message projected to customers may be that your firm does not have the resources to operate a mailing list on its own. You can eliminate this problem by hiring a firm that will set up your mailing list under a virtual domain. One such domain, L-Soft's ListPlex service, is described at **http://www.lsoft.com/products/default.asp?item=listplex**.
Another concern, however, is the sensitivity of topics discussed in your company's mail messages. Ultimately, you may choose to manage your mailing list internally, thus reducing the chance that outsiders will access your mail archives. If sensitivity is a concern, you should also consider encrypting your e-mail traffic.

SUMMARY

This chapter has attempted to present some of the background and development of standards for transferring mail across heterogeneous networks and some of the likelier candidates for use as mail hubs or MTAs. If your work environment uses sendmail, you should now have a better understanding of the tasks facing the person or persons responsible for working with sendmail. If your environment uses or will be using Microsoft Exchange, you should now have an understanding of the capabilities of Exchange Server for messaging and sharing of information.

As mail services develop in complexity, capability, and extent, mail will continue to grow as a component of network traffic; it is likely to outgrow network bandwidth. In UNIX-based e-mail environments with mail user agents such as pine and elm, users could be castigated for quoting an entire message just to add "Me too!" at the bottom, or for using a signature block longer than four or so lines. With the addition of multimedia components to mail user agents, it is increasingly common to see users sending mail messages in HTML format that arrive in another user's mailbox as raw HTML, complete with visible tags obscuring the message content; using a company logo as part of their signature file in every message they send; or casually deciding to forward the latest version of Netscape Navigator (at several megabytes) as a file attachment to an e-mail message. Mail administrators should observe the usage of their users and provide guidance, recommendations, and rules for correct use of the mail system. For example, guidelines for users to turn off HTML or RTF in several e-mail clients can be found on the web at **http://www.rootsweb.com/rootsweb/listowners/html-off.htm**.

CHAPTER 6

Mixed Printing Environments

Even given the increasing power and versatility of today's computers, many are used primarily for word processing. Eventually, whether due to personal preference, department policy, or some other reason, a majority of computer professionals want to see paper copies—or other tangible representations—of what they see onscreen. Since you and everyone else are likely still waiting for "the paperless office" to become a reality, any network near you probably has at least one printer somewhere on it, and users of the network will want to access the printers.

The printing utilities included in most operating systems tend to provide the same major features: spooling directories for storing uncompleted print jobs, print queues for defining the order of uncompleted print jobs, print server processes or daemons for transferring print jobs from spooling directories to physical printers, user commands for creating print jobs, and administrator commands for viewing, modifying, and managing print jobs and print queues. Windows and UNIX systems offer all of these components, but printing is implemented differently on the two operating systems. UNIX itself is hardly monolithic: The various flavors of UNIX implement printing by two major, and not very compatible, methods.

This chapter will discuss printing terms in the Windows and UNIX worlds, address the architecture and configuration of printing services on Windows as well as UNIX, and present advice and strategies for providing print services to network users. The first section of this chapter will discuss Windows printing issues, the second will discuss UNIX printing information, and the third will discuss print service strategies.

WINDOWS 2000 PRINTING

Windows 2000 printing is primarily defined and controlled through use of the graphical user interface. This section will first present the terminology Microsoft uses to describe printing in Windows 2000, then cover several topics relating to TCP/IP printing, and close with a description of the Windows 2000 printing sequence.

Glossary of Terms

The Windows operating system uses a set of precisely defined terms for the world of printing. The following are some of those terms:

PRINTER A *printer* is a physical object that prints hard copy output. A printer may be local (using a workstation as a print server) or networked (connected directly to the network).

LOGICAL PRINTER A *logical printer* is a software interface (on a Windows desktop) that a user uses to control a printer. A logical printer can send to several printers, and several logical printers can target the same printer. For example, two different logical printers can be set up for a single physical printer: One logical printer can be defined to send its print jobs in PCL file format, and the other to its print jobs in PostScript file format.

PRINTER DRIVER The software that allows an application to send a print job in an intelligible format to a printing device is known as a *printer driver.* A printer driver consists of three components: a graphics driver, an interface driver, and a characterization data file. Printer drivers are typically not binary-compatible between platforms, so a printer driver for Windows NT running on an Intel processor will not function for Windows NT installed on an Alpha processor.

PHYSICAL PORT A *physical port* has a cable connecting a print server to a printer.

LOGICAL PORT A *logical port* offers a logical network connection to a remote printer.

PRINTER POOL A *printer pool* is a group of multiple printing devices that appear as a single printer to the user. The printing devices must use the same printer driver and are driven by a common print server.

PRINT SPOOLER A *print spooler* is software that accepts, orders, and dispatches print jobs to a printing device or printer pool.

PRINT MONITOR There are two kinds of print monitors:

- **Language monitors** Used to communicate with the printer, sending data and receiving status messages.
- **Port monitor** Used to view and administer the ports on the system available for printers. The Windows 2000 standard port monitor connects a Windows 2000 print server to networked printers using the TCP/IP protocol.

TCP/IP Printing Services in Windows 2000

Windows TCP/IP printing services provide two important services:

- The capability to use networked printing devices
- The capability for UNIX and other TCP/IP-speaking operating systems to print to a printing device directly attached to a Windows computer

Networked printing devices have their own network adapter cards and are not attached to a Windows or UNIX print server. A networked printing device acts as its own print server and must be able to accept, reject, and queue print jobs directly. Windows 2000 systems can communicate to networked printing devices using NetBEUI, NWLink, and TCP/IP printing services such as lpr and lpd. Other workstations on the network can use whatever other protocol the printing device will accept, such as NetWare's IPX protocol.

Windows NT Automatic Printer Driver Updates

The download of the printer driver happens automatically, with no user intervention. Printer drivers communicate directly with the hardware and do not use the Windows Hardware Abstraction Layer. In the right environment, auto-downloading of printer drivers can simplify an administrator's work. Since Microsoft has so far changed printer drivers with every version of Windows, Windows NT 3.51 clients will need Windows NT 3.51 printer drivers. Automatically downloading a Windows NT 4 printer driver will stop printing from an NT 3.51 workstation. Similarly, downloading a Windows NT 4 printer driver for Intel processors will stop printing if your workstation is NT 4, but on an Alpha processor.

If you want to disable automatic updating of the client printer driver, you can do it in one of two ways. The drivers are pulled from a hidden share called PRINTER$, which is in the %SystemRoot%\system32\spool\drivers directory. You can select the %SystemRoot%\SYSTEM32\SPOOL\DRIVERS folder that the printer drivers are stored in, and then unshare it. Alternatively, you can disable the auto-download feature on each client by editing the appropriate entry in the HKEY_LOCAL_MACHINE hive of the Registry. The solution you choose will probably be motivated by the numbers of affected clients.

Microsoft has had several sets of printer driver releases for Windows NT 3.5*x* and 4.0. A good source of information can be found in articles from the Microsoft Knowledge Base. Some of the more interesting Knowledge Base articles are listed in Table 6-1.

Peer-Level Printing Within a Windows NT Network

So, how does printing happen under Windows 2000? This section presents the sequence of events a print job goes through after a print command is issued in an application by a user. The first four steps describe a Windows 2000 client that is using a local printing device attached directly to the workstation.

Article Number	Title
Q121786	LPR and LPD Registry Entries for TCP/IP Printing
Q132460	Troubleshooting Windows NT Print Server Alteration of Print Jobs
Q124734	Text of RFC1179 Standard for Windows NT TCP/IP Printing
Q154291	Installing Cross Platform Print Drivers in Windows NT 4.0
Q154612	Installing Windows NT 4.0 Printer Drivers on a 3.5*x* Server

Table 6-1. Selected Articles on Printing from the Microsoft Knowledge Base

1. The application calls the graphical device interface (GDI), which calls the printer driver associated with the target printer. The client workstation checks the print server to see if the version of the printer driver on the print server is newer than the version resident on the client. If the print server has a newer printer driver than the client, the client first downloads the printer driver, then continues.
2. The Win32 application generates GDI (graphical device interface) commands and creates a file describing the print job in appropriate language for the destination printer. Typically, the print job is either converted to EMF (Windows Enhanced MetaFile) or RAW format. EMF format is the default data type for print jobs for PCL printers and the default format for print jobs from Windows NT or Windows 2000 clients. RAW format is the default data type for print jobs destined for PostScript printers. EMF files are device-independent, whereas RAW files are already prepared for a single kind of physical printer.
3. The print file is passed to the logical printer on the client desktop.
4. The spooler directs the print job to a print router. If the printing device is local (attached directly to the workstation), the print router passes the job to the local printing device.

   However, if the printing device is remote and attached to a Windows 2000 print server (either Professional or Server), the sequence is a little longer. For example, think of two Windows 2000 systems: The first is used by an employee who wishes to print a page, and a second is a workstation with a printing device attached to the physical port LPT1. Steps 1, 2, and 3 occur as previously described. Step 4 is replaced with the client-side spooler making a remote procedure call (RPC) to the server's print spooler, using the router to poll the client-side print provider. The remote print provider makes another RPC to the server spooler, which then receives the print job over the network.

   Printing then continues with the following additional steps:

5. The print spooler sends the print job (still in EMF format) to the print processor for rendering. The print processor renders the print job into a format the printing device can accept and returns the job to the print spooler.
6. Control of the print job is passed to the separator page processor, which adds a separator page, if specified, to the front of the job.
7. The print monitor sends the file to the printer through a physical port. If the printer is bidirectional, a language monitor handles status messages (if any are sent back from the printer) and then passes the print job to a port monitor. If the printer is not bidirectional, the print job is sent directly to the port monitor.
8. The port monitor sends the print job to the printer according to the defined port for that printer.
9. The printing device produces hard copy output from the print job. By default, the print monitor sends a completion message to the user when the printing device is done. (The confirmation message may soon become more irritating than useful; in this case, it can be disabled.)

Windows 2000 User and Administrator Printing Privileges

For this discussion, "administrator" will refer to any user account with membership in either the Administrator or Power User group in Windows 2000. "User" will refer to a user account without membership in either of these groups.

User Privileges

Users in Windows NT have the following printing privileges:

- Setting the default printer
- Viewing a local or remote print queue (by double-clicking the printer icon)
- Pausing, restarting, and deleting their own print jobs, but not those of other users (by selecting the print job in the print queue)
- Displaying details about a document (by right-clicking the document icon and selecting Properties)
- Displaying details about a printer (by right-clicking the printer icon and selecting Properties)
- Connecting to remote printers

Administrator Privileges

In addition to having the preceding user's abilities, administrators have the following printing privileges:

- Installing and removing printers
- Chaining printer configuration settings
- Administering print servers from remote locations
- Setting permissions for local and remote printers
- Establishing and disabling auditing
- Deleting any print job in the queue
- Reordering the print jobs in the queue
- Installing printer drivers locally and remotely
- Redirecting print jobs

Installing a Printer on Windows 2000

Users send print jobs to physical printers through logical printers. An ordinary user cannot create a logical printer, but a user with Power User group membership for his or her workstation can do so.

To add a printer to the local computer, follow these steps:

1. Open the Printers folder (found in the Control Panel) and double-click the Add Printers icon to start the Add Printer Wizard. The first window displays choices for the physical port connecting the printing device to the computer. Choose an appropriate port, such as LPT1, and click Next to go to the second window.
2. The second window displays choices for the manufacturer and model of the printer. In a nice graphical user interface (GUI) design, selecting a manufacturer in the left list box indexes the right list box to that manufacturer's set of printers. When you have selected a printer, click Next to see the next window.
3. The third window prompts you to name the new printer, and to choose if this logical printer will be the system's default printer. Enter a name and click Next.
4. The fourth window asks you to decide if you will share this printer with other network users. Select the Share As option and enter a name for the printer. This name does not have to be the same name you entered in the previous window. When you choose to share the printer, the list box at the bottom of the window becomes usable. Choose the operating systems of all clients that will be accessing this printer. When you are done, click Next to go to the fifth window.
5. The fifth window allows you to enter optional information about the physical printer's location and other comments as desired. Enter what comments you wish, and click Next to go to the sixth window.
6. The sixth window asks if you want to print a test page to test the configuration. Make your choice and click Next to go to the seventh window.
7. The final window displays your configuration information you've chosen. If any of your choices is incorrect, use the Back button to return to the appropriate window and edit the information. When you are done, click Finish to complete adding a printer.

In contrast to adding a local printer, adding a remote printer is a comparatively simple operation. The printer is already configured with a printer server elsewhere. Selecting Network Printer Server in the window described in Step 1 displays a second window, which displays all shared printers on the network. Choose a printer from the Shared Printers list box, then click OK. Alternatively, you could use Windows Explorer to browse the Network Neighborhood. Once you have found a shared printer on the network, right-click the printer and choose Install from the pop-up menu to install that printer to your desktop.

TIP: Since Windows logical printers are software interfaces to physical printers, you can create multiple logical printers on the same desktop that point to the same printers. Suppose, for example, that you have a printer attached to your workstation. You decide that you want to share it with others in your immediate area, but you still want to have priority on your printer. You can create two logical printers on your desktop: Designate the first logical printer (yours alone) as unshared with high priority, and the second as shared for everyone's use, but with lower priority.

Configuring Printer Properties

You access the printer properties by right-clicking the printer icon and choosing Properties from the pop-up menu. The Printer Properties window will appear. The Properties window has six tabs: General, Sharing, Ports, Advanced, Security, and Device Settings.

GENERAL The General tab displays information and comments about the printer, including the optional location and comment information you may have entered when configuring the printer.

SHARING The Sharing tab allows you to change whether the printer is shared, as well as the operating systems you want to include printer drivers for. This window is where you would go when you need to modify a printer to support a Windows NT Alpha workstation to be added to the network.

PORTS The Ports tab displays the ports, both physical and logical, available to your workstation. You define printer pooling from this window. If you select multiple ports and check the checkbox at the bottom of the window labeled Enable Printer Pooling, print jobs sent to the printer will print to the first available printing device. Each printing device must be able to use the same print driver.

ADVANCED The Advanced tab allows you to define priorities and to manage the print spooler. The Priority slider allows you to change the priority for the print spooler from 1 (lowest) to 99 (highest). Some of the other options available on this window allow you to turn off the print spooler and print directly to the printing device, hold mismatched documents instead of rejecting them, and hold printed documents in the spool after printing.

SECURITY The Security tab allows you to set permissions, enable or disable auditing, and view or change ownership of print jobs. The four permission levels are:

- **Print** The spooler will accept print jobs from this user or group. This is the default access level for the Everyone group.
- **Manage Documents** The user or group can pause, resume, restart, or delete documents from the print queue. A user who is not an administrator can always perform the preceding actions on his own print jobs; Manage Documents allows the user to act on other users' documents. This is the default access level for the Creator Owner of a print job.

- **Manage Printers** In addition to the permissions granted by Manage Documents, the user or group can change printer properties, create or delete printers, change printer permissions, and take ownership of a printer. This is the default access level for the Administrator group, and for Power Users of the local system.
- **No Access** The user or group is not allowed to use the printer at all. No Access overrides any other permissions a user or group might have. For example, you could deny a Server Operator the ability to print to a particular printer.

DEVICE SETTINGS The Device Settings tab displays specific information about the printing device. A useful feature available in this window is the capability to map form names and types to trays in printing devices holding multiple trays. By allowing meaningful associations between trays and form types, this feature reduces the number of users who would otherwise select tray 2 and print their document onto 11 × 17 inch paper when they thought they'd chosen 8 1/2 × 14 inch, or onto A4 paper when they thought they'd selected the envelope tray.

UNIX PRINTING

UNIX printing commands have been part of the operating system since its beginning, when ASCII line printers were the standard hard copy production method. Over the years, the printing subsystems of UNIX have been extended, enhanced, and simply hacked in order to work with dot-matrix printers, plotters, laser printers, and almost any other hard copy output device that can be imagined.

UNIX, of course, is not a one-of-a-kind operating system; there are many flavors of UNIX. The two major families of UNIX are BSD (Berkeley Software Distribution) and System V. Proper coverage of the evolution of UNIX is beyond the scope of this book, but some flavors of UNIX are more like BSD UNIX, some are more like System V UNIX, and some are a mix of the two. One of the widest areas of variation between the two families is in the printing subsystem. A quick way to identify the family of your version of UNIX is to look for the lpsched print queue daemon or the /etc/printcap file. If lpsched is present, the UNIX you are looking at is a System V family relation. If /etc/printcap is present, the UNIX you are looking at is a BSD derivation.

UNIX Glossary

UNIX has its own set of terms used for printing issues. If you're unfamiliar with them, here are a few of the ones you'll need to know.

SPOOLER The *print spooler* receives, stores, prioritizes, and dispatches print jobs to a printer.

PRINTER In the UNIX world, a *printer* is the same as it is in Windows: a physical object that produces hard copy output.

RIP A *raster image processor* accepts a document in a PDL (page description language) and converts the file to a bitmap format from which a printer can produce hard copy output. The RIP processing can occur either on the host computer sending the print job or on the printer itself. For example, many modern printers can accept files in Adobe's popular PostScript RIP format. Processing to convert the PostScript file to bitmap format occurs on the printer.

PDL A *page description language* describes how to print images. Although a bitmap image also does this, PDL files are more abstract, making them easier to move between platforms. Some of the better-known PDLs are Adobe's PostScript, Hewlett-Packard's HPGL (Hewlett-Packard Graphics Language), PCL (Printer Command Language), and Microsoft's EMF (Enhanced MetaFile, formerly known as Windows MetaFile).

BSD Printing

Operating systems in the BSD UNIX family include SunOS, Digital UNIX, and Linux, as well as AIX. (AIX has its own print queue system that is a specific instance of a general job queue system, but it accepts BSD as well as System V print commands as alternatives to its native command set.) This section will first examine BSD UNIX printing subsystem components and then discuss the procedure for adding a local printer to a BSD UNIX workstation.

BSD Printing Subsystem Components

Since BSD UNIX printing architecture is supported by Windows NT print servers, whereas System V printing is not, this section will be more detailed than the following section on System V printing. BSD-derived UNIX printing uses the following files and executables as major components:

LPD The lpd program is the printer daemon responsible for moving a print job from the spooling directory to the physical printer.

LPR The lpr program accepts a print job from either the local workstation or a remote client and places the print job into the spooling directory.

LPQ The lpq program displays or lists the print jobs currently in the print queue.

LPRM The lprm program deletes a print job from the spooling directory. Due to the permissions that should be defined on the printer spool directory, lprm is restricted to deleting a user's own jobs.

LPC An administrative interface to printing, lpc originally was an acronym for line printer control. It is used to view and change the status of the printer and to alter the order of print jobs waiting in the print queue.

/ETC/PRINTCAP The /etc/printcap file describes all printing devices for which the local print spooler is configured to send print jobs. A sample printcap entry for a standard design line printer would look like this:

```
# lineprinter - system default printer
lp|line printer:\
   :sd=/var/spool/lp:if=/usr/lib/lpf:lf=/var/adm/lpd-errors:\
   :lo=lp0LOCK:lp=/dev/lp:pl=66:pw=132:af=/var/adm/lpa
```

Each comment line begins with an octothorp (#), also known as a number sign or pound sign. The first line in a printcap entry has the printer name (lp). The printer given the name lp in the /etc/printcap file is the system default printer. The other entries in this sample indicate the error log file pathname (lf), the lock filename (lo), the device specific file (lp), the page length (pl), the page width (pw), and the accounting file pathname (af).

PRINT JOB A print job is a file that has been generated and sent to a print queue to await actual printing. "Print job" is the BSD UNIX term; System V calls the same concept a "print request."

Installing a New Printer Under BSD UNIX

Adding a new printer locally to a BSD UNIX workstation is a reasonably simple task. The following are the steps required to configure a BSD UNIX workstation as a print server. Since the various flavors of UNIX do differ, a check of the specific operating system documentation for precise steps is recommended.

1. Physically attach the printer to the computer. Printers are commonly attached through the parallel port, the serial port, or the SCSI (Small Computer Systems Interface) port. If the printer is a serial line, disable the line by creating or editing a line for that serial port in the appropriate UNIX configuration file, such as /etc/ttytab.
2. Confirm that the lpd daemon is started at system boot time. If this is the first printer added to the UNIX workstation, you may have to edit the system startup files to start lpd. UNIX system startup files are often in the /etc/rc or /etc/rc.d directory—check your operating system documentation.
3. Edit the /etc/printcap file to add or un-comment an entry for your printer. Many UNIXes provide an extensive /etc/printcap file with all entries commented out and inactive, so look to see if your printer is already listed. If the printer is not in the /etc/printcap file, check the printer documentation—many manufacturers can provide /etc/printcap entries for their printers.
4. Create a spooling directory for the printer, which often is located in the /var/spool directory. Each physical printer will require a separate spooling directory. Under BSD UNIX printing, the print job is copied to the spooling directory; therefore, plan carefully and select a size for the spooling directory

appropriate for the expected users. The spooling directory should be owned by the same group and user that the lpd daemon runs as. The spooling directory should also have access mode 755. Mode 755 means only the user has write access to the directory, but everyone (including the user) has read and execute permission to the directory. This security precaution prevents users from inserting a print job at the top of a busy print queue, deleting print jobs from the queue, or otherwise acting in an inappropriate manner.

5. Create the printer accounting file, as defined in the printer's /etc/printcap file, and assign it the same ownership and permission as the printer's spooling directory.
6. Start and enable the printer queue with this command:

   lpc up *printer_name*.

7. Test the setup by attempting to print a file.

System V Printing

We will not address System V printing in as much detail as BSD printing, because the Windows 2000 print server does not support the System V print architecture. Operating systems in the System V family include Solaris, HP-UX, IRIX, and SCO UNIX, as well as AIX (as alternates to its native command set). System V printing consists of four major components: lpsched, spooling directories, user commands, and administrative commands.

LPSCHED The lpsched executable lives in /usr/lib/lp directory. The lpsched daemon is started when the system boots and controls when and where print jobs are passed to which physical printers.

SPOOLING DIRECTORIES Under System V printing, a spooling directory typically is created as /var/spool/lp/request/*printer_name*. Unlike those in BSD UNIX, System V spooling directories only hold print request information, but the actual print job is not copied to the System V spooling directory unless the –c command line parameter is used with the lp command.

USER COMMANDS User commands under System V include the following: lp to create a print request, cancel to cancel a print request (but only a request owned by the cancelling user, unless the user is an administrator), and lpstat to display the contents of a print queue and list the printers currently available. The lp command can also be used to modify the order of print requests within a print queue.

ADMINISTRATIVE COMMANDS System V administrative commands include lpadmin, lpuser, lpmove, lpshut, and the accept, reject, enable, and disable commands. The lpadmin command is used to define a new physical printer, or to edit existing printers to a UNIX System V workstation. The lpusers command is used to define print priority as a systemwide variable for that printer, or to define priority values for specific users. Print requests can be transferred from one print queue to another with the lpmove command. The lpshut command shuts down the printing service on the workstation (which is recommended before editing the printer configuration with lpadmin). The reject and accept commands stop and start transferal of print requests to a spooling directory, while the enable and disable commands stop and start transferal of print requests from the spooling directory to the printer.

Samba and Printing

Samba is a freeware protocol and suite of programs originally written by Andrew Tridgell, and currently maintained by the Samba team. The Samba suite works together to allow clients access to a server's filespace and printers via the SMB (Server Message Block) and CIFS (Common Internet File System) protocols. Samba is available within Windows NT and 2000, OS/2, and Linux, and it is available for a wide variety of other operating systems including almost all UNIX variations, DOS and non-NT/2000 Windows, Apple Macintosh OS, VMS, and so on. In practice, this means that you can redirect disks and printers to UNIX disks and printers from clients running on almost any operating system. A generic UNIX client program allows UNIX users to use an FTP-like interface to access filespace and printers on any other SMB server. (The Samba suite is discussed in more detail in Chapter 2.)

GENERAL ADVICE AND PRINTER STRATEGIES

In this chapter, many of the technical printing issues in Windows and UNIX environments have been covered. Terminology has been provided so that you can use the right vocabulary in the appropriate camps. Additionally, some of the underlying architecture has been presented, so you know what happens when a user drops a Word document onto a printer icon, on a Windows desktop, destined for a remote printer on a UNIX print server across the network. There are, however, issues outside the network. The following section will address some of the physical issues.

General Printing Advice

Much of this section's advice originates from the fact that printing uses physical resources. One signature file seen on the Internet reads, "This message printed from 100% recycled electrons." Unlike electronic mail, printing uses up paper and laser toner or ink. With this distinction in mind, here are some tips mostly aimed at conserving use.

Use Printer Accounting as a Monitoring Tool

A general rule is, "If you can't measure it, you can't tell how well you're doing." For example, monitoring assisted at a university where at one point the use of the printers at a student computer lab increased from two thousand pages a week to over twelve thousand pages a week. Using the printer accounting tools, the administrators were able to determine that students were editing term papers and reprinting the entire document, often with only a single page changed.

Turn Off Banner Pages If They Are Unnecessary

In many cases, where a large number of users access a shared printer, this advice is not practical. However, in other cases, such as a smaller office area with a printer shared by a few people, or a nonshared printer used by a single person, the printing of banner pages can be a significant use of resources. If a nonshared printer is used by a single person for short letters, banner pages (in this extreme case) can approach fifty percent of the total page count.

Always Provide Recycling Bins

Users go through an astonishing amount of paper per day. The paperless office will probably become a reality for the general information technology workforce at about the same time that the personal helicopter comes into general use for commuting to work. Opinions vary on the cost-effectiveness of refurbishing used laser toner cartridges. Although the dollar-cost of a refurbished cartridge is less than that for a new one, refurbished cartridges do not always last as long as new ones. Examine what the options are in your area before deciding, but consider the idea before rejecting it.

Provide Print Previewers, and Educate Your Users

The first part of this advice is often simple to implement: Print preview is a common option in almost all of the word processing and page layout programs on the market. Encouraging users to use print preview before using hard copy is an administrative policy decision; it is not a policy that can be automated into the network. Although WYSIWYG (what you see is what you get) printing is another myth similar in attainability to the paperless office, print previews can be used to determine whether the hard copy output is at least fairly close to the desired result.

Keep Extra Supplies on Hand

Has it been mentioned that users go through paper and toner cartridges at an astonishing rate? If Napoleon was correct when he said, "An army marches on its stomach," imagine (or remember) what happens when the printers run out of supplies. When a software development firm misses a due date to a client because the documentation couldn't be printed because the laser toner cartridge ran empty and there were no replacements available, senior management tends to come looking for an explanation.

Strategies

So now that you've seen how to add a printer to a network, what choice do you make? A printer may reside as a local printer for a Windows server or a UNIX server, or in many cases it may attach directly to the network. This section will compare some of the pros and cons of each of the three options.

Attaching a Printer to a Windows 2000 Print Server

Attaching a printer directly to a Windows 2000 system as a print server gives some benefits. One primary benefit is that Windows peer-to-peer networking is fairly stable and requires minimal configuration. Using Windows 2000 as a print server gives reliable access to the attached printer by the other Windows workstations on the local network and makes the print server's hard disk available as a print spooler. Installing TCP/IP printing on the print server also grants access to the printer from any other platform on the network that supports TCP/IP, which is likely to be every platform present on the network.

However, the Windows 2000 print server does not support UNIX systems, which use lpsched—this includes such operating systems as Solaris and IRIX. UNIX clients using a Windows 2000 print server must use lpd. UNIX systems that use lpsched must either have a printer available on a UNIX print server or install the lpd print system (available over the Internet in source code, and in various third-party commercial offerings) on each client. While adding lpd will allow use of Windows 2000 print servers, doing so is yet another task in an administrator's list and introduces another chance for problems to appear.

REMEMBER: If you choose to use Windows NT as a print server, do consider the relative limitations and performance optimizations of Windows NT Workstation versus Windows NT Server. Windows NT Workstation is limited by license to only ten simultaneous TCP/IP connections. Also, Windows NT Server has its performance optimized for background applications performance. In other words, if someone is logged into a Windows NT Server console, their word processing application will get secondary preference from the CPU in favor of the (name/file/print/RAS/whatever) server functions the server is providing to remote users.

The ability to manage print services remotely for Windows 2000 from a web browser is a welcome feature, but it brings its own problems. With the advent of web-based printer administration and the new command-line access feature, remote control of printing services can be more easily seized by unauthorized users, or even by strangers offsite.

NOTE: A Windows service is equivalent to a UNIX daemon.

Attaching a Printer to a UNIX Print Server

Attaching a printer to a UNIX print server provides many of the advantages of attaching a printer to a Windows 2000 print server, including reliable access to the printer by other similar systems on the network, and use of the local workstation as a print spooler. Windows NT clients with TCP/IP printing installed can also access the printer.

A Networked Stand-Alone Printer

Many printers today, including some in the small/home office categories, are manufactured with network cards, and even smaller laser printers that don't ship with networking built in can be inexpensively equipped with networking capability. For instance, Hewlett-Packard printers lacking networking capability can use JetDirect or Farallon attachments to add an Ethernet interface for about the cost of a laser toner cartridge. Such printers are attached directly to the network, are as much of an individual node on the network as any file server, and do not require you to dedicate any part of a workstation's activity as a print server. As long as the network itself is functioning, the printer is accessible.

On the other hand, no one can use a network printer on a congested Ethernet network. In addition, since workstations tend to have larger storage devices than printers, a stand-alone printer will be limited to a comparatively small print queue. Client workstations attempting to send jobs to the remote print queue on a stand-alone printer may overload the print queue sooner than they could if the print queue were resident on a workstation.

However, even if the printing device itself can stand alone, you may want to configure the printing device as a printer attached to either a UNIX host or a Windows host. A local workstation/printer arrangement provides a diagnostic checkpoint for printing troubles—a heterogeneous UNIX and Windows environment may contain multiple flavors of UNIX, as well as multiple versions of Windows NT, Windows 3.1 or 3.11, Windows 95 or 98, Linux, NetWare, Macintosh System software, BeOS, and so on. If a local print job from the print server succeeds when a print job from over the network is rejected, you know at least a portion of the printing system is still working and configured properly. If part of the network experiences difficulty, at least one person can use the printer while the network is being repaired.

SUMMARY

TCP/IP printing services in Windows 2000 provide both better accessibility for non-Windows workstations in the network and better control over access to the printing devices than was provided in Windows NT. When laser printing devices were new, they were the high-end printers whose use had to be jealously guarded because they consumed expensive resources. Now that laser printers are common, color laser and dye-sublimation printers as well as large plotters are protected devices. Microsoft's TCP/IP printing services provide better control over which users can access specific printing devices than that provided by the NetBEUI networking protocol.

When adding printing resources to a network, you should be guided by the strengths of the information technology support staff and the needs and distributions of the users. If the network primarily consists of Windows workstations with only a few UNIX file servers, it would make little sense to attach printers to the UNIX servers. Similarly, if a majority of the printers on the network are already set up on the UNIX portion of the network, simply extend the current configuration. Networked printers are increasingly popular in the corporate environment. Today's large, fast printers are commonly installed directly onto the network for the same reason that early laser printers were networked: They are expensive to install everywhere, and sharing a valuable resource makes good business sense.

CHAPTER 7

Networking Windows and UNIX

When integrating UNIX and Windows 2000 systems, knowledge of networking and network protocols becomes essential. UNIX systems typically provide networking via the TCP/IP protocol, whereas the Windows systems can implement several different protocols. If the administrator who has been tasked with making a network integration function properly comes from a UNIX environment, he or she will most likely not be familiar with Microsoft's use of NetBEUI, NetBIOS names, WINS, or DHCP. On the other hand, if the administrator comes from a Windows environment, he or she may have had no exposure to TCP/IP at all, possibly having run the Windows environment under NetBEUI or IPX.

It would be impossible in just one chapter to cover all the networking theory that you need to know. In this chapter, we are going to look at some of the significant details that you should know if you are going to network Windows and UNIX systems.

NETWORKING AND THE OSI MODEL

In order to connect various computing resources on a network, we have to be able to discuss the details of the network architecture. For computers to be able to communicate with each other, they must speak the same language or *protocol.* Most protocols have several different functions and operate in a layered fashion. In addition to the protocols, computers must use compatible hardware in order to communicate.

In 1978, an organization known as the International Standards Organization (ISO) developed a model for describing network architectures. In 1984, the ISO revised this model and named it the Open Systems Interconnection (OSI) reference model. The OSI model is widely used as a framework for describing networks and how network components interact at different levels.

Architecture of the OSI Model

The OSI model contends that networks operate in a layered fashion, with a specific set of responsibilities located at each layer. Each particular layer in the OSI model covers the responsibilities of network function, hardware, and protocols. Figure 7-1 depicts the OSI layered network model.

With the network divided into seven layers, different services and functions can be specified at each layer. Each layer in the network communicates with the layers above and below it through a set of boundaries, called *interfaces.*

The primary role of each layer is to provide a set of services to the layer above it, and to hide the details of how those services are implemented from the higher layer. This structure allows each layer to act as if it were communicating directly with its corresponding layer on another computer, when in reality data is being passed down through the OSI layers, out onto the network, and back up through the OSI model on the receiving computer. The appearance of communicating directly with a corresponding layer on

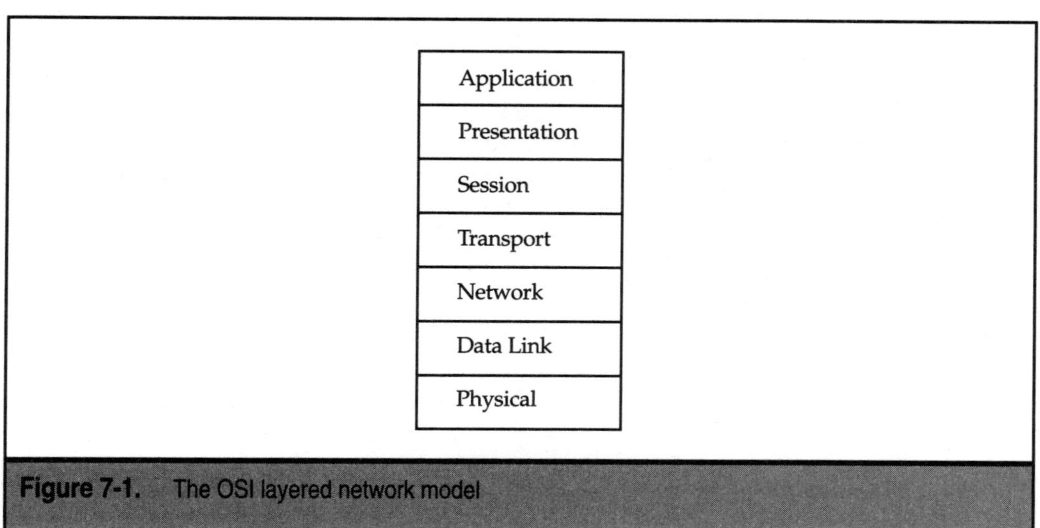

Figure 7-1. The OSI layered network model

another computer is known as *virtual communication.* Let's look at the services provided by the various layers of the OSI model.

Physical Layer

The bottom layer in the OSI model is the Physical layer. The Physical layer is responsible for transmitting the data stream over some type of physical medium, such as Ethernet or fiber optic cable. The Physical layer defines the details of the transmission medium, the details of the computer interface to the transmission medium, and the hardware data encoding scheme that is used. The data encoding scheme defines how the medium sends a 1 or a 0 and ensures that the data sent is received as a 1 or a 0 at the other end. It also defines how bits are translated into electrical or optical signals.

Data Link Layer

The second layer from the bottom is the Data Link layer. This layer is responsible for taking data from the Network layer and transmitting it over the network. It takes data chunks, known as *frames,* from the Network layer, adds some control information, and passes the frames on to the Physical layer for actual transmission.

In addition to the actual data, a Data Link layer frame may contain information such as the source and destination IDs, as well as some error detection codes, so that the Data Link layer on the other end can verify that the data frame is error-free. Since the Data Link layer is responsible for error-free transmission, it will resend any frames that were damaged or have errors.

Network Layer

The next layer up from the Data Link layer is the Network layer. The Network layer is responsible for addressing network data, translating logical addresses and names into physical addresses, and determining the best route from the source computer to the destination computer. In addition, if the Transport layer (described next) sends a block of data, known as a *packet*, that is too large for the lower levels of the network to handle, the Network layer segments the packet into smaller pieces. The corresponding Network layer on the receiving end reassembles the pieces into the original packet. This process is known as *segmentation and reassembly*.

Transport Layer

The Transport layer lives above the Network layer. The Transport layer's goal in life is to ensure that packets are delivered error-free, in sequence, with no duplication or loss. This layer takes long messages in the data stream and breaks them into packets. Since the Transport layer is responsible for ensuring packet delivery, it will request retransmission of packets that have errors or that it did not receive.

Session Layer

The Session layer allows two applications to maintain a dialog called a *session*. The Session layer manages name recognition functions and security between the two sides of the conversation. It also manages the dialog interaction between the two computers.

Presentation Layer

The Presentation layer provides translation functions for the data stream. It translates formats, protocols, character sets, and the like. It may translate data into a widely implemented intermediate format before it is sent onto the network. The Presentation layer is also responsible for data encryption and data compression.

Application Layer

The Application layer lives at the top of the OSI seven-layer model. This layer provides the services that directly interact with client applications. Its services provide network support for applications such as electronic mail and file transfers.

THE TCP/IP PROTOCOL SUITE

Protocols are the languages that computers use to speak to each other. The TCP/IP protocol suite is one of the most widely used sets of network communication protocols in existence. In the mid-1970s, the United States Department of Defense's Advanced Research Projects Agency (ARPA) undertook the task of making different networks interoperate.

ARPA began working with universities and computer firms in order to develop new communications standards. Out of this alliance came a new set of protocols that formed the basis for TCP/IP.

Today, the TCP/IP protocol suite provides the backbone for the Internet. Virtually all UNIX systems implement TCP/IP as their primary networking protocol. Microsoft has adopted TCP/IP as the protocol of choice for Windows, as well. If you are going to use Windows and UNIX in a network environment where they will interoperate and share services, you will be required to understand and manage a TCP/IP network.

TCP/IP has been widely adopted and implemented on a variety of platforms. However, it remains complex and fairly difficult to configure. The next few sections look at some of the key issues in understanding the TCP/IP protocol suite and managing a TCP/IP network.

The Protocol Stack

We refer to TCP/IP as the *TCP/IP protocol suite* because it really is composed of several different protocols. Since TCP/IP was around before the OSI model was developed, it doesn't fit nicely into the OSI seven-layer model. However, we can use the OSI model to help get a feel for how the different protocols that make up the TCP/IP protocol suite interact.

At the top portion of the TCP/IP protocol suite, we have the user application interface protocols, such as *Telnet* for remote login, the *File Transfer Protocol* (FTP) for transferring data files, and the *Simple Mail Transport Protocol* (SMTP) for transporting e-mail. Some other high-level TCP/IP protocols, such as the *Network File System* (NFS) and the *Domain Name Service* (DNS), support complex network functions. These protocols roughly map to the Presentation and Application layers in the OSI model. Some of these protocols also incorporate features defined in the Session layer.

At the middle level of the TCP/IP protocol suite, we find two protocols that support functions defined in the Transport layer of the OSI model. These protocols are the *Transmission Control Protocol* (TCP) and the *User Datagram Protocol* (UDP). TCP is a connection-oriented protocol that is responsible for providing reliable, sequenced, error-free packet delivery over the network. When a TCP protocol session is established, the two computers form a logical connection, transmit a sequence of data, and then dissolve the connection.

UDP is similar in function to TCP, except that it is not connection-oriented and does not guarantee reliable delivery. UDP is a *connectionless* protocol. With UDP, there is no need to have the overhead of setting up and dissolving a network connection. It simply transmits a packet, known as a *datagram*, to its destination host. UDP does not check to see if the packet was received successfully or not.

At the bottom level of the TCP/IP protocol suite, we find the *Internet Protocol* (IP). IP provides a connectionless Network layer protocol that addresses and routes packets. It also provides support for packet fragmentation and reassembly. Since IP is a connectionless protocol, it does not guarantee reliable delivery of network packets.

Addressing

The Internet Protocol (IP) is the Network layer component of the TCP/IP protocol suite and is, therefore, responsible for handling network addresses. IP requires that each computer or network device have a unique address assigned to it.

IP addresses are composed of four eight-bit numbers separated by decimals. Each of the four numbers that make up an IP address is referred to as an *octet* and may have a value in the range from 0 to 255. Depending on the type of IP address, some portion will designate a particular network or subnetwork, and the remainder of the address will indicate the particular host on that network. An example of an IP address is

207.68.156.49

Certain values used in an IP address have special meanings. The numbers 0, 127, and 255 are reserved: The number 0 refers to the current network or host. The number 127 indicates a lookback to the current host. The number 255 indicates that the message should be broadcast to all hosts on the network.

Types of IP Addresses

Networks can be of vastly different sizes. As a result, different categories of IP addresses are designed to be used in different-sized networks. These different categories are called *address classes.* Three address classes are in common use today: Class A, Class B, and Class C.

A Class A IP address is designed for very large networks. In a Class A address, the first octet of the address indicates the network; it can have a range from 1 to 126. The last three octets indicate the particular host on the network. Since only the first octet is used, and the numbers 0 and 127 are reserved, there can only be 126 Class A networks in existence. However, a Class A network can have over 16 million different addresses!

Class B networks are designed for midsize networks, such as those used by corporations and universities. A Class B network uses the first two octets to identify the network and the last two octets to indicate the host. There can be 16,384 Class B networks, each with 65,534 host addresses.

Class C networks are used for small networks. Only the last octet is used for the host ID portion, giving 254 hosts per network. However, there can be over 2 million Class C networks. Table 7-1 summarizes the different characteristics of the network address classes.

In addition to Class A, B, and C addresses, there are Class D and E addresses as well. Class D is reserved for specialized network traffic known as *multicast addressing.* Class E is reserved for experimentation and research.

IPv6

IPv4 uses a 32-bit address system, which in theory allows more than four billion unique IP addresses. However, inefficiencies in the system of allocating those addresses mean the actual number available is smaller. IPv6, in contrast, uses a 128-bit address system, which in theory will meet the needs of literally trillions of Internet clients. A common illustration of the address space IPv6 provides is that it would be possible to, for example,

Class	Number of Networks	Number of Hosts per Network	Valid Network IDs
A	126	16,721,214	001–126
B	16,384	65,534	128.0–191.255
C	2,097,152	254	192.0.0–223.255.255

Table 7-1. IP Address Class Characteristics

assign a unique IPv6 number to every traffic light in the world, as well as every telephone, every home stereo, and so on.

IPv6 has other benefits, including the capability to offer greater security for data traveling over the Internet using the newer IPSec protocols instead of the less-secure Point-to-Point Tunneling Protocol (PPTP), real-time communications, and better router performance. As of this writing, IPv6 is just beginning to be put into use. For more information, see the IPv6 Forum website at **http://www.ipv6.org/**.

Common Problems with IP Addresses

You've configured TCP/IP and assigned your IP addresses, but things don't appear to be working correctly. What could be wrong? Although any number of things can be wrong with a TCP/IP network configuration, for IP addresses, there are only a couple of common mistakes.

First of all, your network address could be set incorrectly. This will cause all network traffic to be routed to the wrong network. Second, you could have the same IP address assigned to multiple computers. This is a very common mistake and can be hard to troubleshoot. Duplicate IP addresses can cause some very strange behavior, which can appear and disappear. Windows will not initialize its network connection if it detects a duplicate IP address; it will indicate the error with a message in the error log, visible in the Event Viewer. (On the Windows 2000 desktop, click the Start button, choose Programs, choose Administrative Tools, and then choose Event Viewer.) However, you can still have duplicate IP addresses with UNIX systems, or by configuring a UNIX system to have an address duplicating an existing Windows workstation. Your network administrator should assign IP addresses in a very controlled manner to prevent duplicate addresses. Never, ever, allow users to just make up an IP address for their computers!

ROUTING

The Internet Protocol is responsible for routing packets of data, known as *datagrams*, to their destination over a group of connected networks, known as an *internetwork*. Routing destinations can be local, on another network with a known route to that network, or completely remote. In this section, you'll look at some of the details of routing and understand the significance of logical and physical addresses and the difference between them.

Physical Addresses vs. Logical Addresses

Under IP, every host connected to the network must have an IP address. This address is a *logical* address. Logical addresses have no relationship to the physical hardware used or the physical media that the host is connected to. Logical addresses are assigned to an organization and are then assigned by that organization to network devices as needed. Recall that an IP address contains both a network portion and a host portion. The network portion is logically assigned according to criteria assigned by the network administrator.

Physical addresses, by comparison, are assigned to a particular piece of hardware. When you buy an Ethernet card from some manufacturer, the card has a specific Ethernet address burned into the hardware of that card. This address cannot be changed, thus the term "physical" address. If you move the card from one computer to another, the physical address of the card will not change.

Routing deals with the logical address rather than the physical address. Since you can assign logical addresses yourself based on your own criteria, routing allows you to segment your network along logical, organization-specific lines.

Bridges vs. Routers vs. Switches

A *bridge* is a network device that manages traffic based on its physical address. Bridges function at the Data Link layer in the OSI model. Bridges enable you to separate your network into different physical segments in order to manage network traffic. When you install a bridge in a network, you create two physical segments. The bridge monitors network traffic and builds a table of physical addresses. This table keeps track of which side of the bridge a particular physical address is on. If network traffic is sent from one host to another, and they are both on the same side of the bridge, the bridge will not forward the traffic to the other side. Since bridges operate at the Data Link layer, they do not know anything about routing and logical addresses. They can only manage network traffic by keeping track of the physical addresses.

Routers, on the other hand, operate at the Network level in the OSI model. Routers are used to separate a network into multiple logical networks. Traffic is controlled and manipulated according to logical addresses, such as the IP address.

Moving up the OSI layers, the next higher networking object is a *switch.* A switch can be defined as a multi-port bridge. Since bridging is defined in the OSI specification as a Layer 2 (Data Link layer) function, many well-known networking standards such as Ethernet, Token Ring, or FDDI can be bridged or switched (IP may be handled with a simple router, as discussed in the next section). Switches are generally used to divide a larger network into many smaller ones. Switch performance can vary greatly and is often based on how a switch handles the forwarding of packets (many switches are simply configured as bridges). Methods for packet forwarding can be one of the following: store-and-forward, cut-through, or modified cut-through.

Consider an example of why you would use a router. Say you have two groups in your company, Sales and Research and Development (R&D), and you want to have them on separate networks. By installing a router, you can separate the Sales network from the R&D network according to the corporate functions of the two departments involved. You would simply assign different IP addresses with different network components to Sales and R&D, and configure a router to route between the two. That way, all Sales traffic would stay on the Sales network, and all R&D traffic, on the R&D network. Only traffic specifically sent from one network to the other would pass through the router. In fact, even broadcast packets would not be sent, as routers do not forward broadcasts.

Routable vs. Nonroutable Protocols

As you can probably gather, IP is a *routable* protocol. A routable protocol is one that can be managed with a router rather than a bridge. For a protocol to be routable, it must have some method for encoding a network address into its logical address. IP is a routable protocol because its addresses are broken down into separate network and host portions.

A nonroutable protocol does not have a network address component. Most nonroutable protocols were developed to operate in a local LAN environment and were never meant to travel outside the local LAN.

Why is the distinction between routable and nonroutable an issue? Because many Microsoft networks still use NetBEUI, which is a nonroutable protocol. If your network relies on routers for traffic routing and management, you will not be able to use NetBEUI as a Windows protocol unless you first enable the Windows Internet Name System (WINS).

NOTE: We will discuss the WINS later in this chapter.

Local Routes

Okay, we've seen how routers and bridges can manage network traffic according to logical or physical addresses, respectively. So how do the mechanics of routing work? There are a couple of scenarios. Let's start with the simplest.

Assume that you are sending an IP datagram to a host on your local network. The IP layer on the sending computer will request the physical address of the destination computer via something known as the *Address Resolution Protocol* (ARP). If the destination computer is on the same network, ARP will return the physical address of the destination to the sender. IP then adds the source and destination addresses to the datagram and drops the datagram down through the OSI stack until it goes out on the network.

Once the datagram, now called a *frame,* hits the network, it passes through all the network interfaces on its network segment. Each network interface examines the destination physical address of the frame and compares it to its own. When the frame lands in the network interface of its intended destination, it is passed up the OSI stack to the IP layer. All other hosts will ignore the frame once they figure out that it wasn't intended for them.

Think about this for a moment. Every network interface has to examine every frame on the local segment to see if it belongs to it. So, if we add more network devices to the segment, we add more traffic in the form of frames. Eventually, performance will start to suffer as network interfaces spend more and more time examining frames that were not meant for them in the first place. This is why most large networks are really several small networks joined by routers. In a multiple-network configuration, only the network interfaces on the destination network segment have to examine the arriving frame.

Remote Routes

Instead of being on the local network, the destination for an IP address might be on a remote network. IP figures this out by matching the network portion of the address with the network portion of the address of the sender. If they are on different networks, IP forwards the datagram to a router. This router then compares the network addresses again. If the destination is still remote, it forwards the datagram onto another router, and the whole process repeats.

Eventually, one of two things will happen. First of all, the IP datagram could make its way to a router with a network address that matches the network portion of the destination address. If this happens, the router treats the IP datagram as though it were a local route, calls ARP, and fills in the physical address of the destination. Second, the datagram may just die in the network. Each datagram has a data field known as the time-to-live (TTL) field. Each time a datagram passes through a router, the TTL field is decremented. If it reaches zero before the datagram reaches its destination, the datagram is thrown out, and an error message is sent back to the sender. This mechanism keeps packets from being trapped in a network "twilight zone" forever.

Default Gateway

So, where does the network send a datagram when it doesn't know the route to its final destination? The IP protocol routes the datagram to the *default gateway* on the network. The default gateway is a router that you designate to receive traffic when no local route can be found on your network. Typically, this is the router that connects your organization to the outside world and the Internet. The default gateway is specified in each computer's network configuration.

Static and Dynamic Routes

By this time, you're probably wondering how routers know where to send datagrams if they cannot be delivered locally. Sure, we can send them to the default gateway, but how does the default gateway know where to send them?

Basically, there are two answers. Routers can be configured with *static routes* or can implement *dynamic routing.* Static routes are routing tables that map network destinations to a specific router. When a datagram arrives at a router that uses static routing, it will look up the destination network in its routing table and send the datagram to the corresponding router. Since static route tables must be manually maintained, they can get to be very time-consuming in a large network.

Dynamic routing is the solution to the shortcomings of manually maintained routing tables. When routers are able to use dynamic routing, the routers communicate with each other and exchange routing information via protocols such as Routing Information Protocol (RIP) or Open Shortest Path First (OSPF). The routing tables are generated automatically and are passed back and forth between routers.

HOST NAMES

Host names are text names that act as aliases for network addresses. Within a UNIX environment, the term *host name* refers to the name of a particular network device that is mapped to an IP address. In the Microsoft world, a host name can refer to a name mapped to either an IP address or a NetBIOS name. We'll talk about NetBIOS names in a second.

Why would we want to complicate things by using host names in addition to network addresses? Simple: because they're easier to remember. It is easier for us to remember a name associated with an organization than it is to remember a string of numbers. Also, by using host names, we can hide the address details from the end user. This way, if we want to change the network address of some computer, we can do so without changing its name.

DNS Names

In TCP/IP, a host name is an alias that is mapped to an IP address. Host names are stored in a distributed database known as the *Domain Name Service* (DNS). The DNS database is queried by systems that are trying to resolve a host name into an IP address.

NOTE: For more information on the DNS, see Chapter 9.

DNS uses a name space that is organized in a tree structure. At the top of the tree are the general subdivisions that determine the type of organization the name belongs to. For example, "com" refers to a commercial organization, and "edu" refers to an educational institution. DNS divides its name space into logical domains. Each domain is a logical collection of TCP/IP hosts. Typically, there will be one top-level domain in an organization, with additional subdomains under it. For example, **ncsu.edu** is the domain that refers to North Carolina State University, and **cs.ncsu.edu** is a subdomain for the Computer Science department. To specify a particular host within a domain, simply concatenate its host name and domain name, separated by a period character. For example, **www.ncsu.edu** is the NCSU Web server. The host **sun1.cs.ncsu.edu** might be a UNIX system in the Computer Science department.

NetBIOS Names

Windows is capable of supporting multiple networking protocols. The *Network Basic Input/Output System* (NetBIOS) is a network application programming interface (API) that is used with the Microsoft Networking architecture and has shaped a significant portion of Windows' network name space. Defined in RFCs 1001 and 1002, NetBIOS is a flat namespace as opposed to the hierarchical structure of DNS. Microsoft uses NetBIOS names for Windows domain names, share names, printer names, and computer names.

When you give a command to map a remote directory, as in this example,

```
net use G: \\FILESRV\PUBLIC
```

you are using a couple of different NetBIOS names. The name FILESRV is the NetBIOS name of the server that has the directory that we are mapping. The name PUBLIC is the actual directory located on the server FILESRV.

NetBIOS names can be a maximum of 15 characters long. NetBIOS names are not case sensitive but are typically written in all uppercase. A NetBIOS name consists of fifteen alphanumeric or special characters. The special characters are:

! @ # $ % ^ & ( ) - ' { } . ~

An additional sixteenth byte in the NetBIOS name ranges from 0x00 to 0xff and is used to indicate the name's *resource type*. NetBIOS names aren't only assigned to machines; a user logged in at a client machine also has that username registered during the login period. Table 7-2 describes the common resource types likely to be seen attached to NetBIOS names in a network.

As we mentioned earlier in this section, NetBIOS is an API that provides access to network services. It is commonly, though by no means always, used in conjunction with the NetBEUI protocol. NetBIOS can be bound to several different protocols, including TCP/IP, so that systems may honor NetBIOS requests or Server Message Block (SMB) messages from other systems.

Windows 2000 is expected to use the SMB protocol to connect to TCP port 445 and use DNS for name resolution. However, given the current plan for Microsoft's Active Directory implementation of the Lightweight Directory Access Protocol (LDAP, discussed in Chapter 5) is to require any non-Windows 2000 clients (meaning Windows 95/98 and Windows NT) to use a NetBIOS name service to access SMB services. Expect to see NetBIOS traffic on your network for some time to come, then.

NetBIOS Name	Description
<00>	Workstation name, generally called the NetBIOS machine name.
<03>	Messenger service, used to send and receive messages to the machine name and currently logged-in user.
<1b>	Domain master browser, used by clients to locate the PDC (Primary [Windows] Domain Controller) for a given domain.
<20>	Server service, used to provide file-sharing access points.
<1c>	Domain group name, registered by the domain controller that contains a list of machines that have registered the domain name.
<1d>	Master browser name. There can be only one domain master browser per domain and one master browser per network broadcast segment.
<1e>	Normal group name, used in the election of a master browser.
_ MSBROWSE_	Used in the place of a single sixteenth byte in order to announce the domain name to other master browsers on the local subnet.

Table 7-2. Typical NetBIOS Resource Types

DNS NAME RESOLUTION

Recall that DNS maps host names to IP addresses. When someone uses a DNS host name, the name must be *resolved,* or mapped to an IP address. This process usually takes a couple of steps, as IP address mappings are stored in multiple locations.

NOTE: Where an example in this chapter provides a directory path into the Windows system directories, we assume that your Windows NT or 2000 root directory is *WINNT.* If you have named the Windows NT root directory something else, change the directory pathnames to reflect where NT is installed on your system.

When a computer needs to resolve a DNS host name, it first checks its own name to see if the request is local. If its own name doesn't match, it typically looks in a static file on the computer first. This file, known as a *hosts file,* is a static mapping of host names and IP address pairs. Since this file is static, it is never automatically updated by DNS. You either manually edit the file or use a local tool to add and delete entries. On UNIX systems, the hosts file is typically located in /etc/hosts. On Windows NT and 2000, the file is located in \WINNT\system32\drivers\etc\HOSTS.

CAUTION: The NT and 2000 version of the hosts file is named *HOSTS.* and has only a period at the end with no extension. If you edit the file with a text editor, make sure that the editor does not rename the file *HOSTS.txt* or give it some other extension.

If the system fails to find a match in the local hosts file, it then contacts one or more DNS servers, provided that it has been configured to do so. On UNIX systems, the in structions for finding DNS servers are typically located in the file /etc/resolv.conf. Under Windows 2000, the DNS server information is specified in the DNS control panel (on the Windows 2000 desktop, click the Start button, choose Programs, choose Administrative Tools, and then choose DNS).

If it finds no match after querying a DNS server, UNIX will return an error, but Windows NT or 2000 will then try to resolve the name as a NetBIOS name. We will discuss NetBIOS name resolution later in the chapter.

The Hosts File

The hosts file, whether HOSTS in Windows NT/2000 or /etc/hosts in UNIX, is a flat text file that contains DNS name and IP address mapping pairs. In some ways, the hosts file is a holdover from the old days of the Internet. Originally, the Internet was a fairly small place. Host additions, deletions, and address changes were propagated by a flat hosts file that was distributed over the Net. As the Internet grew, this solution became unwieldy, and the DNS system was developed.

You may wonder why we would want to have this file, since DNS will resolve things for us. Most UNIX systems require a hosts file in order to map the local host name to an IP address, so that the local computer knows its address. Under NT/2000, the hosts file is not required. By using a local hosts file, you can provide local address mappings that will be used if the DNS system is not available. If you include your common servers and destinations in your hosts file, and DNS goes down, you can still resolve addresses for the entries in your hosts file.

There is something that you should be aware of, however. NT/2000 checks the hosts file first and uses the address that it finds there, if it finds one. This means that if the hosts file has an address that is out of date, NT/2000 will use the incorrect address. On some UNIX systems, it is possible to change the order in which UNIX will check the hosts file and DNS. These changes are made through special configuration options in the /etc/resolv.conf file.

For more information on changing the DNS resolution order on your UNIX system, look in the online help with the following commands:

```
man resolver
man resolv.conf
```

SUBNETTING A NETWORK

As you know, a network provides a means for computers and other devices to communicate. The word *subnet* refers to subdividing a network into sections. You can combine different physical networks into a single internetwork by connecting them with routers. Each physical network segment requires a separate means of identifying that particular segment.

Keep in mind that every IP address, such as 192.168.1.1, is divided into a network ID portion and a host ID portion. The different classes of addresses use different parts of the IP address to represent the host ID and network ID. In the preceding example, the default network portion consists of the first three octets, 192.168.1, and the default host portion consists of the last octet, 1 (that is, it is a Class C network). Sometimes you will find it necessary to divide the network portion up in such a way that it can represent multiple networks. This dividing of the network ID is known as *subnetting;* you can accomplish it by using a custom *subnet mask.*

Subnet Masks

Why would we want to divide the network portion of our IP address to create subnets? Let's look at an example:

Assume that you've got a small company network with less than 100 users, and you have been assigned a Class C network address, 192.168.1.0, by your ISP. You, being a network-savvy administrator, know that a Class C address uses three octets for the network portion and one octet for the host ID. You also know that you can't use the numbers 0 or 255 to represent hosts, so you can have up to 253 different addresses in your Class C office network. In fact, their addresses would be in the range from 192.168.1.1 to 192.168.1.253.

Now, what happens if you need to break your network into two physical segments, say, one for development and one for marketing? Sure, you can stick a router in between and make them separate segments, but in order for the router to work, they have to be different subnets. What do you do? You could go back to your ISP and pay for another Class C address for the other segment, but you've already got plenty of room in your existing Class C network. The smart thing to do is to subnet your Class C network and break it into two networks. You can do this by applying a custom subnet mask; we will cover this process later in the chapter. By picking the right subnet mask, you can cause your network to have a small number of network IDs with a larger number of host IDs, or you can have a large number of smaller subnetworks. It all depends on your organization and how many subnets you need.

Networks and Default Subnet Masks

So what is this cryptic item called a subnet mask, and what does it do? A subnet mask is a four-octet number sequence that looks similar to an IP address. Its job in life is to determine which part of an IP address is the network ID, and which part is the host ID.

When you set up TCP/IP on a system, whether Windows 2000 or UNIX, you have to supply a subnet mask. This lets TCP/IP figure out how to divide IP addresses into their network and host parts. In fact, the system may offer you a default subnet mask when you configure it. How can the system know what subnet mask you need? Well, it can't really, but it makes an educated guess. You see, each of the different classes of IP addresses has a default subnet mask that comes with it for free. If you don't want to change the default manner in which the network and host portions are broken up in a particular address, you can simply use the default masks. Table 7-3 lists the address classes and their default masks.

The default subnet masks allow the different address classes to divide their IP addresses in different ratios. The default subnet mask for a Class A network reserves the first octet for the network ID portion, and the last three octets for the host portion. For a Class B address, the first two octets make up the network portion by default, and the last two octets are reserved for the host portion. In a Class C network, the default mask reserves the first three octets for the network portion, leaving only the last octet for the host ID.

How Subnet Masks Work

Okay, so subnet masks look sort of like IP addresses, and they are used to divide IP addresses into network IDs and host IDs. Exactly how do they do this? First of all, realize that we can write IP addresses in a binary form. To do this, we just translate each octet

IP Address Class	Default Subnet Mask
Class A	255.0.0.0
Class B	255.255.0.0
Class C	255.255.255.0

Table 7-3. IP Address Classes and Subnet Masks

into its binary equivalent. For example, the IP address 192.168.16.1 would be written in binary as follows:

```
11000000 10101000 00010000 00000001
```

We can do the same thing with subnet masks. Since 192.168.16.1 is a Class C address, its default subnet mask is 255.255.255.0. Writing the subnet mask in binary, we get this:

```
11111111 11111111 11111111 00000000
```

Now, if we place the binary subnet mask under the binary IP address, we can use it to figure out the host and network portions of the IP address. The bits of the IP address that correspond to 1's in the subnet mask make up the network portion of the address. The 0's in the subnet mask correspond to the bits in the IP address that make up the host portion of the address. To figure out the network ID portion, look for the 1's in the subnet mask and copy down each corresponding bit of the IP address. When you find a 0 in the subnet mask, just fill in a 0, as in this example:

```
11000000 10101000 00010000 00000001        IP Address
11111111 11111111 11111111 00000000        Subnet Mask
11000000 10101000 00010000 00000000        Network ID
```

Translating our network ID back to dotted decimal, we get 192.168.1.0, which gives us a network ID that corresponds exactly to the first three octets in the address. Now, let's use the subnet mask to get the host ID portion. It's just like what we did for the network portion, except we look for 0's in the subnet mask instead of 1's.

```
11000000 10101000 00010000 00000001        IP Address
11111111 11111111 11111111 00000000        Subnet Mask
00000000 00000000 00000000 00000001        Host ID
```

Translating the host ID back to dotted decimal, we get 0.0.0.1, which gives us a host ID that corresponds exactly to the last octet in the address.

In this example, there are 24 bits in the nonzero network ID portion of the address, as is the default in a Class C network with the default subnet mask. There are 8 bits in the nonzero host ID portion of the address, and they are available for us to assign to hosts. Since we can't use all zeros or all ones for a host number, this gives us a maximum of $2^8 - 2$ (or 254) hosts on this Class C network. If we need more host addresses, we will have to go to a bigger network class or get another Class C address space.

This process works with any class of network. Let's look at another example. What happens if we take the address 172.21.192.7 and apply the default subnet mask? Since the first octet is between 128 and 191, this is a Class B address. The default subnet mask for a Class B address is 255.255.0.0. Translating the address into binary, we get this:

```
10101100 00010101 11000000 00000111
```

If we translate the Class B default subnet mask into binary, here is the result:

```
11111111 11111111 00000000 00000000
```

Putting the binary IP address over the subnet mask and solving for the network ID, we get this:

```
10101100 00010101 11000000 00000111        IP Address
11111111 11111111 00000000 00000000        Subnet Mask
10101100 00010101 00000000 00000000        Network ID
```

This results in a decimal network ID of 172.21.0.0. Doing the same operation to solve for the host ID gives us this:

```
10101100 00010101 11000000 00000111        IP Address
11111111 11111111 00000000 00000000        Subnet Mask
00000000 00000000 11000000 00000111        Host ID
```

Here we see that the decimal host ID portion of the address is 0.0.192.7.

Since the default Class B subnet mask splits the address right down the middle, the network ID portion consists of 16 bits, and the host ID portion consists of 16 bits. So, with a Class B address and the default subnet mask, we get one network with up to $2^{16} - 2$ or 65,534 possible host addresses.

Custom Subnetting

Now that you have seen the mechanics of how subnets separate an IP address into network and host ID portions, you can see that you get a fixed number of bits to assign to hosts for addressing purposes. The network portion of your address space is fixed; you can't change it. You only have flexibility to deal with the address portion. So, no matter what class of network you have, by default you have one network segment address with multiple host addresses.

What if you need to divide your network into multiple segments? You might have some remote segments that you need to connect, or you might want to reduce broadcasts and local traffic by using routers. There are lots of reasons why you might need to create multiple network segments in your network.

Since each network segment connected by a router is its own subnet, each network segment requires its own unique network ID. If you already have an address assigned to you, then you will have to create a custom subnet mask to divide your network properly.

Before you start creating a custom subnet mask, you need to figure out how many subnets you are going to need. You also need to take into account the maximum number of hosts per subnet that you will need. When we start figuring out the custom subnet, you will see that there is a tradeoff between the number of subnets and the number of hosts per subnet. You should plan for future expansion as best you can, because figuring out the subnet mask and changing the subnet mask and addresses on all your systems is a time-consuming process. You don't want to repeat it any more often than necessary!

Okay, it's example time. Let's say that you have a software development company with a Class C address space, 192.168.183.0. You want to divide your network into five subnets, one each for development, sales, marketing, quality assurance and testing, and company administration. You figure that your company will be less than 100 people for quite a while, and you won't need more than 20 addresses in any subnet for the foreseeable future.

To subnet your Class C network into five subnets, you are going to take some bits from the host ID portion of your network and reassign them to the network ID. To do this, you need to create a custom subnet mask. The first thing to do is figure out how many bits you need in order to create your custom subnet mask. Since the math for this is in binary, subnets are allocated on a power-of-two basis. Also, remember that we can't have a subnet whose address is all zeros or all ones. By using three extra bits, we can get $2^3 - 2$, or 6 subnets. Since we can't get exactly five subnets, we can reserve one for future use.

By moving three bits from the host ID portion to the network ID, we leave five bits for the actual host ID. This gives us $2^5 - 2$, or 30 valid host IDs per subnet. Since we need only 20 host IDs per subnet, it looks as if those three extra bits will work for us. Our default subnet mask for a Class C network is 255.255.255.0, which, in binary, looks like this:

```
11111111 11111111 11111111 00000000
```

Let's go ahead and add the three bits from the host portion to the right-hand side of the network portion of the subnet mask. This gives us the following:

```
11111111 11111111 11111111 11100000
```

This result translates back into decimal as 255.255.255.224—our new subnet mask!

Before you can plug the new subnet mask in and make your new subnets, you've got to figure out what our new network IDs and host IDs will be. This can get a bit complicated, so we'll go slowly.

Our original Class C address is 192.168.183.0, which translates into binary as

```
11000000 10101000 10110111 0000000
```

Since we're adding three bits to the network ID, the network address will expand just like the subnet mask. To get our new network IDs, we add all the possible permutations of the three-bit value, excluding 000 and 111. This gives us six new network IDs, as detailed in Table 7-4.

Subnet Binder	Subnet in Binary	Subnet in Dotted Decimal
Subnet 1	11000000 10101000 10110111 00100000	192.168.183.32
Subnet 2	11000000 10101000 10110111 01000000	192.168.183.64
Subnet 3	11000000 10101000 10110111 01100000	192.168.183.96
Subnet 4	11000000 10101000 10110111 10000000	192.168.183.128
Subnet 5	11000000 10101000 10110111 10100000	192.168.183.160
Subnet 6	11000000 10101000 10110111 11000000	192.168.183.192

Table 7-4. Creating Six Subnets Within 192.168.183.0

These new network addresses may look a bit confusing, because they don't end in 0 like all the other network addresses that you have seen. Keep in mind that there are five bits at the end of each of these subnet addresses that are reserved for your host IDs. So how do we assign host IDs? We just start filling in the host ID bits on the end.

REMEMBER: We can't use all 0's or all 1's for the host ID; all 1's is reserved for broadcast.

Table 7-5 lists some of the host addresses for the 192.168.183.32 subnet. There are 30 possible addresses in each subnet.

Subnet Tables

While you can calculate all the details of custom subnets by hand, it is a time-consuming task. To make life easier, you can use the following tables, which give the general subnet information for each class of networks. Each table gives the number of subnets and number of hosts per subnet available for each possible subnet mask. It also shows how many bits must be shifted from the host ID portion to the network ID portion. You will still have

Host Address Number	Host Address in Binary	Host Address in Dotted Decimal
Host 1	11000000 10101000 10110111 00100001	192.168.183.33
Host 2	11000000 10101000 10110111 00100010	192.168.183.34
Host 3	11000000 10101000 10110111 00100011	192.168.183.35
Host 4	11000000 10101000 10110111 00100100	192.168.183.36
...	...	...
Host 28	11000000 10101000 10110111 00111101	192.168.183.61
Host 29	11000000 10101000 10110111 00111110	192.168.183.62
Host 30	11000000 10101000 10110111 00111111	192.168.183.63

Table 7-5. Host Addresses Within 192.168.183.0

to calculate the network IDs by hand. However, just remember that the host IDs count upward from the starting subnet network ID and stop at one less than the next subnet network ID. Table 7-6 lists the subnet information for Class A networks.

Table 7-7 lists the subnet information for Class B networks.

Number of Subnets	Hosts per Subnet	Bits Required	Subnet Mask
2	4,194,302	2	255.192.0.0
6	2,097,150	3	255.224.0.0
14	1,048,574	4	255.240.0.0
30	524,286	5	255.248.0.0
62	262,142	6	255.252.0.0
126	131,070	7	255.254.0.0
254	65,534	8	255.255.0.0

Table 7-6. Subnet Information for Class A Networks

Number of Subnets	Hosts per Subnet	Bits Required	Subnet Mask
2	16,382	2	255.255.192.0
6	8,190	3	255.255.224.0
14	4,094	4	255.255.240.0
30	2.046	5	255.255.248.0
62	1,022	6	255.255.252.0
126	510	7	255.255.254.0
254	254	8	255.255.255.0

Table 7-7. Subnet Information for Class B Networks

Table 7-8 lists the subnet information for Class C networks.

Number of Subnets	Hosts per Subnet	Bits Required	Subnet Mask
2	62	2	255.255.255.192
6	30	3	255.255.255.224
14	14	4	255.255.255.240
30	6	5	255.255.255.248
62	2	6	255.255.255.252
invalid	invalid	7	255.255.255.254
invalid	invalid	8	255.255.255.255

Table 7-8. Subnet Information for Class C Networks

DYNAMIC HOST CONFIGURATION PROTOCOL

As anyone who has ever had to manage a TCP/IP network knows, keeping track of IP address assignments and configuring workstations can be a time-consuming task. TCP/IP requires each device to have a separate unique address that cannot conflict with any other network device. You must, therefore, take care when assigning or reassigning addresses to make sure that you do not duplicate addresses between systems. Also, TCP/IP has several configuration parameters, which makes it even easier to cause errors when configuring a workstation.

Microsoft has developed a system known as the *Dynamic Host Configuration Protocol* (DHCP) in an attempt to solve these problems. Their solution, depending on your point of view, is at least partially successful. DHCP is a system that automatically configures a TCP/IP client when it boots up, providing it with a unique IP address, plus other configuration information such as its default gateway, DNS servers, and WINS servers. So in theory, all you have to do is set up a DHCP server and tell your clients to use it for configuration for all your TCP/IP configuration headaches to be a thing of the past.

To DHCP or Not to DHCP?

Unfortunately, there is a slight difference between theory and practice. You see, no matter how much Microsoft would like you to believe that DHCP is a magic cure-all, DHCP has some serious limitations. For example, only a Windows NT or Windows 2000 server can act as a DHCP server, and DHCP clients must be running Windows NT Server or Workstation 3.5 or greater, Windows 95/98, certain versions of the MS Networking Client or LAN Manager server for MS-DOS, or Windows for Workgroups with a particular version of TCP/IP software.

In addition to the current requirement that clients and servers be Microsoft products, you need to know about a few other limitations to DCHP before you go down that road.

- DHCP servers do not talk to each other. This means that if two DHCP servers are configured to give out the same range of IP addresses, there is no way for one to know what the other has assigned.
- Unless configured otherwise, DHCP will not provide a specific IP address to a client. It will instead pick an address out of the range of valid addresses. If you have a workstation that needs to be assigned a specific address upon boot, you must manually customize the DHCP profile for that workstation.

- The IP address and subnet mask provided by the DHCP server are guaranteed to be used by a DHCP client. However, any modifications that you make on the local DHCP client to the NT/2000 Registry or other network information, such as manually setting DNS, will override DHCP information.
- DHCP will not detect any IP addresses already in use by non-DHCP clients. This means that you will need an accurate list of all IP addresses in use by all UNIX systems, OS/2 systems, Macs, and so on before installing DHCP, and you will have to manually exclude them from DHCP server configuration.
- Unless you have routers that are configured for BOOTP forwarding, DHCP servers are confined to their local subnet and will not work across routers.

So with all these problems, who would want to use DHCP? If you have a very Microsoft-oriented network, with Windows NT and 2000 servers and lots of Microsoft clients, and you want to centrally manage TCP/IP configuration for your clients, and you don't mind the clients getting a different IP address each time they boot, then DHCP could be a good solution. On the other hand, if you have a lot of UNIX systems or other non-DHCP-capable computers, and only a few Microsoft systems, you should probably steer clear of DHCP, as it will be more trouble than it is worth.

How DHCP Works

Okay, if you've decided that DHCP could work in your environment, let's look at how it actually functions. DHCP provides IP addresses to clients for a specified period of time. This is known as an *IP lease.*

When a DHCP client boots up, it sends a broadcast message to any DHCP servers on the network requesting an IP lease. Every DHCP server that gets the request, both on local and remote networks, will respond with an offer to lease the client an IP address. The DHCP client accepts the first offer that it gets, and it sends out another broadcast message that contains the IP address that it has decided to use. The server that leased the IP address to the DHCP client then sends back an acknowledgment to the client. This process occurs whenever a DHCP client needs a new IP lease.

By default, IP leases expire in three days. The expiration interval can be configured by the system administrator, and it can be set so that leases never expire. When its IP lease expires, the DHCP client sends a message to the DHCP server that gave it the lease, requesting that the lease be renewed. If the DHCP server is up and running, and the IP address is still available in the server's list of addresses, it automatically renews the lease. If the address is not available, possibly because the address has been manually assigned to a non-DHCP client and removed from availability, the client has to go through the whole DHCP lease process again.

NOTE: You can configure DHCP so that IP leases do not expire.

The DHCP Server

In order to run a DHCP server, you must have a computer running Windows NT Server 3.5 or later with Microsoft TCP/IP installed. The DHCP server software is installed as a network service in the Administrative Tools folder of the Control Panel (click the Start button, choose Programs, choose Administrative Tools, and then choose DHCP).

DHCP is configured with a set of ranges of IP addresses, known as *scopes*. The DHCP server requires a scope be defined for each subnet that the DHCP server will manage. This includes the local subnet and any other subnets that are connected via routers.

Before creating a scope, you will need to know a valid range of IP addresses to include in the scope and all the current non-DHCP-capable IP addresses that are in the range. You will also have to know the details of the specific options that you want to configure, such as netmasks, default gateway addresses, and WINS server addresses. If you have DHCP clients that require static IP addresses, you will need to know the name of the client, its specific IP address, and its specific hardware address, such as its Ethernet address.

Scopes are created and managed, along with general DHCP server configuration and options, in the DHCP Manager Tool. (The details of using the DHCP Manager Tool are beyond the scope of this book, no pun intended.)

UNIX and DHCP

The Internet Software Consortium is in the process of developing an implementation of the DHCP services to run on POSIX-compliant systems, such as most UNIX systems. The most current version includes

- A DHCP server
- A DHCP client
- A DHCP relay agent

For the most current information, see the website for the ISC's DHCP project at **http://www.isc.org/view.cgi?/products/DHCP/index.phtml**.

THE NETBIOS API

You will recall from the earlier section on NetBIOS names that NetBIOS is a programming API that Microsoft uses to bind to a variety of protocols. Although NetBIOS is commonly thought of as being associated with the nonroutable NetBEUI protocol, it can be bound to TCP/IP and IPX/SPX as well. NetBIOS is supported by several different networking systems, including

- Microsoft's implementation of TCP/IP, IPX, and NetBEUI
- Microsoft LAN Manager for MS-DOS, UNIX, and OS/2
- DEC Pathworks from Digital Equipment Corporation
- IBM LAN Server

Thus, NetBIOS provides a common programming interface over a variety of networking schemes. For example, a computer running LAN Manager for OS/2 can make a NetBIOS request to a Windows NT or 2000 system, provided that both are running compatible network protocols.

NetBT

Although it is possible to run NetBIOS over a variety of protocols, you will probably be using TCP/IP, especially if you have other UNIX systems. As we said previously, NetBIOS requests are commonly sent via the NetBEUI protocol. NetBEUI has less overhead than TCP/IP and is, therefore, slightly faster. It is also very simple to install and configure. However, NetBEUI is not a routable protocol. NetBEUI was designed to be used in a LAN environment and will not work with hosts that are separated by routers.

Fortunately, NetBIOS also binds to TCP/IP. This combination is commonly referred to as *NetBT* or *NBT*. Remember that NetBIOS uses different names than UNIX DNS names. So, in order for NetBIOS to function over TCP/IP, there must be some way to map a NetBIOS name to an IP address.

REMEMBER: NetBIOS is a programmatic API. All requests to NetBIOS use NetBIOS names. NetBIOS does not understand numeric IP addresses.

The NetBT Name Resolution Process

When a computer using NetBT joins a network, it sends a registration request. This registration request is either sent to a NetBIOS server or broadcast to the local network via a UDP datagram, depending on the NetBT computer's configuration. The purpose of the NetBIOS registration request is to notify other computers using NetBIOS that a new NetBIOS computer has joined the network, and to register with a NetBIOS name server, such as a WINS server. We will discuss WINS in more detail later in the chapter.

If there is a WINS server on the network and it receives the registration request from a new host, it checks to see if another computer is already using the NetBIOS name. If so, it sends a notification back to the source computer indicating that the name is already in use.

When NetBT computer, referred to as the *resolving computer*, needs to resolve a NetBIOS name to an IP address, it first looks in its local NetBT name cache. This name cache contains all the NetBIOS names that have been resolved since TCP/IP was initialized on the system. Entries in the NetBIOS name cache typically expire after a period of time, to ensure that the cache doesn't grow without bounds and that the entries stay reasonably current.

If the resolving computer doesn't find the name in the NetBIOS name cache, it sends a request to a WINS server, provided that one exists on the network. In order for a computer to access a WINS server for NetBIOS information, the address of the WINS server must be entered in the computer's TCP/IP Configuration dialog box. The computer requesting the NetBIOS resolution will send up to three requests to the WINS server before deciding that the WINS server is not responding. If the WINS server does not respond, the resolving computer will then try a secondary WINS server, if available.

After giving up on the WINS servers, the computer attempting to resolve the name will use something called a *B-node broadcast.* A B-node broadcast is a message broadcast onto the network, requesting the host who has the particular NetBIOS name in question to respond with its NetBIOS name and IP address. B-node broadcasts are limited to the local network, plus any networks connected by routers configured to forward B-node broadcasts. A computer attempting to resolve a NetBIOS name will send up to three B-node broadcasts.

If the resolving computer has come up empty on all its other attempts, it will look in a local static file called the *LMHOSTS file.* This file is similar to the TCP/IP hosts file in that it is a list of static mappings. However, the LMHOSTS file contains mappings for NetBIOS names to IP addresses.

However, you might not have the LMHOSTS file, and many organizations choose not to configure one, as it can require significant maintenance. If LMHOSTS is enabled, the system must have a valid LMHOSTS file in the \WINNT\system32\drivers\etc directory.

THE WINDOWS INTERNET NAME SERVICE

As you saw earlier in the chapter, NetBIOS clients go through several steps when trying to map NetBIOS names to IP addresses. One of the first steps in this mapping process is to send a query to a WINS server.

In spite of its name, the Windows Internet Name Service (WINS) has nothing to do with the Internet. WINS servers act as a registration point for NetBT clients, so that they can register their NetBIOS name to IP address mapping information. By using a WINS server, NetBIOS clients do not have to broadcast their name queries onto the network. This is beneficial for a couple of reasons. First, each broadcast consumes network bandwidth. Sending the name queries directly to a WINS server eliminates the need to broadcast a query to everyone on the network. Second, routers are typically not set up to forward NetBIOS broadcasts, so any broadcast queries are limited to the local network.

When a WINS client using NetBT starts up, it sends a registration request to its WINS server. If the address is available, the WINS server sends a response back to the client confirming its IP address and NetBIOS name, and telling it how long its registration is valid before it must be renewed. When the renewal time expires, the NetBIOS name is deleted from the WINS server. To prevent its name from being deleted when the renewal time expires, the WINS client must send a renewal request to the WINS server before the expiration time arrives.

NOTE: By limiting the amount of time that NetBIOS name registration is valid, WINS servers prevent their name databases from containing old, out-of-date information.

When a WINS client using NetBT shuts down, it sends a message to its WINS server telling it to remove the client's information from its database.

WINS Servers

The WINS server software is installed as a TCP/IP installation and configuration option in the Windows Control Panel. Once the WINS software is installed, it must be configured. Configuration takes place within the WINS Manager program. A variety of options are available when configuring a WINS server. The details of WINS configuration are beyond the scope of this chapter.

How many WINS servers should you install? In general, you can usually get away with one or two for your entire organization, unless you have a very large number of WINS clients and the server traffic load becomes prohibitively high. It is good practice to have both primary and secondary WINS servers, in case the primary server should fail. Microsoft's official recommendation is for a minimum of one primary and one secondary WINS server per ten thousand clients.

There is no need to have a WINS server on each subnet. Since each client knows the address of the WINS server, either by manual configuration or via DHCP, requests that go to the WINS servers are sent in normal IP datagrams. This means that WINS server requests are routed normally by all routers on your TCP/IP internetwork.

SUMMARY

The area where Windows NT/2000 and UNIX networking meet makes for an interesting mix of topics. If you, as the administrator, come from a UNIX background, you are probably unfamiliar with common Windows topics such as NetBIOS, DHCP, and WINS. On the other hand, if you come from a Windows background, using the TCP/IP protocol suite—especially subnets—may seem to be an obscure art.

In this chapter, we have covered most of the areas where Windows and UNIX collide in the networking world. We discussed the OSI model of networking and how it applies to the TCP/IP protocol suite. We looked at routing and DNS name resolution. Subnets play an important role in creating TCP/IP internetworks, so we explored the steps involved in creating custom subnets.

From the Windows side, we examined the issues surrounding NetBIOS, including NetBIOS over TCP/IP, NetBIOS name resolution, and WINS. We also looked at how DHCP can be used in some circumstances to help reduce the management load for a network administrator.

CHAPTER 8

Scripting for Windows 2000

One of the major benefits of working in a UNIX environment is the ubiquity of the tools: You may not have Tcl installed on every UNIX system (unless you're working on a recent Solaris system), but you almost certainly have Perl residing somewhere. If you don't have the Perl scripting language engine installed, you do have many of the standard set of UNIX command tools, such as grep, available, as well as one or several of the common shells such as C, Korn, Bourne, or bash. One of the basic strengths of the UNIX systems—and mindset—is that availability of a minimal set of basic tools, such as grep and ps, can be counted on. Also fundamental is the ability to link the output of one command directly as input to the next command. Scripting languages are generally considered to be a kind of glue: You should ideally take the applications and tools present on your operating system of choice and use scripts to stick them together. Although many of the scripting languages, shells, and other tools familiar to the experienced UNIX user may be available for Windows, they are not part of the standard suite of tools provided with the operating system. If you are called upon to configure or maintain a Windows-based server, what can you do with the basic system?

Many system administrators complained about the lack of command-line support in early versions of Windows NT Server. Some tasks were only capable of being performed through the GUI, while a few others were only capable of being performed from the command line. From a UNIX perspective, the administrative tools were too slow and limiting: If multiple renditions of a given task were needed, the administrator had to click this button, enter info in that field, select that tab, click that radio button, and so on, for each individual iteration of the task. For a repetitive task such as creating two hundred users with their home directories, groups, and passwords, there was no automated way to perform the task. Under UNIX, you could write a shell script and pass individual definitions from a character-delimited text file, but the Windows GUI was mandatory and could not be ignored. Microsoft, as well as other third-party groups, have developed several commercial, shareware, and freeware solutions to this perceived need. This chapter will present some of the lesser-known capabilities of the Windows command-line interface, along with suggestions for experienced UNIX users who are used to writing a quick shell script to perform a task. This chapter will also address the command-line and scripting capabilities inherent in Windows (for situations when you are presented with a malfunctioning system and don't have time or the ability to add to the base system), and present some useful options that you may wish to add to your Windows system now.

WINDOWS-NATIVE SCRIPTING

Some of the tools (such as the almost but not quite ubiquitous scripting language Perl) described later in the chapter can be helpful if they are present. However, by definition, if they're not part of the basic Windows installation, they may not be present on a given installation. This section presents some of the capabilities and characteristics of a default Windows 2000 installation.

NOTE: This section will not present the Windows Script Host (wscript.exe or cscript.exe, depending on whether you are looking at the GUI-based or the command-line-based version). Just like Microsoft Internet Explorer, Windows Script Host serves as a controller of ActiveX scripting engines, and it supports scripts written in Visual Basic Scripting Edition (VBScript) or JavaScript.

Windows 2000 command scripts are ASCII-format text files containing a set of commands. It's generally considered a good idea to add comment lines to your scripts, so that the minimal documentation for the script stays with the script. Each Windows script comment line begins with either a double colon or a rem (remark) entry, and ends with a return, as in these examples:

```
:: This is a comment line for a Windows script.
rem This is a second comment line for a Windows script.
```

Those of you familiar with Java or C/C++ can remember that the double forward slash (//) used to indicate a comment is not too different from the double colon here.

CAUTION: The WordPad editor that comes with Windows is not recommended for scripting, because its default behavior is to add a .txt extension to every text file it creates. This behavior interferes with the standard of using the .tcl extension for Windows Tcl scripts, for example, and the .pl extension for Perl scripts.

Windows-Native Command Line Conventions: The CMD Shell

What a UNIX environment tends to call a shell, Windows refers to as a command interpreter. The command interpreter cmd.exe, included in Windows 2000, has a number of helpful features.

To start a command shell in Windows, click the Start button, select the Run command, type

```
cmd
```

and then press the ENTER key. A command prompt window will appear on the Windows 2000 desktop. The top of the window displays the path to the executable file (C:\WINNT\System32\cmd.exe). By default, the prompt displays the directory path. The default behavior is to open the command shell in your home directory, which is in the C:\Documents and Settings folder. If you are logged in as jeff, here is what will appear at the command prompt:

```
C:\Documents and Settings\jeff
```

The Windows 2000 command shell accepts a number of flags, as summarized in this line:

cmd [[/c | /k] [/q] [/a | /u] [/t:*fg*] [/y | /x] *string*]

These flags have the following functions:

- **/c** Performs the command specified by *string* and then stops.
- **/k** Performs the command specified by *string* and continues. Obviously, the /c and /k flags cannot both be used in the same command line.
- **/q** Turns echo off.
- **/a** or **/u** Creates ANSI or Unicode output respectively. Both the /a and /u flags cannot be used in the same command line.
- **/t:*fg*** Sets the foreground and background colors (*f* and *g*).
- **/y** or **/x** Disables or enables extensions to the Windows 2000 version of cmd.exe, respectively. The extensions are enabled by default.
- ***string*** The command or script you wish to run.

NOTE: If the /y flag is used and Windows 2000 extensions are disabled, the following commands will not be available for use: assoc, call, cd and chdir, color, del (and erase), endlocal, for, ftype, goto, if, md (mdir), prompt, pushd, popd, set, setlocal, shift, and start.

Windows Command Logic Control

Putting together a script, also referred to as a batch file, makes it possible to take advantage of logic control commands such as if statements, goto statements, and for loops. A script is an unformatted text file that contains at least one executable command and has a .bat or .cmd filename extension. When the filename is entered at the command prompt, the commands in the file are executed sequentially. Any command can be included in a script.

This section presents the command logic available for use in Windows 2000 scripts. The available logic controls are:

- **Call** Calls one script from another without causing the parent script to stop executing. The call command also accepts labels as the target of the call.
- **Echo** Turns the command-echoing feature on or off, or displays a message instead.
- **Endlocal** Ends localization of environment changes in a batch file. Each setlocal command must have an endlocal command to restore environment variables. This command has no parameters.
- **For** Runs a specified command for each file in a set of files. You can use the for command either within a script or directly from the command prompt.
- **Goto** Directs the script to a line in a script marked by a label you specify. When Windows 2000 finds the label, it processes the commands beginning on the next line.
- **If** Performs conditional processing: If the condition specified in an if command is true, Windows 2000 carries out the following command. If the

condition is false, Windows 2000 ignores the command in the if clause and goes to the next line or executes any command in the else clause (if one has been specified).

- **Pause** Halts processing of a script and displays a message prompting the user to press any key to continue.
- **Rem** Enables you to include comments (remarks) in a batch file or in your configuration files.
- **Setlocal** Allows environment variables to be defined locally within the script. Each setlocal command must have an endlocal command to restore environment variables.
- **Shift** Changes the position of replaceable parameters in a script. If command extensions are enabled, shift is allowed to take a switch /*n*, which tells the command to begin shifting at the *n*th argument. *N* can be a value from zero to eight.

New Commands for Windows 2000

Table 8-1 lists the commands added in Windows 2000. These commands can be entered at the command line or included in scripts.

Windows 2000 Versions of MS-DOS Commands

Some of the familiar DOS commands have been either improved or otherwise changed from their behavior under DOS. If you wish to port a DOS or older Windows shell script to Windows 2000, you should check if your script uses any of the commands in this section. These Windows 2000 command replacements (or enhanced versions of the DOS commands that you may be familiar with) are as follows:

- **chcp** Changes code pages for full-screen mode only.
- **cmd** The cmd.exe command interpreter replaces the older command.com.
- **del** Has several enhancements in the forms of new switches.
- **dir** Has several enhancements in the forms of new switches.
- **diskcomp** The switches /1 and /8 are not supported in Windows 2000.
- **diskcopy** The switch /1 is not supported in Windows 2000.
- **doskey** Has several enhancements in the forms of new switches.
- **format** Now supports 20.8MB optical drives. However, switches /b, /s, and /u are *not* supported.
- **label** The symbols ^ and & can now be used in volume labels.
- **mode** Has many new options.
- **more** Has several new enhancements.

Command	Function
at	Schedules commands or applications to run on a system at a specified time and date.
cacls	Displays or modifies access control lists (ACLs) of files.
Convert	Converts file systems from FAT to NTFS.
Dosonly	Specifies that only DOS-based applications can be run.
echoconfig	Displays messages when reading the MS-DOS subsystem config.nt file.
endlocal	Ends localization of environment variables.
findstr	Searches for text in files using regular expressions.
ntcmdprompt	Runs the Windows 2000 command interpreter cmd.exe, rather than command.com, after running a TSR or after starting the command prompt from within an MS-DOS application.
popd	Changes to the directory last set with the pushd command.
pushd	Saves the current directory for use by the popd command, and then changes to the specified directory.
setlocal	Begins localization of environmental variables.
Title	Sets the title of the command prompt window.
&&	Indicates that the subsequent command should run only if the preceding command succeeds.
||	Indicates that the subsequent command should run only if the preceding command fails.
&	Separates multiple commands on the command line.
()	Groups commands.
; or ,	Separates parameters.

Table 8-1. Commands Introduced in Windows 2000

- **path** Can now be used with a %PATH% environment variable to append the current path to a new setting at the command prompt.
- **print** The switches /b, /c, /m, /p, /q, /s, /t, and /u are not supported.
- **prompt** Now allows the use of ampersands ($a), parentheses ($c and $f), and spaces ($s) in a custom prompt.
- **recover** Now recovers files only—not directories.

- **rmdir** Finally has a /s switch to delete directories containing files and subdirectories.
- **sort** No longer requires a TEMP environment variable, and file size is now unlimited.
- **xcopy** Has several added functions.

Commands Obsolete in Windows 2000

A number of MS-DOS commands are not available at the Windows 2000 command prompt, either due to being unsupported or obsolete. Table 8-2 lists the DOS commands that cannot be used in Windows 2000.

Command Line Controls: Windows 2000 Format vs. UNIX Format

Windows 2000 includes a significant number of command-line tools that even experienced Windows users may be unfamiliar with. For those Windows administrators, as well as UNIX administrators, looking for familiar ways to work, Table 8-3 lists a number of command-line controls for Windows NT 4 and Windows 2000, and their related counterparts under Linux.

Command-Line Printing Controls in Windows

For an example of Windows 2000 command-line capabilities, let's look at some of the printing controls available. Printers are often scarce resources on a network, and command-line

assign	drvspace	menucolor	power
backup	emm386	menudefault	restore
choice	fasthelp	menuitem	scandisk
ctty	fdisk	mirror	smartdrv
dblspace	include	msav	submenu
defrag*	interlnk	msbackup	sys
deltree	intersrv	mscdex	undelete
diskperf	join	msd	unformat
dosshell	memmaker	numlock	vsafe

Table 8-2. DOS Commands Obsolete in Windows 2000

* Windows 2000 automatically defragments disks.

Windows	Linux	Function
net users	cat /etc/passwd	Lists all local user accounts.
net users /domain (Note that Active Directory is a different topic altogether.)	ypcat passwd.byname (if running NIS)	Lists all user accounts in a network database.
net localgroup	cat /etc/group	Lists all local groups.
net group	ypcat group.byname (if running NIS)	Lists all groups in the network database.
net use h: \\server\users	mount -t nfs server: /var/home /home	Mounts a remote filesystem.
chkdsk *drive*:\	fsck	Checks a file system's integrity.
net share newshare=c:\export	vi /etc/exports to define the points, then killall rpc.mountd, then /usr/sbin/rpc.mount d	Creates an exported share point.
net statistics	netstat or pcinfo	Displays statistics on shared file servicing.
at *nn*:00am | pm *cmd.exe*	crontab –e *command*	Schedules the specified job for a specified time.
fc *file1 file2*	diff *file1 file2*	Compares the contents of two files.
edit *filename.txt*	vi *filename.txt*	Edits the specified text file.
pulist (Available from the Microsoft Windows Server Resource Kit)	Ps	Lists all active processes.
rmdir /s *directory*	rm –r *directory*	Deletes the specified directory and all the subdirectories and files within that directory.

Table 8-3. Windows NT/2000 Commands and Their Linux Counterparts

Windows	Linux	Function
runas *username*	su *username*	Allows a user to run a process with the permissions of another user.
kill *process_id* (Available from the Microsoft Windows Server Resource Kit)	kill *process_id*	Kills a process of the specified process ID number.

Table 8-3. Windows NT/2000 Commands and Their Linux Counterparts *(continued)*

print commands can be useful if you need to connect users to shared printers through a login script or any other automated batch command, or through a script procedure. For this section, you'll want to have a command prompt to work in. From the Start menu, select Programs, select Accessories, and then click Command Prompt to open a command window. Here are some of the printing-related commands available at the Windows 2000 command prompt:

Command	Function
PRINT	Prints a text file or displays the contents of a print queue.
NET PRINT	Displays or controls print jobs and printer queues.
NET USE	Connects or disconnects the user's machine to or from a shared printer.
NET START	Activates the print spooler service.
NET STOP	Shuts down the print spooler service.

Following are some specific examples of these preceding commands.

To print the text file scrap.txt to a printer on parallel port LPT1:

```
PRINT /d:LPT1: C:\scrap.txt
```

To view the print queue of Networkprinter on print server WIN2KSERVER:

```
NET PRINT \\WIN2KSERVER\Networkprinter
```

To delete print job number 3 on Networkprinter on print server WIN2KSERVER:

```
NET PRINT \\WIN2KSERVER 3/delete
```

To redirect print output for the LPT1 port to Networkprinter on print server WIN2KSERVER:

```
NET USE LPT1: \\WIN2KSERVER\Networkprinter
```

To display information about the LPT1 port:

```
NET USE LPT1:
```

To start the Print Spooler service:

```
NET START spooler
```

To stop the Print Spooler service:

```
NET STOP spooler
```

NOTE: When you use the NET STOP command, other services (besides the spooler) might need to be stopped as well. If this is the case, the Windows 2000 system will display the names of those services and prompt you to confirm whether you want to stop the spooler.

NONSTANDARD SCRIPTING LANGUAGES FOR WINDOWS

You have several options if you want to use scripting languages other than the default Windows scripting capability. Perl, Python, Tcl, Scheme, REXX, ports of the UNIX shells to Windows, and so on: the list goes on. This section will focus on three of the best-known, most widespread, and most useful of the scripting languages: Perl, Python, and Tcl. Although they have a number of dissimilarities, they also have much in common; for example, all three are

- *Cross-platform,* meaning that all three are available on UNIX, Windows, and the Macintosh OS, as well as other operating systems.
- *Free,* which helps make them…
- *Widely-used,* so that it's likely you'll encounter them—and because they're widely supported, they're…
- *Robust,* with the available examples, libraries, and support communities to make them generally useful for a wide variety of tasks and suitable to different needs.

An excellent comparison of scripting languages, "Perl, Tcl, and Python: They're Not Your Father's Scripting Languages" by Cameron Laird and Kathryn Soraiz, is available on the web at **http://www.sunworld.com/swol-10-1997/swol-10-scripting.html**. Mr. Laird has expanded this article into a more elaborate discussion at **http://starbase.neosoft.com/~claird/comp.lang.misc/portable_scripting.html**.

Perl

Perl is a scripting language that has become the de facto almost universal scripting language on the web for CGIs. (Although you can write a CGI in any language, Perl has become the most common.) The language name "Perl" stands for Practical Report and Extraction Language. The Perl language currently stands at version number 5, which is commonly referred to as Perl5. Perl5 has excellent support for object-oriented programming methodology, which Perl version 4 lacked. Some of Perl's many strengths are:

- **Development speed** You edit a text file, and you run it. Being a scripted language, Perl does not need to be compiled, as C and C++ do.
- **Power** One of Perl's universally acknowledged strengths is its regular expressions set. Although optimized for scanning text, Perl can also deal with binary data, and it can make dbm files look like associative arrays.
- **Flexibility** A common axiom of Perl programmers is that there's always more than one way to perform any task in Perl. There is no one true way to do anything.
- **Portability** In general, a Perl script developed on a Windows machine can be placed on a UNIX system and run with no or little modification necessary. In practice, of course, testing is always a good idea—consider the potential damage if you're wrong, and take a calculated risk if you want to.
- **Editing tools** Perl scripts can be created with any tool that allows you to save a script as a text file. This tool list includes every text editor known, plus almost every word processor in existence. It's simply not possible that you'd find an operating system with a functioning port of Perl installed that would not include a tool for Perl development.
- **Price** Like most of the scripting languages, Perl is free. A wealth of documentation and information on Perl is available, both online and in the bookstores for offline perusal. Many of the leading experts on Perl have contributed or authored many of the currently available reference works on the language and are actively involved in the ongoing development of Perl.

Here's an example of a Perl script that asks a question, compares the given answer to the right answer, and then lets the user know whether his or her answer is correct:

```
print ("What is 3 times 4?\n");
$right_answer = 12;     # the right answer
$input_answer = <STDIN>;
chop ($input);
until ($input == $right_answer) {
        print ("Not quite, try again.");
        $input = <STDIN>;
        chop ($input_answer);
}
print ("That's right.\n");
```

One of the most interesting ventures in the Perl community is the UNIX Reconstruction Project, also referred to as the Perl Power Tools project. Initiated by Tom Christiansen, one of the best-known experts in the Perl community, the project aims to recreate most of the standard tools available on UNIX entirely within the Perl language. One motivation for the project was that Mr. Christiansen and his associates were tired of not having these various tools available on different operating systems. This reconstruction effort wasn't sparked by the lack of these UNIX tools on Windows: grep is not a standard part of (for a non-Microsoft example) Apple's Macintosh operating system prior to Mac OS X. Perl for Win32 is a port of most of the functionality in Perl5, but with extra Win32 API calls added in to take advantage of native Windows functionality. Perl will run on any Microsoft Windows platform from Windows 95 up. The Perlcrt.dll library is normally stored in the %SystemRoot%\System32 directory; however, the library can also be placed in the \Perl\bin directory if you wish.

Here are some web-related resources of interest for Perl on Windows:

- The latest version of Perl for Win32, PerlScript, and Perl for ISAPI can be found at the ActiveState website at **http://www.activestate.com/ActivePerl/**.
- The Perl Mongers user group system may have a gathering of Perl enthusiasts in your area: Check **http://www.pm.org/** to see if there's a user group in your neighborhood.
- The Perl language's main reference on the web is at **http://www.perl.com/**, and the Windows-related material can be found at **http://www.perl.com/reference/query.cgi?windows**.
- If you're interested in the current status of the Perl Power Tools project, you can find the project's website at **http://language.perl.com/ppt/index.html**.

Python

Python is an interpreted, interactive, object-oriented programming language loosely descended from the Modula family of programming languages. Python and Perl both originated from a background of UNIX shell scripting. However, as Guido van Rossum, the creator of Python, describes in his essay, "Comparing Python to Other Languages,"

> [Python and Perl each] have a different philosophy. Perl emphasizes support for common application-oriented tasks, e.g. by having built-in regular expressions, file scanning and report generating features. Python emphasizes support for common programming methodologies such as data structure design and object-oriented programming, and encourages programmers to write readable (and thus maintainable) code by providing an elegant but not overly cryptic notation. As a consequence, Python comes close to Perl but rarely beats it in its original application domain; however Python has an applicability well beyond Perl's niche.

Python has a strongly object-oriented language, and in that way it resembles Perl5. Python's pattern matching and regular expressions suffer in comparison to Perl5, but not cripplingly so. With a clean syntax and strong emphasis on common programming methodologies, Python is considered for larger programming tasks than other scripting languages. A routinely stated characteristic of the language (by its adherents) is its elegance: Python devotees claim that Python is easy to read, and the readability of a Python script carries over as reduced maintenance overhead.

Cameron Laird, in his previously mentioned article for *SunWorld Online*, makes the interesting point that Python has few enemies. Some may criticize Perl for offering so many ways to do anything that there is no right, or even reasonably right, way to do anything in Perl, and Perl scripts are sometimes considered terse or even cryptic. One of the few points Python's detractors make is that some consider the control of subroutines via mandatory indentation (the TAB key is used extensively by Python programmers) to be an annoying feature of the language.

Three web resource pointers of note:

- The Python Software Activity, an international community of Python users and supporters, has a membership website at **http://www.python.org/psa**.
- An almost lyrical comparison of Python to other programming languages, written by Guido van Rossum, can be found at **http://www.python.org/doc/essays/comparisons.html**.
- "The What, Why, Who, and Where of Python," a well-written introduction to Python programming written by developer Aaron R. Watters, is available at **http://www.networkcomputing.com/unixworld/tutorial/005/005.html**.

Tcl/Tk

Tcl, which stands for Tool Command Language, is another glue-oriented scripting language like Perl. Tcl (most often pronounced *tickle*) takes output from one application and sends it to another. The two primary features of Tcl as designed by the creator of the language, Dr. John Ousterhout, are embeddability and extensibility. Tcl was designed to be embedded within an application, merging with the features of the application to provide easily manipulated hooks for use of the application. For extensibility, Tcl provides programming interfaces that make integrating an application written in C++, Java, or any other language comparatively simple.

Probably the most widely used Tcl library extension is a graphical user interface (GUI) toolkit called Tk. Tk includes buttons, menus, scroll bars, and other graphical widgets. Using Tk, you can build a graphical user interface or front end that allows easy use of your script or set of scripts, if your users are unlikely to want to run a series of scripts from the command line personally. A great deal of work has gone into the Tk library to support different platforms: a Tcl script written using Tk will look like a Windows application on a PC, a Macintosh application on a Macintosh desktop, and a Motif program on a UNIX workstation. Work has also been done to integrate Perl and other scripting languages with Tk. Multiple initiatives have set out to implement extensions to access Tk, rather than implementing the same kind of GUI functionality within a given scripting language; this fact is strong evidence of Tk's success, and supports the claim that Tcl is an extensible language.

Like the other scripting languages, Tcl is not designed for intensive computational tasks. Focused number-crunching should be performed by applications written in compiled languages, whose output can then be routed via Perl or displayed via Tk. Tcl does not have the robust routines available in Perl, so complex Tcl program logic can be difficult to create. Finally, because Tcl generally stores all data as strings, it lacks the data structures that make Python scripts run faster when performing database queries and related tasks.

For a brutally simple example of Tcl syntax, here is the venerable programming example "Hello, World!":

```
puts stdout {Hello, World!}
```

The command takes two arguments (an I/O stream identifier and a string) and writes the string to the I/O stream along with a following newline character.

Tcl will run on almost all flavors of Microsoft Windows, with the caveat that Windows 3.1 systems will need the Win32 subsystem installed. In Windows, version 8.0.5 and above of Tcl/Tk requires only one Registry value (as expected, in the HKEY_LOCAL_MACHINE section) identifying the path to the installed location of the Tcl executable.

- The official home for current Tcl and Tk releases is Dr. Ousterhout's company, Scriptics; you can visit their website at **http://www.scriptics.com**.
- A Frequently Asked Questions file concerning Windows-specific issues related to Tcl/Tk is located on the web at **http://www.pconline.com/~erc/tclwin.htm**.
- TkCon provides a robust console window for systems that have the Tcl engine installed. UNIX users may not get excited about yet another shell or console window, but TkCon can be helpful on systems such as Windows and the Apple Macintosh OS (prior to Mac OS X) that don't provide built-in or feature-rich consoles. TkCon can be downloaded from the web at **http://www.purl.org/net/hobbs/tcl/script/tkcon/**.

MICROSOFT RESOURCES

In general, the best starting resource for Microsoft applications is Microsoft. Microsoft has provided an extensive array of documentation and training materials for its software. This section will address two major resources of interest to those working in a cross-platform environment: the Microsoft Windows Add-On Pack for UNIX, and the Microsoft Windows Server Resource Kit.

The Microsoft Windows Add-On Pack for UNIX

Microsoft has licensed a subset of MKS Systems' port of UNIX utilities to Windows NT. The resulting product, Windows NT Services for UNIX, provides the following three major areas of enhancements for Windows:

- **File Services** Includes both client and server support for the Network File System (NFS).
- **Connectivity Services** Includes both a server and a client for Telnet. In addition to the Windows GUI-based Telnet client that is available by default on every Windows 95 and later system, a command-line Telnet client is also included, along with a password synchronization daemon that allows single password management across both Windows NT- and UNIX-based systems.
- **Usability Services** Provides a set of UNIX utilities and a port of the UNIX Korn shell, as well as a password synchronization tool.

Much of this capability has been rolled into Windows 2000 Server: The Telnet server and client are included, but only a two-user Telnet server license is included with Windows 2000 Server.

The Telnet Server Administrator is a command-line utility and will not be found in the Control Panels or the Administrative Tools section of the Windows GUI. To start the Telnet Server Administrator GUI, open a command prompt window and enter the command **tlntadmn** to launch the menu-driven utility. NFS clients are included in all of Windows 2000, although NFS server capability seems to be available only on the Windows 2000 Server family of systems.

The Microsoft Windows Server Resource Kit

If you are responsible for administering a Windows NT or Windows 2000 server, just buy this. Buy the latest edition, buy any updates available, and buy a Microsoft TechNet subscription. In addition to the tools mentioned in Table 8-3, the Server Resource Kit also provides such items as a Telnet server. The usual security concerns regarding Telnet apply, in that a Telnet login sends the user's password across the network as clear text that can be read by anyone on the local LAN who has a packet sniffer.

NOTE: If you do not have the Resource Kit, a small Telnet server still in development, it is available on the web at **http://hem.passagen.se/deschatr/ndtelnet.htm**. This Telnet server does perform user authentication against both local and domain accounts.

Seriously, the Resource Kit and TechNet are mandatory for any use of a Windows server above the hobby level.

SUMMARY

In this chapter, we've examined some of the command line-level controls available in Windows 2000, and explored how they differ from the control capabilities in Windows NT. We discussed some of the differences between using the command line in Windows and in UNIX, and surveyed some of the freely available scripting languages, such as Perl, Python, and Tcl/Tk. Finally we introduced Microsoft's Add-On Pack. With a port of the UNIX Korn shell to Windows, those experienced with the Korn shell through their UNIX background can now have a familiar and powerful tool to work with.

CHAPTER 9

DNS Configuration

The Domain Name System, simply referred to as the DNS, provides a mechanism for associating hierarchical, user-friendly names with numeric Internet Protocol (IP) addresses that computers can recognize. Within the DNS, for example, a request for the hostname **www.whoeveritis.com** will be translated into its corresponding IP address.

DNS service is available on both UNIX and Windows platforms. In this chapter, we will look at the history of the DNS, survey the various files and data components that make up a DNS system, and detail the installation and configuration of DNS on both Windows and UNIX.

WHAT IS THE DNS?

When the Internet was first formed, there were very few computers attached to it. It was a straightforward matter to maintain the name/address mapping by having a complete list of all host names and addresses in a local file on each host computer. However, as more and more computers connected to the Internet, it became clear that this system could not keep up with the growth. Whenever a new host was added, it was necessary to update every host file on every computer. It was evident that a new solution had to be devised—hence the emergence of the DNS.

Domains and Zones

The Domain Name System organizes the domain name space into a tree structure. Conceptually, each node in the tree, known as a *domain*, has a database of information about the hosts under its authority. Domains were previously assigned by the Internet Network Information Center, also known as the InterNIC. (More information on the InterNIC can be found on the web at **http://www.internic.net**.) In 1998, however, the Internet Corporation for Assigned Names and Numbers (ICANN) was formed with the following objective:

> ...to serve as the global consensus entity to which the U.S. government is transferring the responsibility for coordinating four key functions for the Internet: the management of the Domain Name System, the allocation of IP address space, the assignment of protocol parameters, and the management of the root server system.*

The transition of responsibility for managing the DNS is scheduled to be completed by September 2000. For more information on the progress of this conversion, see the ICANN website at **http://www.icann.org**.

The actual information for a domain or subdomain is contained in files known as *zone files*. It is important to note that the terms *domain* and *subdomain* refer to logical divisions

*Source: **http://www.icann.org/general/fact-sheet.htm**.

of the domain name space, whereas *zone* refers to the actual files that contain the information. There can be multiple zones for one domain, and they can be used for distributing domain management responsibility and redundancy.

The Authoritative Root Domain

The uppermost node in the DNS heirarchy is the *authoritative root domain*. The *root zone files* contains information about every registered domain name; this information is replicated across 13 *root zone servers* that are located in the United States, London, Stockholm, and Tokyo. The root zone servers distribute Internet address records and other crucial data to lower-level DNS servers, thus allowing websites around the world to connect and communicate with each other. In DNS address mapping, the root domain is represented by **.** (a period character).

The Top-Level Domains

The second layer of nodes in the DNS consists of the *top-level domains*. Currently, the most familiar of these are the seven *generic top-level domains* (GTLDs), which are generally categorized according to the functions of the individual websites they encompass. Each top-level domain has its own *domain specifier*. The GTLDs, for example, are identified as follows:

Domain Specifier	Usual Website Owners
net	Networking organizations
org	Nonprofit organizations
com	Commercial organizations
gov	United States government
edu	Educational organizations
mil	United States military
int	Administrators of files needed by the Internet itself and organizations established by international treaties

In addition to the GTLDs, there are alternative top-level domains that identify the different countries or regions where lower-level domain servers are located. These *country code top-level domains* (CCTLDs) are represented by two-letter domain specifiers, such as us for the United States and uk for the United Kingdom. For a detailed guide to all the CCTLDs, the Internet Assigned Numbers Authority (IANA) maintains a CCTLD database at **http://www.iana.org/cctld.html**.

Like the root zone files, the top-level zone files contain information about all the domains below them in the DNS hierarchy.

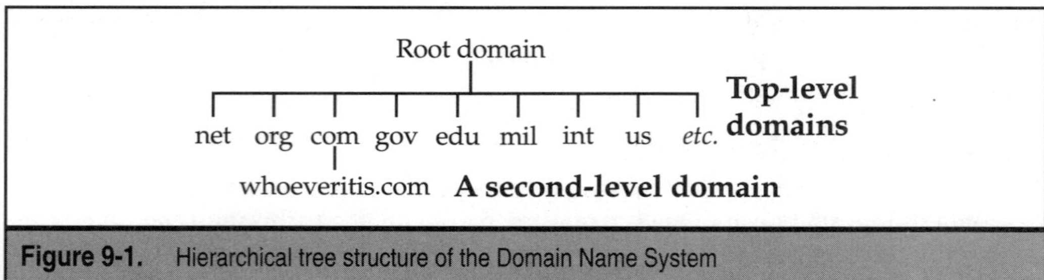

Figure 9-1. Hierarchical tree structure of the Domain Name System

Second-Level Domains

Typically, a single large entity, such as a company or a university, will register one second-level domain name. For example, **microsoft.com** is the domain allocated to Microsoft, and **ncsu.edu** is the domain allocated to North Carolina State University. Figure 9-1 shows the hierarchical structure of the Domain Name System, and maps its relationship to a hypothetical website managed by the company that has registered the domain name **whoeveritis.com**.

Site-Specific Subdomains

Domains can be divided into logical elements known as *subdomains*. For example, suppose the network folks at the sample company wanted to group their sales computers in a separate component of the domain name space, as diagrammed in Figure 9-2. They might create a subdomain like **sales.whoeveritis.com** and assign host names to computers within this subdomain. Subdomains provide for logical grouping of hosts, and further organize the domain name space.

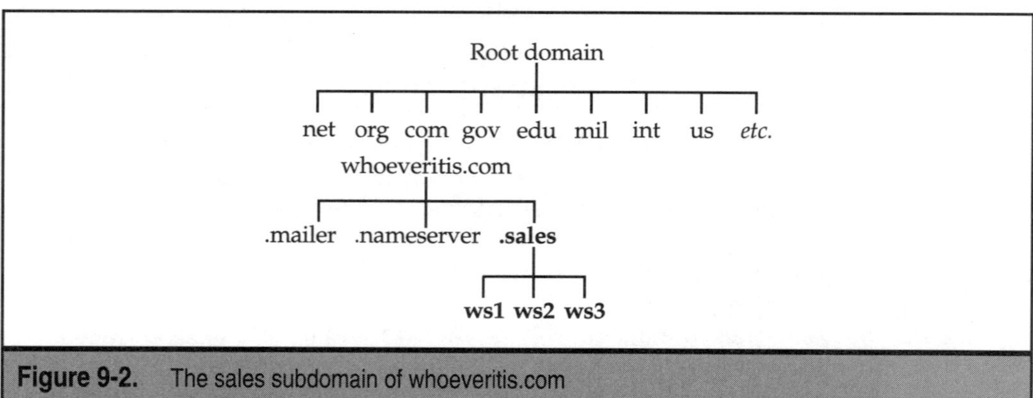

Figure 9-2. The sales subdomain of whoeveritis.com

Name Servers

Name servers are programs that contain, maintain, and answer queries regarding the data in the domain name space. Each name server has complete information about a subset of the domain name space. In addition, a server may contain cached information about other domains and subdomains.

Primary Name Servers

A *primary* name server is a server that stores its data in local zone files. When an administrator updates or adds host information to a domain, the update is performed at a primary name server. Primary name servers are considered the last word in authority for the host information that they serve to clients.

Secondary Name Servers

A *secondary* name server functions similarly to a primary name server in that it answers DNS queries from clients. However, it does not keep its host information in local zone files. Instead, a secondary name server obtains its information via a *zone transfer* from a specific primary name server, known as its *master name server.*

You should consider having multiple name servers, including servers at remote locations, in your DNS configuration. By using multiple secondary servers, you can add redundancy in case your primary server fails. In addition, you can use secondary name servers to reduce the load on your primary name server.

Caching-Only Servers

A *caching-only* server does not have any authority in the domain name space. Nor does it perform zone transfers with a master name server. A caching-only server exists to make queries and cache the results locally. Caching-only servers start with no zone information locally, then build up their cache of domain name space information over time by caching the results of queries. This type of server is useful when there is a network link between you and your primary DNS server.

UNIX DNS

In this section, we will examine the process for configuring a DNS server to run under UNIX. Please remember that several different varieties of the UNIX operating system are commonly used today. As a result, the examples that we give in this section may not be exactly correct for the particular version and release of UNIX that you are using. However, since virtually all UNIX implementations of the DNS are based on the same original source, these examples should be very close to the actual details for most versions of UNIX.

The named Daemon Process

Under UNIX, the DNS name server duties are typically provided by the *named daemon* process. The named daemon starts when the computer is booted and reads its initial configuration information from a configuration file. Typically, this file is called named.boot and is located in the /etc directory. Once named has started and is initialized with its configuration information, it begins listening for DNS requests on the default network port specified in the /etc/services file.

NOTE: In the named.boot file, as in the other DNS configuration files under UNIX, comments are indicated by the semicolon character and continue to the end of the line.

The named.boot file is the roadmap that the named daemon uses to find all its other configuration files. Several options can be listed in the named.boot file. Table 9-1 lists the most common options. Depending on your version of UNIX, these options may be slightly different or you may have additional options.

NOTE: The domain names and IP addresses used in these examples are not valid names and addresses. They are used as examples only.

The following is a sample named.boot file:

Option	Function
Directory	Specifies the directory where the DNS zone files are located.
ores	Tells named to be a primary server for the specified domain.
Secondary	Tells named to be a secondary server for the specified domain.
Cache	Tells named to cache the results of queries.
Forwarders	Causes the local name server to try to contact other servers if it cannot resolve the query locally.
Slave	Tells named to be a slave server and forward the request to one of the forwarder name servers.

Table 9-1. Common Configuration Options Present in named.boot

```
; A sample named.boot file
directory /etc/named
cache . named.ca
primary whoeveritis.com named.hosts
primary 1.169.192.in-addr.arpa named.rev
```

This boot file sets up the local name server to act as a primary name server for the **whoeveritis.com** domain. By using a directory option, we have told named that it can expect to find its files in the /etc/named directory. Another common place to put configuration files is in the /var/named directory.

The next line contains the cache option; here it tells named to cache information that it receives and to preload its cache from the named.ca file.

The primary option, on the next line, directs named to become a primary name server for the domain **whoeveritis.com**. As the primary name server needs to read its zone information locally, the name of the zone file, named.hosts, is specified on the line as well.

Don't be confused by the second "primary" line in the named.boot file. According to the second "primary" line, this name server is also a primary server for **1.168.192.in-addr.arpa**, with named.rev as the name of the zone file. DNS was originally designed to map names to IP addresses, without the capability to map the other way. With a second primary entry, named can be configured to map IP addresses back to DNS names as well.

Zone Files

As we said before, primary name servers load their host information from zone files. These zone files contain all the information for hosts in the particular zone of authority that a given name server has responsibility for. All information in these database files is stored in a format known as a *resource record.* Each resource record has a type associated with it, which is used to indicate the function of that particular resource record.

CAUTION: The file formats used by the DNS are fairly complicated and obscure. In fact, most DNS configuration problems can be traced to errors in the configuration files.

Several different types of resource records are available, each serving a different function. Table 9-2 lists the most common types of resource records that you are likely to encounter.

Resource Record Syntax

When describing the details of a resource record in one of the zone files, we use a syntax that is common to all types of resource records. The basic format of a resource record is shown here, with the optional components indicated by square brackets:

[*record_owner*] [*time_to_live*] [*class*] *type data*

Type of Record	Description
A	An address record that maps a name to an address. The address is specified in the data field in dotted decimal format.
CNAME	A canonical name record that is used to assign an additional name to a host. Since there can only be one address record for each host, any additional host name mappings must be given via canonical name records.
HINFO	A host information record that provides general information such as hardware type and operating system version.
MX	A mail exchanger record that is used to indicate that another computer handles mail delivery for the host listed in the record.
NS	A name server record that points to the authoritative server for another zone.
PTR	A pointer record that is used to map addresses back to host names.
SOA	A Start of Authority record that informs the name server that it has final authority for a list of resource records.

Table 9-2. Common Types of Resource Records

The *record_owner* field of the resource record indicates the particular thing that the resource record refers to. It can indicate either a domain name or a host name. If no record owner field is given, the domain name of the previous resource record is used.

The *time_to_live* field indicates how long, in seconds, this particular resource record is valid as an answer to a query. This field is used to specify how long a particular record may be cached after it is retrieved from a server. If you do not specify a time-to-live value, the minimum time-to-live value of the last Start of Authority (SOA) resource record is used.

The *class* field is used to indicate that this resource record uses a particular type of networking addresses. The value IN is used to indicate a TCP/IP network. As with the *record_owner* field, the class of the previous resource record is used if you do not specify a class.

The *type* field, which is required, is used to indicate which type of resource record we're working with. The various resource record types are listed earlier in the chapter.

The *data* field, which is also required, is the actual value that is contained within this resource record. Since there are several different types of resource records, the format of the data field is dependent on the particular type of resource record being defined.

The Start of Authority Record

The Start of Authority (SOA) record is used to indicate that the records that follow are authoritative for a particular zone. This means that the name server that contains the SOA record has the final word on the data contained in these records. The data in the authoritative records overrides any cached data on other name servers and any currently held data on secondary name servers.

The SOA record has one of the most complicated data formats of all the resource records. Although it uses the same general syntax format described earlier in this chapter, the *data* field is surrounded by parentheses, and usually contains more than one line.

Let's look at the fields that make up the complicated data format in the SOA record. The *origin* field gives the canonical name of the primary name server for this domain, which is typically given as a *fully qualified domain name* (FQDN). An FQDN is a host name that has the entire domain and subdomain information appended, such as **www.whoeveritis.com**. If the host name is provided as an FQDN, it will need to end with a period character. This tells the name server daemon not to append the current domain name to it by default.

The SOA record also contains information regarding how to contact the domain administrator. This information is contained in the *contact* field. It is specified typically as an Internet electronic mailing address, with one exception: the at character (@), typically found in the e-mail address, is replaced by a period. This is because, within a resource record, the @ character expands to the value of the *origin* field.

When the domain administrator updates information in the zone files, there must be some mechanism to let the various name servers know that the file has changed and that their zone-transferred and cached copies are no longer current. Since date and time stamps vary with the clock settings on various computers, they are unreliable as a means to indicate change. The SOA record uses an incremented serial number instead. The *serial* field contains an integer serial number that is used to indicate the version number of the zone file.

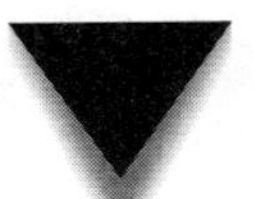

REMEMBER: You *must* increment the SOA serial number every time you change information in one of the zone files. If you forget, secondary servers will not know that the file has been updated, and your DNS servers will not respond consistently. Forgetting to increment the SOA serial number is one of the most common problems in managing a DNS system.

Several parameters in the SOA record relate to time-out and retry options. The *refresh* field indicates how long, in seconds, a secondary server should wait before refreshing and checking the SOA record of the primary name server. Typically, SOA records are not updated that frequently. A typical value for the *refresh* field is about 24 hours.

NOTE: On most UNIX systems, you can force the named daemon to reload its configuration, either by rereading its zone files or by initiating a zone transfer. Typically, you will accomplish this by sending a SIGHUP signal to the named process. First, use the ps command to locate the process ID (PID) of the named process; then use the command **kill –HUP *processID*.**

Two fields in the SOA record control how a secondary name server functions when it is unable to contact the primary name server. The *expire* field is used to control how long a secondary name server should wait before it invalidates its zone information, assuming that it hasn't been able to contact the primary name server. The *retry* field tells a secondary name server how long it should wait, in seconds, to retry a request if the primary name server is not available.

You will recall that resource records have a time-to-live value that determines how long a resource record is valid. If you do not specify a time-to-live value in an individual resource record, the record inherits the time-to-live value from the SOA record. The *minimum* field in the SOA record indicates the default resource record time to live, in seconds.

The Primary Zone File

When we configured the named.boot file earlier in the chapter, the "primary" line indicated that the primary zone file was named .hosts. This file contains the authoritative information for the **whoeveritis.com** zone. Here is a sample named.hosts file for **whoeveritis.com**:

```
; A sample named.hosts file for the
; domain whoeveritis.com
;
@ IN SOA nameserver.whoeveritis.com. root.whoeveritis.com. (
 19             ; The SOA serial number - remember to increment it!
 43200          ; Refresh field - Refresh every 12 hours
 120            ; Retry field -   Retry every 2 minutes
 2592000        ; Expire field -  Expire after 30 days
 43200          ; Time-to-live  - Default time-to-live is 12 hours)

 IN NS nameserver.whoeveritis.com.
;
; Set up an entry for the domain itself whoeveritis.com
;
IN A 192.168.1.1
;
; Our nameserver
;
nameserver A 192.168.1.1
;
; Our mail server
;
```

```
mailer IN A 192.168.1.2
;
; Several client workstations
;

ws1 IN A 192.168.1.3
IN MX 100 mailer.whoeveritis.com
ws2 IN A 192.168.1.4
IN MX 100 mailer.whoeveritis.com
ws3 IN A 192.168.1.5
IN MX 100 mailer.whoeveritis.com
ws4 IN A 192.168.1.6
IN MX 100 mailer.whoeveritis.com
ws5 IN A 192.168.1.7
IN MX 100 mailer.whoeveritis.com
```

Let's look at this file in detail. The first resource record in the file is the Start of Authority (SOA) record for **whoeveritis.com**. Recall that the @ character in a resource record translates to be the current origin. The origin is defined in the main named configuration file, named.boot. It is listed on the "primary" line in named.boot.

Following the @ symbol, we see the *class* and *type* fields, which contain the following:

```
IN SOA
```

The *class* field contains IN, which indicates that this resource record uses TCP/IP addressing. The *type* field contains SOA, which indicates that this is a Start of Autority record. The next entries make up the *data* portion of the SOA record. As we've just seen, this part of an SOA resource record is pretty complicated.

The first element in the *data* field is the canonical name of the primary name server for this domain, **nameserver.whoeveritis.com**. Following the name of the name server is the contact e-mail address, **root.whoeveritis.com**.

REMEMBER: In the contact e-mail address, we have to replace the usual at character (@) with a period character (.) because the @ is translated to be the current value for the domain origin.

The next five fields in the SOA resource record are the numeric parameters that control refreshing and expiration. The first of these numbers is the serial number of the SOA record. Remember to increment this number when you update your zone files so that changes can take place! The next four fields are the *refresh*, *retry*, *expire*, and *time_to_live* fields, respectively. (These fields are discussed in detail earlier in the chapter.)

Following the SOA record is a name-server resource record, which lists **nameserver.whoeveritis.com** as the name server for the **whoeveritis.com** domain. Remember that the first field in a resource record is the optional *record_owner* field. Since we did not list a value for this field, named assumes that we're using the last domain that we specified. Because no domain is named in the *domain* field, it is assumed to be the last domain specified. What was that last domain that we specified? Look back at the beginning of the SOA record and you will see the @ character. The @ character is the domain; remember that it expands to be the domain from the named.boot file, **whoeveritis.com**.

The next thing we do is set up an address for the domain itself, in case anyone should try to use **whoeveritis.com** as a host name. We do this via an address (A) resource record. Normally we would list a host name at the beginning of the A record, but since the last thing we referenced was the domain itself (via the @ character), we can just leave the host name portion blank.

CAUTION: We let named figure out the default domain or host name in several examples in this chapter so that you can get practice reading this type of syntax. In reality, you must be careful if you implement zone files this way. If you add an entry in the middle of a file, and that entry has a domain name specified, you will cause problems if other entries use the previously referenced domain in their resource records.

Since **whoeveritis.com** is not a real computer, we assigned it the IP address 192.168.1.1, which is really the IP address of our name server.

If you look back toward the beginning of the named.hosts file, you will see that we listed **nameserver.whoeveritis.com** in an NS resource record. This tells named that **nameserver.whoeveritis.com** is the name server for our domain. However, we need to give an IP address for **nameserver.whoeveritis.com**. We do this via another A record, which looks like this:

```
nameserver A 192.168.1.1
```

After setting up the address for our name server, we assign an address to our mail server as well. The last several lines in the file assign IP addresses to a series of workstations. You will notice that after each A record for a workstation address, there is a line that looks like this:

```
IN MX 100 mailer.whoeveritis.com
```

This line contains a mail exchanger (MX) record, and tells named that when mail is received for this workstation, it should be forwarded to the host **mailer.whoeveritis.com** instead.

The Cache Configuration File

The DNS process caches results from its queries in order to speed up the resolution of frequently requested name translations. In the named.boot configuration file, we entered a line that looked like this:

```
cache . named.ca
```

This line tells named to cache queries and to preload its caching information from the named.ca file. Unlike the other DNS configuration files, this file is pretty simple. As stated earlier in this chapter, the caching operation of named is very important. Fortunately, the named.ca file that sets up caching is also usually the simplest of the various DNS configuration files. It lists the root name servers for the various domains along with their IP addresses, so that your DNS server will already have the addresses of the root servers. The following is a sample caching configuration file:

```
; A sample caching configuration file
;
; NS record configuration
;
99999999 IN NS KAVA.NISC.SRI.COM.
99999999 IN NS TERP.UMD.EDU.
99999999 IN NS NS.NIC.DDN.MIL.
99999999 IN NS NS.NASA.GOV.
99999999 IN NS NS.INTERNIC.NET.
;
; Address record configuration
;
NS.NIC.DDN.MIL. 99999999 IN A 192.112.36.4
NS.NASA.GOV. 99999999 IN A 128.102.16.10
KAVA.NISC.SRI.COM. 99999999 IN A 192.33.33.24
TERP.UMD.EDU. 99999999 IN A 128.8.10.90
NS.INTERNIC.NET. 99999999 IN A 198.41.0.4
```

The Reverse Resolution Configuration File

The DNS was designed to map names to addresses. However, we also need to be able to map addresses back to names. Recall that we had a line in the named.boot configuration file that looked like this:

```
primary 1.168.192.in-addr.arpa named.rev
```

This line tells named that we are also the primary server for a domain called **1.168.192.in-addr.arpa**. What is this strange looking domain? The in-addr.arpa component tells named that this domain does reverse lookups that match IP addresses to host names. The 1.168.192 component is the network portion of our IP address in reverse. The last argument on the line, named.rev, is the zone file that contains the reverse resolution information. This file is very similar in format to the named.hosts file, except that it is used to map addresses to host names. Here is a sample named.rev file:

```
@ IN SOA nameserver.whoeveritis.com. root.whoeveritis.com. (
 19            ; The SOA serial number - remember to increment it!
 43200         ; Refresh field - Refresh every 12 hours
```

```
 120           ; Retry field -   Retry every 2 minutes
 2592000       ; Expire field -  Expire after 30 days
 43200         ; Time-to-live  - Default time-to-live is 12 hours)
;
; Our nameserver
;
nameserver A 192.168.1.1
;
; Here are the reverse address mappings
;

1 IN PTR nameserver.whoeveritis.com.
2 IN PTR mailer.whoeveritis.com.
3 IN PTR ws1.whoeveritis.com.
4 IN PTR ws2.whoeveritis.com.
5 IN PTR ws3.whoeveritis.com.
6 IN PTR ws4.whoeveritis.com.
```

As you can see, the named.rev file has the same SOA record as the named.hosts file. The SOA record sets up authority for the reverse resolution domain. Remember all the discussion about the @ character expanding to be the value of the origin? Well, here it is set to **1.168.192.in-addr.arpa** from the "primary" line in the named.boot file.

The first resource record is an NS record that indicates the name server. The rest of the records in the file are PTR records that map IP addresses to host names. The host names in the PTR resource records must be the full canonical name of the host, each ending with a period character.

WINDOWS 2000 DNS

Under Windows 2000 Server, DNS service is not installed by default during installation but is an optional service that you may choose from the Networking Services group.

Note that prior to installing DNS, you need to check your current TCP/IP configuration, including your DNS client configuration information. When the DNS service is installed, it uses the DNS client configuration information for some of its default settings.

You can find your DNS client configuration information by opening the Control Panel folder, then double-clicking the Network and Dial-Up Connections folder. If your system is part of a network, there should be a Dial-Up Connection or Local Area Connection icon in the right-hand side of the window. Right-click the Connection icon and select the Properties command to view the Properties information for that connection profile. A table in the middle of the Properties window displays the network protocols bound to that connection. Click the Internet Protocol (TCP/IP) line in the table, then press the Properties button below the table to display the DNS addressing information for the system.

If you want to add DNS service to an existing Windows 2000 Server, it's quite easy: Simply click the Start button in the Windows taskbar, then select Settings, then Control Panels to display the Control Panels folder. Double-click the Add/Remove Programs icon, then double-click the Add/Remove Windows Components icon in the left margin of the window. Click the Components button and the Windows Components Wizard will start. After you have finished installing DNS service, you will have to restart your server before the service will be available.

Configuring Microsoft DNS

The Microsoft DNS Server is configured via the DNS tool, which is available from the Start button of the Windows taskbar by selecting Programs, then Administrative Tools, then DNS. If you are working with DNS for the first time on that Server, the Configure New Server Wizard will start the first time you manage DNS on that server.

Since the installation of DNS only installs a basic configuration, no DNS servers will show up in the server list. By selecting New Server from the DNS menu, you can add a local DNS server. Once you add a local DNS server, you can double-click the server in the Server list to see the zone definitions for that server. By default, Microsoft DNS is installed as a caching-only server, so if you want to use it as a primary or secondary server instead, you will have a bit more configuration to do.

Microsoft also provides the capability to integrate the DNS server with its LDAP (Lightweight Directory Access Protocol) offering, Active Directory. One great advantage of this integration is the ability it affords to designate additional primary servers for a DNS domain. If a given primary server is out of service for some reason, another server can respond to DNS requests to the downed server. This feature is especially effective if the downed primary server also supplied dynamic addressing through DHCP.

THE DNS AND WINS

Microsoft Windows also provides a service known as the Windows Internet Naming Service (WINS). WINS provides a NetBIOS naming layer above the TCP/IP addressing layer in the network protocol stack. This layer maps Microsoft NetBIOS names to TCP/IP addresses. This mapping allows communications via the NetBIOS name and the Microsoft Universal Naming Convention (UNC) when the target computer is using TCP/IP as its network protocol. Since NetBIOS is not a routable protocol, it uses a flat name space and has no concept of hierarchical name space as found in DNS host and domain names.

The Microsoft DNS and WINS servers are designed to work together to resolve names. Under WINS, hosts are allowed to dynamically register their names with the WINS database, and so they may or may not appear as static IP addresses in the regular DNS database.

Microsoft has defined a new resource record of type WINS that is attached to the root zone in the domain. This record tells Microsoft's DNS server how to contact the WINS server to resolve name queries for hosts that do not have static DNS entries. For example, a WINS resource record might look like this:

```
@ IN WINS 192.168.1.100
```

NOTE: You should be aware that this resource record is not standard and can occasionally adversely affect non-Windows DNS servers attempting to perform a zone transfer from an NT primary server.

Adding WINS Lookup to Existing DNS Configurations

If you have an existing DNS architecture and decide to add WINS lookup, you will need to use Microsoft's DNS server on an NT server. The easiest way to provide this functionality is to add a new subdomain to support WINS lookup. For example, if your domain is **whoeveritis.com**, you might want to add the subdomain **wins.whoeveritis.com** to support WINS lookup. Set up a primary DNS server for this zone, and enable WINS lookup, pointing the DNS server to the WINS server.

UNIX OR NT?

As you have seen, there are versions of DNS for both Windows NT and most flavors of UNIX. So, which should you use? Let's look at a few pros and cons.

The DNS implementation under UNIX is very robust and has been extensively tested and is widely deployed. It is based on the Internet Request for Comments (RFC) standards documentation. The vast majority of DNS traffic on the Internet today is served from UNIX-based computers. However, UNIX systems can be difficult to administer, and DNS configuration under UNIX is notoriously difficult. As you have seen earlier in the chapter, UNIX DNS configuration is based on manually edited text files that have a very complicated syntax.

Microsoft shipped their first release version of DNS with Windows NT 3.51. It was shipped as an add-on component with the NT 3.51 resource kit. This release had several major shortcomings and was not robust enough for production use. With Windows NT 4.0 and now the Windows 2000 Server, Microsoft has released a greatly updated version of DNS as an NT service, including graphical management tools that make it much easier to maintain and update zone information. The Microsoft Windows DNS tools also include integration with the WINS protocol to add support for computers that rely on the NetBIOS protocol. However, the DNS-WINS integration component of Microsoft DNS uses nonstandard resource record types that are not supported by most other DNS servers. If a non-Microsoft DNS computer attempts a zone transfer from a Microsoft DNS server with DNS-WINS resource records, it may encounter problems. Some users on Internet-support mailing lists have reported unusual behavior from the NT DNS service as well, at least in its early stages.

In addition to Microsoft's DNS implementation, there are other versions of DNS that run under Windows NT 3.51 and 4.0, and should run under Windows 2000. These versions include both commercial implementations and freeware versions. In addition, there is a Windows NT port of the UNIX BIND name server software. A review of some of the most popular NT DNS servers can be found on the web at **http://www.dns.net/dnsrd/docs/exotic.html**.

NOTE: For extensive information on DNS, see **http://www.dns.net/dnsrd/**.

Given the power of the UNIX DNS offerings, we recommend that you implement a UNIX-based DNS if it is feasible in your environment. If you do not have UNIX expertise or are primarily an NT-based organization, you might want to review some of the alternative commercial NT DNS offerings before making a final decision.

DESIGNING A DNS ARCHITECTURE

Now that we have explored the various options available in both NT and UNIX DNS servers, what is the best way to set up your DNS architecture? One of the most important points, from both a management and performance point of view, is deciding how you will structure your domains and subdomains. There are two common approaches to this decision. You can either have one large domain for your whole organization, with hosts addressed directly from the domain name, or you can opt to create subdomains.

Single Domain Model

If you have a fairly small organization, especially if your organization is located in a single geographical area, you might want to consider having one domain, such as **whoeveritis.com**. You would then address your hosts directly off the domain name, for example, **ws1.whoeveritis.com**. The advantage to this approach is that all domain management is centralized in one location. You don't have to worry about separate subdomains, multiple master servers, different zone files, and the like. However, you can suffer some performance problems. If you use multiple secondary name servers, your primary DNS server can suffer load problems answering refresh queries from the secondary servers. In addition, lots of users making queries against your primary server can reduce its performance.

Subdomain Model

If your organization is geographically dispersed or you have lots of users, it may be to your advantage to create subdomains and manage your DNS entries accordingly. In this model, you would have a single root domain server with an appropriate number of secondary servers supporting it. Your root server is responsible for answering requests for hosts that directly connect to your organization's root domain, and for directing querying hosts to the appropriate subdomain servers. These subdomain servers can be organized according to geographic region, departmental function, corporate structure, or whatever makes sense for your organization. For example, if your root domain is **whoeveritis.com**, you could create subdomains **sales.whoeveritis.com**, **marketing.whoeveritis.com**, **development.whoeveritis.com**, and **support.whoeveritis.com**. By separating the DNS structure into subdomains, you increase the number of systems for which administration will be required; however, you can delegate this responsibility to the appropriate departments or regions. You also reduce the load on the primary DNS servers by separating information into multiple servers.

TROUBLESHOOTING DNS

As you have probably figured out by now, DNS is a complex system whether UNIX- or NT-based. It is easy to make mistakes that are very difficult to locate. Most of the problems result from syntax errors in your configuration files, or from assigning an address to the wrong computer. Remember the following guidelines when implementing and troubleshooting your DNS:

- For all entries, check and verify the spelling of host names. Also remember that absolute host names end with a period. Absolute host names are names that are complete as written; they do not need to have a domain name appended to them.
- Update the serial number in the SOA records of your zone files if you make a modification. This will ensure that secondary servers reload the files correctly.
- Verify that the DNS name and IP address entered in the primary zone file match the corresponding reverse resolution information in the reverse resolution zone file.
- SOA and CNAME records can cause all sorts of problems if you are not careful. Misspelling a name or getting a host address wrong here can redirect queries to computers that don't exist.
- Microsoft's DNS server uses some nonstandard resource records, which can cause problems for UNIX-based secondary DNS servers that make zone transfers from the NT DNS server. These records occur primarily when WINS resolution is enabled on the NT server.

The best practice is to thoroughly test your DNS configuration. The nslookup utility, available on both NT and UNIX, is an excellent tool for examining your DNS database.

SUMMARY

In this chapter we have looked at many aspects of DNS, including its history and use. We have explored the configuration of DNS zone files in detail and have examined the differences between Microsoft's DNS server for Windows NT 4.0 and the various UNIX DNS servers that are available. In addition, we've looked at several potential pitfalls when setting up and configuring a DNS system, as well as some design principles for choosing the best DNS architecture for your organization. Remember that regardless of your DNS architecture, testing your DNS database thoroughly is one of your best defenses against problems.

DNS is a very complex system, and it can cause problems that are difficult to locate. However, with a bit of research, planning, and forethought, DNS is quite manageable.

CHAPTER 10

Microsoft Windows Routing and Remote Access Service

Connecting a computer to another computer is the basis of networking and the Internet. With the wide variety of networking protocols available, network interoperability issues can become complicated in short order. Windows provides a mechanism known as the *Routing and Remote Access Service* (RRAS) that is used to provide remote network connections. The Remote Access Service from Windows NT has been integrated into RRAS as a subset.

When integrating Windows and UNIX environments, you will probably have a Windows computer acting as the client, dialing in to a UNIX- or TCP/IP-based network. In this chapter, we will look at RAS in some detail, including installation, configuration, and troubleshooting.

INTRODUCTION TO RAS

Figure 10-1 shows an example of how a Windows NT client using RAS can interact with various network services.

RAS supports a wide variety of network programming interfaces and protocols, allowing it to work in diverse environments. By use of the Point-to-Point Protocol (PPP), many different networking protocols can be routed via RAS. RAS also supports a variety of hardware networking media, as described in Table 10-1.

RAS is available on both Windows NT 4.0 Workstation and Windows NT 4.0 Server as well as Windows 2000 Professional and Windows 2000 Server.

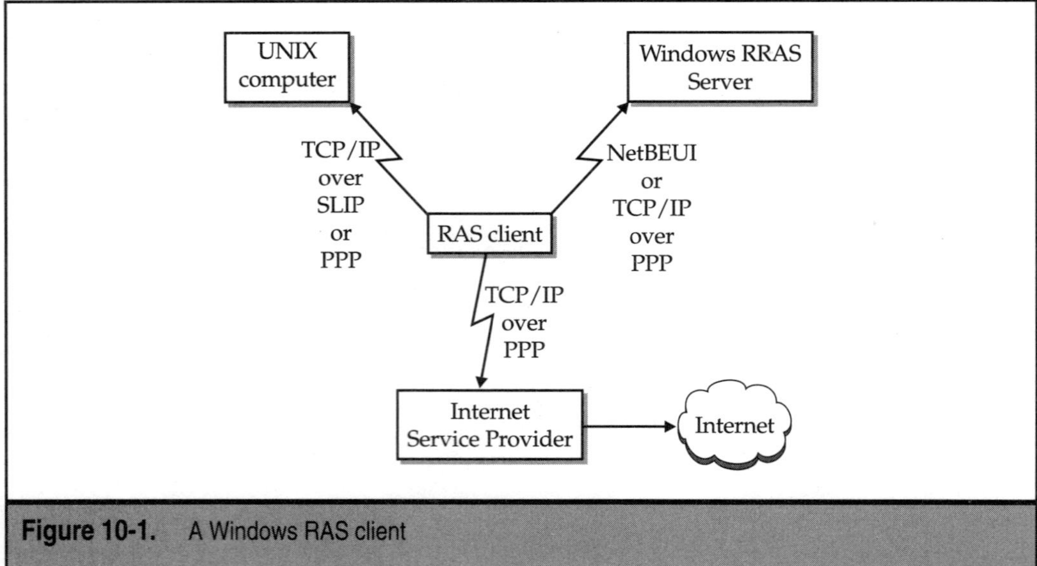

Figure 10-1. A Windows RAS client

Media	Description
PSTN	The *Public Switched Telephone Network,* or PSTN, is the standard analog telephone service provided by your local telephone company. RAS can connect via the PSTN with an analog modem; it currently has a maximum connection speed of 56Kbps.
ISDN	The *Integrated Services Digital Network,* or ISDN, is a digital communications network service available from most telephone companies. ISDN provides a higher bandwidth connection than a standard analog phone line, but it requires special hardware, which is referred to as an *ISDN terminal adapter* or *ISDN modem.* ISDN provides a connection speed of up to 128Kbps.
X.25	The X.25 network is a packet-switched data network. Access to an X.25 network is made via a packet assembler disassembler (PAD) device. X.25 supports direct connection via a PAD or analog dial-up connections.
xDSL	*Digital subscriber line,* of which ADSL (asymmetric digital subscriber line) is one common form (the x in xDSL indicates there are several forms of DSL). ADSL provides speeds up to 8 Mbps downstream (to the user) and up to 1 Mbps upstream.
Cable modem	A cable modem connects to a standard TV cable, allowing it to transmit data.
Null modem cable	A null modem cable is a special cable that allows two computers to be connected via their serial ports.

Table 10-1. The Network Media Supported by RAS

Line Protocols

A *line protocol* is a network protocol that provides the underlying connection over an asynchronous data connection. The RAS service supports several different line protocols, of which three are listed here:

- Serial Line Internet Protocol (SLIP)

- Point-to-Point Protocol (PPP)
- Point-to-Point Tunneling Protocol (PPTP)

Serial Line Internet Protocol

The Serial Line Internet Protocol (SLIP) is a standard networking line protocol that supports serial line connections via TCP/IP. Today, SLIP has been almost entirely replaced with other dial-up technologies such as PPP, ISDN, and xDSL.

SLIP differs from its younger cousin, PPP, in several important ways. SLIP does not allow any type of negotiation of network configuration, nor does SLIP support any type of encryption. Additionally, SLIP only functions with TCP/IP, and all computers using SLIP must have static IP addresses. The requirement for using static IP addresses prevents central IP address management using Windows' Dynamic Host Configuration Protocol (DHCP). Although the Windows RAS client supports SLIP, RAS does not have a SLIP server component, and therefore it cannot be used as a SLIP server.

Point-to-Point Protocol

The Point-to-Point Protocol, or PPP, is the successor to SLIP. It has become the industry standard for asynchronous network communications. PPP offers several features not available in SLIP, including the capability to use multiple network protocols and encrypted passwords. PPP supports negotiation of network configuration between host and client computers, and it does not require clients to use static IP addresses. In addition to TCP/IP, PPP supports IPX, NetBEUI, AppleTalk, DECnet, and other protocols. When installing RAS, Windows automatically binds it to TCP/IP, IPX, and NetBEUI if these protocols are installed.

Point-to-Point Tunneling Protocol

The Point-to-Point Tunneling Protocol, or PPTP, is an extension of PPP with some interesting features. All traffic over PPTP is encrypted, and thus, PPTP enables you to transmit PPP packets over TCP/IP in a more secure fashion. Since your network traffic is encrypted, it is extremely difficult to eavesdrop on your network data. By using PPTP as a line protocol, sites can create their own Virtual Private Network, or VPN, over the Internet. A VPN enables a company to use the Internet as a means to join sites in different locations, while maintaining a high level of security and protection for its network traffic.

In addition to its security features, PPTP allows multiple protocols to be sent over a PPP connection. PPTP relies on PPP packets for its network transmission. As such, PPTP can act as a translation layer between a non-TCP/IP protocol, such as IPX, and the PPP-line protocol layer. This enables you to route non-TCP/IP protocols, such as IPX or NetBEUI, over the Internet.

Network Connection Wizard

Microsoft Windows 2000 provides a wizard that enables you to establish remote connections with other computers or networks. This application is known as the *Network Connection Wizard.* To start the Network Connection Wizard, click the Start button to display the menu:

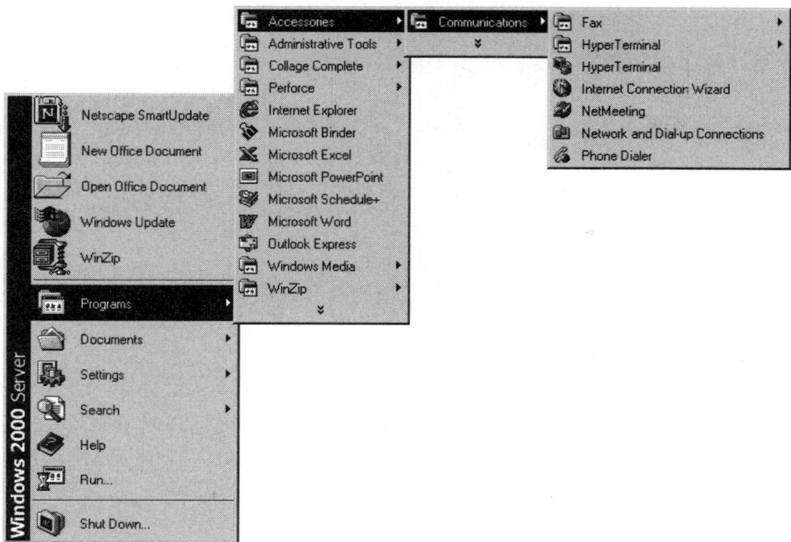

From here, select Programs, then Accessories, then Communications, and finally Network and Dial-up Connections.

When you select the Network and Dial-up Connections menu command, the Network and Dial-up Connections window appears, as shown in Figure 10-2.

In the window, double-click the Make New Connection icon to display the Network Connection Wizard, shown in Figure 10-3.

Click the Next button to display the Network Connection Type window, shown in Figure 10-4.

This window presents the following options:

- Dial-up to private network
- Dial-up to the Internet
- Connect to a private network through the Internet
- Accept incoming connections
- Connect directly to another computer

Notice that "Connect directly to another computer" includes support for infrared ports on your computer or laptop, if the computer has any. For this example, we'll create a new dial-up connection to a Virtual Private Network (VPN), using a modem attached to the Windows 2000 computer. Select the radio button to the left of that option, and then click the Next button to display the Destination Address window of the Network Connection Wizard, shown in Figure 10-5.

Here you can enter the IP address or the Internet domain name of the computer acting as a VPN server. After entering a name or number, click the Next button to display the Connection Availability window of the Network Connection Wizard, shown in Figure 10-6.

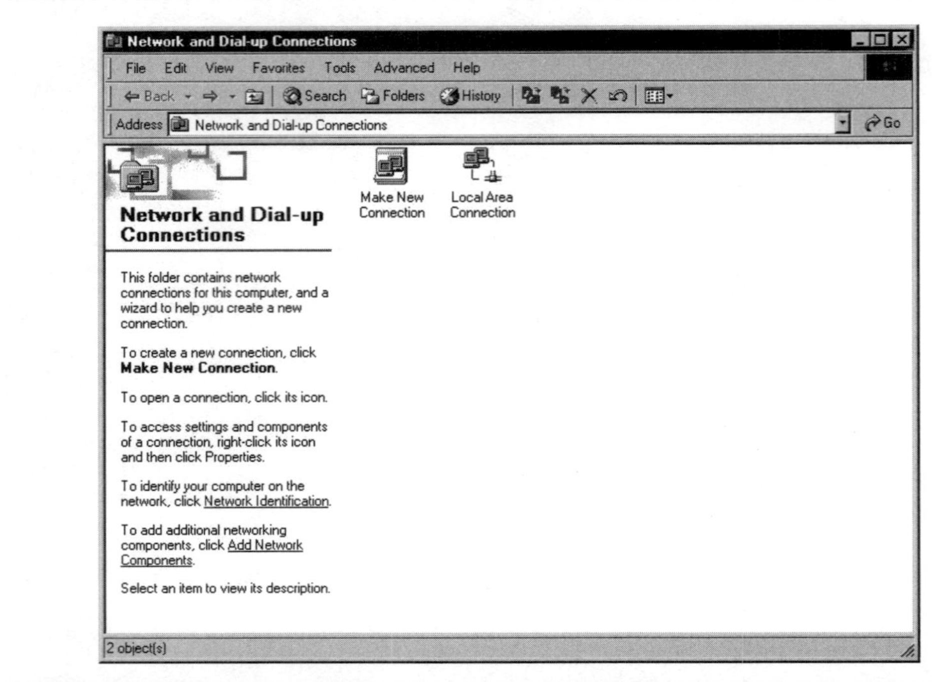

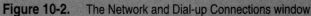

Figure 10-2. The Network and Dial-up Connections window

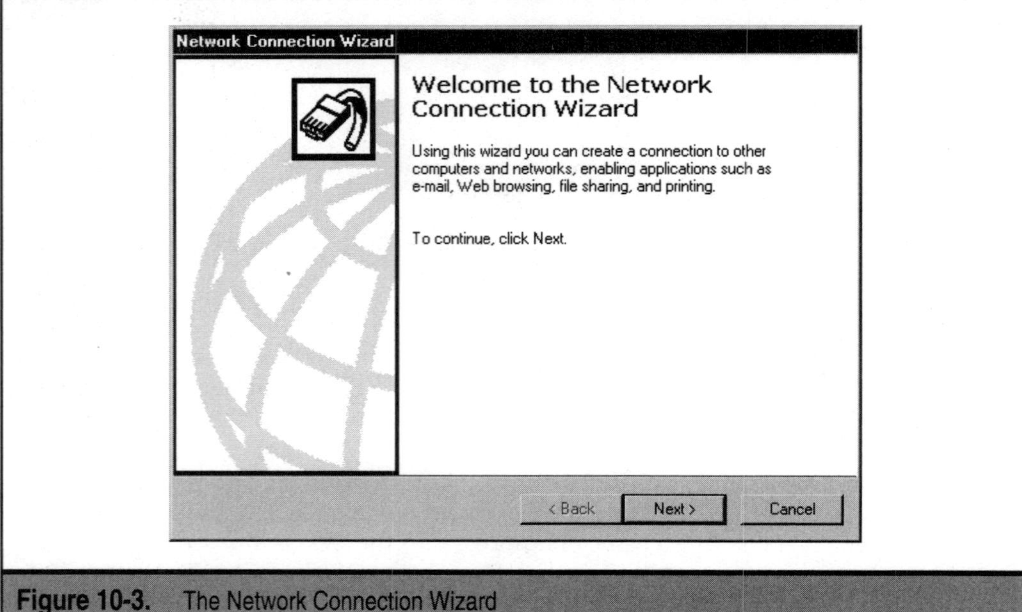

Figure 10-3. The Network Connection Wizard

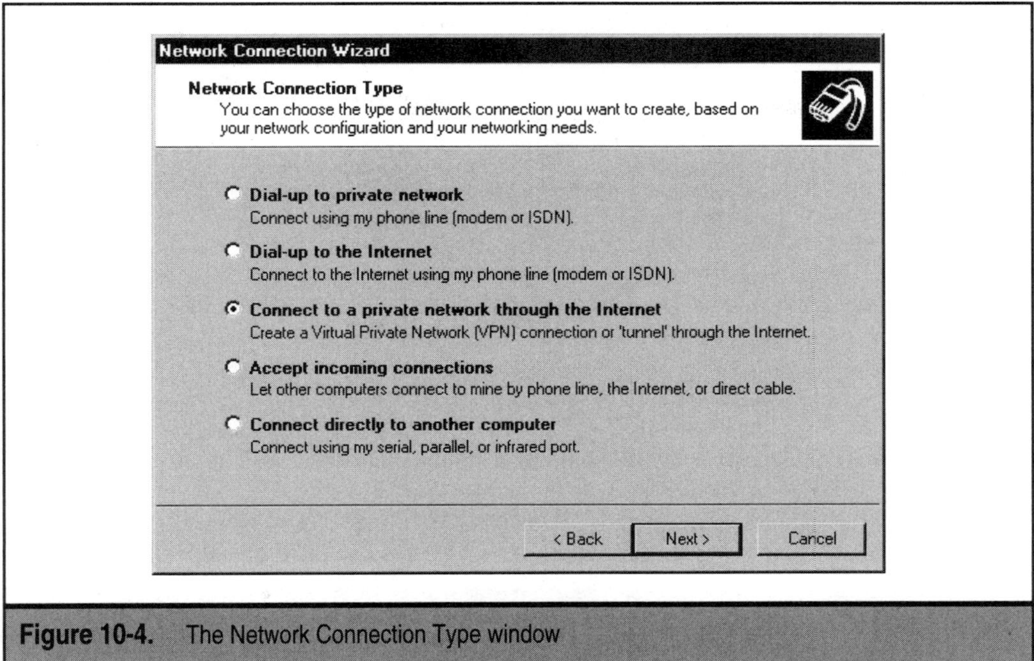

Figure 10-4. The Network Connection Type window

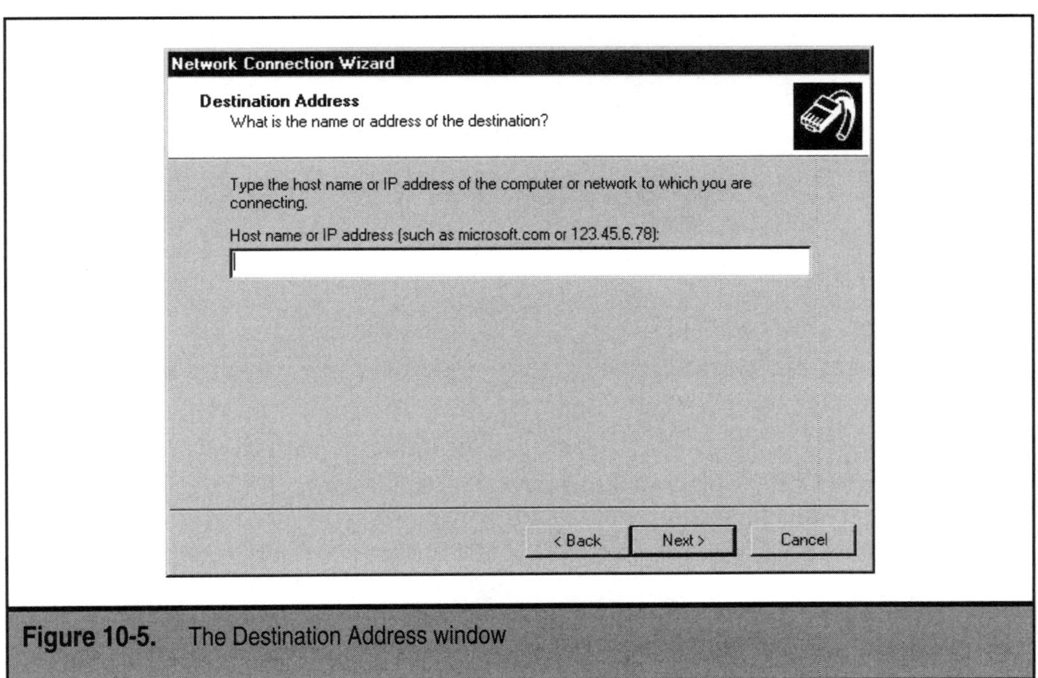

Figure 10-5. The Destination Address window

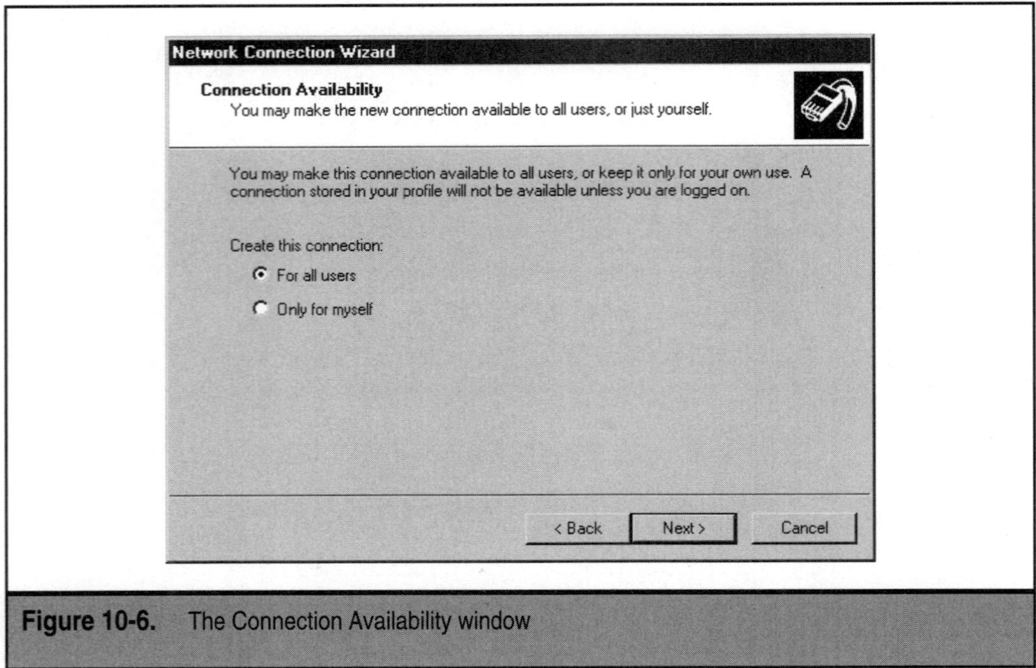

Figure 10-6. The Connection Availability window

In this window, you decide whether or not to allow other users access to this connection. Choose "For all users" and click the Next button to display the Internet Connection Sharing window of the Network Connection Wizard, shown in Figure 10-7.

The first setting in this window allows your Windows 2000 computer to act as a router, permitting other computers on the same local area network to use the connection at the same time. Click the checkbox to the left of "Enable Internet Connection Sharing" to enable this setting. By choosing to provide IP masquerade service to the local network, you are giving your server the ability to act as a router for the local network. By default the option is on; leave it on. Click the Next button to display the final window of the Network Connection Wizard, shown in Figure 10-8.

This final window of the Wizard enables you to name the connection, and to automatically create a desktop shortcut for the connection. Since this was only an exercise, click the Cancel button to cancel the Wizard.

INTRODUCTION TO RRAS

Originally code-named "Steelhead" while in beta for Windows NT, the Windows Routing and Remote Access Service (RRAS) is a robust network application that provides networking services for remote client computers. The RRAS server component acts as a remote dial-in point for client computers, and the Network Connection Wizard provides

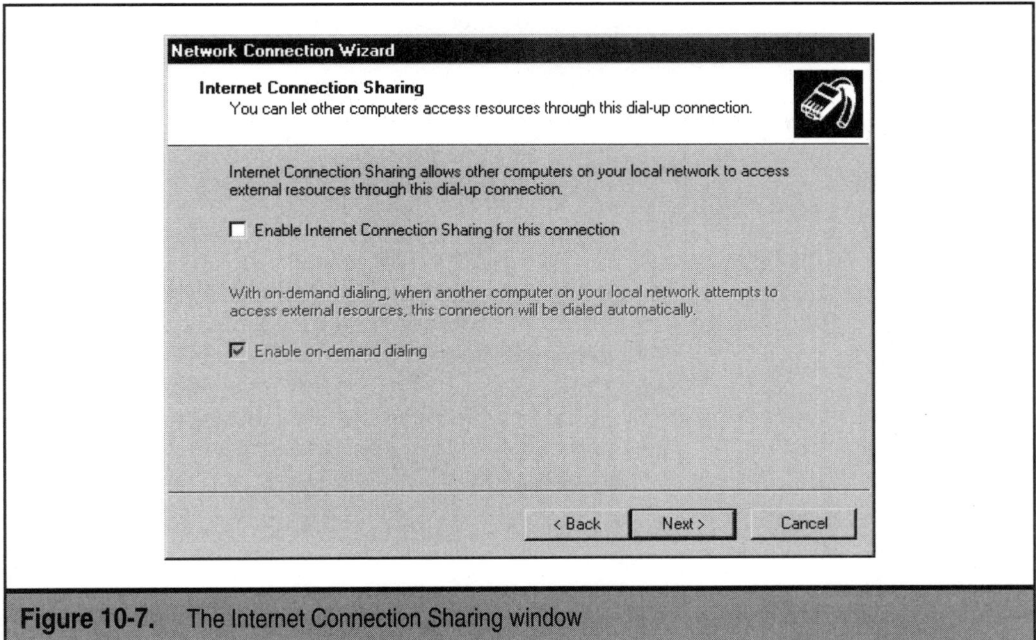

Figure 10-7. The Internet Connection Sharing window

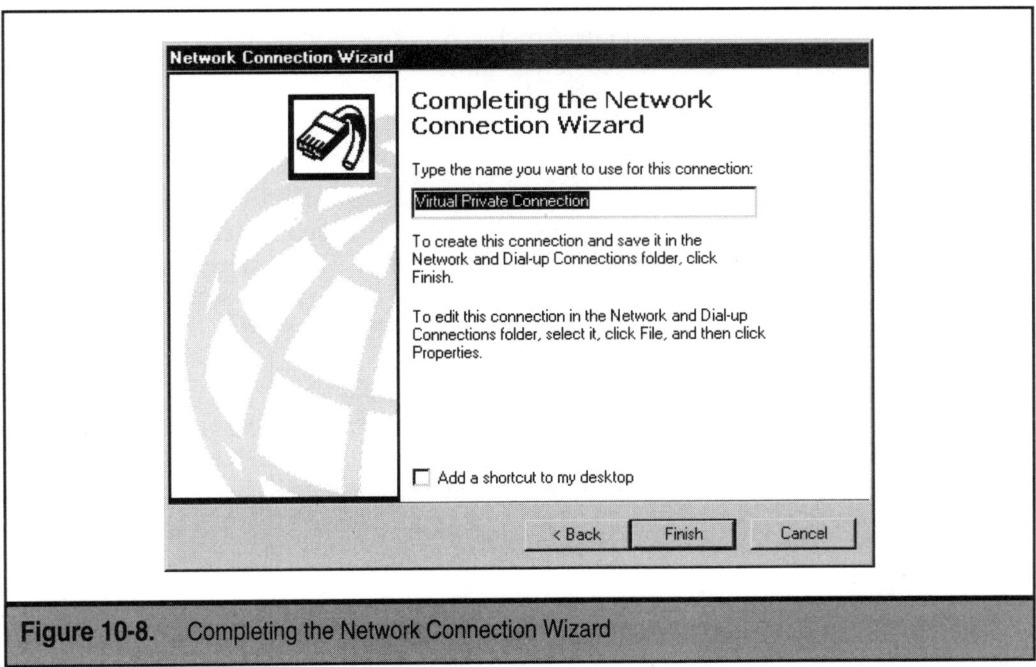

Figure 10-8. Completing the Network Connection Wizard

a simple interface for creating connections to other computers. RRAS is available for Windows NT 4 Server (Service Pack 4 and above) and Windows 2000 Server.

Microsoft RRAS supports three major groups of protocols:

- Routing protocols
- Transport protocols
- Authentication protocols

Supported routing protocols include AppleTalk, RIP v1 and v2 for IP and IPX, OSPF, and SAP for IPX. Transport protocols include TCP/IP, IPX/SPX, AppleTalk, and NetBIOS, whereas supported authentication protocols include PAP, CHAP, MS-CHAP, and RADIUS. A useful feature of RRAS is packet filtering, which can be set to accept or refuse incoming packets according to the IP address or packet type, and can also filter outbound as well as inbound traffic. RRAS supports 256 simultaneous remote access connections, 48 demand dial interfaces, and 16 LAN interfaces. RRAS provides for two major types of connections: dial-up connections to the Windows 2000 server, and Virtual Private Network connections.

Managing RRAS

RRAS is administered via the Routing and Remote Access (RRAS) tool, a component of the Microsoft Management Console (MMC). To start this tool, click the Start button, then select Programs, then Administrative Tools, and choose Routing and Remote Access. The RRAS window appears, as shown in Figure 10-9.

From the (RRAS) tool, you can perform a variety of administrative tasks: managing the RAS services, granting user dial-in permissions, sending messages to users, and monitoring server status.

Monitoring Server Status

The main display window of the RRAS tool displays a list of RAS servers. Each server that you are administering will have an entry in the list. For each server in the list, Remote Access Admin displays the server name, the status of the RRAS service, the total number of present ports, the number of ports currently in use, and the system uptime since last restart or crash. By default, the local computer is listed here as a server.

Configuring RRAS with the RRAS Setup Wizard

Choose a server in the list in the left pane of the RRAS window, and right-click to display the pop-up menu. Select the Configure and Enable Routing and Remote Access command to display the first pane of the Routing and Remote Access Server Setup Wizard, shown in Figure 10-10.

Click the Next button to display the Common Configurations window, shown in Figure 10-11.

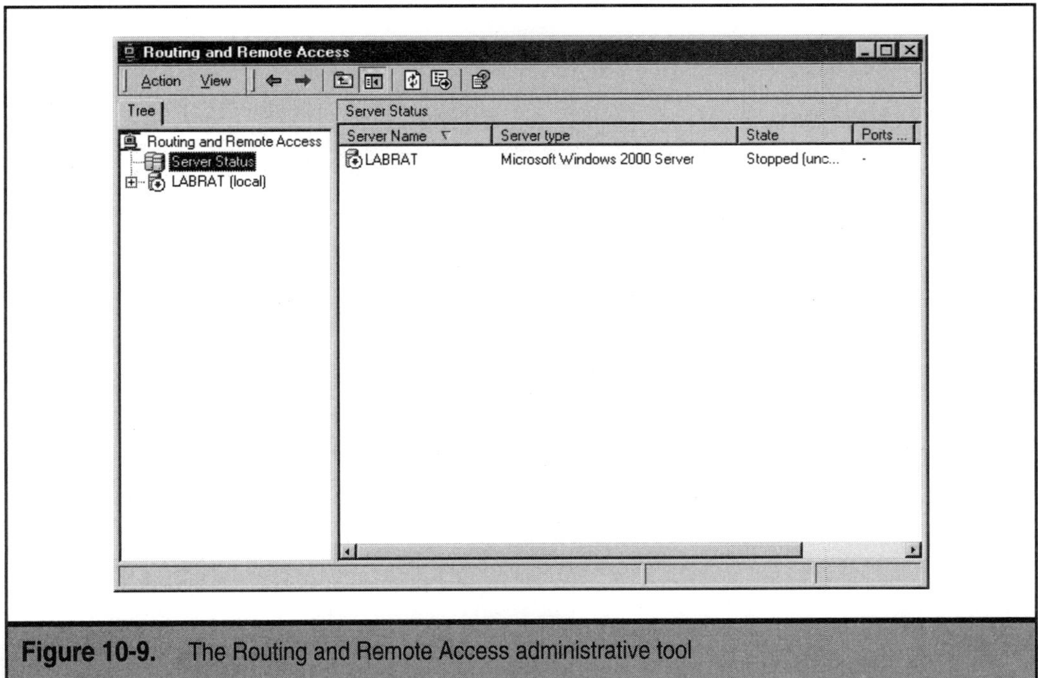

Figure 10-9. The Routing and Remote Access administrative tool

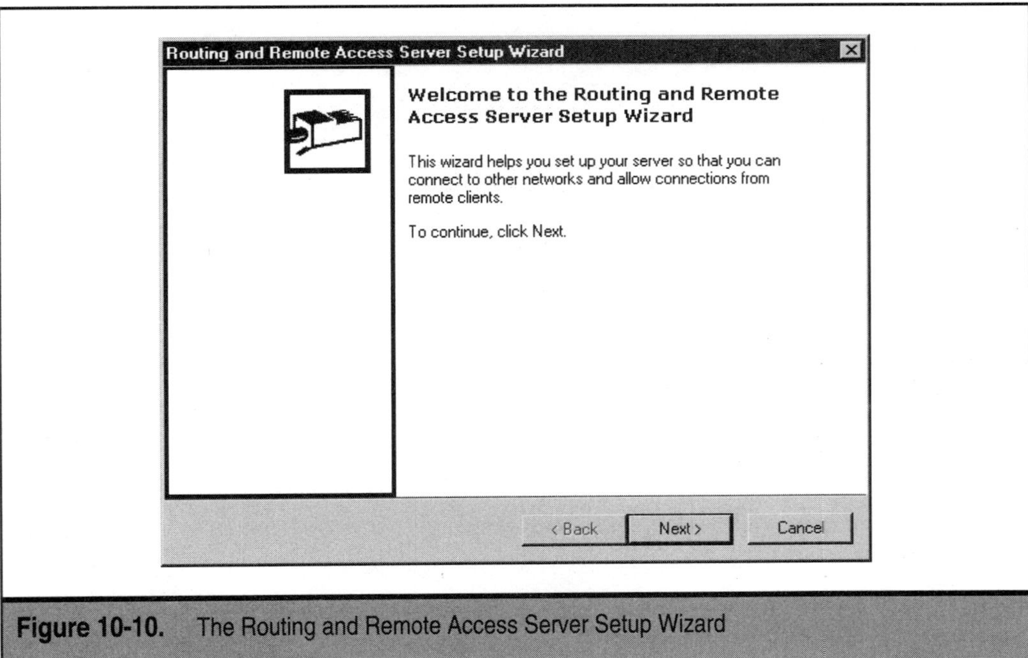

Figure 10-10. The Routing and Remote Access Server Setup Wizard

The options are:

- Internet connection server
- Remote access server
- Virtual private network (VPN) server
- Network router
- Manually configured server

For this example, we'll define this server as a network router. Click the radio button to the left of the Network router option, then click the Next button to display the Routed Protocols window, shown in Figure 10-12.

This window shows you the protocols available on your server for routing to and from remote clients. If all of the protocols you need are not present, you'll need to quit the RRAS Setup Wizard, add the protocols through the Network Connection Wizard, then restart the RRAS Setup Wizard and continue. For this example, we'll assume the protocols present are the ones you need. Click the Next button to display the Demand-Dial Connections window, shown in Figure 10-13.

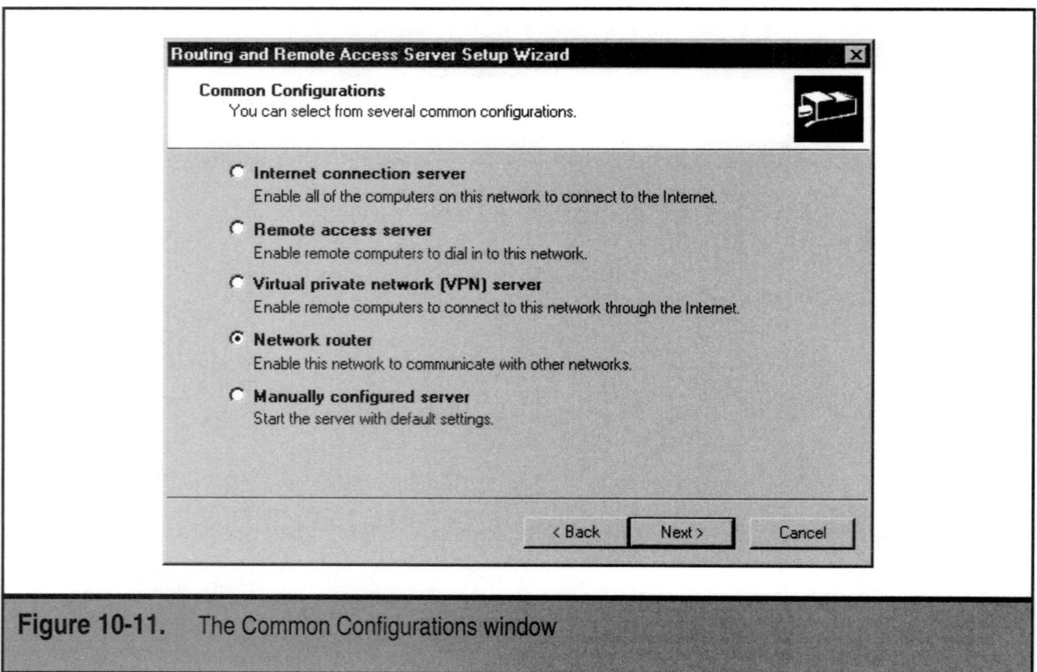

Figure 10-11. The Common Configurations window

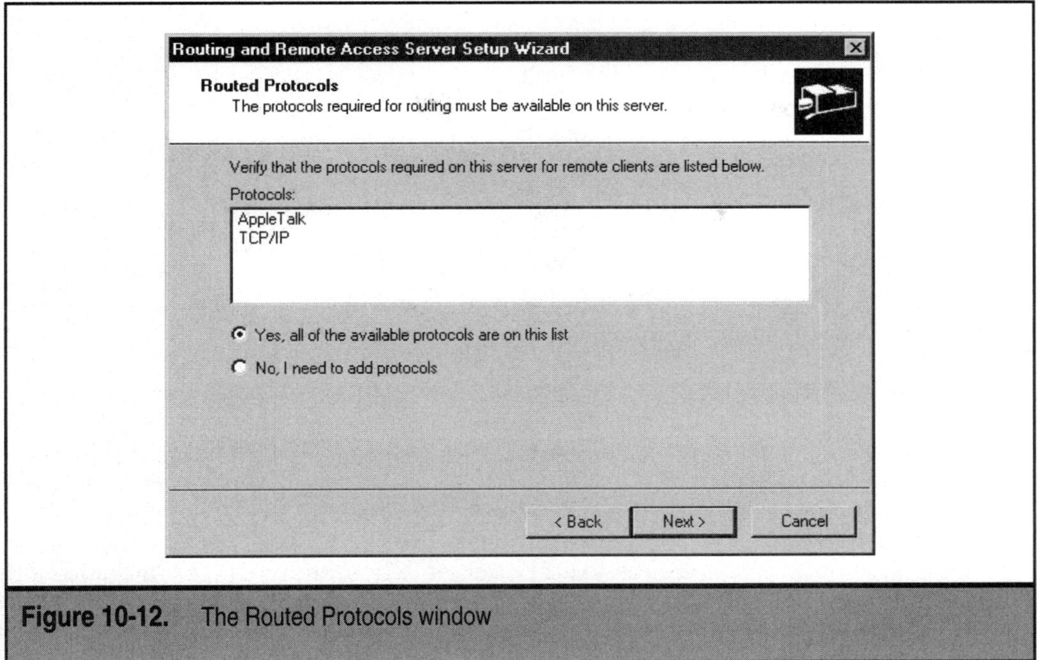

Figure 10-12. The Routed Protocols window

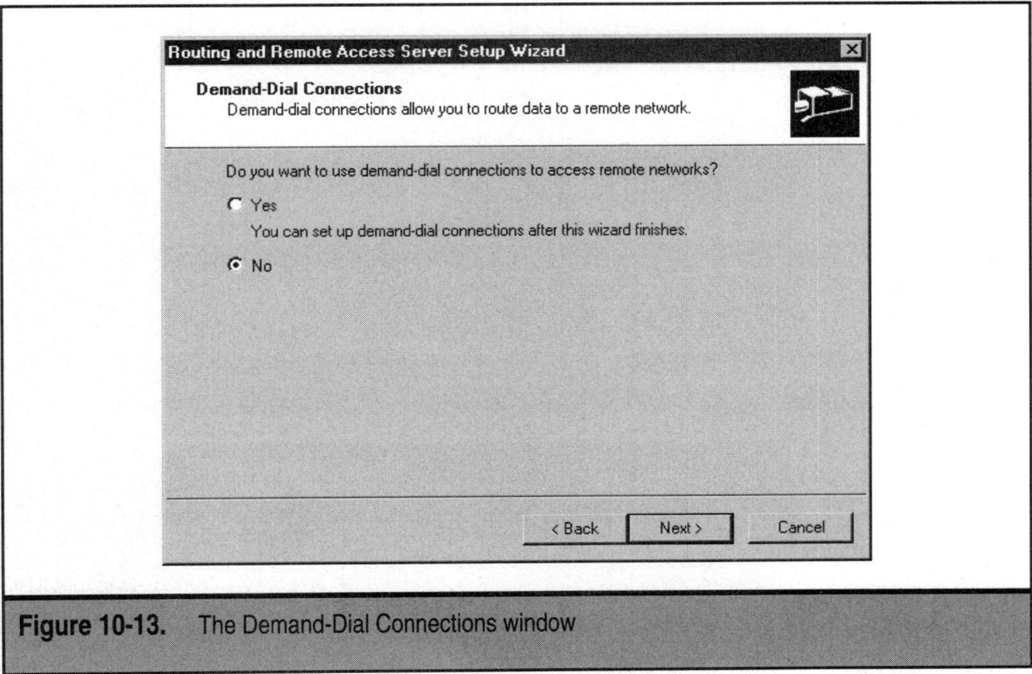

Figure 10-13. The Demand-Dial Connections window

Leave the default No selected, and then click the Next button to display the last window, shown in Figure 10-14.

Click the Finish button and you're done. The Wizard closes, the RRAS tool moves to the foreground, and the RRAS service starts up, as shown in Figure 10-15.

Administering RRAS

Generally speaking, systems will tend to grow in use until maximized, for two reasons:

- Users discover the capability is present.
- The administrator is directed to add a new capability but is given no additional budget or physical resources.

If you need to add a parameter to a given server you've configured with the RRAS Setup Wizard, the RRAS administrative tool allows you to do so. To edit a configured server's settings, open the RRAS administrative tool, as shown in Figure 10-15, right-click the server needing editing (in this example, the server name is LABRAT), and select the Properties command to display the server Properties window, shown in Figure 10-16.

Appropriately for the General title of the tab, this tab enables you to choose if the server will be a router, a remote access server, or both. Click the Security tab to display the window in Figure 10-17.

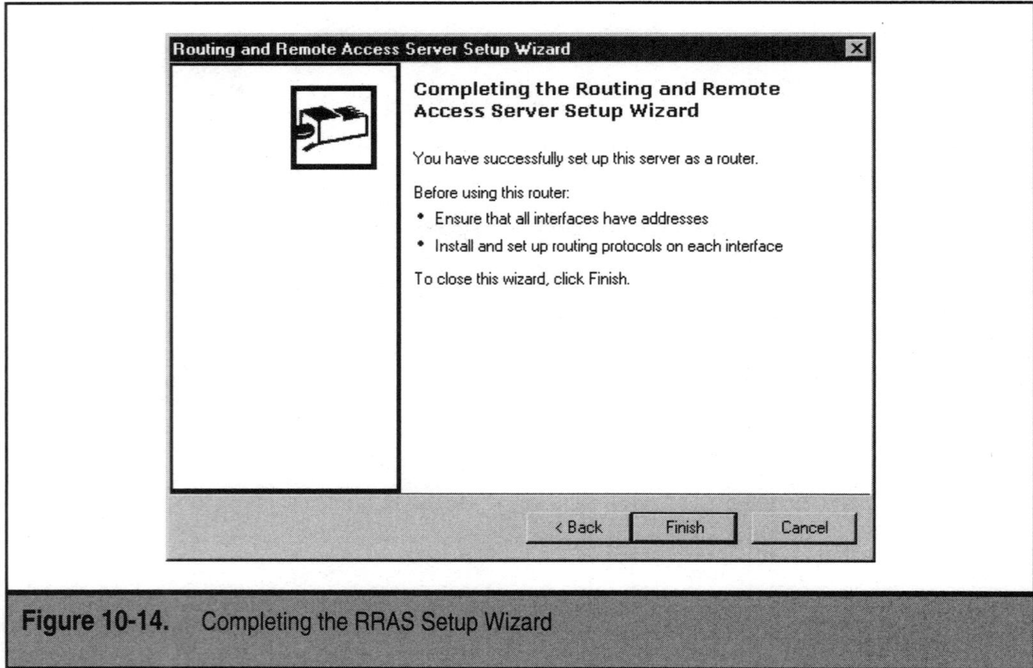

Figure 10-14. Completing the RRAS Setup Wizard

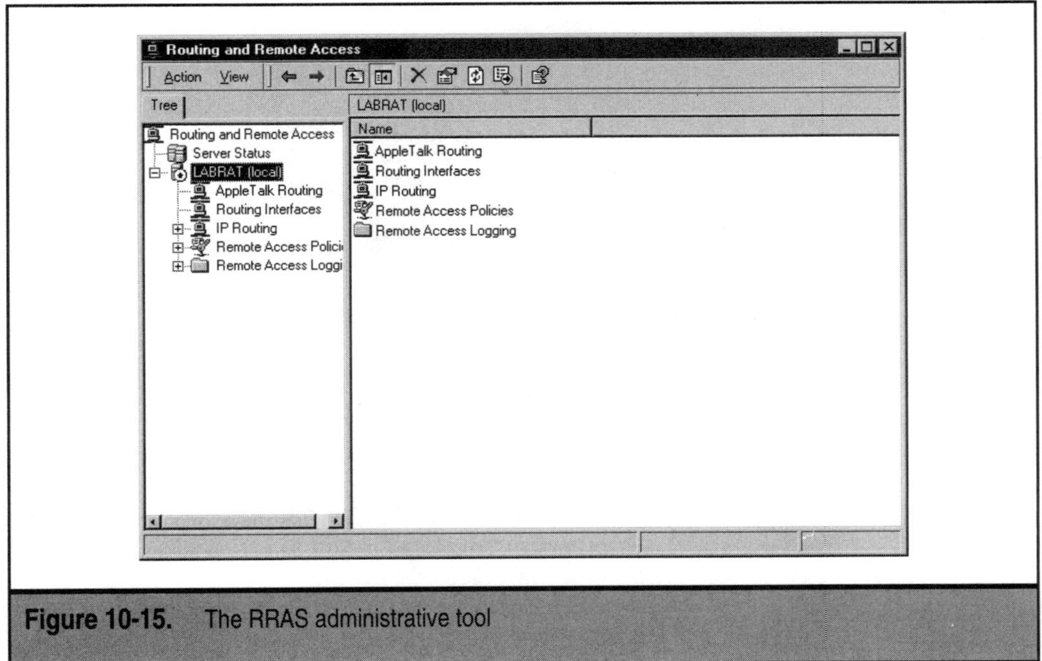

Figure 10-15. The RRAS administrative tool

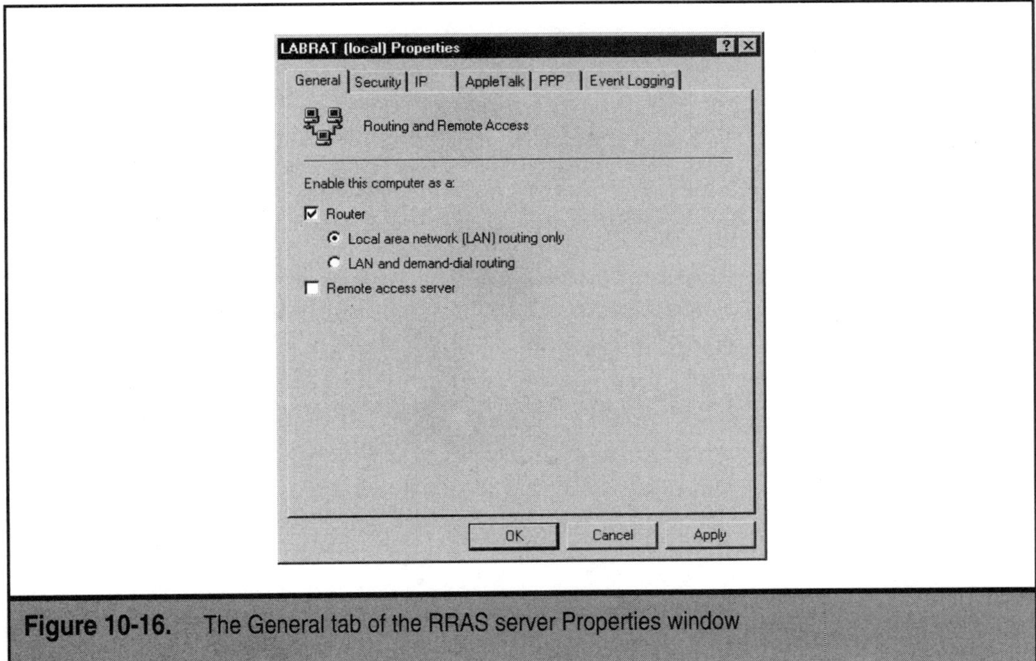

Figure 10-16. The General tab of the RRAS server Properties window

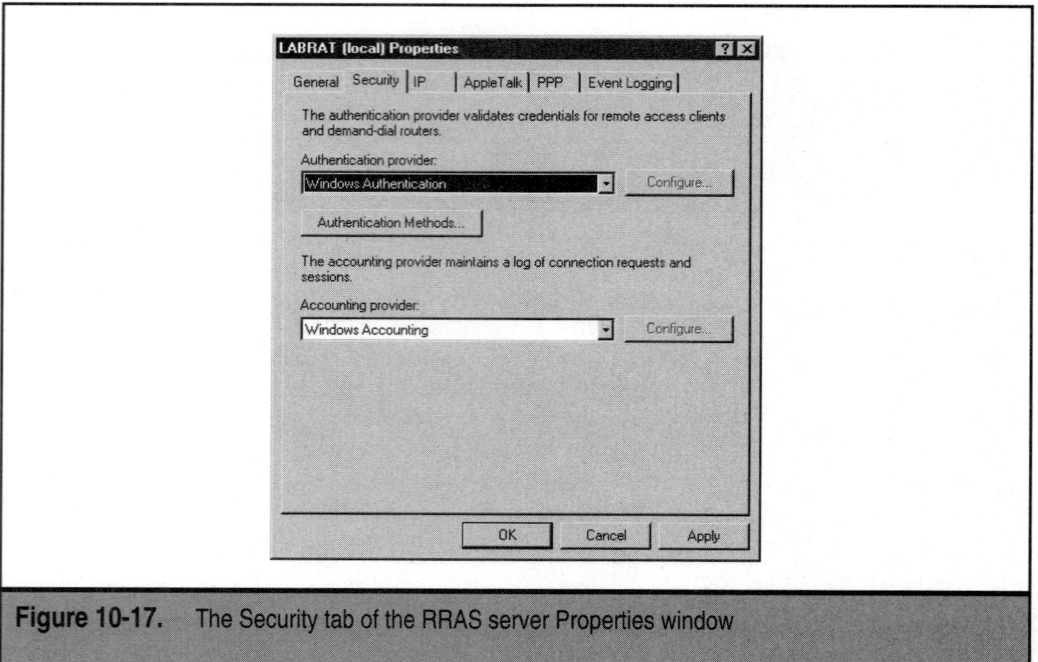

Figure 10-17. The Security tab of the RRAS server Properties window

The Security tab presents options for authentication and accounting, or logging of connection attempts. Click the Authentication Methods button to see available authentication methods, as shown in Figure 10-18.

Windows 2000 RRAS provides several different authentication methods in order to be accessible from a wide variety of client systems. However, not all of these authentication methods are supported by every possible operating system. Windows 2000 authenticates remote connections in the order shown, from top to bottom:

- **Extensible authentication protocol (EAP)** EAP extends PPP connection authentication in a modular manner, allowing a third-party authentication method to be hooked in at this point.
- **Microsoft encrypted authentication version 2 (MS-CHAP v2)** MS-CHAP v2 answers some of the more serious criticisms of MS-CHAP. MS-CHAP v2 is a one-way encrypted password, mutual authentication process. The sequence of MS-CHAP v2 authentication is as follows:
  1. The authenticator (the RAS or IAS server) sends a challenge to the remote access client that consists of a session identifier and an arbitrary challenge string.

2. The remote access client sends a response that contains the username, an arbitrary peer challenge string, and a one-way encryption of:

   The received challenge string
   The peer challenge string
   The session identifier
   The user's password

3. The authenticator checks the response from the client and sends back a response containing a success/failure flag and an authenticated response based on:

   The sent challenge string
   The peer challenge string
   The encrypted response of the client
   The user's password

NOTE: MS-CHAP (versions 1 and 2) is the only authentication protocol included with Windows 2000 that allows users to change their passwords during the authentication process.

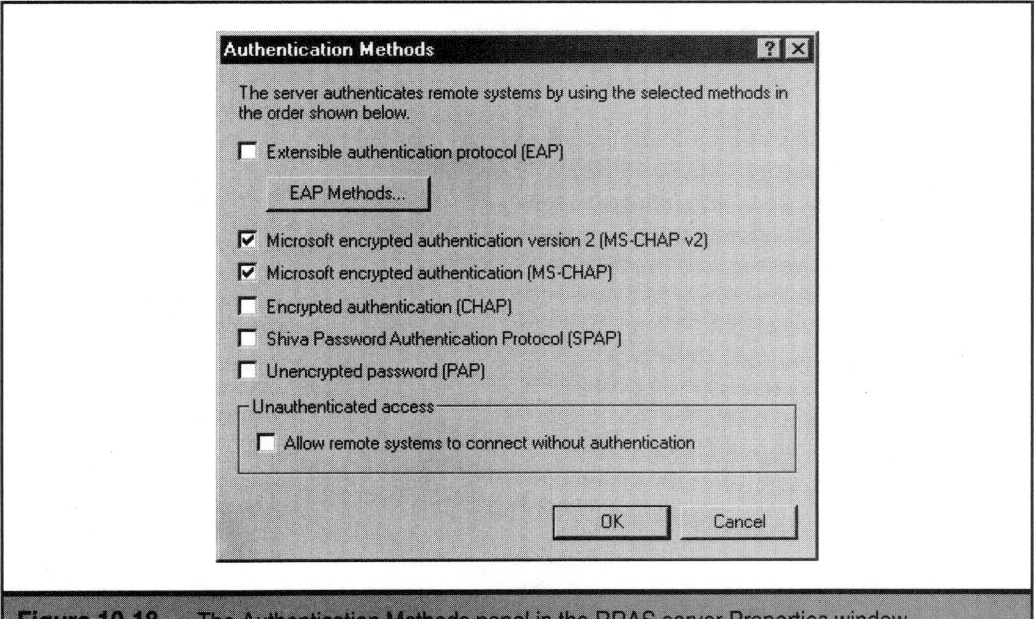

Figure 10-18. The Authentication Methods panel in the RRAS server Properties window

- **Microsoft encrypted authentication (MS-CHAP)** The Microsoft Challenge Handshake Authentication Protocol, or MS-CHAP, uses a Microsoft version of the MD4 algorithm, developed by RSA Inc. By using MS-CHAP, users can also elect to have all data encrypted as it travels over the network. Since MS-CHAP is a Microsoft-specific protocol, it is primarily used for communication and authentication between Microsoft clients and Microsoft servers.
- **Encrypted authentication (CHAP)** The Challenge Handshake Authentication Protocol, or CHAP, algorithm allows RAS clients to connect to virtually all third-party PPP servers. When a client attempts to connect to a PPP server that supports CHAP, the CHAP server sends a random challenge to the client. The client, using a special nonreversible encryption algorithm, encrypts the challenge with the user's password and sends it back to the server. Since the challenge sent by CHAP is random, it is not possible to record the session and play it back to gain access.
- **Shiva Password Authentication Protocol (SPAP)** The Shiva Password Authentication Protocol is a special version of PAP that is implemented by members of the Shiva family of clients and servers, such as the Shiva LAN Rover. SPAP is implemented as a reversible encryption algorithm that sends passwords in encrypted form. While more secure than PAP, it is not as secure as CHAP: The same user password is always sent in the same reversibly-encrypted form. This vulnerability in SPAP authentication allows a malicious person to capture a login session and use the information to log in themselves, but as the trusted user.
- **Unencrypted password (PAP)** The Password Authentication Protocol is the least sophisticated method of authenticating a RAS session. It uses clear text data transmission instead of any type of encryption. This means that usernames and passwords are sent unencrypted over the network. If someone were to capture your data stream with a network analyzer or packet sniffer, they could see both your username and your password! Although this is obviously not the recommended method of authentication, there are plenty of systems that require this method. For example, many SLIP and PPP servers do not support encrypted authentication and will therefore require using PAP instead.
- **Unauthenticated access** This protocol doesn't even ask for a password. Don't use it.

NOTE: Educating the users of a system about network security will markedly improve system safety. Remind users to choose strong passwords. All passwords should do the following:

- Exceed eight characters in length.
- Contain a mixture of uppercase and lowercase letters, numbers, and permitted punctuation symbols.
- Have no meaning. A password should not consist of any recognizable name, or any word that can be found in a dictionary in any language.
- Remain concealed, even to friends and coworkers. The strongest password a user can create is worthless if it's written on a Post-It note and stuck to the monitor.

Since different clients and servers will support different authentication protocols, sometimes you will have to experiment to find the most secure protocol supported in your current configuration. If you have a problem with a client authenticating with RRAS, try setting your authentication protocol permissions to "allow any" authentication protocol, down to and including clear text. If this solves your authentication problems, try increasing the level of authentication to reach the highest level that is supported by both systems.

When you're done examining the authentication methods available, click the OK or Cancel button to return to the Security tab, and then click the IP tab to display the settings shown in Figure 10-19.

In the IP tab, you can enable or disable IP routing, enable or disable IP-based remote access and demand dialing connection access, and choose between DHCP and static IP address pool assignment. Click the AppleTalk tab to display the settings shown in Figure 10-20.

The AppleTalk tab enables and disables AppleTalk routing: You can configure AppleTalk in the main RRAS window by selecting the AppleTalk Routing interface of the server and right-clicking to display the Properties for the protocol. Click the PPP tab to display the settings shown in Figure 10-21.

The PPP tab controls PPP options on a server level, allowing or disallowing multilink connections, link control protocol extension, and software compression of the connection. An individual PPP access policy, by contrast, affects which PPP options an individual user has access to. These server- and user-level settings work much like system and user variables in UNIX that affect all users on the system and a given single user respectively. Individual access policies may be defined in the Remote Access Policies section of the console tree for a given server in the Tree pane of the Routing and Remote Access administrative tool. Click the Event Logging tab to display the settings shown in Figure 10-22.

The Event Logging tab allows you to configure the level of event logging you feel appropriate. A log of events can be useful for analyzing system load and needed expansion, as well as for analyzing security breaches. If the server is acting as a PPP dial-up server, PPP

Figure 10-19. The IP tab of the RRAS server Properties window

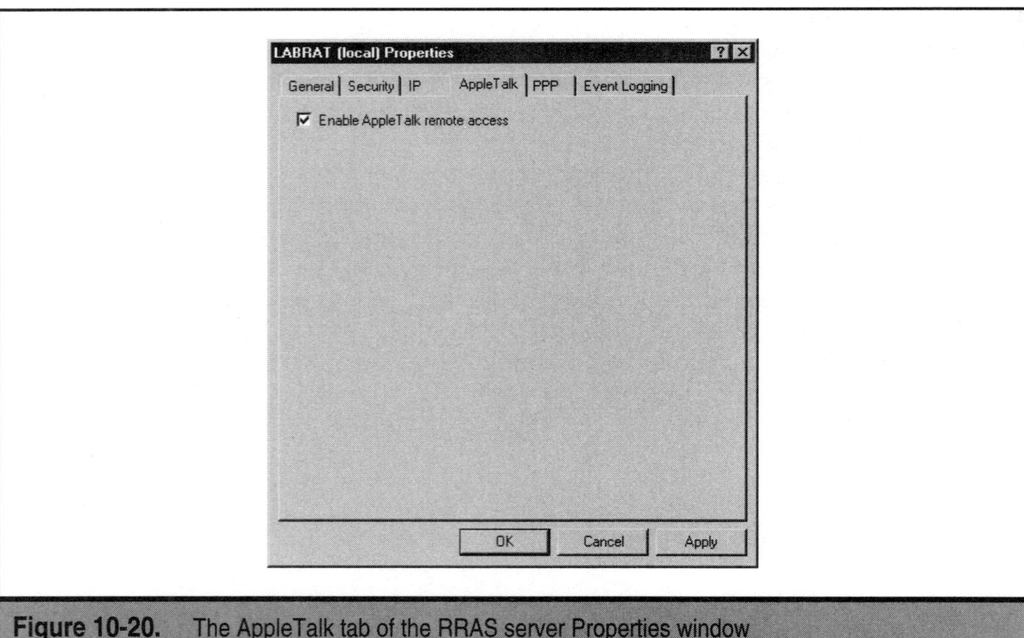

Figure 10-20. The AppleTalk tab of the RRAS server Properties window

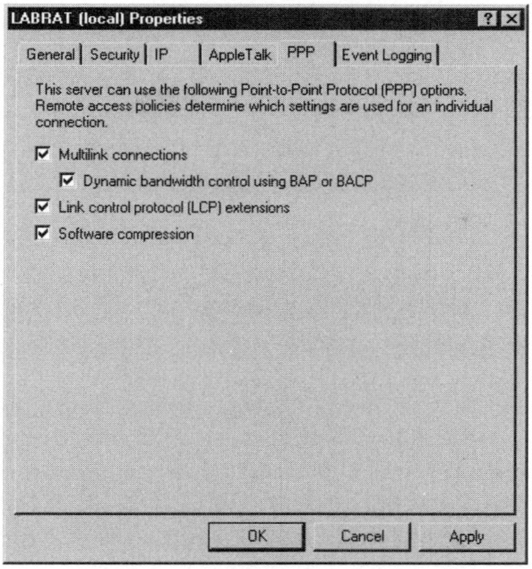

LABRAT (local) Properties

General | Security | IP | AppleTalk | PPP | Event Logging

This server can use the following Point-to-Point Protocol (PPP) options. Remote access policies determine which settings are used for an individual connection.

- [x] Multilink connections
  - [x] Dynamic bandwidth control using BAP or BACP
- [x] Link control protocol (LCP) extensions
- [x] Software compression

OK | Cancel | Apply

Figure 10-21. The PPP tab of the RRAS server Properties window

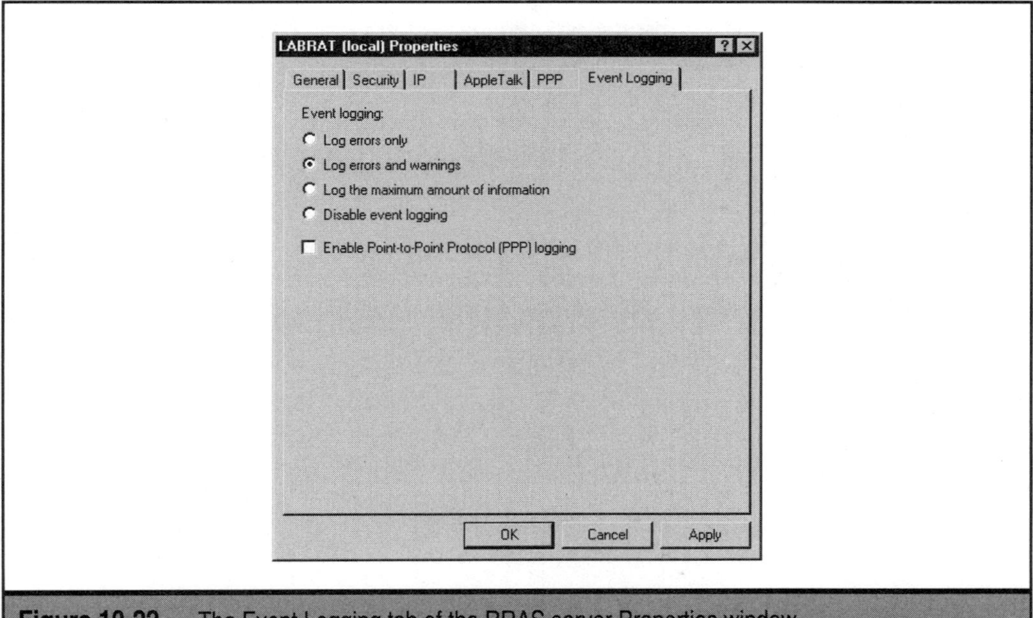

Figure 10-22. The Event Logging tab of the RRAS server Properties window

logging should be enabled, as PPP connections can be difficult to troubleshoot, even on a good day. Fortunately, like modem initialization, RAS provides logging of PPP sessions to help you solve the problem. To enable PPP logging, edit the Registry by setting the following entry to a value of 1:

\HKEY_LOCAL_MACHINE\SYSTEM\CurrentControlSet\Services\RasMan\PPP\Logging

The log file created when PPP logging is enabled is named PPP.LOG. Examine the PPP.LOG file and look for problems. Typical PPP connection problems can be traced to incorrect authentication protocols, or to the server requiring additional information to be sent. In the latter case, you may need to create a login script to automate the PPP login process.

Finally, remember that logs grow over time as the system is active, and you will need disk space for the expected size of the logs. You can limit the size of log files by configuring the log file as just described. It can also be reset daily, weekly, or monthly. By default, the log file is kept in the system root (boot drive:\\WINNT\system32 in most cases) \LogFiles directory. The file location is listed in the Remote Access Log folder.

SUMMARY

Microsoft Windows 2000 provides extensive capabilities for remote network connections in the form of its Routing and Remote Access Service, or RRAS. RRAS can operate as a dial-in server, providing connections to both NT- and non-NT-based computers, as well as connect to other systems as a client.

In this chapter, we've examined the capabilities of the Windows RAS client and RRAS server. We examined the various security protocols that are provided under RAS and the procedures involved in managing a RRAS server, with special focus on adding a dial-up connection with the Network Connection Wizard. Along the way, we also discussed how to troubleshoot problems that you might encounter when using RAS to make remote connections, either to Windows systems or to non-Windows systems such as UNIX. By using RAS and RRAS, you can integrate Windows 2000 into your existing environment, either in the role of a remote network client or as a network dial-in server.

CHAPTER 11

Microsoft Internet Information Server

Microsoft Internet Information Server (IIS) provides a range of servers—web (HTTP), FTP, and Gopher—for use with Windows. It comes with, and is tightly integrated with, Windows NT Server 4.0 software. More important, IIS 5.0 is installed on Windows 2000 Server by default. IIS works well with Microsoft BackOffice and comes with open database connectivity (ODBC) drivers for Microsoft SQL Server.

NOTE: IIS administration is a big topic. A single chapter certainly doesn't cover everything you may need—or want—to know. A number of books are devoted to the subject; you may want to pick up an IIS reference.

This chapter focuses on the web server (HTTP) portion of IIS, providing installation and configuration information. Although this chapter isn't intended to provide exhaustive coverage of the IIS web server and its configuration options, it will give you a feel for some of the issues involved.

To see if IIS is already installed on Windows NT 4, select Programs from the Start menu. If you see an Internet Information Server menu item, it's installed. An alternative test is to open the browser and enter the URL **http://localhost/iisHelp/** in the browser address bar. For your Windows 2000 system, click the Start button, then select Programs, then Administrative Tools, and look for the web services.

NOTE: IIS is installed by default on any fresh installation of Windows 2000. If the installation is an upgrade to Windows 2000, IIS 5.0 is installed by default only if IIS has been previously installed on the system.

If you need to install IIS, open the Control Panel and double-click Add/Remove Programs, then choose the Add/Remove Windows Components option, and then choose Internet Information Services.

Setting Up Windows 2000

The Windows Server must be configured to support IIS. This involves setting up the TCP/IP protocol and the Connectivity Utilities. Microsoft also recommends that:

- A DNS server be running somewhere on your intranet
- All drives used with IIS be formatted in NTFS format for better control of permissions than with FAT format file systems

Configuration

IIS is primarily configured using the Internet Service Manager. With it, you can control and configure almost any part of IIS.

To start ISM:

1. From the Start menu, select Programs | Administrative Tools | Internet Service Manager.
2. The Internet Service Manager window will appear, as shown in Figure 11-1.
3. Select the service you want to manage by double-clicking it.

NOTE: There is also an HTML version of the Internet Service Manager.

Remote Administration

Remote administration means controlling IIS on a machine other than the one you're sitting at. You must have Administrator privileges on the IIS machine to make changes.

Remote administration can be broken down into two types:

- Local network (LAN)
- Internet

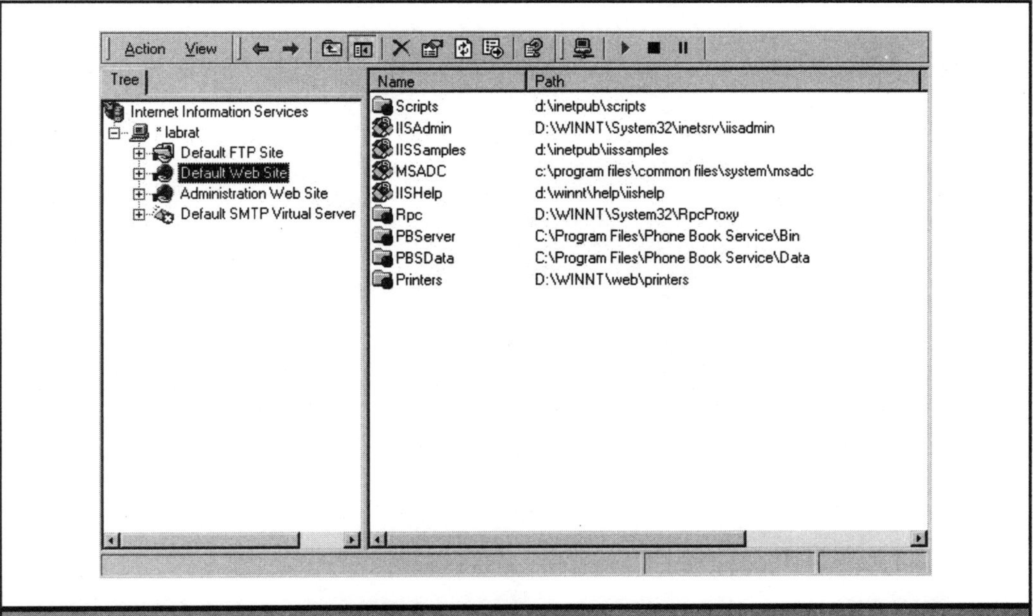

Figure 11-1. The Internet Service Manager provides extensive control of web services.

LOCAL NETWORK You can use the Internet Service Manager to control IIS over a network. This type of administration provides the same capabilities as administration on your local machine.

INTERNET What if you need to administer IIS from outside your local network? IIS 3.0 and above gives you the option of administering IIS from a web browser. Before connecting via your web browser, remember that to use remote administration, you must have Administrator privileges on the server you're connected to.

For example, you would connect with an URL such as this one:

http://*www.myserver.com*/iisadmin

where *www.myserver.com* would be replaced with the name of your server.

NOTE: The iisadmin directory is automatically created when you install the Internet Service Manager (HTML version).

Using the HTML version is similar to using the stand-alone version of Internet Service Manager. However, this type of remote administration relies on the password authentication setting of your web server. Because remote administration is always done through a secure communications channel, you must have Basic, Challenge/Response, or both selected. Otherwise, you won't be able to connect.

Password authentication is set in the Authentication Methods dialog:

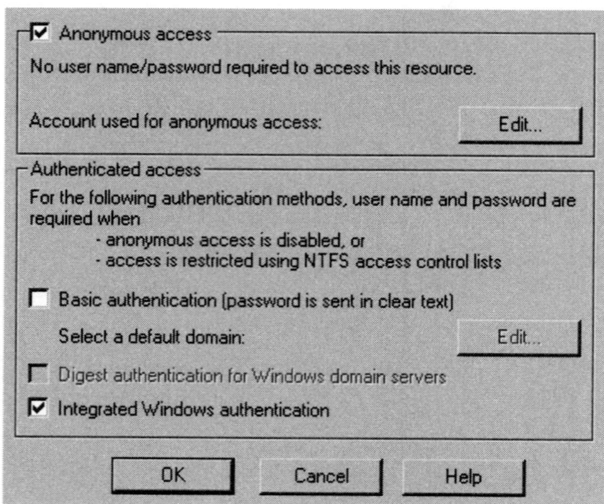

To reach the Authentication Methods dialog, open Internet Information Services, select the Directory Security tab, and then click the Edit button to display the Authentication Methods window.

CONFIGURATION OPTIONS

This section discusses a selection of configurations you may elect to make to your server. Although it is not intended to be comprehensive, it does give you an idea of the types of configurations you can make.

IIS Add-Ins

The following are some of the IIS components you can install for use with your IIS web server. Because each component is independent of the other pieces and has its own installation, you can install any or all of them.

Active Server Pages (ASP)

Active Server Pages (ASP) is a specification that allows HTML authors to create server-side programs that are translated into HTML before they are served to a browser. Pages are based on ActiveX and rely on VBScript or JScript as the scripting language. Other scripting languages (such as Perl, REXX, and Python) can be added by modifying the Registry key HKEY_ LOCAL_MACHINE\SYSTEM\CurrentControlSet\Services\W3SVC\ASP.

The primary language used (VBScript by default) can be changed by setting the HKEY_LOCAL_MACHINE\SYSTEM\CurrentControlSet\Services\W3SVC\ASP\ Parameters key (DefaultScriptLanguage value) to the name of the language you want to use.

CAUTION: Editing the Registry incorrectly can cause serious problems, including corruption, which may make it necessary to reinstall Windows NT or ASP.

For more information, see Microsoft's ASP FAQ at **http://support.microsoft.com/support/IIS/FAQ/Active/Custom/faq100.asp**.

Internet Server Application Programming Interface (ISAPI)

The Internet Server Application Programming Interface (ISAPI) is a Microsoft specification for writing applications and tools for an IIS environment. The API enables programmers to create two types of programs: extension DLLs and ISAPI filters.

- Extension DLLs are designed to extend the capabilities of the base IIS web server. They are roughly equivalent to regular CGI scripts. No special configuration is needed to run them; just put the files in the /Scripts or similar directory.
- ISAPI filters are also DLLs. However, unlike extension DLLs (or CGIs), filters are called for every URL, regardless of the contents. They allow programmers to create programs that sit between the web server and the Internet/intranet connection. When a filter is loaded, it tells the web server what type of events

it wants to process. This is useful for such activities as logging, compression, custom authentication schemes, and encryption.

NOTE: To add new ISAPI filters, you will need to add them to the HKEY_LOCAL_MACHINE/SYSTEM/CurrentControlSet/Services/W3SVC/Parameters Registry key (Filter DLLs value) and restart your system.

ISAPI (and a similar API for Netscape, NSAPI) is an alternative to CGI programs and offers its own set of advantages and disadvantages. ISAPI tends to be faster than CGI. However, disadvantages include the fact that ISAPI isn't widely supported outside of Microsoft. Also, if the ISAPI DLL crashes, it could also crash the Windows 2000 Server that IIS is running on.

Common Gateway Interface (CGI)

The Common Gateway Interface (CGI) is a specification that determines how servers communicate to a script or program and how a script or program formats its reply for use by the server. CGI itself is not a language; it describes a protocol that can be used to write programs for use with a web server. CGI scripts allow people to write simple applications in any number of languages. Scripts run on a web server and can produce output in a user's web browser. User input is passed in through environment variables or standard input, the program does whatever it was designed to do, and it sends HTML back through standard output. This simple design, combined with languages like Perl and TCL, makes CGIs very easy to develop. Alternatives to CGI include ISAPI and NSAPI (described earlier in this chapter).

As far as server configuration issues are concerned, CGI scripts can be executed out of a server root directory specified as the /Scripts directory without any special configuration. However, access to this directory is usually restricted.

CAUTION: All CGI programs, both scripted and compiled, are potentially insecure. The level of security required for a site varies widely. Some sites require users to submit their script or program to a webmaster, who checks that the code doesn't contain security holes before it can be used. Other sites restrict CGI access to trusted users, who are responsible for checking their own code.

IIS expects script to be in the /Scripts directory by default. This name is an alias for a physical directory you specify with the Internet Service Manager. The physical directory must be on an NTFS disk.

NOTE: If you are porting UNIX CGIs to Windows NT, you will find that there are a number of similarities among functions. Functions such as open(), fopen(), read(), and write() are available in the C runtime library of most Win32 C compilers. Also, there is a one-to-one mapping of several UNIX APIs to Win32 APIs, for example, read() to ReadFile(), write() to WriteFile(), open() to CreateFile(), close() to CloseFile().

Script Languages

A CGI program can be written in pretty much any language. Some of these are listed here:

Language	Download Site(s)
Python	http://www.python.org/
Object REXX	http://www.software.ibm.com/ad/obj-rexx/
TCL/TK	http://www.scriptics.com/

The following capabilities are needed for CGIs:

- Ability to create 32-bit programs. (Due to Windows NT's memory requirements, the IIS web server only works with 32-bit CGIs.)
- Ability to access environment information variables
- Ability to access command line parameters

NOTE: IIS doesn't support WinCGI. WinCGI is an interface specification for running CGI on Windows platforms. WinCGI is supported on other Windows NT web servers, such as Netscape.

Server Side Includes (SSI)

Server-side includes (SSIs) allow HTML authors to direct the web server to perform some type of processing on the HTML file before it is returned to a browser. HTML files that use the #include statement must use the STM filename extension instead of HTML. For example, an appropriate filename would be report.STM instead of report.HTML. To change the default extension, .STM, change the value of the Registry key HKEY_LOCAL_MACHINE/SYSTEM/CurrentControlSet/Services/W3SVC/Parameters/ServerSideIncludesExtension.

CAUTION: Using SSIs can compromise website performance. Each file is scanned by the web server for SSI directives before it is sent to the browser.

Image Maps

Image maps are pictures that allow users to access different documents by clicking different areas of an image. IIS uses standard CERN or NCSA map file formats.

There are two distinct types of image maps: server-side and client-side. Server-side image maps are processed by the web server and require some web server processing. Client-side image maps are processed by the user's browser and don't require any web server configuration or processing. However, client-side image maps are not supported by older browsers, which will simply ignore the coordinates.

NOTE: MapEdit (**http://www.boutell.com/mapedit/**) is a good shareware program for creating map files.

Virtual Servers

A *virtual server* enables you to have multiple domain names on a single computer. Such an arrangement is also known as *multi-homing* or *multi-homed servers.* For example, say you wanted to have your internal intranet and your external Internet websites on the same physical workstation. To do this, you could set up a regular server for one site, and a virtual server for the other site. Although they are on the same machine, the URLs for these sites would be different, as shown here:

http://www.imanexample.com
http://web.imanexample.com

To set up a virtual server, follow these steps:

1. Assign a static IP address for each web server.
2. Bind each IP address to your server's network card.
3. Change your DNS server so that it can route the addresses of the virtual server(s).
4. Set up IIS to handle the virtual server directories.

Virtual Directories

When you set up a server, you specify a home directory. For the server to access files, they must be in subdirectories of the home directory. Virtual directories give you a way to get around this. They essentially allow you to specify an alias for a path, which appears to users to be on your server. IIS provides virtual directory support for web, Gopher, and FTP servers.

Secure Transactions—SSL

The Secure Sockets Layer (SSL) is a security protocol designed to ensure data moving between a browser and a server remains private. In theory, someone could intercept information—such as a credit card number—while it is in transit between the browser and the server. One solution to prevent information from being usable if it is intercepted is to encrypt it. The most widely implemented encryption system for the web at present is a protocol known as the Secure Sockets Layer (SSL).

The IIS web server supports SSL. However, there are several steps involved in enabling this support. Here's a general list of what you'll need to do:

1. Generate a key pair file and a request file using the Internet Service Manager Key Manager or the keygen program.

2. Request an SSL certificate from VeriSign, Inc. See their website at **http://www.verisign.com**.
3. Install the certificate in IIS using the Key Manager or the setkey program.
4. Enable SSL on the server by using the Internet Service Manager to select the directories you want to secure, and setting the Require Secure SSL Channel option.

Entrust also issues temporary security certificates. Here's how you can request a temporary security certificate for testing purposes if you use Netscape Enterprise Server:

1. Start Netscape Administrator for your server.
2. Click the Keys & Certificates button to go to Keys and Certificates.
3. Click Request Certificate.
4. Complete the requested information:
   - Enter your name as the certificate authority.
   - Click New Certificate for a new secure site.
   - Enter the password for the server certificate, the common name, and the company information, and then click OK. The certificate request will be displayed on the screen.
5. Open a new browser window and go to **http://freecerts.entrust.com/webcerts/**.
6. Click Request a Web Server Certificate.
7. In the next window, enter the requested information (name, e-mail address, server name).
8. Copy the certificate request from Netscape Administration from "---Begin" to "Request---" and paste the certificate request into the appropriate field on the form.
9. Click Submit. The certificate will be displayed on the screen.
10. Copy from "---Begin" to "Certificate---."
11. In the Netscape Administration window, click Install Certificate, and then click Certificate From This Server.
12. Enter the certificate name, and in the message text field paste the text you copied from the Entrust window (if there are spaces at the beginning of lines, delete them so that the lines are all flush left in the message text field), and then click OK.
13. Shut down and restart the virtual server you've just added the certificate to.

Certificates from Entrust are valid for 60 days. When the certificate expires, the server for the user group will not run.

MIME Types

The web allows you to publish information in many different formats. Each format type has its own MIME (Multipurpose Internet Mail Extensions) type.

NOTE: In Apache, MIME types are added to the file named mime.types.

Adding a new MIME type to IIS used to involve editing the Registry with the Registry Editor, but thankfully that technique is no longer required. Now adding a new MIME type is easier: Open Internet Information Services, select the Administration website, and right-click the selected icon. Choose the Properties command to display the Properties dialog, and then click the HTTP Headers tab. Click the File Types button on the HTTP Headers tab to display the File Types dialog:

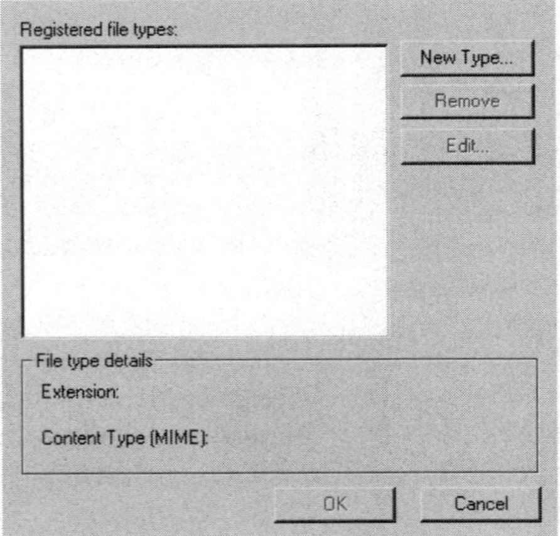

This is where you'll add your new MIME type.

MAINTENANCE

Maintenance is the ongoing process of tweaking the web server after its initial installation and configuration. It consists of tasks such as tuning performance, starting and stopping the server, monitoring files such as the error and access logs, and generating usage statistics for your website(s). Some general maintenance tips include these:

- *Back up your web documents frequently.* You might also consider putting them in a version control system.

- *Keep an eye on the size of the log files.* The busier your web server is, the faster they will grow in size.
- *Log as little information as possible.* Turn DNS lookup off and do lookups later with a script. Log referrer URLs sparingly, if you need to know the origin of a consistent bad file request in the error logs, for example. There are search engines, such as Digital's AltaVista, that can tell you who's linking to you.
- *Scan your access and error log files regularly.* Signs of suspicious activity might involve system commands or repeated attempts to access a password-protected document. Extremely long URL requests can indicate an attempt to overrun a program's input buffer.

Starting and Stopping Servers

In IIS, the various Internet servers run as servers under Windows. To start and stop any of these services (HTTP, FTP, Gopher, Index Server, and so on), you can use either the Internet Information Services or the Services applet.

Log Files and Reports

Log files give you a record of every event that has occurred with your server. To turn this raw information into a more usable form, you run a report.

IIS log files can be in either text or database format. You can run reports from commercial tools, such as Crystal Reports, or create your own reporting tools and log formatting programs.

Log files give you a record of every event that has occurred with your web server. IIS gives you the option of logging to either a file or an SQL/ODBC-compliant database. Reports allow you to derive meaningful information from your web server logs. You can run custom reports from log information stored in databases, or use other reporting tools. Sources for log analysis tools include Yahoo, at **http://dir.yahoo.com/Computers_and_Internet/Software/Internet/World_Wide_Web/Servers/Log_Analysis_Tools/**, and WebReference, at **http://www.webreference.com/internet/software/usage.html**.

Performance Monitoring

The Performance Monitor is a standard Windows 2000 tool for tracking the status of various system resources. It enables you to monitor your system as it is being used and is useful when you need to determine where system performance is being affected.

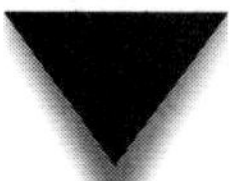

TIP: To check the status of your connections, display information about the protocol being used, or display the port number used on the local machine. The netstat command-line program is also useful.

To start the Performance Monitor:

1. Select Start | Programs | Administrative Tools (Common) | Performance.
2. The Performance window appears, as shown in Figure 11-2.

Like any service, the Performance Monitor can have an impact on your system performance. Like any other program, it uses system resources such as memory and CPU cycles.

Security

Security is a very broad and important topic. In no way is this section a comprehensive treatment. It does, however, suggest some of the issues you may want to consider.

General Considerations

Site security typically includes a combination of firewalls and solid internal network security. This is a fairly common layered security approach. In theory, either method alone should protect your site; however, reality tends to do nasty things to theories.

A comprehensive approach to protecting a website generally means following best practices in a number of different areas. The International Computer Security Association (ICSA) is in the process of planning a certification process for websites that touches on a number of these areas. See the ICSA at **http://www.icsa.net/html/certification/** for more details.

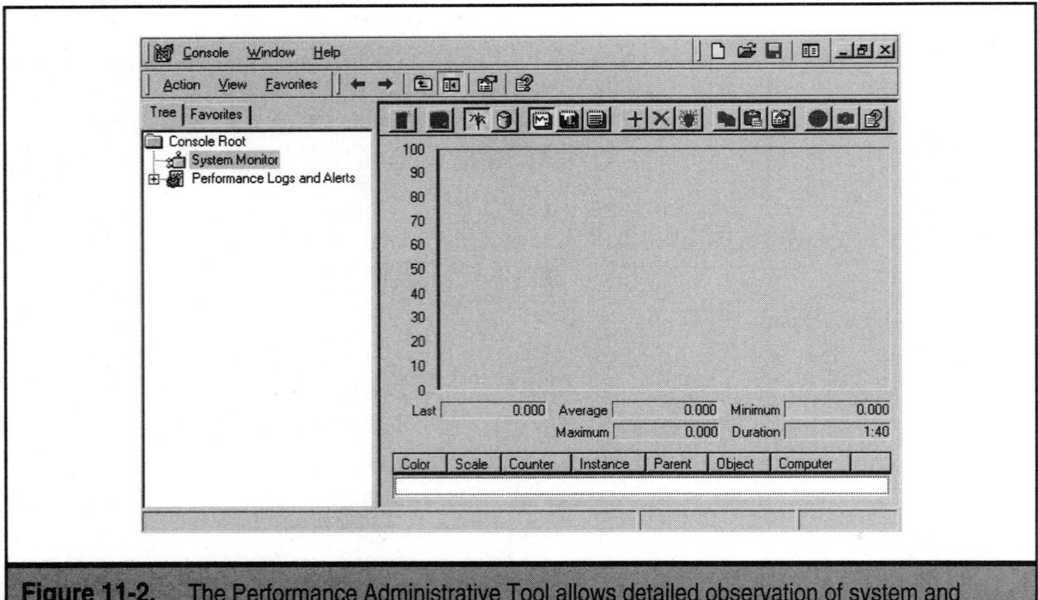

Figure 11-2. The Performance Administrative Tool allows detailed observation of system and server activity.

NOTE: You may also want to take a look at RFC1244, the Site Security Handbook—available at **http://www.net.ohio-state.edu/hypertext/rfc1244/toc.html**—for more information.

The guidelines being developed by ICSA are intended to ensure a basic level of security, rather than a hacker-proof one. They set minimum standards for logical and physical security issues that address such issues as hacking, intrusion, data loss, and tampering. Although these guidelines may be more or less stringent than your site's needs, they can certainly be used as a starting point for developing your own security guidelines. A summary of the ICSA guidelines for a single-server site is as follows:

- The website must withstand network-based attacks by means of a firewall, filtering router, or other appropriate security mechanism.
- The Domain Name Service (DNS) entries for all URL-referenced systems must be resolvable.
- NIC handles must be authenticated, and the NIC contact information must be accurate and contain at least two contacts.
- The site must maintain logging. Access to logs must be limited to authorized personnel. Logs must be retained in a secure but retrievable format.
- A standard encryption mechanism, such as SSL or SHTTP, must be used for sensitive data transmission.
- CGI scripts and programs must be checked to ensure that they don't intentionally or unintentionally compromise your system.
- A person must be designated as the site's client executable (CxE) Evaluator. All client executables must be examined and evaluated as "harmless" to the user.
- Pages that contain or accept sensitive data must be made non-cacheable. Users must be informed if any pages containing sensitive data will be cached to local storage.
- The site must meet physical security requirements, such as access-controlled areas, a roster of authorized personnel, suitable equipment, and emergency contact information.
- The site must meet logical security requirements, such as secure password policies, webmaster contact, HTTPD server configured for least privilege, and separate development and production systems.
- If a transaction mechanism is in place, it must be documented, and the server's private key protected by a strong pass-phrase. Sensitive information must be periodically removed from the server. The OS and platform must be documented and integrity assured. Backup and restore capabilities must be in place.

Specific Considerations

The following are some specific suggestions you might consider for a Windows-based web server. Although this list isn't intended to be all-inclusive, it does give you an idea of issues you may want to consider. For more suggestions, see the Windows Security Issues at **http://www.somarsoft.com/** and the WWW Security FAQ at **http://www.w3.org/Security/Faq/wwwsf1.html**.

Use the NT File System (NTFS) as your file system. NTFS allows you to limit access to files and directories for individual users and also at the group level. Here's how to set access permissions for a directory or file:

1. In Windows NT Explorer, select a directory or file you want to secure.
2. On the File menu, select Properties.
3. On the Security property sheet, click Permissions.
4. In the Directory Permissions dialog box, click Add to add users and groups.
5. In the Add Users and Groups dialog box, select a computer (or domain) from the List Names From list box.
6. In the Names box, select a user or group that you want to grant access to your file or directory.

NOTE: The default access settings for NTFS directories and files grants Full Control access to the Everyone user group, which includes all users. This means that all users have permission to modify, move, and delete files or directories, and to change NTFS permissions.

7. From the Type of Access list box, set the access permission level for the selected user or group.
8. Click OK.

NOTE: If there are conflicts between your NTFS and web server permissions, the most restrictive settings will be used. This means that permissions that explicitly deny access will always take precedence over those permissions that grant access.

Some of the other points to note to further secure a Windows server include:

- Check permissions on network shares.
- Disable file mappings for .bat and .cmd.
- Enable auditing. For websites connected to the Internet, the events to look at are Logon and Logoff, and File and Object Access for users logged on as IUSR.
- Run only the services and protocols required by your system.

- Don't overlook the built-in guest account. If you set up an FTP server, anyone can log into the guest account by entering any name/any password. Fix this by disabling the guest account under User Admin.
- Run any HTTP servers, such as IIS, under an ordinary user account rather than the System account.
- Ensure that remote Registry access is disabled except for administrators. In Windows NT Server 4.0, the HKEY_LOCAL_MACHINE\SYSTEM\CurrentControlSet\Control\SecurePipeServers\winreg key is installed by default. If remote Registry access is enabled, a user can change the Registry of any workstation or server on which the user has an account. Usually, this means all servers in a domain environment, or on which the guest account is enabled.

NOTE: The key to disable remote access on NT 4.0 workstations is not installed by default, but it can be added.

OTHER WINDOWS SERVERS

IIS isn't the only Windows web server available. However, it is, like Apache under UNIX, one of the most widely used Windows NT web servers, and the default IIS installed base should almost exactly parallel Windows 2000 Server. See NetCraft's web server survey at **http://www.netcraft.com/survey** for current statistics. As with UNIX, a number of commercial and free web servers are available. WebCompare at **http://webcompare.internet.com/compare/chart.html** provides comparison information for a number of commercial and noncommercial web servers. Want more? Yahoo lists a number of Windows NT HTTP servers at **http://dir.yahoo.com/Computers_and_Internet/Software/Internet/World_Wide_Web/Servers/Windows_NT**. Among the available web servers for Windows (NT as of this writing, and probably Windows 2000 at some point) is a port of the Apache web server. Apache is covered in more detail in Chapter 12.

For example, Netscape's Enterprise Server provides a document-sharing system to control who edits files and when. Enterprise also includes a feature called AutoCatalog, which lists HTML documents by author, modification date, and popularity. Enterprise comes with some powerful web tools, including Verity's topicSearch search engine and a server configuration–saving feature that gets your site running again if modifications make it crash. Enterprise also provides ODBC links via Netscape LiveWire engines. Netscape's FastTrack is nearly as fast as IIS, and maybe even faster with fewer than 12 clients. It takes a broad approach by including ODBC, web authoring tools such as Navigator Gold, and extremely simple remote site management via any frame- and Java- compliant browser. Although it's easy to use, however, FastTrack might not have everything you're looking for. For example, it lacks Enterprise's configuration and document- management tools.

SUMMARY

Microsoft's Internet Information Server provides an integrated environment for web services under Windows. It is a fairly easy system to install, configure, and manage. In this chapter, we looked at the various components that make up IIS, including several optional add-ons. We examined the installation and configuration process and looked at the various issues that you will face when managing an IIS system. Since IIS 5.0 is included with Windows 2000 Server, it is an obvious choice for a web server tool if you decide to use Windows Server as your server platform.

CHAPTER 12

UNIX Web Servers

Web growth over the past few years has been tremendous. As a result, web server applications are a very common type of server application on both UNIX and Windows. If you are an experienced Windows administrator who must also administer UNIX systems, you will probably encounter a UNIX-based web server before long. Unlike many Windows web servers—such as Microsoft IIS—which tend to be configurable through a GUI, many UNIX web servers are configured and administered via variables in configuration files.

NOTE: Although not covered in this chapter, Netscape's web server configuration is more GUI-based than Apache's.

In the UNIX world, there are a variety of web servers available. However, one of the most widely used web servers is the Apache server. In fact, Apache is one of the most popular web servers even when compared to those running under all other operating systems. Among other operating systems, both the Red Hat distribution of Linux and Apple's Mac OS X Server ship with Apache, as does Solaris 8.

Since web servers are very common UNIX applications, you are very likely to run into an Apache web server if you do any serious UNIX administration. It would be impossible to cover all the details of all the different UNIX web servers that you might encounter in a single chapter. So in the interest of providing practical information, we will discuss the Apache web server in some detail.

WEB GROWTH

As you've probably heard (and experienced), the growth of the World Wide Web (WWW) has been phenomenal. Access to the web really is worldwide: web servers and websites are found in several hundred countries on all seven continents. You can find information available on almost any subject imaginable (and some you probably never thought of!). Companies, universities, governments, states, cities, schools, hospitals, museums, clubs, and individuals all maintain websites. The AltaVista search engine (**http://www.altavista.com/**) alone reports that its robot has indexed over 31 million web pages on over 476,000 servers. And these figures don't include all the web servers and web pages contained within private intranets throughout the world!

Web servers have thus had a growth explosion. Just a few years ago, there were roughly a dozen or so web servers. All were products of experimentation or research. Now, there are multitudes of web servers. Although many are commercial, many free web servers—such as Apache—continue to be developed, supported, and used. Just how many different types of web servers are out there? Well, that depends on the platform that you're on.

TIP: See WebCompare (**http://webcompare.internet.com/cgi-bin/quickcompare.pl**) for a listing of web server software, platforms supported, and price.

As for the operating system of choice, UNIX currently holds the lead. Surveys show that UNIX is the most used web server platform. This isn't surprising, as the Internet cut its teeth on UNIX, which has a reputation for being a robust, highly scalable, and flexible operating system that provides an excellent price-to-performance ratio.

Though UNIX still holds the lead, Windows has moved into the web server market. Microsoft is aggressively pursuing the UNIX market, citing Windows' increased scalability, performance, and reliability. Microsoft has also set out to provide integrated software solutions, from website creation to hosting and development. Some UNIX vendors, such as SunSoft (**http://www.sunsoft.com**) and SCO (**http://www.sco.com**), have also begun to offer more integrated software solutions.

When it comes to web server software, the numbers aren't quite as clear-cut. A survey done in December 1999 by NetCraft (**http://www.netcraft.com/Survey/**) shows the top overall web servers as being Apache, Microsoft's IIS, and Netscape. The top seven are listed here:

Server	Percentage of Total Users
Apache	54.49
Microsoft-IIS	23.78
Netscape-Enterprise	7.02
Zeus	2.07
Thttpd	2.07
Rapidsite	1.91
CnG	1.27

Your selection of a web server (and an operating system) is likely to be influenced by a number of factors. For example, a commercial website that offers online purchasing or access to confidential information usually has different requirements from a site providing local television listings or an internal corporate site that is isolated from the outside Internet.

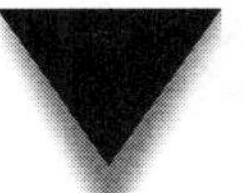

NOTE: Some NetCraft figures are a compilation of multiple web server products offered by the same company. For example, the figure for Netscape is the sum of sites running Netscape-Enterprise, Netscape-FastTrack, Netscape-Commerce, Netscape-Communications, Netsite-Commerce, and Netsite-Communications. That for Microsoft is the sum of sites running Microsoft-IIS, Microsoft-IIS-W, Microsoft-PWS-95, and Microsoft-PWS.

WHY APACHE?

You have a number of UNIX web servers to choose from, both commercial and free. Apache was selected for this chapter because of its widespread use. According to the NetCraft Web Server Survey (**http://www.netcraft.com/survey/**), Apache has consistently been the most frequently used web server, found in roughly 55 percent of total sites surveyed. By comparison, the combined total of the other top web servers—from Microsoft and Netscape—is roughly 30 percent of the sites in the same survey.

SECURE TRANSACTIONS

Before we go any further, we should talk a little about secure transactions. Most of the information transmitted over the Internet is general web surfing—reading general information, window shopping—and as such, isn't particularly confidential. However, at times you may want to safeguard certain information.

For example, consider a current hot topic: credit card numbers on the Internet. When you place an order for goods or services from a website and enter a credit card number, the credit card number is transmitted across the Internet from the browser to the server. In theory, someone could intercept this information while it is in transit. One solution to prevent information from being usable if it is intercepted is to encrypt it. A good encryption scheme effectively scrambles the information and resists *cracking* (unscrambling by people who have no business seeing the information in the first place). The most widely implemented encryption system for the web at present is SSL (Secure Sockets Layer).

SSL is an open, nonproprietary protocol developed by Netscape Communications. It uses industry-accepted RSA public key cryptography for authentication and encryption. The SSL protocol was designed to provide a data security layer between TCP/IP and application protocols such as HTTP, Telnet, NNTP, or FTP. SSL provides data encryption, server authentication, message integrity, and optional client authentication for a TCP/IP connection.

CAUTION: Because SSL data transport requires encryption, you may find that there are government-imposed restrictions on its use. Many governments—including the United States—have restrictions on the import, export, and use of encryption technology.

A number of commercial web servers support SSL: several Netscape servers (**http://www.iplanet.com/products/infrastructure/web_servers/index.html**) and IBM's HTTP (based on Apache, **http://www-4.ibm.com/software/webservers/httpservers/**), to name a few. Although Apache itself doesn't support SSL, there is an Apache web server variant, called Stronghold, that does. Stronghold was formerly known as Apache SSL-US and is available for both UNIX and Windows from UK Web (**http://www.c2.net**). Covalent also provides a commercial Apache module to include SSL support from **http://www.covalent.net/raven/ssl/**. SSL web servers require some additional steps that are not necessary for other types of web servers. Most notably, you must generate a public/private key pair, and register with a Certificate Authority such as Verisign. Although

Stronghold is similar to Apache, this chapter does not address Stronghold installation and configuration.

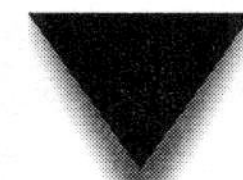

CAUTION: Some server configurations may suffer as much as a fifty-fold degradation in performance from incorporating SSL, down to just a few transactions per second. Testing capacity is critical if you are adding SSL capability, and load balancing solutions may also be needed to provide satisfactory performance versus non-SSL web server performance.

SETTING UP A WEB SERVER

UNIX web servers in general and Apache specifically are typically configured using configuration files. These files contain directives that control basic settings such as the server name and the directory locations of files such as the error log. In contrast, Windows web servers, such as IIS and WebSite, are configured using a series of dialog boxes and wizards. A mixture of the two methods, the Netscape family of servers is configured via HTML forms but maintain data in configuration files.

In general, setting up a web server involves the following steps:

1. Get the software.
2. Install the software.
3. Compile the software to create a web server. (Skip this step if you have a binary for your system.)
4. Configure the web server.
5. Run the web server.
6. Maintain the web server.

Getting the Software

You can get Apache from a number of different sources. You can download the latest release from the Apache website (**http://www.apache.org/**). You will also find a version of Apache on the CD-ROM included with this book.

If you download a binary distribution, you can go on to the "Installing Apache" section; otherwise, you will need to compile the source on your workstation.

Installing Apache

To install Apache, follow these steps:

1. Copy the source code package to a part of your file system. Free-space requirements vary among the different operating systems, and with the specific options you want to include in your software. A general figure would be around 15MB of free space.

2. Unpack the software. This will create a directory called apache_1.3_9/. Within this directory, go to the src/ subdirectory. A sample set of commands might look like this:

```
gunzip apache_1_3_9.tar.gz
tar -xvf apache_1_3_9.tar
cd src
```

Compiling Apache

Apache is known to compile on just about every UNIX variant: AIX, SunOS 4.1.*x*, Solaris 2.*x*, Linux, FreeBSD/OpenBSDI/NetBSD/BSDI, HP-UX, Ultrix, SCO, SGI Irix 5.*x* and 6.*x*, DEC OSF1, NeXT, Apple A/UX, UTS, UnixWare, Sequent, Apollo Domain/OS, QNX, Mac OS X, and probably a few that haven't been tried yet. There's a port to OS/2, and a Windows NT port is available (although you are warned that "Apache on NT has not yet been optimized for performance. Apache still performs best, and is most reliable on Unix platforms. Over time we will improve NT performance").

If you have downloaded a binary for your system, you won't have to go through these steps; they have already been done for you. However, if you want to modify the functionality of your web server, you will need to recompile a new web server.

Compiling Apache is pretty straightforward:

1. Customize the Configuration file for your installation. In most cases, you should be able to skip this step: the configuration program has some intelligence built into it for detecting the platform and compiler on your system. If you have problems (that is, you get error messages after running Configure), or know there are specific configuration changes you'd like to make (such as modules), you'll need to hand-edit this file. Run the Configure script. Run make.
2. After make finishes, you should have a web server executable called httpd in the Apache src/ directory. You're now ready for the next step, which is configuring the web server behavior. (See "Configuring Apache" later in this chapter.)

The rest of this section gives you more details on the Configuration file, the Configure script, make, and modules.

The Configuration File

The Configuration file is located in the Apache src/ directory and is used by the Configure script to create a MakeFile. (See the "Modules" section in this chapter for information about the default modules included with Apache.)

Should you decide to edit the Configuration file by hand, the following are some of the main variables you should consider setting:

- Specify which C compiler you're using (probably gcc).
- Uncomment the configuration for your operating system (including appropriate settings for the AUX_CFLAGS and AUX_LIBS variables).
- Modify the modules to be compiled as needed. (See the "Modules" section for more information.)

The Configure Script

This file doesn't need any configuration; all you need to do is run it. The Configure script is a simple Bourne shell script that takes the Configuration file and creates two files—MakeFile and modules.c. The MakeFile created will be specifically targeted to your platform, with any necessary runtime defines set, and with any modules you've chosen compiled together. It also creates modules.c, which contains information about which modules to link together at compilation time.

The make Script

As with Configure, all you have to do with make is run it. After it finishes, you should have an executable program in your Apache src/ directory called httpd. This file, httpd, is your web server program. At this point, you're ready to begin the server configuration. (See "Configuring Apache" later in this chapter.)

Modules

Apache has a *modular architecture*, which makes it possible for you to add or remove web server functionality without a lot of hassle. Most of the code that comes as part of an Apache distribution is in the form of modules. This gives you a great deal of flexibility in customizing the functionality of your web server, especially as your web server needs change over time.

Here are some important points to keep in mind when selecting modules:

- The more modules included in the build, the more memory the compiled server will use.
- Module placement is important: modules are listed in the Configuration file in reverse priority order. Later modules can override the behavior of those that come earlier.
- Some modules are mutually exclusive.
- Some modules require extra linking.
- Apache 1.3 supports HTTP/1.1. For this reason, some older modules that process input via POST or PUT methods may not work correctly.

NOTE: The HTTP/1.1 standard offers speed enhancements over HTTP/1.0 and new features such as host name identification, content negotiation, persistent connections, chunked transfers, byte ranges, and support for proxies and caches. You can learn more by looking at RFC2068, the HTTP/1.1 standard (**http://www.ics.uci.edu/pub/ietf/http/rfc2068.txt**), or reviewing W3C's set of overviews (**http://www.w3.org/pub/WWW/Protocols/Overview.html**).

THE DEFAULT MODULES Modules packaged with your distribution are listed near the end of the Configuration file, which is located in the Apache src/ directory. Unless there are specific changes you know you need to make, it's easiest to use the default settings. Following is an example listing of modules included in a default Configuration file. Module descriptions are provided with the Apache distribution. They are in HTML and are located in the Apache htdocs/manual/mod/ directory.

NOTE: The following example is from the Configuration file for the Apache version 1.3.9 distribution on the CD-ROM.

```
#################################################################
# Module configuration
#
# Modules are listed in reverse priority order --- the ones that come
# later can override the behavior of those that come earlier.  This
# can have visible effects; for instance, if UserDir followed Alias,
# you couldn't alias out a particular user's home directory.

# The configuration below is what we consider a decent default
# configuration.  If you want the functionality provided by a
# particular module, remove the "#" sign at the beginning of the line.
# But remember, the more modules you compile into the server, the
# larger the executable is and the more memory it will take, so if
# you are unlikely to use the functionality of a particular module
# you might wish to leave it out.
##
## Config manipulation modules
##
## mod_env sets up additional or restricted environment variables to
## be passed to CGI/SSI scripts.  It is listed first (lowest priority)
## since it does not do per-request stuff.

Module env_module          mod_env.o

## mod_dld defines commands that allow other modules to be loaded
## dynamically (at runtime).  This module is for experimental use.
## only.
```

```
# Module dld_module          mod_dld.o

##
## Request logging modules
##

Module config_log_module   mod_log_config.o

## Optional modules for NCSA user-agent/referer logging compatibility
## We recommend, however, that you just use the configurable
## access_log.

# Module agent_log_module    mod_log_agent.o
# Module referer_log_module  mod_log_referer.o

##
## Type checking modules
##
## mod_mime maps filename extensions to content types, encodings,
## and magic type handlers (the latter is obsoleted by mod_actions).
## mod_negotiation allows content selection based on the Accept*
## headers.

Module mime_module          mod_mime.o
Module negotiation_module  mod_negotiation.o

##
## Content delivery modules


##
## The status module allows the server to display current details
## about how well it is performing and what it is doing. Consider
## also enabling STATUS=yes (see the Rules section near the start
## of this file) to allow full status information.  Check
## conf/access.conf on how to enable this.

# Module status_module       mod_status.o

## The Info module displays configuration information for the server
## and all included modules. It's very useful for debugging.

# Module info_module         mod_info.o
```

```
## mod_include translates server-side include (SSI) statements in text
## files. mod_dir handles requests on directories and directory
## indexes. mod_cgi handles CGI scripts.

Module includes_module     mod_include.o
Module dir_module          mod_dir.o
Module cgi_module          mod_cgi.o

## The asis module implemented ".asis" file types, which allow the
## embedding of HTTP headers at the beginning of the document.
## mod_imap handles internal imagemaps (no more cgi-bin/imagemap/!).
## mod_actions is used to specify CGI scripts which act as
## "handlers" for particular files, for example to
## automatically convert every GIF to another file type.

Module asis_module         mod_asis.o
Module imap_module         mod_imap.o
Module action_module       mod_actions.o

##
## URL translation modules.
##
## The UserDir module for selecting resource directories by user
## name and a common prefix, e.g., /~<user>, /usr/web/<user>, etc.

Module userdir_module      mod_userdir.o

## The proxy module enables the server to act as a proxy for
## outside http and ftp services. It's not as complete as it could
## be yet.
## NOTE: You do not want this module UNLESS you are running a proxy;
##       it is not needed for normal (origin server) operation.

# Module proxy_module        modules/proxy/libproxy.a

## The Alias module provides simple URL translation and redirection.

Module alias_module        mod_alias.o

## mod_rewrite allows for powerful URI-to-URI and URI-to-filename
## mapping, using regular expressions.

# Module rewrite_module      mod_rewrite.o
```

```
##
## Access control and authentication modules.
##
Module access_module       mod_access.o
Module auth_module         mod_auth.o

## The anon_auth module allows for anonymous-FTP-style username/
## password authentication.

# Module anon_auth_module    mod_auth_anon.o

## db_auth and dbm_auth work with Berkeley DB files - make sure
## there is support for DBM files on your system.  You may need to
## grab the GNU "gdbm" package if not and possibly adjust
## EXTRA_LIBS. (This may be done by Configure at a later date)

# Module db_auth_module      mod_auth_db.o
# Module dbm_auth_module     mod_auth_dbm.o

## msql_auth checks against an mSQL database.  You must have mSQL
## installed and an "msql.h" available for this to even compile.
## Additionally you may need to add a couple entries to the
## EXTRA_LIBS line, like
## -lmsql -L/usr/local/lib -L/usr/local/Minerva/lib
##
## This depends on your installation of mSQL. (This may be done by
## Configure at a later date)

# Module msql_auth_module    mod_auth_msql.o

## "digest" implements HTTP Digest Authentication rather than the
## less secure Basic Auth used by the other modules.

# Module digest_module       mod_digest.o

## Optional response header manipulation modules.
##
## cern_meta mimics the behavior of the CERN Web server with
## regards to metainformation files.

# Module cern_meta_module    mod_cern_meta.o

## The expires module can apply Expires: headers to resources,
## as a function of access time or modification time.
```

```
# Module expires_module      mod_expires.o

## The headers module can set arbitrary HTTP response headers,
## as configured in server, vhost, access.conf or .htaccess
## configs

# Module headers_module      mod_headers.o

## Miscellaneous modules
##
## mod_usertrack.c is the new name for mod_cookies.c.  This module
## uses Netscape cookies to automatically construct and log
## click-trails from Netscape cookies, or compatible clients who
## aren't coming in via proxy.
##
## You do not need this, or any other module to allow your site
## to use Cookies.  This module is for user tracking only

# Module usertrack_module      mod_usertrack.o

## The example module, which demonstrates the use of the API.  See
## the file modules/example/README for details.  This module should
## only be used for testing — DO NOT ENABLE IT on a production
## server.

# Module example_module      modules/example/mod_example.o

## mod_browser lets you set environment variables based on the
## User-Agent string in the request; this is useful for
## conditional HTML, for example. Since it is also used to detect
## buggy browsers for workarounds, it should be the last (highest
## priority) module.

Module browser_module      mod_browser.o
```

Not all modules provided with Apache are automatically compiled. Module names starting with a pound sign (#) are not included in the build. To include a default module, simply uncomment its entry in the Configuration file. Adding a new module involves a few more steps; see "Adding a New Module" later in this chapter for more information.

CAUTION: Before commenting or uncommenting default modules, make sure you understand what effects the changes will have on your server.

Table 12-1 lists the standard Apache modules. For more information on these modules, see the official Apache website at **http://www.apache.org/docs/mod/** or the Apache Module Registry at **http://modules.apache.org/**.

Type of Module	Filename	Description
Access Control	mod_access.c	Controls per-directory access for server document tree.
Action	mod_actions.c	Performs action based on assigned MIME type.
Alias/Redirect	mod_alias.c	Directory aliasing and redirects.
As-Is	mod_asis.c	Sends file types without adding headers.
Authorization	mod_auth.c	Basic user authentication.
Anonymous Access Control	mod_auth_anon.c	Much like anon-FTP access, for user tracking.
DB Authentication	mod_auth_db.c	User authentication using DB format database.
DBM Authentication	mod_auth_dbm.c	User authentication using DBM format database.
MD5 Authentication (experimental)	mod_auth_digest	MD5 authentication (experimental).
Automatic Directory Listings	mod_autoindex	Automatic directory listings.
Environment variables based on User-Agent	mod_browser	Apache 1.2 only. Sets environment variables based on User-Agent strings.
CERN Meta File	mod_cern_meta.c	CERN Meta File Emulation.
CGI	mod_cgi.c	CGI execution compliant with CGI/1.1 spec.
Cookie	mod_cookies.c	Cookie generation and tracking. In Apache 1.2 and up, replaced by mod_usertrack.
Digest Authentication	mod_digest.c	Module cookie generation and tracking.

Table 12-1. Standard Apache Modules

Type of Module	Filename	Description
Directory Module	mod_dir.c	Directory index generation on the fly.
Dynamic Loader	mod_dld.c	Apache 1.2 and earlier. Dynamically loads Apache modules. Replaced in 1.3+ by mod_so.
Dynamic Loader	mod_dll.c	Apache 1.3b1 to 1.3b5 only. Replaced in 1.3b6 by mod_so.
Environment	mod_env.c	Passes environment variables to CGI/SSI scripts.
API example	mod_example.c	Apache 1.2 and up. Demonstrates Apache API. (Not recommended for use in a production server.)
Expires	mod_expires.c	Apache 1.2 and up. Applies Expires: headers to resources.
HTTP header	mod_headers.c	Apache 1.2 and up. Adds arbitrary HTTP headers to resources.
Imagemap	mod_imap.c	Handles image map files.
Include	mod_include.c	Server-side includes.
Information	mod_info.c	Server and module configuration information.
Windows	mod_isapi.c	Windows ISAPI Extension support.
Log user agent	mod_log_agent.c	Logs user agent from browser
Common log	mod_log_common.c	Standard logging Common Log Format (CLF). In Apache 1.2 and up, replaced by mod_log_config.
Config log	mod_log_config.c	User-configurable log module.
Log referrer	mod_log_referer.c	Log referrer.
MIME	mod_mime.c	Handles MIME types.

Table 12-1. Standard Apache Modules *(continued)*

Type of Module	Filename	Description
MIME	mod_mime_magic.c	Determines document types using "magic numbers."
Memory	mod_mmap_static.c	Maps files into memory for faster serving.
Negotiation	mod_negotiation.c	Content negotiation of MIME types.
Proxy	mod_proxy.c	Proxy support for Apache.
URI	mod_rewrite.c	Apache 1.2 and up. URI-to-filename mapping using regular expressions.
Configuration	mod_setenvif.c	Apache 1.3 and up. Sets environment variables according to client information.
Dynamic Loader	mod_so.c	Apache 1.3 and up. Experimental support for loading modules (DLLs on Windows) at runtime.
Spelling	mod_speling.c	Apache 1.3 and up. Automatically corrects minor typos in URLs.
Server Status	mod_status.c	Provides server status information.
Userdir	mod_userdir.c	Controls file system mapping of user directories.
Logging	mod_uniqueid.c	Apache 1.3 and up. Generates unique request identifier for every request.
User Tracking	mod_usertrack.c	Apache 1.2 and up. User tracking using cookies. Replaces mod_cookies.c.
Virtual Host	mod_vhostalias.c	Apache 1.3.7 and up. Support for dynamically configured mass virtual hosting.

Table 12-1. Standard Apache Modules *(continued)*

ADDITIONAL MODULES There are a number of additional modules that you may want to add to your web server. Table 12-2 lists a sampling of these modules. You can find them, and the instructions for linking modules to core Apache code, at the official Apache website (**http://www.apache.org/dist/contrib/modules/**).

Type of Module	Filename(s)	Description
Authentication	mod_auth_msql (mSQL) mod_auth_pg95 (Postgres95) mod_auth_dbi (DBI)	Usernames and passwords can be stored in either ASCII flat file format (included in the default distribution) or database format.
	mod_auth_external.c	Lets you call an external program for username and password verification.
	mod_auth_anon	Anonymous FTP-style access to authenticated areas, where users give anonymous usernames and real e-mail addresses as passwords. (Included but not enabled in the default Apache 1.2 distribution.)
	mod_auth_nis.c	NIS/passwd authorization using normal user IDs.
	mod_auth_dce.c	DCE authentication and secure DFS access.
Counters	mod_counter.c mod_cntr	Some server-side scripting languages, such as PHP/FI, can also provide access counters.
Faster CGI	mod_perl mod_perl_fast	Builds a Perl interpreter into the Apache executable.
	mod_fastcgi	Implements FastCGI on Apache.

Table 12-2. Samples of Custom Apache Modules

Type of Module	Filename(s)	Description
	mod_pyapache.c	Builds a Python interpreter into the Apache executable.
Access control	mod_auth_uid.c	Disallows serving web pages based on UID/GID.
	mod_access.c	Allows or denies access to a user/domain pair.
	mod_bandwidth.c	Limits bandwidth based on the number of connections.

Table 12-2. Samples of Custom Apache Modules *(continued)*

Adding a New Module

The steps for adding a new module are similar to installing Apache itself.

1. Get the module source code file and place it in the Apache src/ directory.
2. Add the module definition to the Configuration file in the Apache src/ directory. You'll add a line that looks something like this:

   Module *name_module* *mod_something.o*

   - *name_module* must match the name listed in the module's source code. You'll find this name in the module file itself, usually near the end of the file.
   - *mod_something.o* is the filename of the module, with the final *.c* replaced by *.o*.
3. Recompile Apache. (See "Compiling Apache" earlier in this chapter.)
4. Restart the server. (See the "Maintenance" section later in this chapter.)

CONFIGURING APACHE

After you've installed your web server, you'll want to configure it. As we mentioned earlier, most UNIX web servers use separate configuration files to customize web server settings. Apache (and NCSA) use three files—httpd.conf, srm.conf, and access.conf—to configure web server behavior:

Type of File	Name	Description
Server configuration	httpd.conf	Provides essential information that the server needs in order to run.
Resource configuration	srm.conf	Specifies how resources should be handled when they are requested by a client.
Access configuration	access.conf	Specifies who has access to directories and files.

NOTE: The mime-types file is used to specify which file types are associated with which suffixes.

The srm.conf and access.conf files are where you will make the most server configurations. The locations of both of these files are referenced by the httpd.conf file: the location of the srm.conf file is set by the ResourceConfig directive, and the access.conf file is set by the AccessConfig directive.

All configuration files are located in the Apache conf/ directory. In a new installation, files have a "–dist" extension. Before configuring, it's a good idea to make copies of all the files, saving them without the "–dist" extension, and then edit the new files. The "–dist" files will then be your reference and backup copies.

Before configuring the server, you need to make some decisions regarding where web server directories and files should live on your system. You'll need to know these in order to make any necessary changes to the configuration files. The main directories you need to decide on are the following:

- Server root
- Document root
- Log files

The *server root* is the subdirectory where you unpacked the Apache files. It contains the conf/, src/, cgi-bin/, and other server-related files and subdirectories. The default location is /usr/local/etc/httpd; however, you can move it wherever you want. To change the default location, update the ServerRoot directive in the httpd.conf file.

NOTE: If the server (httpd) crashes, the core file will be in the server root directory.

The *document root* is the subdirectory where HTML and related files (such as images) will live. The default location is /usr/local/etc/httpd/htdocs. Because users will have access to these files, the document root should be in a different location (its own directory) outside of the server root directory.

TIP: For security reasons, you should set file permissions in the document and server root directories such that only trusted users can make changes. Many sites create a "www" group and a "www" user for this purpose. Only trusted web authors in the "www" group will be able to change files in the document root directory; only the official website administrator, the "www" user, will be able to change files in the server root directory.

Log files, by default, are stored in the Apache logs/ directory. As these files grow dynamically, you may want to put them in a different location with a good amount of free space. How much free space? That depends on how much traffic the website(s) supported by your web server generate(s).

httpd.conf

The httpd.conf file sets basic system-level information about your web server. It contains the directory location of the server root (ServerRoot directive). If you are not the system administrator at the site where you're installing this web server, you might want to get that person's assistance.

Table 12-3 lists some directives from this file that you might find useful.

Directive	Description
ServerAdmin *e-mail_address*	Specifies the e-mail address used when the server sends error messages in response to failed requests. No default.
ServerRoot *directory_path*	Specifies the directory in which all server-associated files reside. Default is /usr/local/etc/httpd.
User *username*	Specifies the user (UID) and group (GID) you want the server process to run as. Default is nobody.
PidFile*filename*	Specifies the location of the file where the server should place the process ID (PID) of the server when running stand-alone. Default is logs/httpd.pid.

Table 12-3. Useful httpd.conf Directives

TIP: Apache treats httpd.conf, srm.conf, and access.conf the same way. You can create a single config file out of the three. To do this, append the contents of srm.conf and access.conf to httpd.conf. To prevent Apache from complaining about missing srm.conf and access.conf files, edit the AccessConfig and ResourceConfig variables so that they point to /dev/null. The edited lines in httpd.conf would then look like this:

```
AccessConfig    /dev/null
ResourceConfig  /dev/null
```

srm.conf

The srm.conf file specifies how your web server handles resources such as HTML files. For initial configuration, this file contains the directory location of the document root (DocumentRoot directive).

Table 12-4 lists some directives from this file that you might find useful.

Directive	Description
AccessFileName *filename*	Specifies the filename for access control files. Default is .htaccess.
Alias *symbolic_path real_path*	Creates a virtual name or directory by mapping a virtual pathname in a URL to a real path on your server.
DocumentRoot *directory_path*	The main location for HTML and related files for the web server.
ScriptAlias *symbolic_path real_path*	Provides a way to create a virtual cgi-bin directory. You can give users their own cgi-bin access without giving them access to the main cgi-bin directory located in the server root directory.
UserDir *directory_name*	Specifies the web directory name the server looks for in a user's home directory. Default is public_html.
Redirect *pathname url*	Tells the server to forward clients that request a given directory or document to a new location.

Table 12-4. Useful srm.conf Directives

access.conf

The access.conf file controls how the contents of directories are accessed. Table 12-5 lists some directives from this file that you might find useful.

Configuration Options

Apache is a highly configurable web server. Its modular structure makes it easy to add or remove functionality, while its configuration files give you a great deal of control over how that functionality is implemented.

This section discusses a number of server configurations that you may choose to make to your server. While it is not intended to be comprehensive, it does give you an idea of the types of configurations you are able to make.

Directive	Description
AccessFileName *filename*	Specifies the filename for access control files. Default is .htaccess.
Alias *symbolic_path real_path*	Creates a virtual name or directory by mapping a virtual pathname in a URL to a real path on your server.
DocumentRoot *directory_path*	The main location for HTML and related files for the web server.
ScriptAlias *symbolic_path real_path*	Provides a way to create a virtual cgi-bin directory. You can give users their own cgi-bin access without giving them access to the main cgi-bin directory located in the server root directory.
UserDir *directory_name*	Specifies the web directory name the server looks for in a user's home directory. The default is public_html.
Redirect *pathname url*	Tells the server to forward clients that request a given directory or document to a new location.

Table 12-5. Useful access.conf Directives

User Directories

Many sites allow users to manage their own web pages from their home directories. This is usually the case when you see a URL that looks like **http://some.place.com/~jdoe**. This means there is a directory called jdoe that contains a subdirectory matching the User directive in the srm.conf file.

By default, this is enabled in Apache; the subdirectory name is public_html. You can set this name to be "www," or anything else you want. (Just notify your users!) If you don't want to allow users to have their own web pages, set the User directive to DISABLED.

NOTE: Users do not have default cgi-bin access within their public_html directory.

User Authentication

User authentication lets you restrict documents to people with valid usernames and passwords only. Before the user can view web pages, that user must enter a valid username and password.

Setting up user authentication involves these steps:

1. Create a file containing the usernames and passwords.
2. Configure the server to specify what resources are protected and which users are allowed (after entering a valid password) to access those resources.
3. Create an .htaccess file (or .htgroup file) and put it in the directory to be protected; or, create a <Directory> listing in access.conf.
4. Restart the server.

CREATING A USERNAME AND PASSWORD FILE The password file(s) you create for web server access are similar to UNIX password files in that they contain usernames and encrypted passwords. Since there isn't a link between valid UNIX users and valid users for your server, you can specify any username you want.

NOTE: In Apache 1.2 and above, you can restrict pages by username and password, and also let users from particular domains access the pages without giving a password. This is implemented with the Satisfy directive. Restrictions can be applied to individual files with <File>, and to files that match a regular expression.

To create password files, Apache is distributed with a program called htpasswd in the source/ directory. This program will automatically generate an encrypted password for each username and password you enter.

NOTE: You may need to compile htpasswd (by entering **make htpasswd**) before using it.

Creating a password file is pretty straightforward. For example, to create a new user file called users, and to add the username mkalharri with the password %dfWqh5, you would type

```
htpasswd -c users mkalharri
```

The –c argument tells htpasswd to create a new users file. When you run this command, you will be prompted to enter a password for mkalharri and to confirm it by entering it again. Other users can be added to the existing file in the same way, except that the –c argument is not needed. The same command can also be used to modify the password of an existing user.

After adding a few users, the /usr/local/etc/httpd/users file might look like this:

```
mcardon:G1UJqVPOCD7U2
dshard:NXD9tmO9GQqcU
kora:/l4YDay8cnQVY
```

The first field is the username, and the second field is the encrypted password.

CAUTION: Don't place the password file in the document root; otherwise, users from other sites will be able to access it. Although the password is encrypted, it is not completely safe from decryption. Place the password file in the server root or some other nonaccessible area.

CONFIGURING THE SERVER To get the server to use the usernames and passwords in the username and password files, you need to configure a realm. A *realm* is a section of your site that is to be restricted to some or all of the users listed in the password file. Once the user has entered a valid username and password, that user has access to all the resources in that realm. If there is more than one realm with the same name, users will have access to those resources as well, unless access is limited via the require directive.

The directives to create the protected area can be placed in an .htaccess file in the directory concerned, or in a <Directory> section in the access.conf file.

TIP: Apache will search through every subdirectory of a directory that is .htaccess-enabled, and this can cause a significant disk access load if you don't limit the search. To limit .htaccess searches to specific directories, create a <Directory> section for each .htaccess-containing directory, and use the AllowOverride directive. You can set up <Directory> sections in access.conf or even srm.conf. For example, say you needed an .htaccess file only in the /htdocs/company/finance/sales/4Q/bonuses subdirectory. You might put something like this in your access.conf file:

```
<Directory /htdocs>
Options All
AllowOverride None
```

```
</Directory>
<Directory /htdocs/company/finance/sales/4Q/bonuses>
Options All
AllowOverride All
</Directory>
```

Make sure the *access.conf* file allows user authentication to be set up in an *.htaccess* file. This is controlled by the AuthConfig override. To allow authentication directives to be used in an *.htaccess* file, the *access.conf* file must include the following:

```
AllowOverride AuthConfig
```

HTACCESS After you've created a password file, create a file named .htaccess. Place the .htaccess file in the directory to be protected. All subdirectories of the protected directory will also be protected.

NOTE: Apache 1.2 and above will also let you protect individual files. You can also assign users to groups; the process is similar to setting up user-based access.

The .htaccess file should contain the following lines:

AuthName *realm_name*
AuthType Basic
AuthUserFile */usr/local/etc/httpd/my_users*
require *valid-user*

These directives tell the server where to find the usernames and passwords and what authentication protocol to use. The server now knows that this resource is restricted to valid users.

NOTE: The require directive tells the server what usernames are valid for particular access methods; it may be a file containing valid usernames or individual usernames separated by spaces. The valid-user argument tells the server that any username in the specified password file (set by the AuthUserFile directive) can be used. To restrict access to specific users within the password file, type **user**, then the username(s), separated by spaces. Here is an example:

```
require user mkalharri zippy
```

The server can also be configured for DBM authentication. Its setup is similar to that for user authentication. For more information, see the Apache Week information on DBM User Authentication (**http://www.apacheweek.com/features/dbmauth**).

Image Maps

Image maps are pictures that allow users to access different documents by clicking different areas of an image. There are two types of image maps: server-side and client-side. Server-side image maps are processed by the web server and require some server configuration to enable them. Client-side image maps are processed by the user's browser and don't require any web server configuration or processing.

SERVER-SIDE IMAGE MAPS The image map module included with Apache (mod_imap) allows you to do server-side image maps. This module is part of the core Apache distribution and is compiled by default. Before using image maps, however, you will need to configure the server to enable image maps. To do this, uncomment the following line in the srm.conf file:

```
AddHandler imap-file map
```

This specifies that files with a .map extension are image map files.

> ***NOTE:*** When you change a configuration file, you must restart the server for the changes to take effect. (See the section "Starting, Stopping, and Restarting Apache" later in this chapter for more information.)

To use image maps, follow these steps:

1. Create a map file that specifies the sections of the image that are "hot."
2. Add code to an HTML file to tell the browser which image and map file to use. Here is an example:

   ```
   <A HREF="/global_sites/world.map"><IMG SRC="/graphics/world.gif" ISMAP></A>
   ```

(See Apache Week's tutorial on image mapping at **http://www.apacheweek.com/features/imagemaps** for more information.)

CLIENT-SIDE IMAGE MAPS In client-side image maps, all information needed for the image map is contained within the same HTML file. No server configuration is necessary.

CGI

The Common Gateway Interface (CGI) is a specification that says how servers should talk to a script or program and how the script or program formats its reply for use by the server. CGI itself is not a language; it describes a protocol that can be used to write programs for use with a web server in any language.

As far as server configuration issues are concerned, CGI scripts can be executed out of a server root directory called cgi-bin without any special configuration. However, access to this directory is usually restricted. Other solutions for providing CGI access for your users include setting up ScriptAliases or adding a CGI MIME type with AddType. Both of these methods are covered in this section.

CAUTION: All CGI programs, both scripted and compiled, are potentially insecure. The levels of security required for different sites vary widely. Some sites require that users submit their scripts or programs to a webmaster, who ensures that the code contains no security holes, before it can be used. Other sites restrict CGI access to trusted users, who are responsible for checking their own code.

Although CGI has been a standard solution, there are other options. As an alternative to CGI, many scripting languages can be built into Apache as modules. This makes executing the scripts much more efficient, since an interpreter does not need to be started for every request. This is true of such languages as Perl (mod_perl.c) and Python. However, this method does present some risk, as users have the potential to cause damage to your system either intentionally or unintentionally.

SCRIPTALIAS ScriptAlias is a directive in srm.conf. It tells the server you want to designate a directory (or directories) as script-only: that is, any time the server tries to retrieve a file from these directories, it will execute the file instead of reading it. Here is an example:

```
ScriptAlias /cgi-bin/ cgi-bin/
```

This will make any request to the server that begins with /cgi-bin/ be fulfilled by executing the corresponding program in ServerRoot/cgi-bin/.

NOTE: You may have more than one ScriptAlias directive in srm.conf to designate different directories as CGI.

The advantages of using ScriptAlias are ease of administration, centralization, and slight increase in speed. However, many system managers don't want anything as dangerous as a script in the file system. Another disadvantage is that anyone wishing to create scripts must either have their own entry in srm.conf or must have write access to a ScriptAlias directory.

ADDTYPE Another method of allowing CGIs is to specify a "magic" MIME type that tells the server to execute files instead of sending them. This is done using the AddType directive either in srm.conf or in a per-directory access.conf file. The advantage (and disadvantage) of this setup is that scripts can be run from absolutely anywhere.

For instance, to designate all files ending in .cgi as scripts, use the following directive:

```
AddType application/x-httpd-cgi .cgi
```

Alternatively, you could add .sh and .pl after .cgi to allow automatic execution of shell scripts and Perl scripts, respectively.

REMEMBER: You need to have an Options directive specifying the directory as permitting execution of CGI scripts, such as

```
<Directory /web/docs>

        Options ExecCGI
</Directory>
```

NOTE: Given the potential dangers of poorly written CGI, you probably don't want to make CGIs available everywhere. Per-directory access gives you more control over which directories can execute CGIs.

SSIs

Server-side includes (SSIs) allow users to create simple, dynamic pages. The HTML author embeds special SSI variables, such as the current date or time, or even another file, in an HTML file. When the page is accessed, the server processes the file and substitutes any variables with actual values.

NOTE: Apache 1.2 and above extends SSI (xSSI) to include additional variables and conditional codes.

If a server had to look at every HTML file for SSIs, that would slow down access; by default, this capability is off. To turn it on, you need to tell Apache which documents contain the SSI commands. One method is to use a special file extension such as .shtml, which tells the server to process the file. This would be configured as follows:

```
AddHandler server-parsed .shtml
AddType    text/html     shmtl
```

The AddHandler directive tells Apache to process every .shtml file for SSI commands. This occurs whether there are any SSI commands in the file or not. The AddType directive makes sure that the resulting content is marked as HTML, so that the browser displays it properly.

Another method of telling the server which files include SSI commands is to set the execute bit on HTML files and then set the XBitHack directive. Any file with a content type of text/html (that is, with the extension .html) and the execute bit set will be checked for SSI commands.

For either method, the server also needs to be configured to allow SSIs. This is done with the Options Includes directive, which can be placed in either the global access.conf or a local .htaccess file.

REMEMBER: For .htaccess, also enable AllowOverride Options.

MAINTENANCE

Maintenance is the ongoing process of tweaking the web server after its initial installation and configuration. It consists of tasks such as reconfiguring the server, tuning its performance, starting and stopping the server, monitoring files (such as the error and access logs), and generating usage statistics for your website(s). Here are some general maintenance tips:

- Back up your web documents frequently. You might also consider putting them in a version control system such as RCS.
- Keep an eye on the size of the log files. The busier your web server is, the faster they will grow in size.
- Rotate log files daily. Summarize your log files frequently so that you don't have to keep disks full of old logs hanging around.
- Log as little information as possible. Turn DNS lookup off and do lookups later with a script. Log referrer URLs sparingly—for example, if you need to know the origin of a consistent bad file request in the error logs. There are search engines that can tell you who's linking to you, such as Digital's AltaVista.
- Scan your access and error log files regularly. Signs of suspicious activity might involve system commands (rm, login, chmod, etc.) or repeated attempts to access a password-protected document. Extremely long URL requests can indicate an attempt to overrun a program's input buffer.
- Read the WWW Security FAQ (**http://www.w3.org/Security/Faq/wwwsf1.html**) for good, up-to-date information on setting up and maintaining web servers with as few security holes as possible.

Starting, Stopping, and Restarting Apache

To start the server, run the httpd program by typing

```
httpd
```

You may notice several httpd processes running at the same time. There is a parent process and a number of child processes automatically spawned by the parent process. You stop or restart Apache by sending the parent httpd process a signal. Which process is the parent? It's easy to tell, because its PID is automatically written to the httpd.pid file.

NOTE: The location of the httpd.pid file is set by the PidFile directive in httpd.conf.

There are three signals you can send to Apache:

- TERM
- HUP
- USR1

The TERM signal causes Apache to stop running. First all child processes are killed, then the parent exits, and the server is no longer running. Here is an example:

```
kill -TERM `cat /usr/local/etc/httpd/logs/httpd.pid`
```

The HUP signal causes Apache to reread its configuration files and reopen any log files. As with TERM, all child processes are killed; however, the parent process remains alive. After the configuration and log files are dealt with, new children are created, and the server continues serving hits. Here is an example:

```
kill -HUP `cat /usr/local/etc/httpd/logs/httpd.pid`
```

The USR1 signal causes Apache to reread configuration files and reopen log files without dropping connections in progress, as currently happens with a HUP restart. The parent process advises the child processes to exit after their current request, or exit immediately if they have no current requests. The parent rereads its configuration files and reopens any log files. As each child dies off, it is replaced by a new one, which begins serving new hits. Here is an example:

```
kill -USR1 `cat /usr/local/etc/httpd/logs/httpd.pid`
```

CAUTION: Don't use this signal unless you are using Apache 1.2b9 or greater. The code for USR1 was unstable in previous versions.

Log Files

Currently, if you want the server to rotate its log files and start logging somewhere else, you send it a HUP. Unfortunately, this also has the effect of killing whatever transfers are currently in progress. For many sites, this only occurs once a week when logs are rotated, and thus it can effectively be ignored. However, webmasters responsible for sites with large files may be more worried about this problem, as it can cause users to be disconnected in the middle of large download procedures.

A solution is to log to another process rather than a file, using the " | " prefix for the log filename. As an example of this, you'll find a sample program called rotatelogs.c in the Apache support/ directory.

CAUTION: Anyone who can write to the directory where Apache is writing a log file can almost certainly gain access to the UID that the server is started as, which is normally root. Don't give people write access to a directory where the logs are stored without being aware of the consequences.

Security

Security is a very broad and important topic. In no way does this section provide a comprehensive treatment of security. It does, however, acquaint you with some of the issues you may want to consider.

General Considerations

Site security typically includes a combination of firewalls and solid internal network security. This is a fairly common, layered security approach. In theory, either method alone should protect your site; however, reality tends to do nasty things to theories.

A comprehensive approach to protecting a website generally means following best practices in a number of different areas. ICSA.net is in the process of planning a certification process for websites that touches on a number of these areas. See **http://www.icsa.net** for more details.

TIP: For more information, you may want to take a look at RFC2196, the *Site Security Handbook*, at **http://www.cis.ohio-state.edu/htbin/rfc/rfc2196.html**.

The guideines being developed by ICSA are intended to ensure a basic level of security, rather than a hacker-proof one. They set minimum standards for logical and physical security issues, which address such issues as hacking, intrusion, data loss, and tampering. While these guidelines may be more (or less) stringent than your site's needs, they can certainly be used as a starting point for developing your own security guidelines. A summary of the ICSA guidelines for a single-server site is as follows:

- The website must withstand network-based attacks by means of a firewall, filtering router, or other appropriate security mechanism.
- The Domain Name Service (DNS) entries for all URL-referenced systems must be resolvable.
- NIC handles must be authenticated, and the NIC contact information must be accurate and contain at least two contacts.
- The site must maintain logging. Access to logs must be limited to authorized personnel. Logs must be retained in a secure, but retrievable, format.
- A standard encryption mechanism, such as SSL or SHTTP, must be used for sensitive data transmission.
- You must review CGI scripts and programs to ensure that they don't intentionally or unintentionally compromise your system.
- A person must be designated as the site's CxE Evaluator. All client executables must be examined and deemed harmless to the user.
- Pages that contain or accept sensitive data must be made non-cacheable. Users must be informed if any pages containing sensitive data will be cached to local storage.
- The site must meet physical security requirements, such as access-controlled areas, roster of authorized personnel, suitable equipment, and emergency contract information.

- The site must meet logical security requirements, such as secure password policies, webmaster contact, HTTPD server configured for least privilege, and separate development and production systems.
- If a transaction mechanism is in place, it must be documented, and the server's private key protected by a strong password. Sensitive information must be periodically removed from the server. The OS/Platform must be documented and integrity assured. Backups and Restore capabilities must be in place.

Specific Considerations

The following are some specific suggestions you might consider. (For more suggestions, see the WWW Security FAQ at **http://www.w3.org/Security/Faq/wwwsf1.html**, or the Computer Incident Advisory Capability's bulletin on web security at **http://www.ciac.org/ciac/bulletins/j-042.shtml**.)

- Set file permissions in the document and server root directories such that only trusted users can make changes. Many sites create a "www" group and a "www" user for this purpose. Only trusted web authors in the "www" group would be able to change files in the document root directory; only the official website administrator, the "www" user, would be able to change files in the server root directory.
- When Apache starts, it opens the log files as the user who started the server before switching to the user defined in the User directive. Anyone who can write to the directory where Apache is writing a log file can almost certainly gain access to the UID that the server is started as, which is normally root. Don't give people write access to a directory where the logs are stored without being aware of the consequences.
- CGI scripts run with the UID of the server child process. The default ID is "nobody." For this reason, you may want to consider "nobody" an untrusted user and set its permissions so that it doesn't have read permission on sensitive files, or write permission in critical areas.
- Don't require Apache to use DNS for any parsing of the configuration files. If Apache has to use DNS to parse the configuration files, your server may experience reliability problems, or even denial and theft of service or other such attacks.
- Some SSI commands, like *#exec*, let a user execute programs that might be security risks. You might want to consider limiting this capability. The Includes NOExec option lets all SSI commands work except for those that execute programs.
- Unless you take steps to change it, if the server can find its way to a file through normal URL mapping rules, it can serve it to clients. Sometimes this default access can cause problems. For instance, consider the following example:

```
# cd /; ln -s / public_html
Accessing http://localhost/~root/
```

This would allow clients to walk through the entire file system. To work around this, add the following block to your server's configuration:

```
<Directory />
     Order deny,allow
     Deny from all
 </Directory>
```

This will prevent default access to file system locations. Add appropriate <Directory> blocks to allow access only in those areas you wish. Here is an example:

```
<Directory /usr/local/users/*/public_html>
     Order deny,allow
     Allow from all
 </Directory>
 <Directory /usr/local/etc/httpd>
     Order deny,allow
     Allow from all
 </Directory>
```

- ▲ Place your web server(s) in a DMZ, and set the firewall to drop connections to your web server on all ports but http (port 80) or https (port 443).

SUMMARY

Currently, there are a variety of UNIX web servers available. One of the most widely used is Apache. One of the reasons for its popularity is its flexibility. Its modular structure makes it easy to add or remove functionality, while its configuration files give a webmaster a great deal of control over how the web server functions. In this chapter, we have examined Apache in detail, including how to download the source distribution and compile it on your UNIX system. We then looked at the specifics of configuring Apache, including the syntax of its major configuration files. In addition, we examined various security issues, user authentication processes, log file management, and other maintenance tasks that you will encounter. Apache is a very robust web server with an extremely large installed base. If you find yourself needing to install a UNIX-based web server, you owe it to yourself to evaluate Apache.

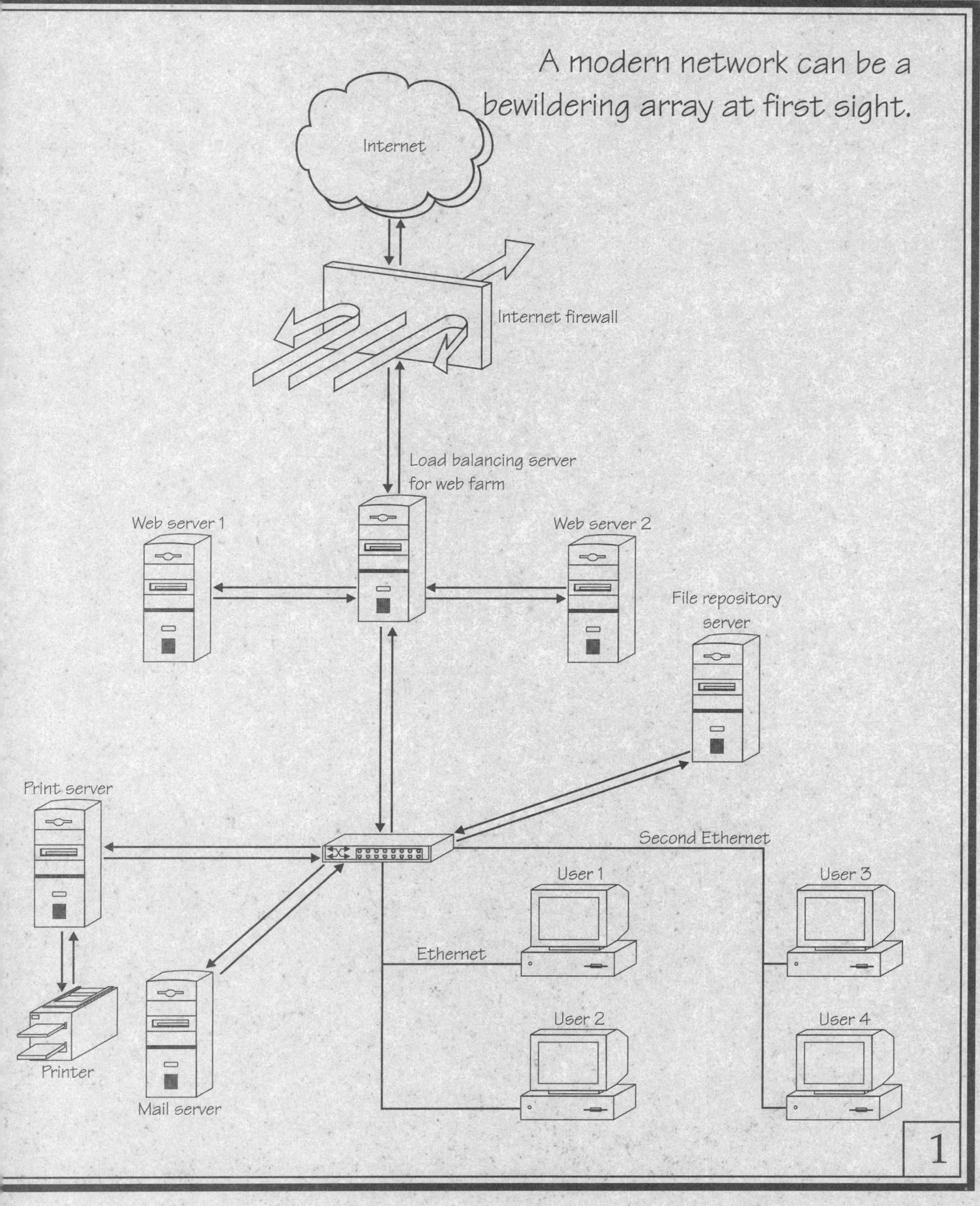
A modern network can be a bewildering array at first sight.
Internet
Internet firewall
Load balancing server for web farm
Web server 1
Web server 2
File repository server
Print server
Second Ethernet
User 1
User 3
Ethernet
User 2
User 4
Printer
Mail server
1

SAMBA allows users of many different operating systems to share file and print resources.

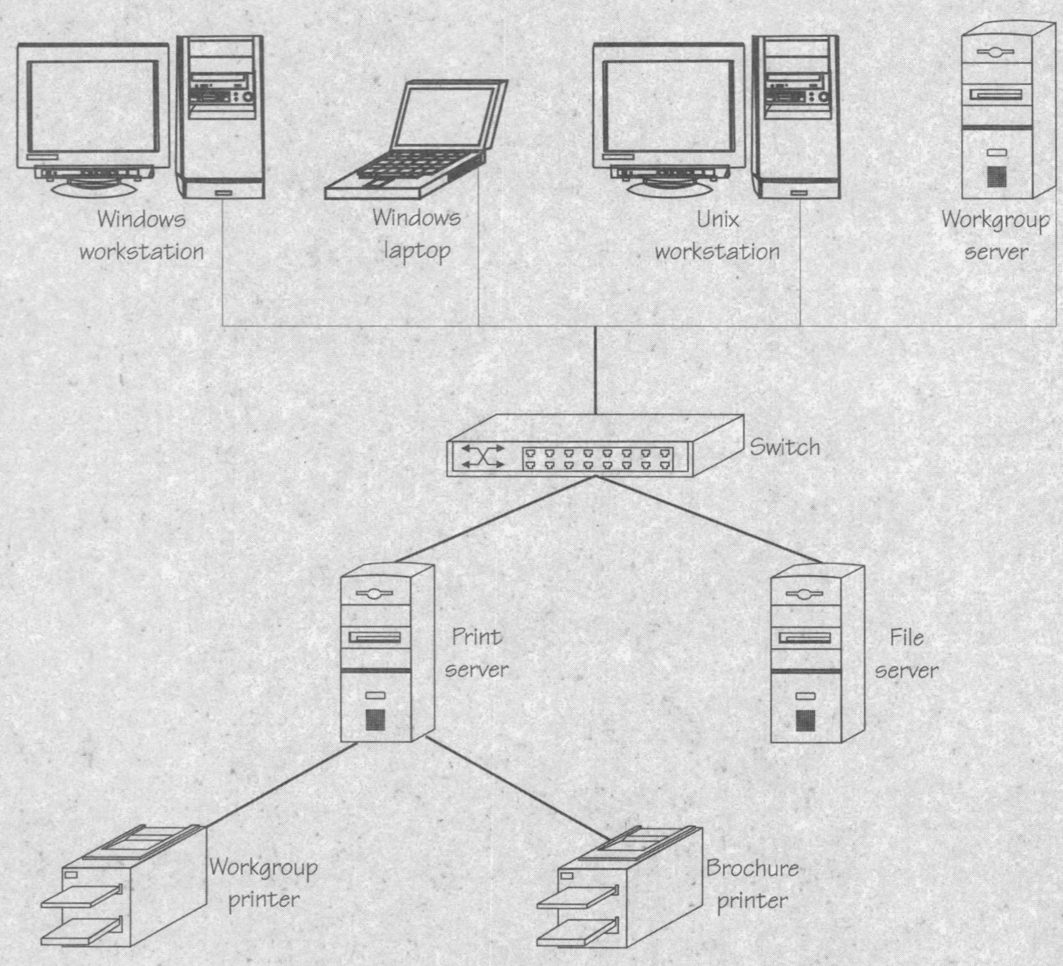

Mail User Agents send mail to Mail Transport Agents, which route it to other Mail Transport Agents, which distribute it to Mail Delivery Agents.

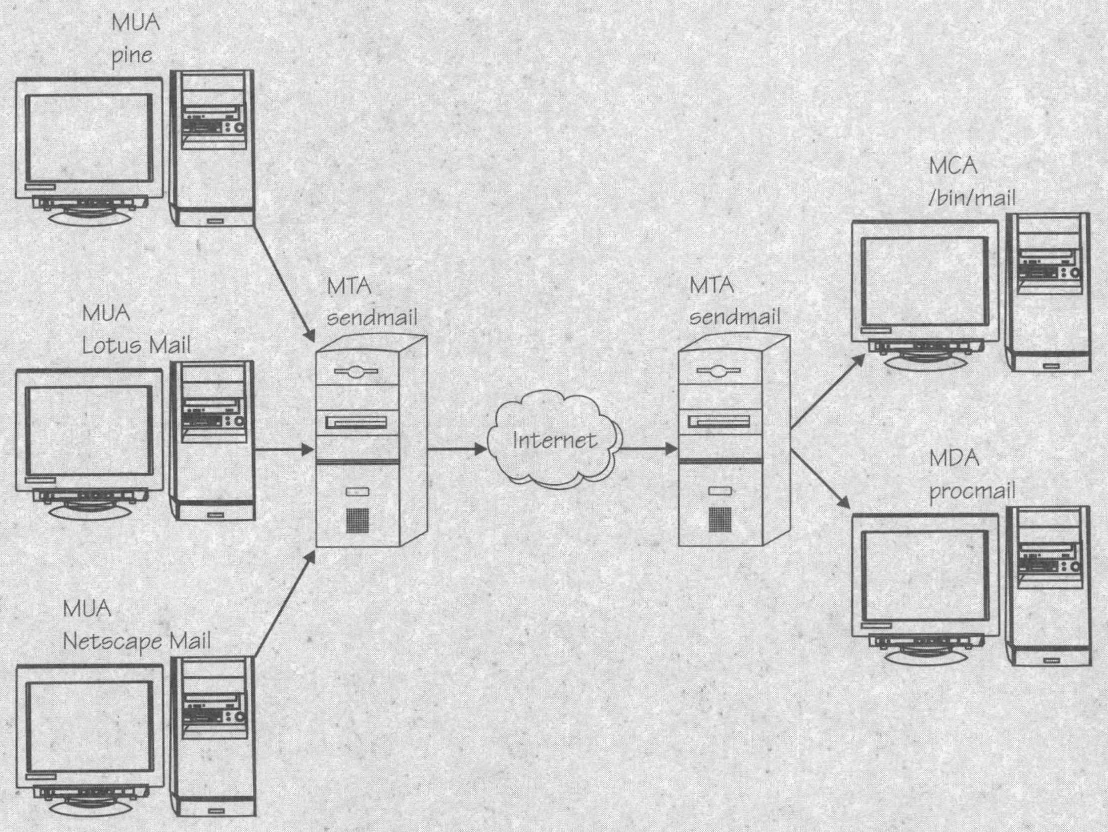

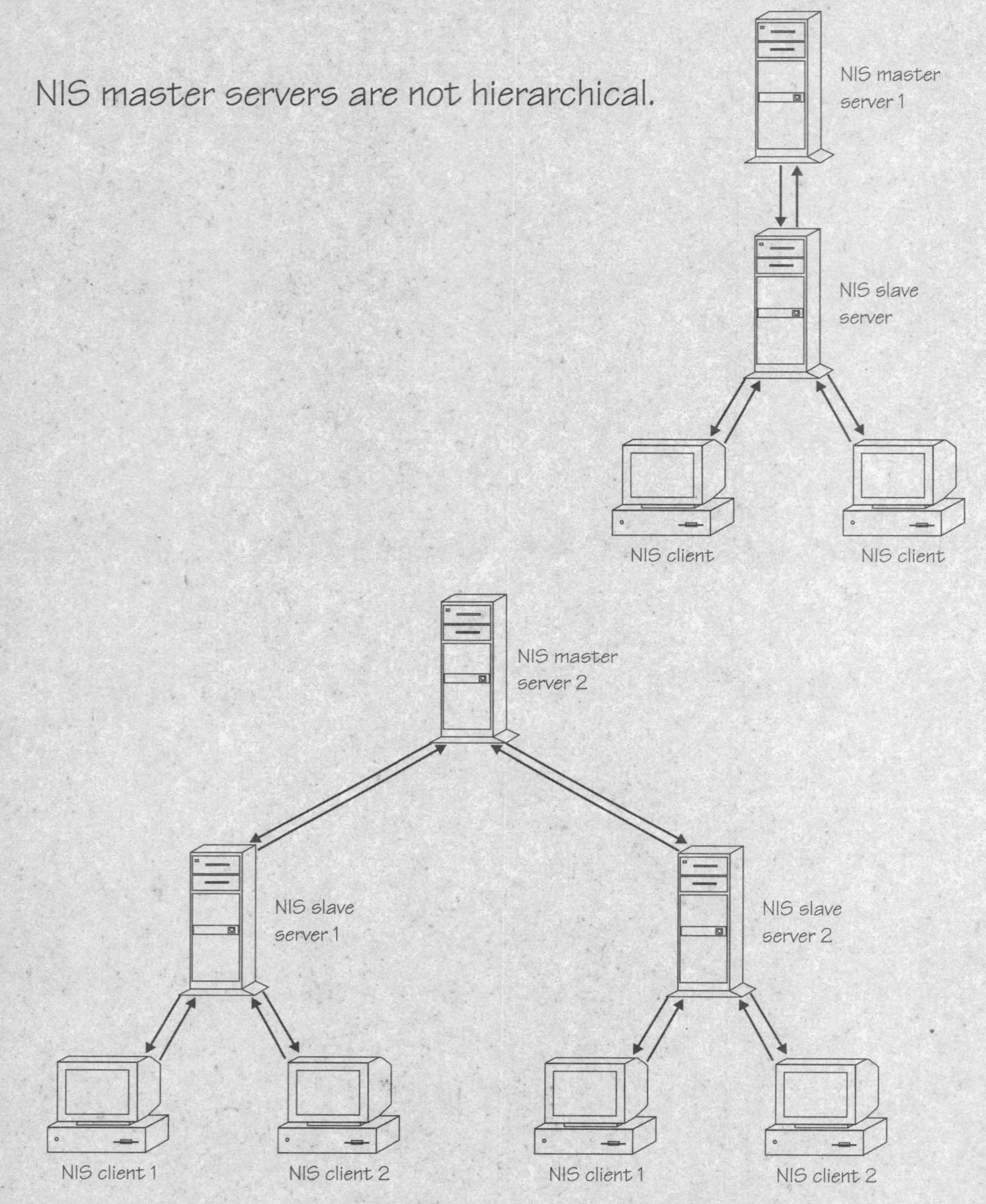
NIS master servers are not hierarchical.
NIS master server 1
NIS slave server
NIS client
NIS client
NIS master server 2
NIS slave server 1
NIS slave server 2
NIS client 1
NIS client 2
NIS client 1
NIS client 2

4

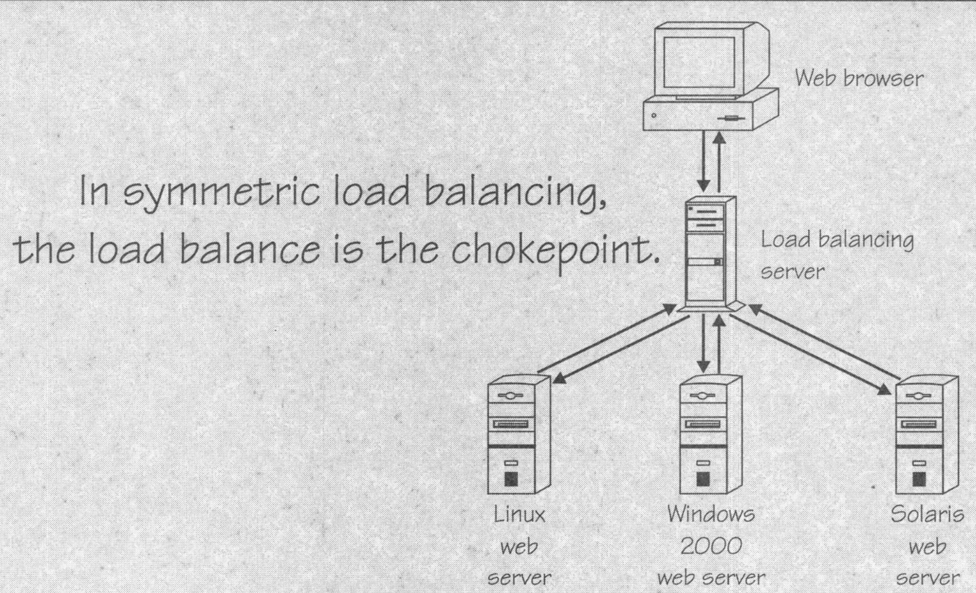
Web browser
In symmetric load balancing,
the load balance is the chokepoint.
Load balancing
server
Linux
web
server
Windows
2000
web server
Solaris
web
server

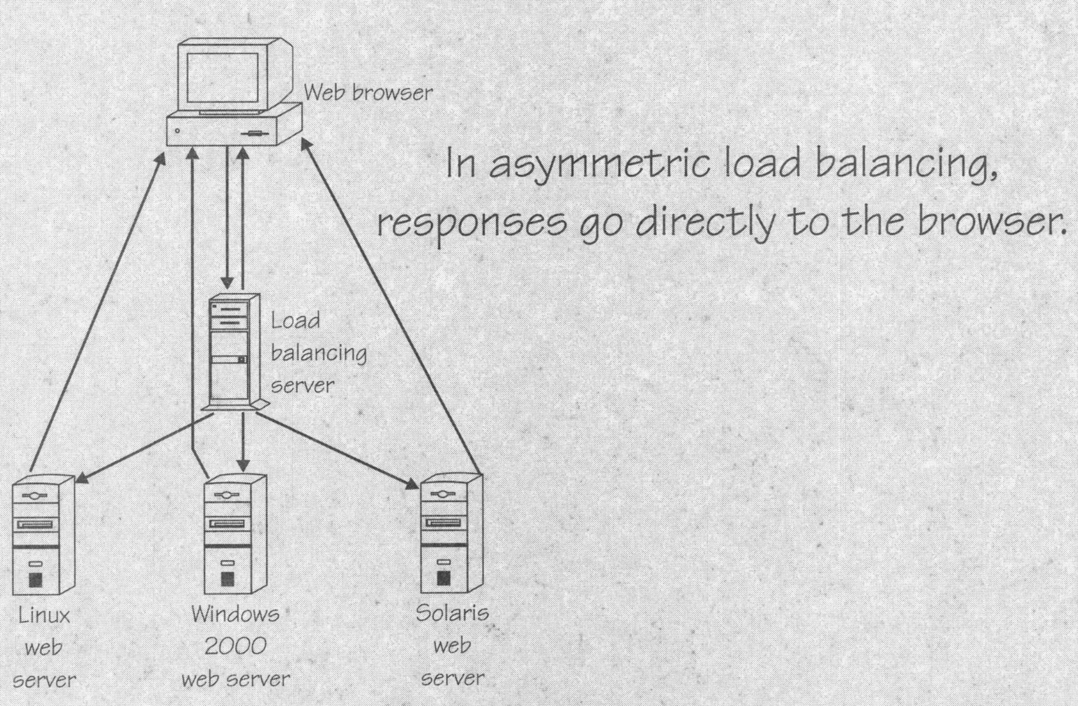
Web browser
In asymmetric load balancing,
responses go directly to the browser.
Load
balancing
server
Linux
web
server
Windows
2000
web server
Solaris
web
server

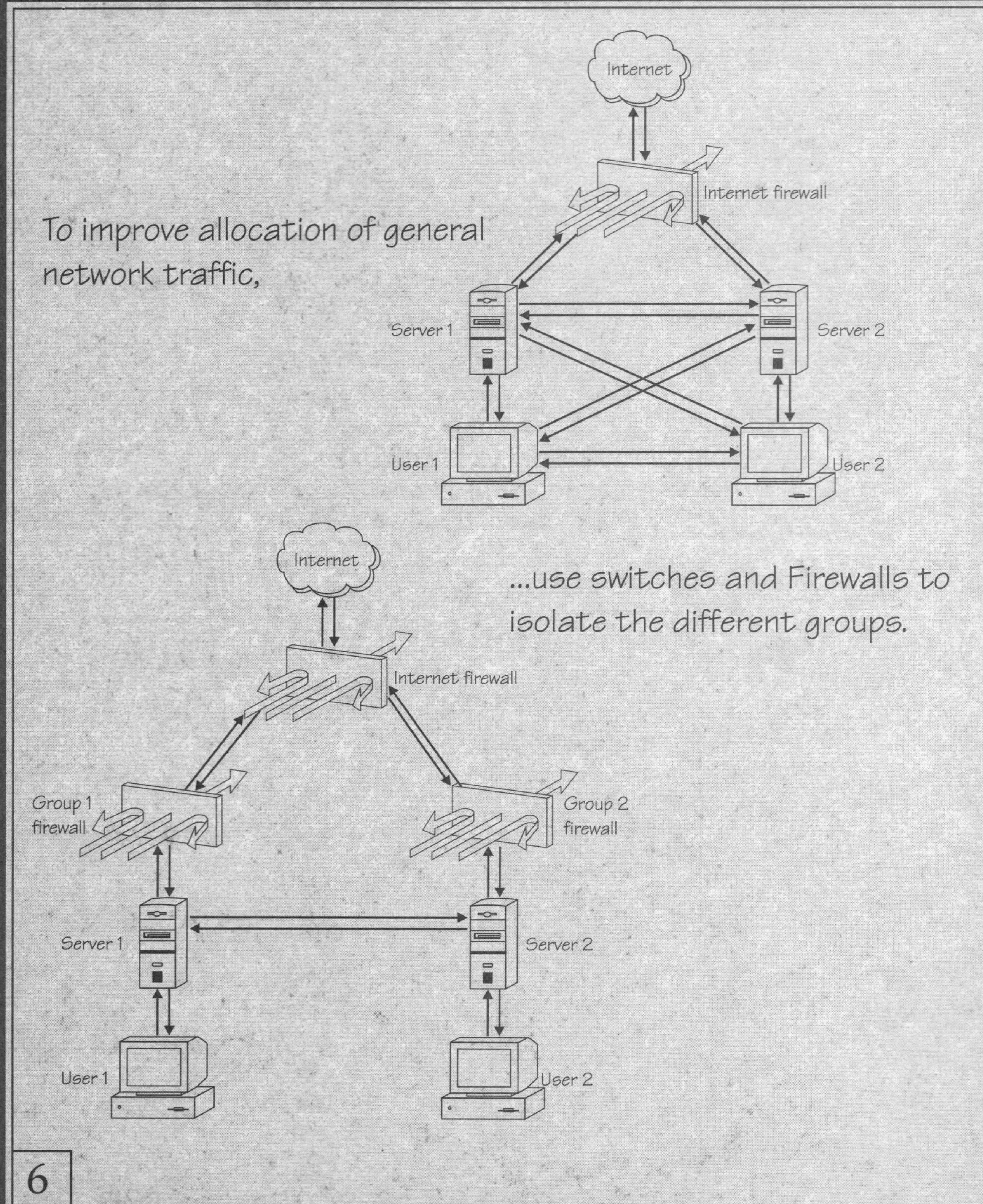
Internet
Internet firewall
To improve allocation of general network traffic,
Server 1
Server 2
User 1
User 2
Internet
...use switches and Firewalls to isolate the different groups.
Internet firewall
Group 1 firewall
Group 2 firewall
Server 1
Server 2
User 1
User 2
6

Application
Presentation
Session
Transport
Network
Data Link
Physical

The OSI model designates a specific set of responsibilities at each layer of the network.

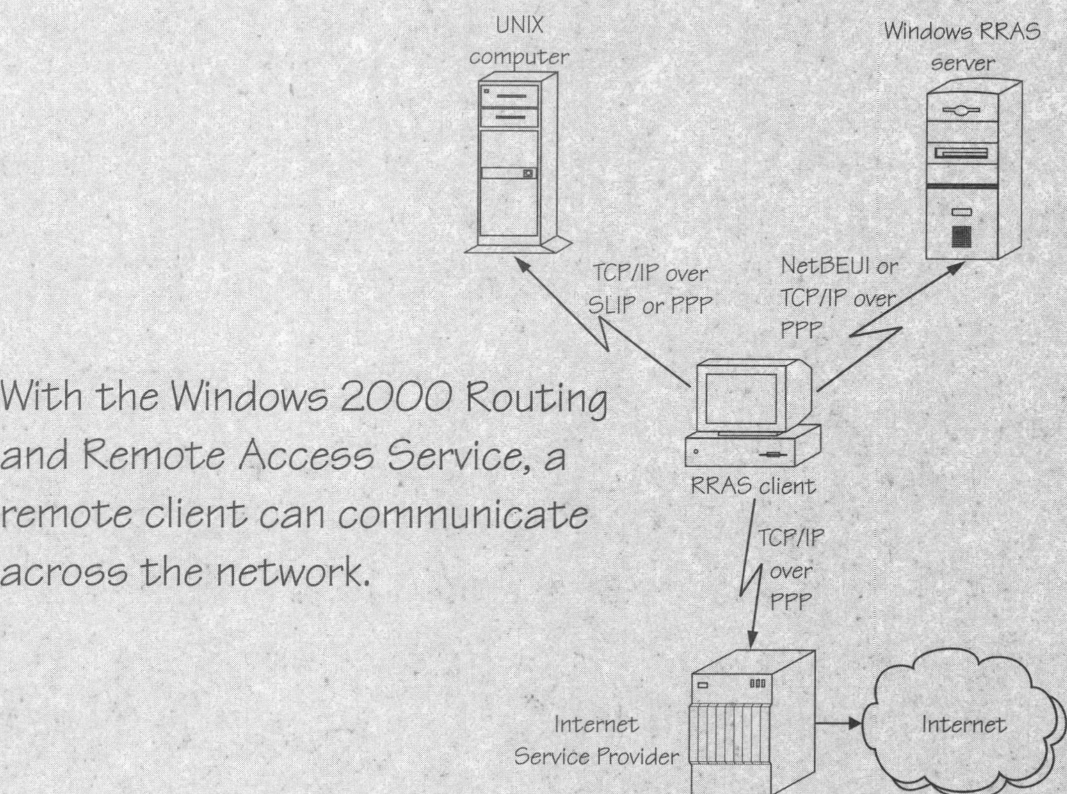

With the Windows 2000 Routing and Remote Access Service, a remote client can communicate across the network.

In the Simple Network Management Protocol (SNMP), information about the status and processes of different network devices is organized in the Management Information Base (MIB).

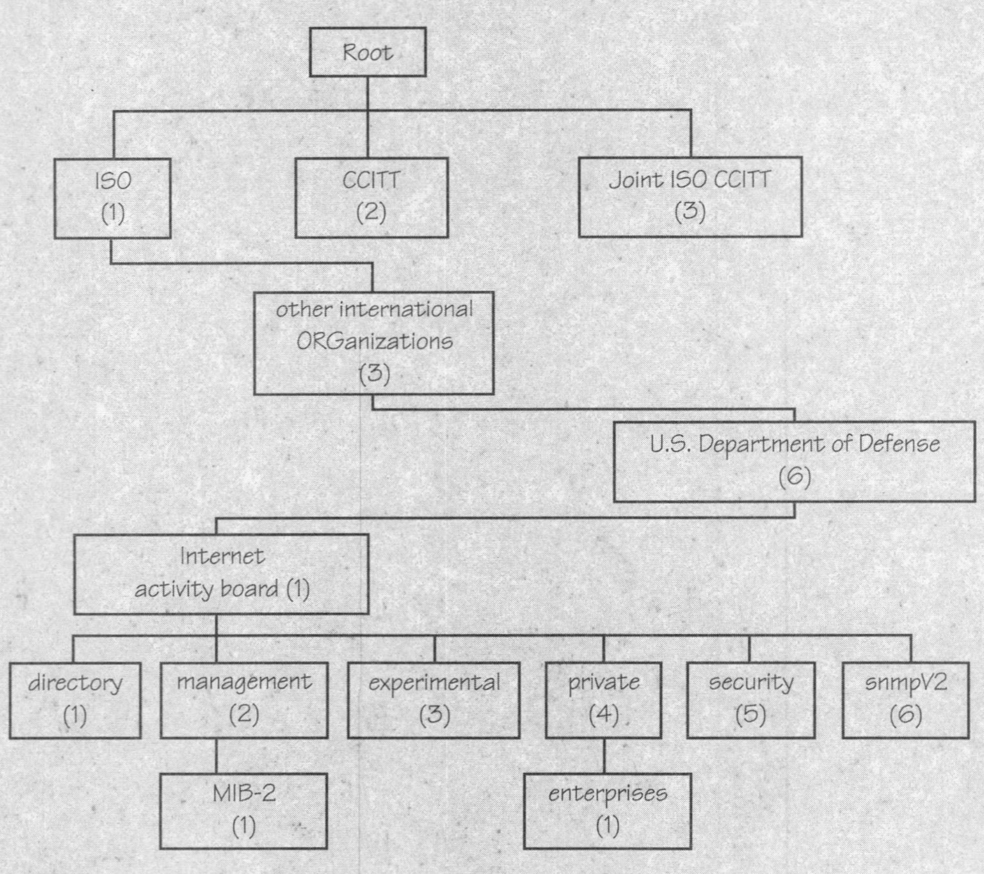

CHAPTER 13

Other Network Servers

Over the past few years, the World Wide Web has completely changed how we view information services provided over a network. Now, through the World Wide Web, a wide variety of different services are available to the user's desktop.

However, several network services still operate outside the realm of the common web server. Many of these other network servers are rarely discussed in the detail with which web services are examined, even though desktop web browsers can act as clients for several of these services. In this chapter, we will look at some of the common network servers that run outside of a web-server environment. As with most things with an Internet heritage, many of these services grew up on a UNIX platform. However, all are currently available on both UNIX and NT platforms.

USENET NEWS AND NNTP

As a system or network administrator, you are almost guaranteed to have read and posted to Usenet news at some point in the past. If you are from a UNIX environment, you may have even managed an NNTP server at some point. If so, please bear with us for a moment while we introduce Usenet.

Usenet news was originally developed at Duke University in 1979 as an experiment attempting to devise a system where UNIX systems could exchange text-based messages. These text messages are called *articles* and are grouped into categories, known as *newsgroups,* based on topic. As the software grew out of the experimental stage and was released to the Internet at large, Usenet grew in popularity. In 1986, new software that provided an implementation of the Network News Transport Protocol (NNTP), defined in RFC977, was released. NNTP allowed Usenet sites to migrate from UUCP to a direct TCP/IP connection for transferring news articles.

Usenet now carries hundreds of thousands of articles every day, categorized into tens of thousands of newsgroups. Each user of Usenet news uses client software known as a *news reader,* which enables a user to browse and read articles and to post new articles to the group of his or her choice.

NNTP Servers on UNIX

Since Usenet news was developed, several different versions of news server software have been released for the UNIX platform. Currently, the most widely used is the InterNetNews system, or INN for short.

INN is a complete Usenet news system that handles posting messages and transferring and receiving messages from remote hosts. It was originally developed by Rich Salz, and is now maintained by the Internet Software Consortium (ISC). The ISC's website can be found at **http://www.isc.org**.

It isn't possible in this chapter to completely cover all the setup and configuration information that you need to install INN. For complete details of how to install and configure INN, refer to the documentation that comes with the INN software. (Both the software and the documentation are on the CD-ROM included with this book.)

NNTP Servers on NT

Windows is just beginning to make inroads into the NNTP server arena. NNTP servers have traditionally run on UNIX systems, and the choices of NNTP servers for NT are still quite limited. The most popular UNIX NNTP server, INN, has not been ported to NT, and there are no plans to do so.

Microsoft Windows 2000 and NNTP

Microsoft Windows 2000 includes support for the NNTP protocol, and can be integrated with Microsoft's Internet Information Server (IIS). Accordingly, the NNTP service can be monitored and controlled with the Windows 2000 Server administration tools for performance monitoring and event reporting. All Microsoft NNTP Service status and error messages are written to event logs for viewing in the Event Viewer. Microsoft NNTP Service also includes support for Simple Network Management Protocol (SNMP) monitors.

Microsoft NNTP Service manages access to newsgroups using access control lists (ACLs). By setting the permissions for the directory that contains a newsgroup, you control who has access to that newsgroup. To allow anyone access to a newsgroup, you can specify anonymous access to the directory.

Graphic administration of the Microsoft NNTP Service can be performed with one of two tools:

- You can use the Microsoft Management Console from a system on the same local area network.
- You can access the NNTP Service Manager with your web browser from anywhere on the Internet.

Either of these options can be used on the server itself.

Netscape News Server

Netscape provides its own commercial news server in the form of the Netscape Collabra Server. The Netscape Collabra Server is a fully NNTP-compliant news server that is integrated with Netscape's SuiteSpot server software suite and is available on a variety of platforms. For more information on the Netscape Collabra Server, see the FAQ at **http://home.netscape.com/collabra/v3.5/faq/index.html**.

DNews

The DNews NNTP server is available from NetWin, Ltd., an Auckland, New Zealand company. In addition to running on Windows NT, this news server software runs on a wide variety of platforms, including Linux and BSDI. e DNews is a robust news server package, and it includes the e DNews web package, which enables you to create a web interface to selected newsgroups, similar to the Dejanews website at **http://www.deja.com**. A number of useful tools are also available from NetWin, including a newsgroup moderating tool. NetWin offers you a free four-week trial of their DNews software. For more information on DNews, including downloading the free trial software, see NetWin's website at **http://netwinsite.com/dnews.htm**.

Cassandra

Cassandra is a Windows-based news server written for the Windows NT platform. Cassandra provides a robust set of configuration options, including access control permissions at the IP level, and support for intermittent connections. For more information on Cassandra, see Atrium Software's website at **http://www.atrium-software.com/cassandra/cassandra_e.html**.

Using NNTP Servers Internally

Companies could benefit from using news servers internal to their corporate intranet for announcements and collaboration. Since the Usenet news paradigm allows you to read and respond to messages and follow subjects by topic with the conversation visible to all reading the newsgroup, it makes an excellent system for interactive communications with employees and clients. You can establish an NNTP server that provides your clients and customers with discussion areas for your products and services. For example, if you provide software support services, you might opt to create a set of support newsgroups available to your customers.

By creating a set of corporate newsgroups, you can communicate information to employees without the overhead of maintaining web pages for information delivery. For example, if you wish to communicate company news and announcements, you can create a set of moderated newsgroups that only a specific person within your organization can post messages to. You can also facilitate corporate support of other activities within your organization by creating additional newsgroups that employees can use to meet and discuss different topics. You can also integrate newsgroup access via web browser to minimize clutter on desktops of end users' systems.

In general, depending on your organization, using an NNTP server to provide access to internal newsgroups can be beneficial both for client communication and for employee participation in discussions of various topics. Such a scheme can enable you to build virtual communities within your organization.

ANONYMOUS FTP

One of the most common tasks in everyday network computing is downloading files to your local computer, or copying files from one computer to another over a network. The chances are, even if you didn't know it, that you have used the *File Transfer Protocol* (FTP) to copy files. The File Transfer Protocol component of the TCP/IP protocol suite has been around a long time, and it provides a way for transferring both binary and ASCII files between computers. A special configuration known as *anonymous FTP* allows users to transfer files from computers on which they do not have an account.

Many sites provide anonymous FTP servers in order to distribute software or to act as public archives. With many people from all over the world accessing these archives, a convention was needed to allow unknown users access to certain file areas, while still maintaining adequate system security. Anonymous FTP was devised as a way to help solve this problem.

CAUTION: By allowing unknown users to store files on your system, you may or may not be opening yourself to legal action if those files are illegal in some way. Consider carefully what your users' needs are.

Currently, anonymous FTP can be invoked either by a dedicated FTP client or from most web browsers. With a web browser, you typically just make a connection by entering **ftp://** (instead of http://) as the URL designator. The web browser will act behind the scenes to log into the anonymous FTP server. With a dedicated FTP client, you open a connection to a specific anonymous FTP server and log in with the username "anonymous." By convention, the password is your complete Internet e-mail address.

NOTE: Virtually all large anonymous FTP sites, and most small sites as well, log all accesses and transfers from their servers.

A properly configured anonymous FTP server allows read-only access to a very specific part of the file system. Since access is controlled and logged, anonymous FTP provides a safe and effective way to distribute software, text, or binary files, both for internal company use and for distribution to the Internet at large. However, FTP servers must be properly configured in order to provide a safe environment for file distribution. Incorrectly configured FTP servers can give malicious users access to system files or passwords, and can provide an avenue for uploading and exchanging pirated copies of software.

Configuring Anonymous FTP for UNIX

Like most things related to TCP/IP and the Internet, anonymous FTP grew up in the UNIX world. Most large FTP sites are still hosted on UNIX systems. In fact, many companies are using low-cost or freeware UNIX operating systems such as Linux and BSDI UNIX for dedicated servers, including anonymous FTP servers. In any case, UNIX and anonymous FTP are going to be around for a while.

Creating the Password File Entry

The first step in configuring anonymous FTP under UNIX is to add the ftp entry to the password file. Open the /etc/passwd file, and add a line similar to this one:

```
ftp:*:500:500:Anonymous FTP User:/home/ftp:/bin/true
```

Adding this line to the password file turns on anonymous FTP access. As with all password file entries, the fields are separated by colon characters. In this example, the first field indicates that the username is ftp, which enables anonymous FTP access. The second field is the password field. By using an asterisk character in the password field, you prevent anyone from being able to interactively log in as the user ftp and get to a UNIX shell. In this example, the user ID (UID) and group ID (GID) are both set to 500. On your system, you should assign a unique UID to the ftp user. You should also create a separate, unique ftp group in the /etc/group file. The home directory in this example is set to /home/ftp, but it can be set to whatever directory you are using for your FTP archive.

CAUTION: When choosing the location of the FTP home directory, make sure that there are no system directories located under it in the directory hierarchy.

The last field in the ftp password file entry sets the shell for the ftp user to be /bin/true. This is not an interactive shell; it thus provides an extra level of security should the ftp user manage to attempt an interactive login.

Creating the FTP Directory Hierarchy

The second step in setting up anonymous FTP access is to create the FTP directory hierarchy and set the file permissions properly. Choose a location for the home directory for anonymous FTP so that it does not sit above any system directories. A common path to the anonymous FTP root directory is /home/ftp. Create the directory in the desired location and set both the owner and group to something other than ftp.

CAUTION: No directory in the anonymous FTP directory hierarchy should ever be owned by the ftp user or have group access set to the ftp group.

Set the owner of the /home/ftp directory to be root and its group to be a system group, such as sys. Set the permissions on the /home/ftp directory so that the owner has read, write, and execute permissions, and group and others have only read and execute permissions. Looking at the directory permissions and ownership should show something like this:

```
# ls -ld /home/ftp
drwxr-xr-x   2 root     sys         1024 May 14 15:35 /home/ftp
#
```

Next, create the etc, bin, and pub directories under the /home/ftp directory. The ownership, group, and permissions for the pub directory should be the same as for the /home/ftp directory. For the bin and etc directories, set the ownership and group to be the same as /home/ftp, but set the permissions to be execute only. The directory permissions and ownership in the /home/ftp directory should show something like

```
# ls -l /home/ftp
d--x--x--x   2 root     sys         1024 May 14 15:35 bin
d--x--x--x   2 root     sys         1024 May 14 15:35 etc
drwxr-xr-x   2 root     sys         1024 May 14 15:36 pub
#
```

Adding Programs and Configuration Files

The next step is to add the necessary programs and configuration files to the anonymous FTP directory tree. In order to list the contents of directories, users will need access to the ls program. To install a copy of ls in the anonymous FTP area, copy the ls program into the /home/ftp/bin directory. It should have the same ownership and group as the /home/ftp directory, and its permissions should be set to execute only. So, the permissions and ownership for ls should be

```
# cd /home/ftp/bin
# ls -l ls
---x--x--x   1 root     sys         36792 Aug 19  1996 ls
#
```

You also need to provide a very simple version of the passwd and group files in the anonymous FTP area. These files are used by anonymous FTP to show the username and group name of the files in the anonymous FTP area. They are not used in any way to authenticate or log in anonymous FTP users.

CAUTION: You should never use your real password and group files in the anonymous FTP area!

Since these files are only going to be used to fill in the user and group names displayed by ls, you can just create them from scratch. Change the directory to the etc directory in the anonymous FTP area and create the password and group files here. Both files should have minimal entries. For example, your password file could look like this:

```
root:*:0:0:The Boss::
ftp:*:500:500: Anonymous ftp::
```

And your group file could look like this:

```
sys:*:10:
ftp:*:500:
```

These files should be owned by root and have read-only permission set for everyone. If you want even more security, you can usually get away with not even using the dummy password and group files. Anonymous FTP only uses them to keep from displaying numbers instead of user and group names. Accordingly, virtually all UNIX anonymous FTP systems will work fine without them.

The pub Directory

The pub directory is where you will place files that you want anonymous FTP users to be able to transfer. This directory, and all directories below it, should have read and execute permission set for users. Do not set write permission for group and other users on these directories, as anonymous FTP users could then upload programs into your anonymous FTP area.

Providing an Incoming Directory

Some anonymous FTP sites provide an incoming directory that is world-writable, with the intent that users can contribute software to the FTP archive. In general, this is a bad idea and can cause you real problems. If you have a directory with world-write access, malicious users can upload pirated software and essentially use your FTP server as a covert, pirate BBS. Also, users will occasionally upload huge amounts of data, which will cause the disk holding your anonymous FTP area to fill up, which is one form of a denial of service attack. We recommend that you do not provide write access in your anonymous FTP area, and that you check all your directory permissions carefully to ensure the safety of your FTP site.

Configuring Anonymous FTP for NT

Under Windows NT 3.51, the FTP server component of the Microsoft TCP/IP network software ran as a network service. Under Windows NT 4.0 and Windows 2000, the FTP server is managed as a component of the NT Internet Information Server (IIS).

NOTE: For more information on the Microsoft Internet Information Server, see Chapter 10.

All components of IIS, including FTP, are managed with the Internet Information Services snap-in tool, which was formerly called the Internet Service Manager. The Internet Information Services snap-in is an administration tool for IIS 5.0 that has been integrated with other administrative functions of Windows 2000.

To set up an anonymous FTP connection, follow these steps:

1. In the Windows taskbar, click the Start button, then select Programs, select Administrative Tools, and then click Internet Services Manager.
2. In the Console Root folder, double-click Internet Information Services, and then double-click the server name. A list of services will display.
3. Right-click Default FTP Site and select the Properties command.
4. Click the Security Accounts tab.
5. Click in the Allow Only Anonymous Connections checkbox.
6. Click Add to display the Add Users and Groups dialog window.
7. Select Everyone, then click Add, then click OK.

NOTE: The Registry path to FTP parameters is HKEY_LOCAL_MACHINE\SYSTEM\CurrentControlSet\Services\MSFTPSVC\Parameters.

THE SECURE SHELL

Connecting over a network and performing sensitive tasks, such as system administration, has some inherent risks. When you send passwords over a network, they can be compromised. Telnet, for example, sends the username and password over the network in clear text, allowing anyone with a packet sniffer to capture the login information and gain access to the network. For this reason, hosts and addresses can be spoofed, allowing commands to be issued from unauthorized sources. One tool that can help solve these problems is the Secure Shell (ssh).

The ssh software is designed to function as a replacement for the UNIX rlogin, rsh, and rcp commands. The ssh command is similar to the telnet command, in that it allows you to start an interactive command session on a remote system. The ssh command provides strong authentication and encryption in order to protect the integrity of the data stream. The ssh package is available both in a public domain form and as a commercial product. The public domain software is available on the web at **ftp://ftp.cs.hut.fi/pub/ssh/**. This version currently runs under most variants of UNIX. A very detailed FAQ covering ssh is available at **http://www.employees.org/~satch/ssh/faq/**. The commercial version of ssh, known as F-Secure, is distributed by F-Secure Corporation. Two versions of F-Secure are available: a client version, F-Secure SSH Client, that runs under Windows 3.1, 95, or 98, NT, Macintosh OS, NetWare, and UNIX; and a server version, F-Secure SSH Server, that runs under several varieties of UNIX. For more information on the commercial version of ssh, see the F-Secure Corporation website at **http://www.datafellows.com**. Ssh clients are available for almost any platform currently used, including the Palm OS for handheld organizers.

Cygnus makes a secure client and shell for Windows (**http://sourceware.cygnus.com/cygwin/**).

NETWORK TIME PROTOCOL

Computer clocks will tend to drift over time, causing different computers in your organization to have different values for the current time. Depending on your computing environment, you may need to make sure that computer clocks are always set accurately. Most computer operations groups use automated processes that are started at a specific time. If the computers in your organization rely heavily on processes that must be time-synchronized, you might want to consider using a Network Time Protocol client to set your computer clocks.

The Network Time Protocol (NTP) is a network protocol that is used to synchronize computer clocks with a reference time. If you are synchronizing clocks over a wide area network, accuracy is usually within the tens of milliseconds range. With NTP, you have the option of configuring your own NTP server to use for synchronization. Since having an NTP primary server requires either a radio or satellite receiver or a dedicated modem, most people choose to connect to a public NTP server for NTP time data.

Clients for NTP are available for most versions of UNIX. For an NT client, you will have to compile it from the NTP source code. Full details about NTP, including the source for clients and servers, can be found at **http://www.eecis.udel.edu/~ntp/**.

MICROSOFT NETMEETING

The NetMeeting product from Microsoft is a bit different from other network software that you may have encountered. NetMeeting is a type of collaboration software sometimes referred to as groupware, designed for corporate communication in order to allow a group of people to work together effectively over the Internet. NetMeeting supports a variety of communications and collaboration media, including voice and video conferencing; data conferencing via application sharing; program sharing; group whiteboarding; text, voice, or video chat; and file transfer.

The idea behind NetMeeting is that you can use the Internet as a means for group interactivity, even if the participants are in different locations. You can conduct conference calls, video conferences, sales presentations, design meetings, and distance learning by using the various collaboration tools in NetMeeting.

Installation and configuration of NetMeeting, although guided by setup wizards, has many options. NetMeeting has been included with a complete download option of Microsoft Internet Explorer, so it's possible that a given Windows system already has NetMeeting installed. For more information on NetMeeting, see the website at **http://www.microsoft.com/windows/netmeeting/**.

NOTE: Microsoft provides a NetMeeting Resource Kit in the form of a 330-page white paper. This resource kit is in Microsoft Word format and is available for download from Microsoft's website.

SUMMARY

A variety of network services run outside the confines of a web server. In this chapter, we have examined some of the most popular types of network software that you may find useful. NNTP news servers provide threaded, discussion group messaging and are useful for internal discussion groups, client feedback, and technical support. In addition, NNTP is the backbone protocol for the world-wide Usenet news system.

Anonymous FTP provides a way for system administrators to create software and information archives and make them available to the public. Configuring an anonymous FTP server requires attention to detail, in order to avoid common configuration problems that could lead to security breaches in your system. We examined the specifics, in detail, of how to install and configure anonymous FTP servers on both UNIX and NT platforms.

In addition to anonymous FTP and NNTP, we examined some of the other network service software available. These other services include the Network Time Protocol for computer clock synchronization, the ssh secure shell for secure network access, and Microsoft's NetMeeting collaboration server. As you would expect, not all of these services are available for both NT and UNIX, though the vast majority are. By analyzing your environment and system requirements, you, as the system administrator, can select appropriate tools from the wide variety of services that are available and apply them to your environment in an effective manner.

CHAPTER 14

Linux

Today, Linux is an excellent alternative to the high-priced, closed-ended operating systems of the past. Many companies, such as IBM, Oracle, and Corel, provide an astonishing array of products for Linux—both for sale and for free. The late 1990s saw Linux used in many different fields, ranging from the special-effects development platform for James Cameron's Oscar-winning film *Titanic* to the foundation of inexpensive, massively parallel supercomputers, as in NASA's Beowulf project. While many information services departments have been running Linux systems clandestinely within their organizations (before the recent media attention), they are now no longer afraid to adopt Linux in their operations.

THE LINUX SAGA

To understand Linux, you must first understand the question, "What is UNIX?" The reason is that Linux is a project initiated to create a working version of UNIX on Intel-based machines, more commonly referred to as the IBM PC-compatible computers that most people are familiar with.

The Linux operating system is available for several types of computer platforms, but the majority of Linux community effort is focused on the Intel processor PC platform. Thousands of programmers scattered around the world designed and built Linux, driven by the goal to create a UNIX clone, free of any commercially copyrighted software, for the entire world to use. This operating system that is the basis of this worldwide development began as a hobby of a European graduate student.

Linux is the brainchild of Linus Torvalds; it started out as a hobby while he was a student at the University of Helsinki in Finland. He wanted to create a replacement for the MINIX operating system, a UNIX-like system available for Intel-based PCs. Linus hoped to create a more robust version of UNIX for MINIX users. MINIX is a program developed by computer science professor Andrew Tanenbaum. The MINIX system was written to demonstrate several computer science concepts found in operating systems. Linus incorporated these concepts into a clone that mimics UNIX and made the program widely available to computer science students all over the world via the early Internet. Soon LINUX, as he called the program, generated a wide following, including its own Usenet newsgroups.

NOTE: For more information on the MINIX operating system, see the website **http://www.cs.vu.nl/~ast/minix.html**.

Linus Torvalds set out to provide his fellow MINIX users with a superior operating system that could run on the emerging 386-based IBM PC computers. After much effort, he had a system that would boot, but that had almost no hardware support. He persevered, however, and announced his work to the world in 1991, asking for contributions from anyone who felt inclined to assist.

What Is Linux?

Linux is essentially a UNIX clone, which means that with Linux you get many of the advantages of UNIX. Linux multitasking is fully *preemptive*, meaning that you can run multiple programs at the same time, and each program seems to process continuously. Other systems, such as Microsoft Windows 3.1, allow you to run multiple programs, but when you switch from one program to another, the first program typically stops running. Microsoft's Windows 95/98 and Windows NT/2000 operating systems are more like Linux, because they allow preemptive multitasking. Linux allows you to start a file transfer, print a document, copy a floppy, use a CD-ROM, and play a game—all at the same time. Linux also provides support for multiprocessor motherboards; not for as many processors as Sun's Solaris or Microsoft's Windows 2000 Datacenter Server, but then again, Linux is free.

Like Windows 2000 and the various UNIXes, Linux is fully multiuser-capable, which means that more than one person can log into and use the system at the same time. Unlike Windows, however, Linux is *free*—or nearly so—available for the price of a CD-ROM or the time it takes to download the system free from the Internet. Linux is distributed by many different organizations, each of which provides a unique collection of programs along with the core group of files that constitutes a Linux release. Distributions such as the following are available on the Net and from various CD-ROM vendors:

- Red Hat
- Caldera
- Corel Linux
- Debian Linux
- S.u.S.E. Linux
- Linux Mandrake
- MCC Interim Linux
- LinuxPPC
- Yellow Dog
- Black Lab
- LinuxWare
- Slackware Linux
- TurboLinux

In addition to this, several companies now sell Linux preinstalled on systems. These companies range from Linux-centric firms such as VA Linux and Penguin Computing to the largest of PC manufacturers such as IBM, Dell, and Compaq; the list also includes such established vendors as SGI.

Linux provides a learning opportunity unparalleled today. Here you have a complete working operating system, including source code with which to play and learn what makes the system tick. Learning what makes Linux tick is something you can't do in a typical UNIX environment, and it's definitely something you can't do with a commercial operating system, because old-time vendors aren't willing to give away their source code. In general, if you're comfortable with any variation of UNIX, you'll recognize much of Linux as familiar, especially if you're familiar with a BSD-derived or -influenced version of UNIX.

NOTE: The distributions listed above are some of the better known Linux distributions. An exhaustive list of Linux distributions, with advice and comments on each, is on the web at **http://www.linuxdoc.org/HOWTO/Distribution-HOWTO.html**.

Why Use Linux?

You'll want to use Linux because:

- It is freely available.
- It provides multitasking and multiprocessing capabilities for multiple users on a variety of hardware platforms, from IBM PCs to Sun Sparc to Apple Macintoshes.
- It is economical. A desktop computer that is unacceptably slow for use as a Windows desktop can normally run Linux at acceptable speeds. Older retired desktop computers may thus be used for a variety of group and departmental tasks.
- Applications for Linux are freely available on the Internet, as is the source code to Linux itself. If you desire, you have access to the source code to modify and expand the operating system to your needs, or to determine if a given problem is an application or operating system bug.

Several commercial vendors, including many of the distributors listed earlier in this chapter, now provide support for Linux, so getting help can be just a phone call away. Unlike the various Usenet newsgroups, mailing lists, and other public forums, such technical support is rarely free. Another downside lies in the fact that Linux is like many of the other UNIXes: If your group or department is entirely Microsoft Windows with no UNIX expertise in-house or otherwise available, be prepared for the expense of learning UNIX-like ways of performing tasks.

The Linux Copyright

Unlike the products of Microsoft and of most UNIX vendors, the Linux kernel is available free of charge, but this does not make Linux a public domain program. Microsoft owns the rights to Windows 2000 and restricts access to its source code, but who owns the rights to Linux? First and foremost, Linux isn't public domain software; many different people hold the copyright to many of the major components of Linux. Linus Torvalds holds the copyright to the basic Linux kernel. Red Hat, Inc., owns the rights to the Red Hat distribution version, and Patrick Volkerding holds the copyright to the Slackware distribution. Many Linux utilities are released under the GNU General Public License (GPL). In fact, Linus and most Linux contributors have also placed their work under the protection of the GNU GPL.

This license is sometimes referred to as the GNU Copyleft (a play on the word *copyright*). This license covers all the software produced by GNU (itself a play on words—GNU's *N*ot *U*NIX) and the Free Software Foundation. The license allows programmers to create software for everyone. The basic premise behind GNU is that software should be available to everyone and that if someone wants to modify the program to his or her own ends that should be possible. The only caveat is that the modified code can't be restricted; others must also have the right to the new code.

The GNU Copyleft, or GPL, allows a program's creators to keep their legal copyright, but it allows others to take, modify, and sell the resulting new program. However, in doing so, the original programmers can't restrict any of these same rights to modify the program from the people buying the software. If you sell the program as is or in a modified form, you must provide the source code. That's why Linux and all the utilities come with completely open source code.

NOTE: The GNU free software philosophy is on the web at **http://www.gnu.org/philosophy/free-sw.html**. A general discussion and comparison of various free software licenses and their differences is also on the web, at **http://www.opensourceit.com/news/990607_freesoftware.html**.

This Open Source movement prompted several vendors to follow suit, and thus Sun, SCO, and other vendors make their base OS available to the general public for very low cost—although most have not released their source code. Apple, for example, has released the Darwin operating system, the Darwin Streaming Server for QuickTime, and other source code as open source: The ongoing efforts are visible at **http://www.publicsource.apple.com/**. The Open Source movement feels that the availability of source code makes for a more robust and secure product. (Other vendors fear losing a "competitive edge" if they release their source code.)

Tux the Penguin: The Linux Mascot

While the Linux development project was growing, the issue arose of a mascot or logo for the operating system. Ultimately, a penguin won the day! One example of the Linux penguin, nicknamed Tux and drawn by Larry Ewing (**lewing@isc.tamu.edu**) using the GIMP (General Image Manipulation Program) Linux-based graphics program, is shown in Figure 14-1.

Figure 14-1. Tux the penguin is the official mascot of the Linux operating system.

WHAT CAN BE DONE WITH LINUX?

Many Fortune 500 companies use Linux for internal projects and mission-critical applications. And recently large companies, such as IBM, Oracle, and Corel, are embracing the concept of open solutions by releasing their own software into the development community, just as Linus Torvalds and others released their software to the world. However, most people will want to do things with their computers, not choose them solely for the operating systems. They want applications and programs to do things with on these computers. The end users can be writers, administrative assistants, graphic designers, lab technicians, or musicians; they may have no preferences, mild preferences, or strong preferences concerning the operating system they use. Regardless, they all have tasks that they want to complete. This section will discuss a sampling of the applications available for the Linux operating system, and some of the purposes that a Linux system can serve.

User Applications

The look and feel of an operating system's interface can be distinctive. The Macintosh operating system's GUI, for example, is strongly recognizable, as is the Microsoft Windows desktop GUI. As Linux is much like many kinds of UNIX, some people will work almost exclusively from the command-line prompt in a shell. Like the UNIXes, Linux can use a variety of GUIs. The oldest of the batch is CDE, the Common Desktop Environment (discussed in Chapter 16). CDE was originally designed as a common desktop and ported to several UNIXes as part of the COSE (Common Open Software Environment) project sponsored by Hewlett-Packard, IBM, Novell, and Sun Microsystems. While not very common in the Linux environment, primarily because of its price, CDE is available for

Linux. If you have a UNIX workgroup already using CDE, using CDE on Linux might be a good idea for standardization purposes.

NOTE: A commercial port of CDE is also available for Windows NT as well, providing a single login and desktop appearance for a mixed network of Windows and UNIX systems.

KDE, which stands for the K Desktop Environment, is much better known and more often used in the Linux world than CDE—primarily because CDE isn't free. Although an Open Source project, KDE does have some commercial development and support. Primarily, though, KDE is advanced by the several hundred developers actively contributing to its development as of this writing. KDE is the default window manager for several of the major Linux distributions including Caldera OpenLinux, and it is packaged with most of the rest. An example of a KDE desktop is presented in Figure 14-2.

The GNOME (GNU Network Object Model Environment) project was started because there were no completely Open Source desktop environments for Linux and other free operating systems. (KDE was built using the Qt GUI toolkit, which was not licensed

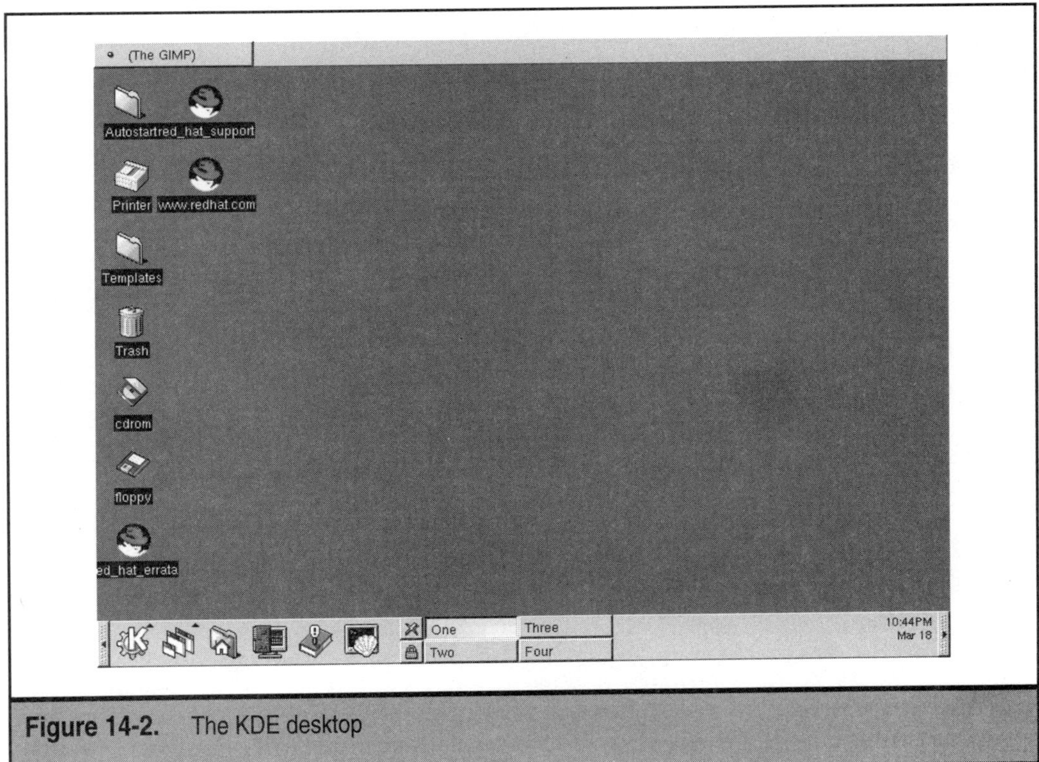

Figure 14-2. The KDE desktop

under the GNU General Public License.) The entire GNOME project is covered by the GPL. Properly speaking, GNOME is not a window manager: It provides a foundation for window managers such as the Enlightenment project (on the web at **http://www.enlightenment.org/**) to work from. Every aspect of GNOME is configurable, which is sometimes a mixed blessing: So many options can at times be difficult to choose from. GNOME ships with many of the major Linux distributions, including Red Hat Linux. Figure 14-3 presents a typical GNOME desktop. Figure 14-4, however, presents an alternative to either KDE or GNOME: the FVWM95 window manager, which is an attempt to make users of Microsoft Windows 95 and 98 feel right at home.

NOTE: The switchdesk utility, included with Red Hat Linux, allows you to switch between different window managers.

Now that you have an operating system and a GUI, what next? It almost goes without saying that the entire suite of GNU utilities has been ported to Linux, as it has to almost every flavor of UNIX known (as well as to other operating systems, including BeOS).

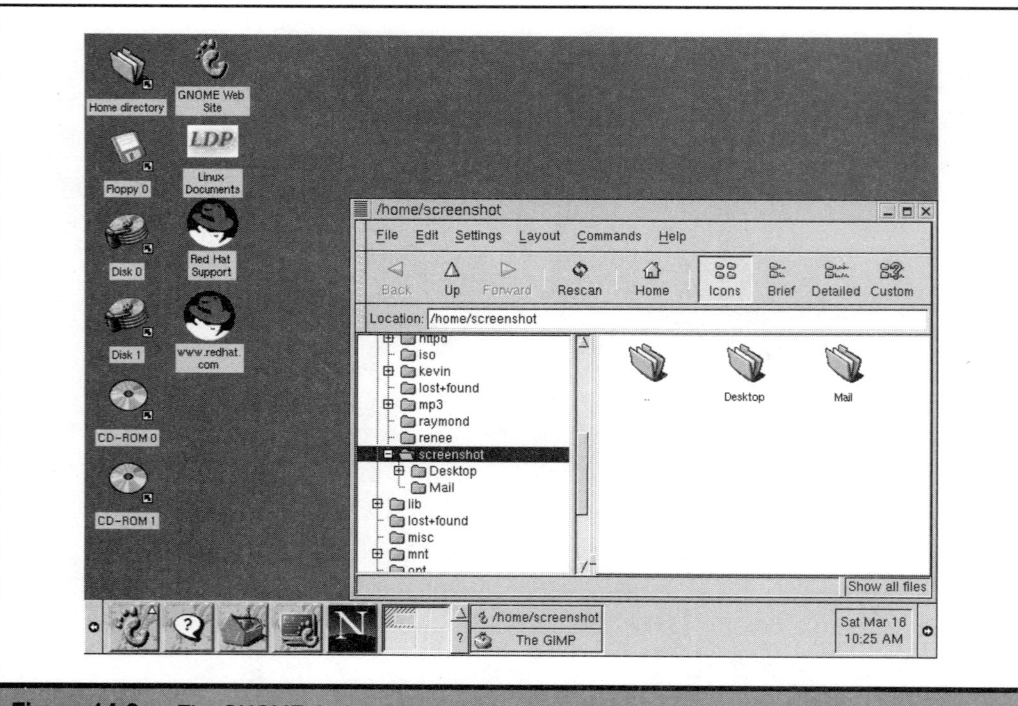

Figure 14-3. The GNOME desktop

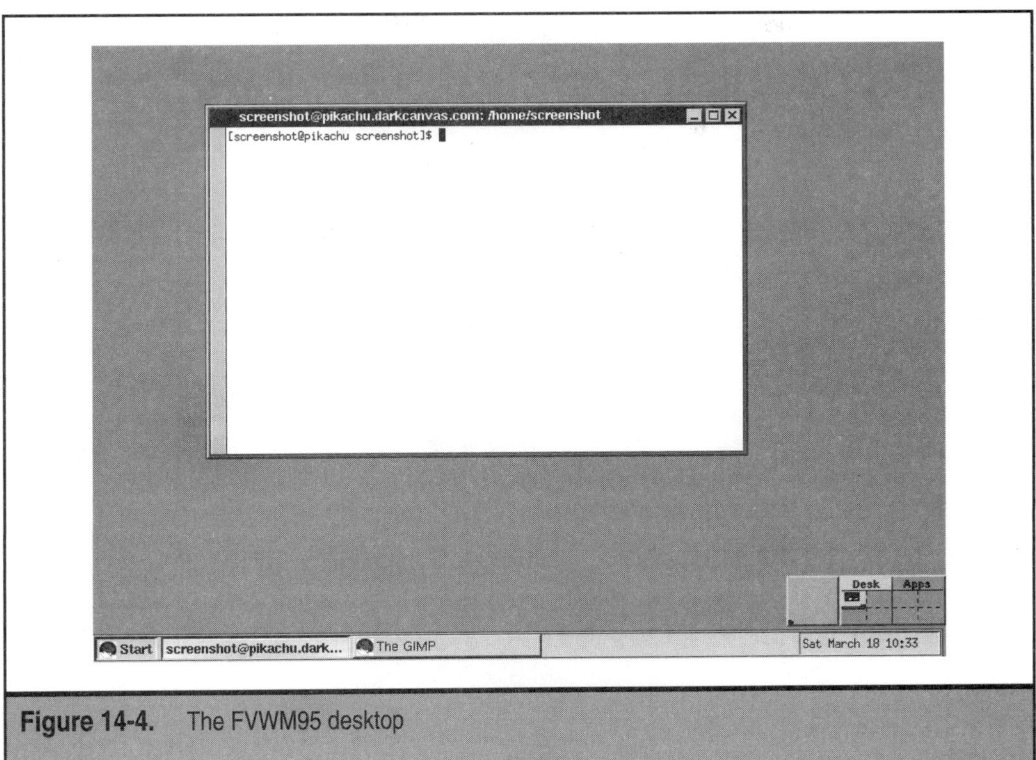

Figure 14-4. The FVWM95 desktop

However, one of the first questions asked for a business environment at this time is, Does it run Microsoft Office? Microsoft has not ported the Office suite to Linux at this time, and may never do so, but other fine office suites are available: Applixware and StarOffice.

Applixware Office is a set of general productivity tools: a word processor, a spreadsheet, a presentation creator, a graphics application, a mail client, and an ODBC database query tool, along with an impressive array of filters for many word processors, spreadsheets, and graphics package file types. Applixware is a mature product, having been used for years under the Solaris operating system prior to being ported to Linux. Applixware is also available for Windows, and a Java version runs in any Java-enabled browser or Java-aware operating system. An example of Applixware is presented in Figure 14-5. For more information on Applixware, see their website at **http://www.applix.com/**.

StarOffice is another productivity suite similar to Applixware, and it also includes a calendar tool and a newsgroup browser in its array of tools. Now owned by Sun, StarOffice is free for anyone's use (but is not an open-source application). Visit **http://www.sun.com/products/staroffice/**; there are over 1.8 million downloads as of this writing. StarOffice is supported on Solaris (both Sparc and Intel processors), Windows 95 and 98, Windows NT 4.0 and higher—and, of course, Linux. Figure 14-6 presents a view

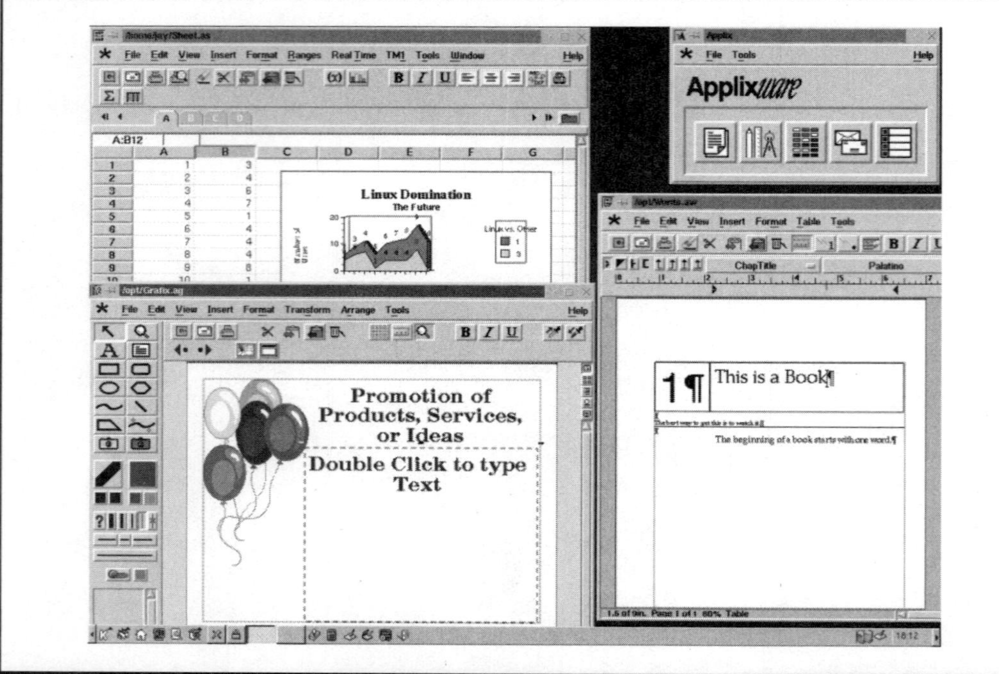

Figure 14-5. Applixware is a multiplatform productivity suite.

of the StarOffice startup window under KDE, and Figure 14-7 presents a view of the StarOffice word processor.

NOTE: Adobe has released a beta version of FrameMaker for Linux. While not an entire office suite, FrameMaker is a popular and powerful word processor best suited to structured documentation such as user guides and manuals. FrameMaker has been available for Windows, the Mac OS, and Solaris as well as other UNIXes. The FrameMaker beta for Linux is available for download at **http://www.adobe.com/products/framemaker/fmlinux.html**.

In addition to the mail clients available as part of the productivity suites above, a well-designed mail client is included as part of the KDE window manager. A view of the KMail Settings window is shown in Figure 14-8.

The GIMP (GNU Image Manipulation Program) was one of the earliest attempts at a mainstream application. The GIMP is designed for photograph editing and retouching and image creation and editing. In general, the user interface resembles that of Adobe Photoshop. While the GIMP lacks many of the more advanced features and specific capabilities of Photoshop, it has many features oriented toward graphics production for the

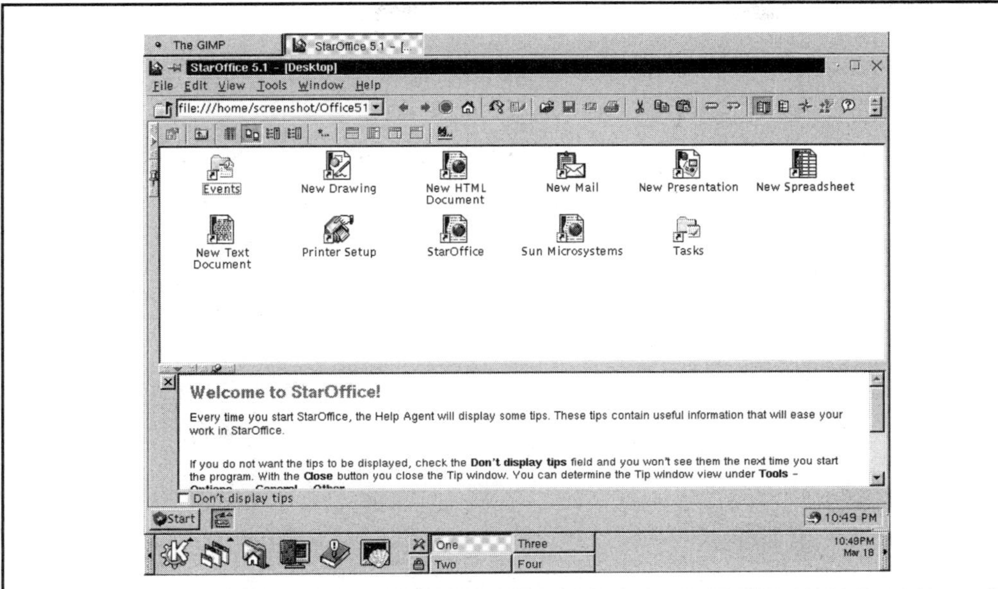

Figure 14-6. The free StarOffice productivity suite

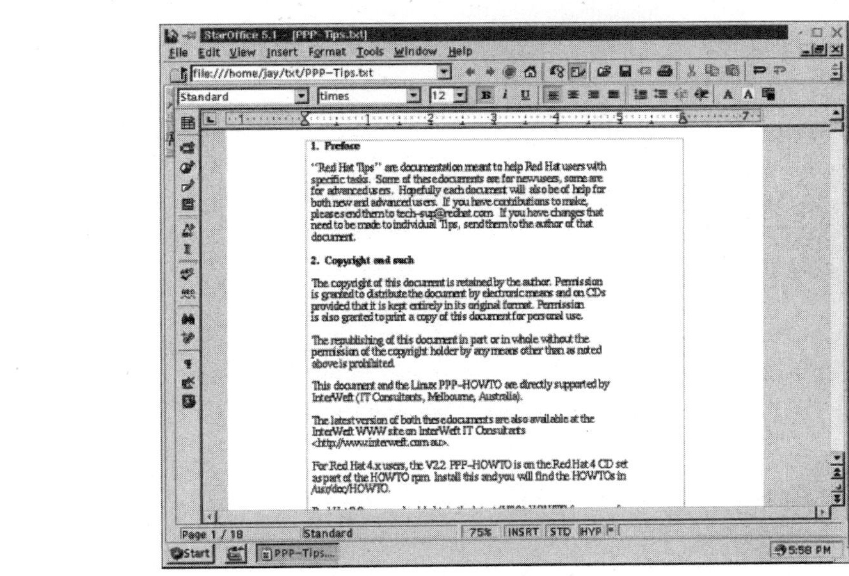

Figure 14-7. The StarOffice Writer word processor tool

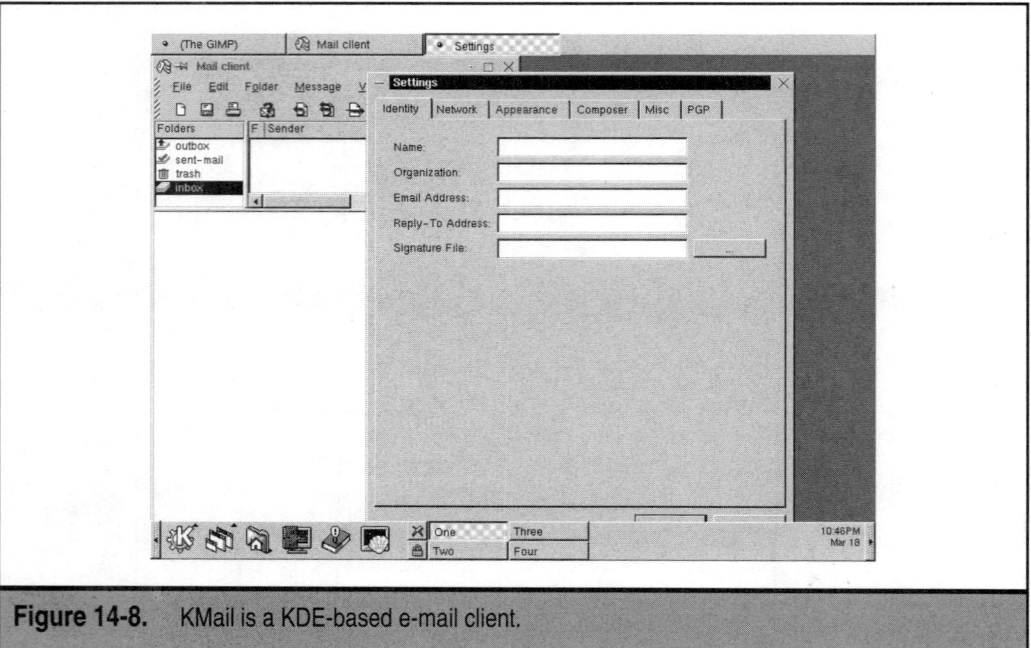

Figure 14-8. KMail is a KDE-based e-mail client.

web. Its strong scripting capabilities allow easy automation of complex repetitive tasks. A view of the GIMP is shown in Figure 14-9.

The GIMP development project also provided another benefit to the Linux community at large: The original developers decided to use a very generalized approach to create the graphics routines. By tying their routines together only loosely, and by using Open Source, they made the graphics routines created for the GIMP easily adaptable for use by other Linux development projects needing graphics routines. One of the primary uses for this cluster of graphics routines (collectively referred to as the GTK, or GIMP Toolkit) has been the GNOME development project.

NOTE: Adobe has been asked often about the possibility of Photoshop for Linux. The consistent statement so far is that there is not enough demand to justify a port of Photoshop to Linux. Perhaps someday...

Software developers are by no means left out of the Linux world: Not counting such free and almost universally available UNIX tools as gcc, and such prototyping tools as the scripting languages, other development tools are also present for the Linux operating system. As one example, Sun's Java development environment, Forte for Java, Community Edition, is free for download, and supports the latest Sun JDK. A partial view of Forte (partial because it likes to take up *all* the monitor's real estate) is presented in Fig-

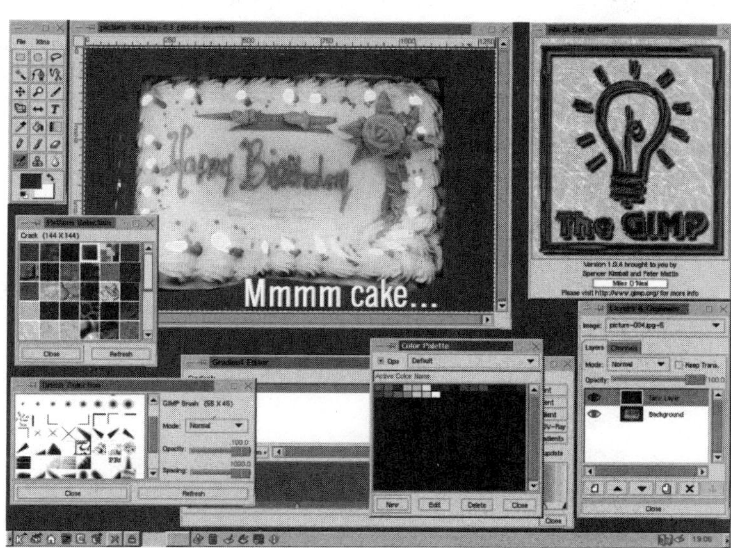

Figure 14-9. The GIMP graphic management tool

ure 14-10. Another excellent development environment for the Linux platform is Visual SlickEdit, shown in Figure 14-11.

Corel/Inprise is creating the Kylix Rapid Application Development (RAD) development environment for the Linux platform, which will allow the developers familiar with Borland's Delphi and C++Builder development environments to work productively. Kylix is described as a component-based development environment that is intended for use as a two-way visual development environment of GUI, Internet, database, and server applications. Corel/Inprise has announced that its plans are for Kylix to be powered by a Linux-native C, C++, and Delphi compiler, and that the product will also include a Linux-native version of the Borland VCL (Visual Component Library) architecture. Another important need of developers is for version control management. In addition to the standard UNIX command-line tools such as RCS and SCCS, both Mainsoft and Perforce, among others, have Linux clients.

For general systems management and configuration needs of a given server, the linuxconf administration tool is excellent. Linuxconf is included with many distributions of Linux, including Red Hat. An example of the Linuxconf GUI is shown in Figure 14-12.

The presence of instant messaging software has grown rapidly and recently. Some firms are using instant messaging as a customer interface for online help and contact; some are automating the process such that automated versions of an instant messaging client

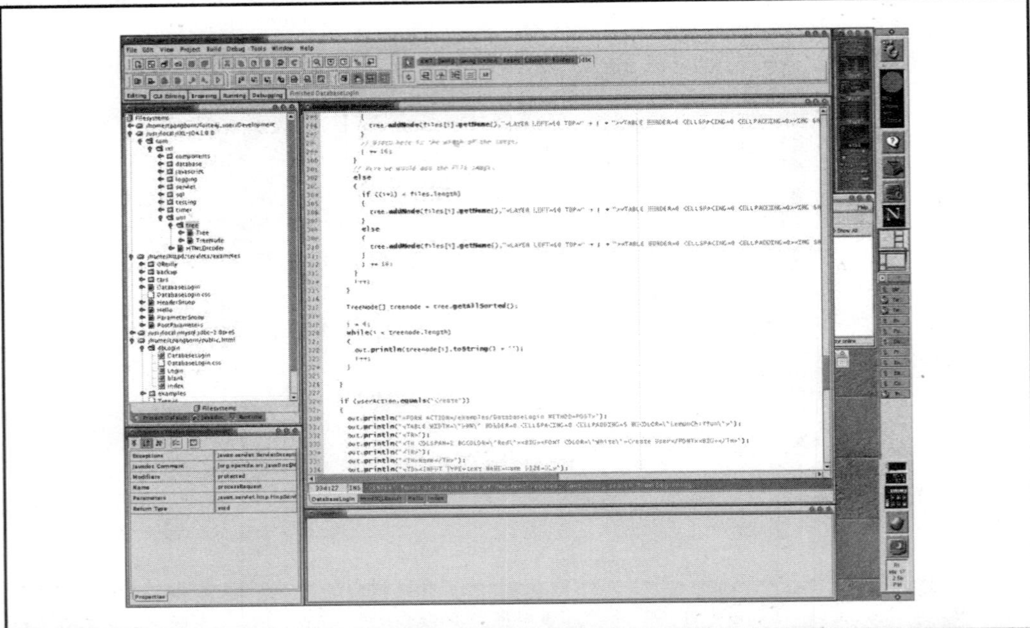

Figure 14-10. Forte for Java, Community Edition: a free Java development environment

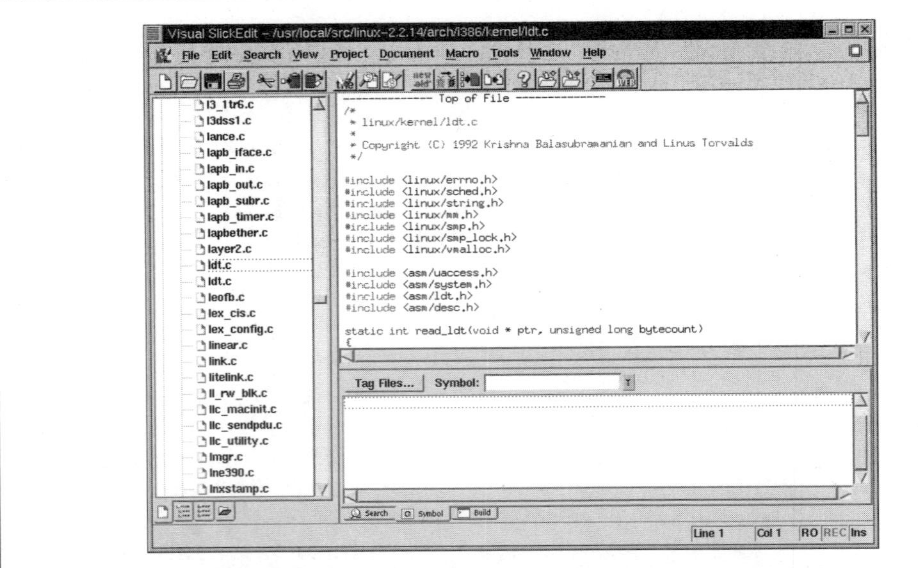

Figure 14-11. The Visual SlickEdit development environment

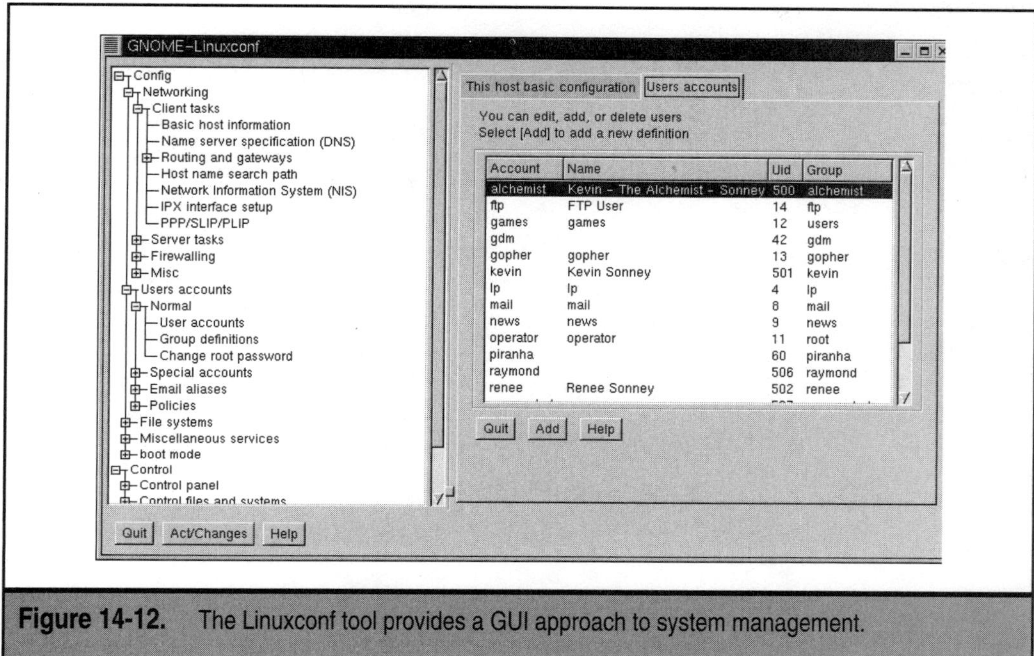

Figure 14-12. The Linuxconf tool provides a GUI approach to system management.

will accept a customer contact and broadcast it to a group of individual online representatives. Everybuddy is a Linux GTK application that consolidates Yahoo pager, AOL Instant Messenger, and ICQ all into one interface. There are several variations of instant messaging clients for Linux, but one of the best is Everybuddy, shown in Figure 14-13. For more information on Everybuddy, visit the website at **http://www.everybuddy.com/**.

Finally, there's entertainment. Many different games written for UNIX have been recompiled for Linux, including the endless run of Minesweeper and Solitaire clones. In the realm of the FPS (First Person Shooter) genre of games, Id Software has ported its popular DOOM and Quake, Quake II, and Quake III to Linux. Figure 14-14 shows a scene from Quake.

Epic Games has released a client of its hugely popular multiplayer and multiplatform action game Unreal Tournament for Linux as well, as shown in Figure 14-15.

Server Services

Because of its ability to run well on older, Intel-based PC workstations that have outlived their usefulness as Windows workstations, Linux is often used as a single-function server in a number of settings. This section will discuss some of the tasks that Linux servers may perform in an organization.

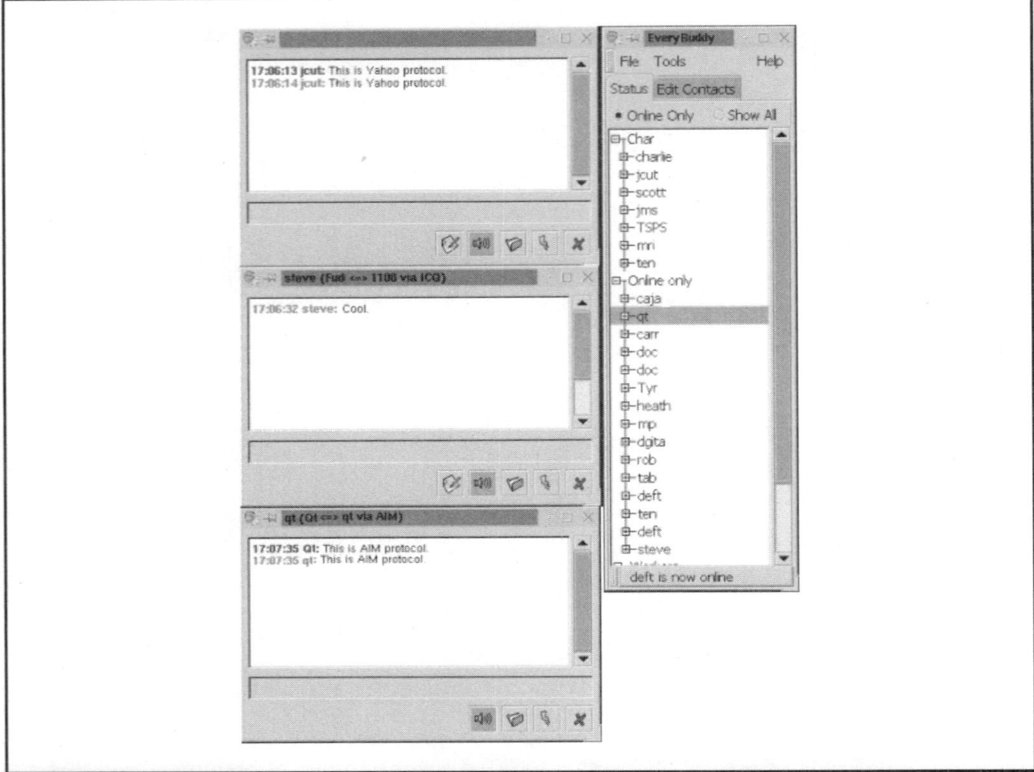

Figure 14-13. Everybuddy combines Yahoo! Pager, AOL Instant Messenger, and ICQ instant messaging.

NOTE: Many systems, Linux-based and otherwise, provide multiple functions, and do so quite well. Nothing in the Linux operating system precludes it from serving multiple functions. This versatility rides on two factors:

- **Evolutionary needs of a workgroup** An office rarely develops its needs for a file server, a web server, a mail server, and a DNS server simultaneously.
- **Personal philosophy** Multifunction devices are great as long as everything works. Isolating, identifying, and repairing a problem with one feature of a multifunction device is a hassle compared to facing the same problem on a single-use device. Also, in the case of a hardware failure, repairs do not affect the rest of your system. That multifunction printer/fax machine/copier/scanner is great until the fax component breaks and you have to send it out for repair—losing all the functions until the one is repaired.

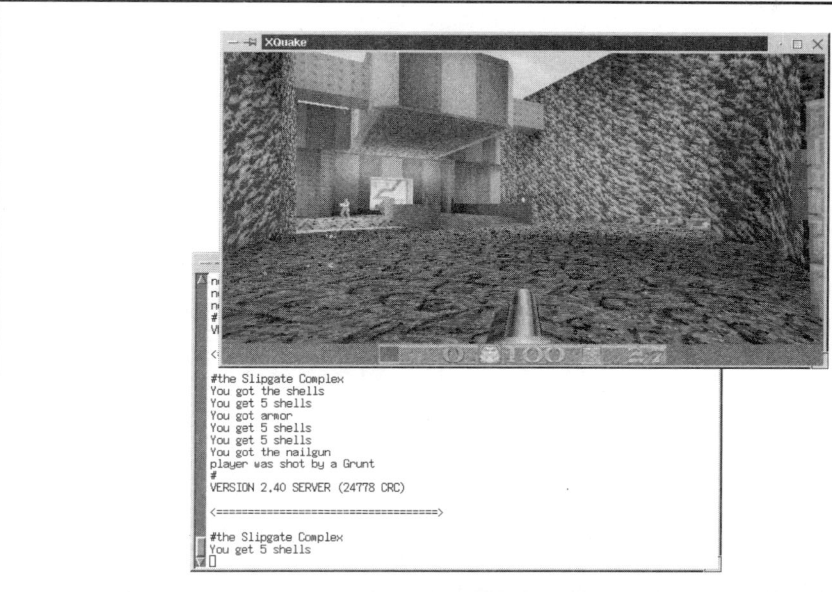

Figure 14-14. The Quake FPS (First Person Shooter) game

Figure 14-15. The Unreal Tournament action game

Linux systems are commonly used by system administrators to provide the fundamental services of the Internet:

- Mail server using sendmail
- Web server with Apache
- DNS server using BIND
- File and print server using Samba

Other roles for a Linux server would be as a directory server, running a directory service such as OpenLDAP (**http://www.openldap.org/**), as a multimedia server running a streaming audio or video server such as the Darwin Streaming Server (**http://www.publicsource.apple.com/projects/streaming/**), and as a Quake server. However, one of the most common roles for a Linux system is as a Samba server, providing file and print services to the users of a given group. The Samba client/server suite, originally developed in Australia by Andrew Tridgell, is an SMB (Server Message Block, the standard protocol that Windows NT uses for sharing file and print services) server package that runs under UNIX. By using Samba, UNIX systems can create shares that can be used by Windows-based computers. More information on the SMB protocol and the Samba suite may be found in Chapter 2, or on the web at **http://www.samba.org/**. An article on using an older desktop machine as a Linux Samba server may be found on the web at **http://www.opensourceit.com/tutorials/jg.cgi**.

Security is like insurance: Not everyone bothers to buy it, because security risks are part of the overhead of doing business. Those that do bother don't always buy enough to meet their actual needs. Good security is a nebulous quantity and a negative concept at best: If it works, you still have what you had before, minus however much your security cost you. An older desktop with two network interface cards (NICs) can be set up as a simple firewall, providing at least some semblance of security.

CAUTION: The default installations of most versions of Linux are dangerously insecure. Do a custom install, and only install the services on your system you need. It's a bad idea to install software just in case you think you might need it. Install only the software you need, and disable any software you don't understand. A good introduction to Linux system security may be found on the web at **http://www. nwo.net/security/**.

An excellent security tool available for the Linux platform is the Internet Security Scanner, shown in Figure 14-16, which probes your network for vulnerabilities. More information on ISS is available from **http://www.iss.net/**.

Other commercial software that now runs on Linux includes such notable applications as:

- The Oracle 8*i* and IBM DB2 databases
- SAP's R/3 business platform

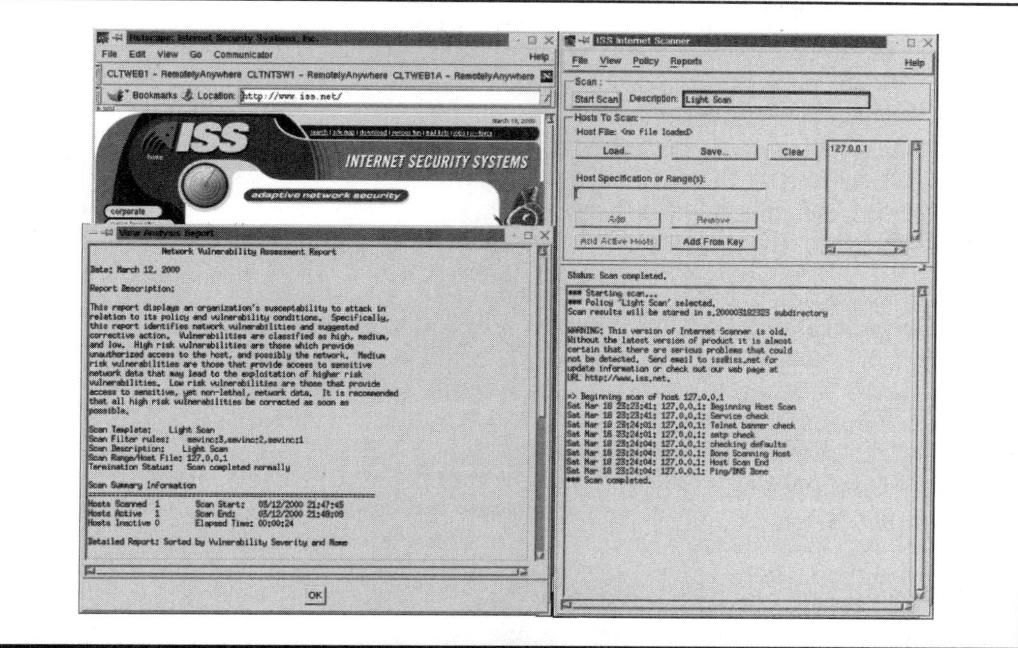

Figure 14-16. The Internet Security Scanner network analyzer

- The massive SAS environment and suite of database, data mining, and business management applications
- IBM's Websphere application server
- The Veritas suite of backup utilities originally released under the company name of Seagate Software
- The Perforce configuration management tool
- Computer Associates' Unicenter TNG management tools
- The Tivoli Enterprise and Tivoli Management Suites of network and systems management tools
- And many others

Reliability and Scalability

Several issues arise under the general topic of reliability and scalability: People want data to be always available, people want their systems to have as little unplanned downtime as possible, and people want to never lose their work. A RAID (Redundant

Array of Inexpensive Devices) can improve data availability. Hardware RAID arrays are amazingly reliable, stable, and capable of massive amounts of high-speed data transfer, and they are generally fiendishly expensive. Software RAID systems are almost always significantly cheaper but are still much safer (and can be significantly faster) than no RAID at all. The primary source for information on Linux as a software RAID controller is on the web at **http://linas.org/linux/raid.html**. The Linux Documentation Project has a well-written HOWTO on the subject, also available on the web at **http://www.linuxdoc.org/ HOWTO/Software-RAID-HOWTO.html**.

So RAID helps protect against one hard disk failure destroying the data. What happens to your company when someone trips over the power line for the company's mail or web server, or if the motherboard in the departmental file server dies? You want not only to mirror data across multiple hard disks, you want to provide multiple servers in parallel, such that a single server failure (or scheduled shutdown for maintenance) doesn't inconvenience or embarrass the group. A VAX minicomputer cluster is this reliable: If you have a cluster of four VAXes, someone can simply turn one of the four off, and none of the users will notice—no data is lost, no service is shut down. The other members of the cluster are not doing anything until the first system fails: the load is shared between the systems. StarFire Technology's RSF-1 (Resilient Server Facility) clustering and mirroring supports Linux, as well as Solaris, AIX, and Windows NT. For more information, see their website at **http://www.starfiretechnology.com/**. Another company offering failover and clustering management application is Technauts.

RESOURCES

Entire books, and many of them, have been written about Linux and its myriad of subtopics. This section will provide some pointers to further resources for learning about Linux.

Reference Materials

For documentation of all matters relating to Linux, the premier source of information is the LDP (Linux Documentation Project), which may be found on the web at **http://www.linuxdoc.org/**. The LDP is the place to find all the HOWTOs, mini-HOWTOs, guides, tutorials, and other information on all things Linux.

On the other hand, you might not be completely comfortable with reading the often-cryptic HOWTO documents. The Linuxnewbie website at **http://www.linuxnewbie.org/nhf/index.html** contains "newbie-ized" HOWTOs that are written for those just learning Linux and, in some cases, UNIX as well. Another good resource for information on Linux is Linuxcare's website at **http://www.linuxcare.com/**.

For daily news on Linux issues, the best sources of information are web publications such as Linux Weekly (and Daily) News at **http://www.lwn.net** and Linux Today at **http://www.linuxtoday.com**, and the Slashdot news site at **http://slashdot.org**/. In addition, more Linux and other UNIX software than you probably have time to browse through is announced every day on the Freshmeat site at **http://freshmeat.net/**.

If you're interested in periodicals on paper, there's the Linux Journal, (**http://www.linuxjournal.com/**), SysAdmin magazine (which conveniently collects its Linux-specific articles together online at **http://www.sysadminmag.com/linux/**), and the Journal of Linux Technology (**http://linux.com/jolt/**). The USENIX journal (**http://www. usenix.org/**) also periodically features Linux articles.

Trying Out Linux

So, after reading this chapter, and maybe looking at some of the informational websites mentioned in the previous section, would you like to actually try Linux? As previously mentioned, several computer manufacturers will sell a Linux workstation or server, prebuilt to specifications and thoroughly tested. If you don't want to spend that much money, there are other options. As mentioned previously, Linux will run at acceptable speeds on older hardware that is painfully slow to run Microsoft Windows on. Once you've found a computer to use, then there's Linux itself to worry about. As mentioned previously, the Linux Documentation Project has an excellent overview of the various Linux distributions on the web at **http://www.linuxdoc.org/HOWTO/Distribution-HOWTO.html**. You can download many of the distributions of Linux easily, or if you have a slow connection, free CD-ROMs with Linux on them may be found in many computer magazines and books.

NOTE: If you don't have a completely spare computer, you can normally install Linux as a dual-boot machine—on startup, you're presented with a selection menu of the operating systems you have installed on the machine. Most common are Linux/Windows dual-boot machines, but variations include Linux/Solaris (on Intel), Linux/BeOS, Linux/FreeBSD/Windows, Linux (one distribution)/ Linux (another distribution), Linux/Netware/Windows/OS/2, and so on. Several of these variations are presented as "mini-HOWTOs" and may be found on the web at **http://www.linuxdoc.org/HOWTO/HOWTO-INDEX-3.html#ss3.2**.

If you have a spare Macintosh, you will find that several versions of Linux have been ported to many of the different models of Macintosh hardware. Of the major Linux distributions, TurboLinux and S.u.S.E. both produce versions of their distribution for the PowerPC. The mkLinux port is intended for older Macintoshes containing the Motorola 68000 family of processors. Yellow Dog Linux and LinuxPPC both produce excellent distributions of Linux intended for the PowerPC-based Macintosh hardware.

If you have a Macintosh that is not spare, the Connectix Virtual PC application emulates an Intel PC quite well, enough to install Windows NT within the Virtual PC space and run applications. While unsatisfactory for real-time or processor-intensive applications such as games or Photoshop, Virtual PC is quite functional for general use. Connectix is shipping Virtual PC bundled with Red Hat Linux, so it is perfectly possible to test out Linux on a Macintosh. A counterpart to the Virtual PC product is the WinLinux product, which installs a Linux operating system that runs within your Windows operating system. WinLinux information may be found on the web at **http://www.winlinux.net**.

TIP: You may be able to run Linux applications from another operating system. The FreeBSD system includes kernel modules for Linux, SCO UNIX, and SVR4 UNIX. With these modules, your FreeBSD system can run an application compiled for Linux without recompiling. Sun's Solaris 8 operating system also supports Linux binaries.

VMWare is another commercial solution to the problem of how to squeeze yet another computer onto the desk without installing a rack. The VMWare Virtual Platform installs on an Intel-based PC and presents a complete image of the PC hardware to whatever operating system. In this way, it resembles the model of Windows NT/2000's Hardware Abstraction Layer, creating a virtual model of the PC's hardware. The difference is that you can play DOOM on DOS, Window95 or 98, or Linux under VMWare, but the Windows NT/2000 HAL prevents DOOM from running.

VMWare virtualizes many of the hardware PC components, but not the CPU. VMWare is effective enough to allow you to install (for example) two Linux images, or two Windows and a third Linux image; have all three run simultaneously; and teach networking between the two, three, or more virtual images, all on one piece of hardware. One networking instructor of my acquaintence uses a single laptop with VMWare to have multiple "computers" in his briefcase; this way he can teach network configuration without having to carry an entire computer lab with him.

More information on VMWare can be found on the web at **http://www.vmware.com/**. A noncommercial version is also being developed; see **http://www.freemware.org/** for more information.

SUMMARY

In this chapter, we've looked at the history and background of the Linux movement, the characteristics of the operating system, and the current status of various distributions. We examined many different products and services available for Linux.

As you can see, it is no longer true that Linux is not robust enough, nor supported enough, nor stable enough to provide mission-critical services. The Linux subset of the computer industry is maturing at a rapid pace. Acknowledging the wish of management to quantify the skill levels of IS professionals, several organizations are either offering or developing certification and training programs for various flavors of Linux. Information and resources relating to Linux certification can be found on the website of the Linux Professional Institute at **http://www.lpi.org/**.

CHAPTER 15

Desktop Applications

Networks are growing bigger and more heterogeneous as time passes. This is due to the fact that, although new solutions to technical problems appear at a dizzying rate, old solutions may still work acceptably. Glass-house mainframe shops with character-based terminals may want to keep their existing mainframes and dumb terminal networks; these older solutions are reliable, and they work well for many business tasks. On the other hand, a character-based dumb terminal can't do anything other than talk to a mainframe. Most users want, and in fact need, the more sophisticated applications available in today's computing environment.

OPERATING SYSTEMS VS. DESKTOP APPLICATIONS

Windows networking with Windows 2000 is approaching the ease of networking Apple has had for years with AppleTalk: building a small Windows-only network is still more complicated than just plugging in the cables, but it's not that difficult to construct. UNIX has evolved as the predominant operating system in the largest computer network of all: the conglomeration of systems, networks, and connectivity that is known as the Internet. Therefore, much of the networking effort over the last three decades or so has gone into either improving UNIX's networking functionality or in enhancing other operating systems to network into UNIX systems. Much of Microsoft's networking effort has been to extend Windows to better work with UNIX and thereby the Internet, as different portions of this book have discussed.

However, users are not so much enamored with a given operating system as they can be with the applications on the operating systems. Users want to use applications to write, draw, or calculate. Users generally interact with operating systems in similar ways: they create, edit, and delete files; they view listings of files in directories or folders; and they may copy or move files around in the directories. Users also manipulate files in other ways: attaching files to be included with electronic mail messages, outputting the files via a printer or other device, and so on.

Most often, users of modern systems today use a GUI (graphical user interface) to interact with a given operating system. DOS had the Windows GUI, until it was incorporated with the OS in Windows NT; the Apple Macintosh operating system, also a GUI, has been reviled by some for not having a command-line interface at all (Apple's Mac OS X is built on a BSD-flavor UNIX kernel); and the different versions of UNIX have had several windowing systems, including the many versions of X Window, Sun's OpenWindows, and the Common Desktop Environment (CDE).

Users who must deal with multiple operating systems are occasionally limited by the following details:

- Not all applications are available on all operating systems.
- If they are available, the multiple versions may not be available on their network.
- Sometimes applications that claim cross-platform compatibility are less than accurate, or are accurate only with a restricted subset of functionality.

▲ Having multiple platforms can lead to its own logistical nightmare of needing to maintain multiple workstations for *each* user.

Much of this book has focused on specific areas of integrating UNIX and Windows systems in order for them to play nice with each other: printing, electronic mail, file systems, and so on. This chapter will focus on ways to allow users to share the same desktop, or the same functionality, from different places in the network.

First, this chapter will discuss X Window, which is the basis for many of the windowing systems available for UNIX, and which has also been ported to many other operating systems. That topic will be followed by a discussion of means to provide access to X Window–based applications to users of Windows desktop workstations, then the view will reverse and we'll look at ways to make Windows desktops available across the enterprise network. This chapter will then close with an overview of several tools, many comparatively low-level that help provide veteran UNIX users with much of the same functionality they are accustomed to having in UNIX environments.

THE X WINDOW SYSTEM

The X Window System was originally developed at the Massachusetts Institute of Technology in order to help answer the needs of research and engineering computer users for graphics capability. X is a graphical user interface (GUI) system that is capable of running on top of many other operating systems. X is available for almost every form of UNIX, Windows, Macintosh OS, OS/2, and many other operating systems, as well as being the underlying basis for such offshoots as the G-Windows GUI for the OS-9 and OS-9000 operating systems. This section will discuss some of the history and architecture of X and then discuss some of the options for making X available on PC-based platforms, including PC X servers and web browser plug-ins.

History of X Window and the X Consortium

The first release of the major form of X, known as X version 11, was in 1987. The X Consortium was formed in 1988 to further the development of the X Window System and was charged with its major goal: to promote cooperation between all participants in the computer industry for the creation of standardized software interfaces for all layers in the X Window System environment. MIT for many years provided a vendor-neutral, central position for leading the development efforts of X, and it later split off the X Consortium as a formal organization. Gone were the days of the sometimes heroic, ad hoc efforts to support X that existed until that time.

Release Six of X, referred to as X11R6, was released in 1994. In 1995, the X Consortium was named as the prime contractor for leading development of the next releases of the Common Desktop Environment (CDE) and Motif. At the beginning of 1997, the X Consortium transferred responsibility for the X Window System to the Open Group and was subsumed into the Open Group. This occurred largely due to a feeling that the original goal of the X Consortium was largely completed: the X windowing environment is widespread and no longer needs a full-scale industry consortium for nurturing. X is the core windowing basis for UNIX and Linux: much X development activity at this time centers around the Enlightenment and KDE desktop packages for Linux and UNIX.

The Open Group continues their existing work of publishing, testing, and branding products that conform to international standards, and it formed the X.Org group in early 1999 to act as the official steward of the X Window System technology. For more information on X.Org, visit their website at **http://www.x.org**. The next section of this chapter will discuss the architecture of X.

The Server Is the Client and the Client Is the Server

The X11 network windowing system has been one of the most popular desktop environments in the history of computing, given its wide availability. Almost all UNIX platforms developed since 1990 have some form of graphical display system available, based upon the X11 protocol. Some of the major reasons for the ubiquity of X in the UNIX world are the same as for sendmail's widespread popularity as a mail transport agent:

- Flexibility
- Portability
- Source code available free and without limitations

For other environments, such as the Macintosh and Windows operating systems, X ports have been commercially available for some time now.

Architecture

X was designed from the beginning of its history to be platform- and kernel- (and therefore vendor-) independent. The X11 protocol is modeled after a network packet transmission model, with the X client and the display being the two ends of the connection, and an X server between the two. What confuses a person about the X architecture is that X's client/server definition feels at odds with the way everyone else uses the term "client/server." In general, the client is the server and the server is the client. Figure 15-1 provides an illustration of this behavior.

An X client opens a network socket appropriate for the intended display and writes X protocol packets to that particular socket. The X server accepts the packets and responds to the requests from the X client by drawing to the defined display. The user operates the input devices (keyboard and mouse) to send information to the X server, which then translates the user's input into X protocol packets and sends them to the appropriate X client. In addition to this, X clients can communicate with other X clients by setting values called *properties* on the X server. This distributed architecture of X provides several advantages: although the X client (a database application, for example) and the X server can run on the same workstation, they do not have to. In some cases, it may increase performance to run the X client and the X server on different workstations. Also, since the X cli-

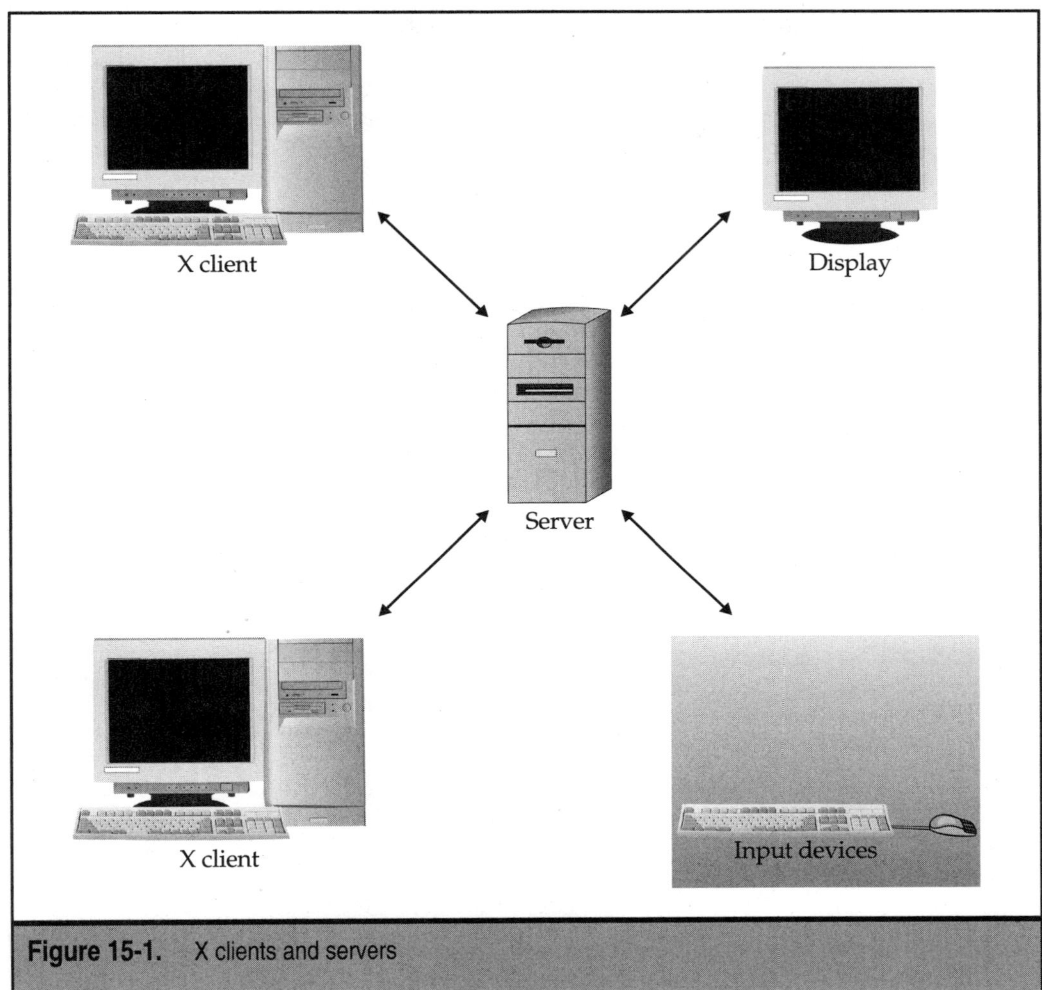

Figure 15-1. X clients and servers

ent and server communicate using the X protocol, there is no requirement that the two run on the same operating system or processor type. Only the X server application has to be aware of the hardware it is running on. Separating the client and server portions thereby improves portability and reuse of applications code.

The Common Desktop Environment

The Common Desktop Environment is a standard desktop for UNIX and is intended to provide consistent cross-platform services to users, application developers, and systems administrators. Introduced in 1995, CDE was jointly developed and licensed by Hewlett-

Packard, IBM, Novell, and SunSoft under the COSE (Common Open Software Environment) initiative. Other participants in the CDE development effort include Hitachi, Fujitsu, Digital Equipment Corporation, and SCO. CDE was developed under the Open Group's Pre-Structured Technology (PST) process, a multivendor technology development program.

CDE 2.1, released in early 1997, integrated the Motif 2.0 GUI, X Window System, and CDE to help standardize application presentation in distributed multiplatform environments. By incorporating some Motif 2.0 user interface objects, or *widgets,* the style guides for CDE and Motif converged with the 2.1 release. Standard features of the CDE, as shown in Figure 15-2, include a floating toolbar that is user- or system-configurable to incorporate launch buttons for any application.

X Terminal

An X terminal is a dumb terminal with just enough computing capability to run an X server. A GUI version of an ASCII character-based dumb terminal, an X terminal can be designed with no internal hard disk, and it may be no more than a CPU, enough RAM to run an X server, boot ROM that looks for a remote server to download the X server from, a

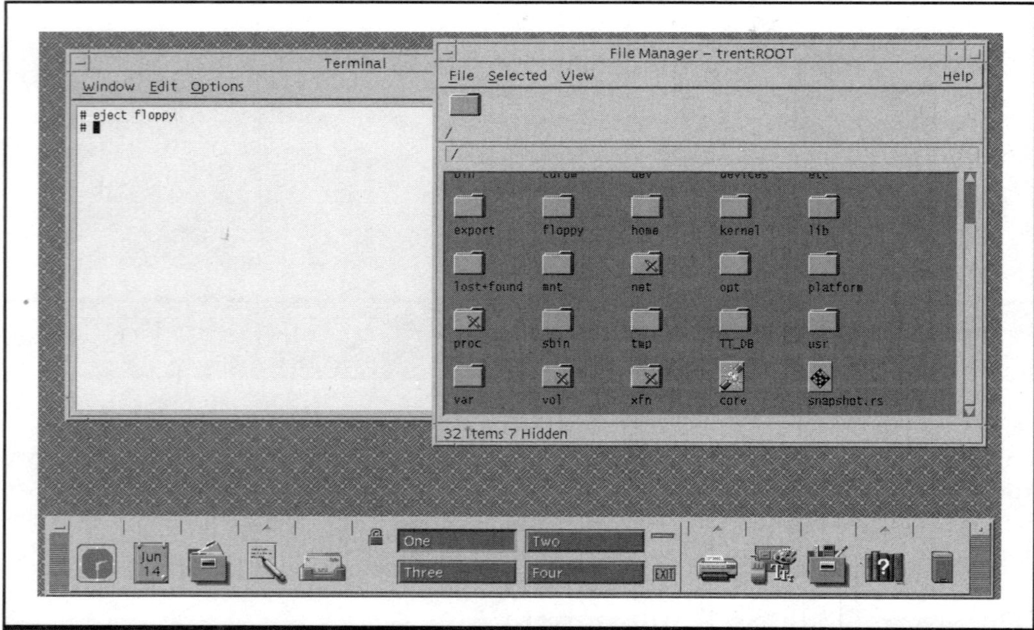

Figure 15-2. The CDE desktop is available for several platforms

monitor, a keyboard, and a mouse. An X terminal can use the Trivial File Transfer Protocol (TFTP) to download an X server from a specified remote host; it may have the X server software embedded in ROM on the motherboard; or it may be a small workstation (that is to say, with a hard disk and perhaps a CD-ROM or floppy drive) that is dedicated to running the X server software. The rest of the network provides all other computing resources—data storage and lookup, processing of requests, and so on. The X terminal is merely responsible for drawing the windows on the monitor. Communication over the network is typically handled via a TCP/IP stack.

NOTE: If an X terminal is starting to sound like a simplified Network Computer (NC) design, that's a good analogy. NCs, however, do not require X and do include Java as part of the Network Computer Reference Platform specification. NCs are considered by some as a low-cost upgrade to current ASCII character–based dumb terminals and X terminals.

PC X Servers

Character-based terminals are becoming extinct, and dedicated X terminals running UNIX applications are being replaced, in many cases, with PCs running networked terminal packages. PCs allow users to run personal productivity applications while attaining network terminal connectivity. Traditionally, UNIX systems provide large business or scientific application access, while the personal computing software market provides personal productivity applications such as word processing, spreadsheets, and contact managers.

PC X server software packages can run alongside (in separate windows) the native PC desktop, or replace the native desktop, converting the PC into an X terminal. These X Window products, such as Hummingbird's Exceed, WRQ's Reflection X, and AGE Logic's XoftWare, allow users to run UNIX X Window applications from a UNIX host on the PC desktop by providing a Motif or Open Look–based X Window GUI, with functionality such as cut and paste, XDCMP compliance, shape extension, and other X protocol support.

With the Broadway extensions to the X protocol (see the following section), viewing and controlling X applications through a web browser (with the Broadway plug-in module) becomes possible. While requiring an X server and a web browser on both the local desktop workstation and the remote server, Broadway does allow identical access to X applications from either Windows or UNIX desktops. Some vendors in the PC X server market, including WRQ and Hummingbird, plan to incorporate the Broadway specifications in their products.

However, running an X server application alongside your regular PC's operating system may require a hardware upgrade, such as at least 16MB or more of additional RAM. Some PC X servers may crash or fail to release memory, especially if running with (and not instead of) the native operating system. Also, although X servers have improved significantly since their early releases, a dedicated X terminal is likely to exhibit superior performance to an X server running on a general-purpose PC workstation.

Broadway: X over the Web

In 1995, it was possible to joke about using Netscape's Navigator web browser as an operating system. Today it's much less of a joke: many different Internet technologies are grafting themselves onto the web by means of the "plug-in" module technology for the major web browsers. One of these was the X Consortium's final project, Broadway, released as X11R6.3. This section will discuss the general design of Broadway, including the capability to access X clients (do you remember what a client is in X vocabulary?) via the web through a web browser.

Broadway was the X Consortium's attempt to merge variations of some of the more common X protocol extensions into a vendor-neutral format. Broadway is intended as an extension to, rather than a replacement for, current X applications, and it is designed to be compatible with unmodified X11 applications. Broadway introduced a wide array of features to the X group of protocols, discussed in the following sections.

X.FAST The X.Fast Extension is a protocol for using X applications over a low-speed network, including dial-up lines, or across the Internet. Traditionally X11 exhibited good performance in 10MB/second Ethernet environments but performed poorly over slower serial lines or modems. X.Fast achieves its goal through additional capabilities, including protocol data compression and caching.

REMOTE X Remote X is a Multipurpose Internet Mail Extensions (MIME) type, which allows integration with web browsers to allow X clients to be launched by and displayed within the browser using a plug-in module. As with other MIME types, the web server being used must be properly configured to understand the RX MIME type. Also, the X client must include the RX capability as well. Many extensions were made to X's security model, allowing a more secure use of the remote capabilities of X over a wide area network (WAN) or the Internet.

NETWORK PRINTING A Print Extension protocol operates through the X protocol. Previous to Broadway, printing through X client applications required a separate mechanism through the UNIX file system. With the XPRINT service, a client application can print directly to a network printer. A platform-neutral solution, XPRINT works with UNIX or Windows NT systems, as well as raster device, PostScript Level 2, and PCL printers.

PROXY MANAGEMENT A proxy management protocol allows the X server to use proxy services such as running an application through a firewall using TCP or UDP network ports.

NETWORK AUDIO A network audio component allows users to play and record audio across a network, as well as to synchronize the audio with other events or applications, thus allowing both voice annotation of documents and teleconferencing.

For more information on X11R6.3 (Broadway), see **http://www.x.org/plugin.htm**.

NOTE: Netopia's Timbuktu Pro cross-platform application also has a web browser plug-in, available at **http://www.netopia.com/www/look/ldownload.html**.

VNC: EVERYWHERE TO EVERYWHERE

There are several commercial products that allow remote viewing (and in some cases control) of a remote desktop, including Citrix's MetaFrame, Microsoft's Terminal Server, and Netopia's Timbuktu Pro. However, a notable counterpart to these is AT&T Laboratories' Virtual Network Computing. The viewers are tiny by modern code standards (the Win32 viewer is 150K) and can access VNC servers running on any of the several supported platforms. VNC can operate through the SSH protocol, making it secure. For more information, the VNC website at **http://www.uk.research.att.com/vnc/** has downloadable clients and servers, as well as complete documentation.

WINDOWS ON UNIX

The previous section of this chapter addressed the possibility of bringing X Window to the Windows desktop. However, what if the situation were reversed, and you had many UNIX workstations in your network, but wanted to bring Windows to those users? One option would be to supply each UNIX user with a Windows workstation and double the size of the network, either by adding additional hubs or switches where possible, or by building a second network for the Windows machines. (You *did* plan for expansion when you laid out the network configuration, right? If so, your job will be easier now.) Although expanding the network is a valid solution, this option may be precluded on the grounds of cost, or a majority of the users may simply not have enough room in their workspaces to add another workstation. One possible solution to this issue is a remote Windows NT server. This section will present some of the benefits and costs associated with remote Windows NT service and discuss some other options, such as emulators.

Remote Windows NT Servers

By careful license agreements and judicious modification of the Windows NT source code, third-party vendors have extended Windows NT to allow remote display over networks. Products such as Citrix's WinFrame use a modified Windows NT Server operating system to provide Windows NT remote access in much the same way as the X protocol is defined: the remote server handles application processing, while the local client (an X server) performs graphical updates and screen management. A protocol called Intelligent Console Architecture (ICA), which was created by Citrix and licensed to the other vendors, provides a network communications mechanism similar to the X client/server protocol model.

The ICA desktop client starts a remote session with a Windows NT server and displays either individual applications in separate windows or a full Windows NT desktop inside a window on the local X desktop. The remote Windows NT desktop appears almost exactly as if you were on a Windows NT Server directly. Since a remote user has to log into Windows NT just as if that user were at a local Windows NT workstation, separate user profiles, desktop views, and access controls are maintainable by the remote Windows NT server. The rest of this section will discuss some of these remote Windows NT servers.

Citrix WinFrame and MetaFrame

Citrix was the first vendor to design remote Windows NT access with ICA. The original intent behind WinFrame was to provide Windows NT to a low-end X Window workstation. As a logical extension of Citrix's concept, Wyse Technology's NC is almost a Windows version of an X terminal. Built around WinFrame, Wyse's minimal computer runs only the ICA client software and requires a dedicated WinFrame server for everything else, making it considerably smaller than the Microsoft and Intel NetPC standard hardware specification. WinFrame is primarily targeted at "organizations using NT 3.51 that are not migrating to NT 4.0." WinFrame runs the Program Manager as a single X Window, with a maximum resolution of 800 × 600 pixels. You can find more information on WinFrame at **http://www.citrix.com/products/winframe/**.

MetaFrame's target market is "customers using Windows NT Server 4.0 and Terminal Server Edition." Citrix adds a Program Neighborhood, similar to the Windows Network Neighborhood, for central distribution and control of application access.

Citrix provides support for a large number of client platforms, including:

- Linux (Red Hat, Caldera, SuSE, and Slackware distributions)
- SCO UNIX clients (UnixWare and OpenServer)
- PCs running DOS, Windows 3.1, Windows for Workgroups, Windows 9*x*, Windows NT Workstation, Windows CE, Internet Explorer (via ActiveX) and other web browsers (via a plug-in)
- Other UNIXes
- Apple Macintosh
- A Java version of the ICA client for use on devices that support a Java Virtual Machine

Microsoft Terminal Server

Citrix licensed the MultiWin technology to Microsoft to create Microsoft Terminal Server. By using the MultiWin codebase, Terminal Server allows multiple concurrent users to log on and run applications in separate, protected Windows sessions on the server. Although Terminal Server is not yet available for Windows 2000, Microsoft has stated its intention to deliver a Windows 2000 version. Some of the possible enhancements being considered include local device redirection, session shadowing, and server load balancing.

Cautions for Using Remote Windows Deployment

In many cases, a remote Windows server may be a much better solution for deploying Windows to 200 UNIX users than alternatives. It may well be a better solution than purchasing and installing 200 Windows workstations, with the attendant support costs. A single remote Windows NT server used as an applications server may fulfill the business needs. This is especially true if the users only need Windows NT for one or two applications, such as Microsoft Excel or Lotus Notes. However, there are some disadvantages to consider before choosing a remote Windows server:

- *Remote Windows NT servers have high memory requirements.* For reasonable performance, one calculation would be 32MB (for the server) + (*the number of concurrent users × the amount of memory each user would need for a typical Windows NT workstation*). The vendors claim that their products will run in lower per-user memory environments than those for real workstations; they suggest four to ten megabytes per user. For example, suppose you wanted to support 35 simultaneous connections. The equation would be

  32 + (35 × 10) = 382MB recommended on the server

  Obviously, given the server's intended use, a multiprocessor server (up to NT 4.0's limit of four processors) can also improve performance for multiple users.
- *The remote Windows servers all work by* modifying *the Windows NT operating system, ranging from the low end of 25 or so dynamic link libraries (DLLs) to approximately 1,000.* Although common applications such as Microsoft Office are likely to run (if for no other reason than the remote NT vendors will test their products against common products first), rare, esoteric, or custom applications may be less than likely to run, if at all. One consideration here is that Microsoft's Terminal Server may be preferable as a single point resource.
- *The cost can be prohibitive.* License fees can amount to as much as, or more than (depending on your configuration), the cost of a new workstation. The tradeoff to consider is that the ongoing support cost of the centralized services may be cheaper than support of a large number of distributed workstations, especially if the workstations are widely separated geographically.

Wine: A Windows Emulator for UNIX

A freeware Windows emulator available for UNIX is named Wine, which stands for either WINdows Emulator, or Wine Is Not an Emulator. Wine has been tested to run on Intel 80386 processors and up—on Linux, NetBSD, FreeBSD and Unixware, and SCO OpenServer. Wine runs under X, so you will need X on whatever UNIX platform you are attempting to run Wine on. More information can be found at **http://www.winehq.com**.

NOTE: Wine supports a fair number of DOS and 16-bit applications but as of this writing still has limited support for Win32 applications in general.

OTHER TOOLS

Many UNIX users are accustomed to working close to the operating system. If they need a new tool such as a new command, they write it, or they write a script around an existing command. A variety of tools are available that should be comfortable to UNIX users working in a Windows environment. This section will present remote access tools similar to Telnet, then look at a suite of similar low-level tools from a particular vendor, and close with an examination of scripting capabilities under Windows NT.

rsh and ssh

Remote login access is sometimes a useful tool. Many people are familiar with the Telnet client in Windows. While Microsoft only supplied a Telnet client in previous editions of Windows, Windows 2000 Server includes a Telnet server that will support up to 63 simultaneous connections. By modern standards, Telnet and related applications are a primitive way to communicate between two host machines. However, Telnet and these related primitive techniques have the advantage that they are almost universally available across almost every platform. This section will examine the r* set of UNIX commands for remote access of other systems, and the ssh application for more secure access.

rsh

The *r** group of UNIX commands (rlogin, rsh, and rcp) all provide remote execution of commands on a UNIX workstation or server, similar to Telnet. The rlogin command uses the login service to connect to another workstation, using the TCP/IP protocol. Some configuration is required for UNIX systems that you wish to access: the two relevant files are /etc/hosts.equiv and $USER/.rhosts. The /etc/hosts.equiv file contains names of hosts, or machines that are considered to be the same as the local machine for security purposes. For example, consider two workstations named GRAPHICS and ADMIN. If the /etc/hosts.equiv file on GRAPHICS contains the host name ADMIN, then any user who has an account on ADMIN (and is logged into ADMIN) can issue an rlogin command to GRAPHICS and connect to GRAPHICS without needing to reenter a password, because ADMIN is defined as a trusted host.

The $USER/.rhosts file is located in a specific user's home directory and contains sets of user IDs matched with host names. To illustrate the difference between the two, consider the example given in the preceding paragraph. If Jeff has a userid of jeff and has an account on both GRAPHICS and ADMIN, then the following two sample files, if present on the GRAPHICS workstation, will allow Jeff to rlogin from ADMIN:

File	Content
/etc/hosts.equiv	ADMIN
/usr/jeff/.rhosts	jeff ADMIN

The difference between the two is that the /etc/hosts.equiv example allows all users with accounts on both ADMIN and GRAPHICS to rlogin to GRAPHICS, but the /usr/jeff/.rhosts file allows only Jeff to rlogin to the GRAPHICS workstation.

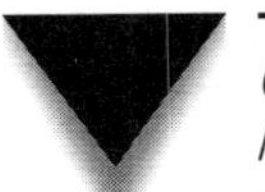

CAUTION: Be careful whenever you're implementing any remote access method. For example, if the /usr/jeff/.rhosts file contained a second line reading "john ADMIN," then the user with the ID john (with an account on both ADMIN and GRAPHICS) could also rlogin to GRAPHICS without a password. But if John were to log in, he would have Jeff's permissions and privileges on GRAPHICS. John could then create, edit, or delete files, send mail to others, and in general do anything Jeff could do. This is exactly as safe as handing someone your house or apartment key—it depends on who the someone is.

While not officially distributed by Microsoft as part of NT Server 4.0, the RSHSVC (rsh service) is the server side for the TCP/IP utility RSH.EXE and works the same way as UNIX's rsh daemon. Both UNIX and Windows NT rsh clients may communicate with the Windows NT rsh service. RSHSVC is distributed on the Windows NT Resource Kit.

NOTE: In Windows 2000 as well as older versions of Windows, the rsh command is available only if the TCP/IP protocol is installed.

Installing Windows NT rsh Service

To install the rsh service:

1. Copy RSHSETUP.EXE, RSHSVC.EXE, and RSHSVC.DLL to the *System_root*\System32 directory, where *System_root* is where Windows NT is installed on the system (often in C:\WINNT).
2. Type the command

   rshsetup *System_root*\system32\rshsvc.exe *System_root*\ System32\rshsvc.dll
3. Type the command

   net start rshsvc
4. To stop the remote shell service, type the command

   net stop rshsvc

Windows NT rsh Configuration

You need to have the .RHOSTS files in the %SystemRoot%\System32\drivers\etc directory. The .RHOSTS file should have one or more of the following type of entries. Each line should be in the following format,

<H1> <user1> [*<user2> <user3>* ....]

where H1 is the name of the host machine from which an rsh client can be run, and user1 and so forth are names of the users that are permitted to access the remote shell service from the H1 machine. If a host machine name is not part of the .RHOSTS file and a user attempts an rsh client connection from that machine, or the user is not associated with the host machine, an Access Denied message is returned by the rsh service. The service will also refuse a connection from any host machine with an unresolvable IP address.

CAUTION: Microsoft advises that you don't use the rsh service or client to run interactive commands, such as for editing files.

ssh

One major security concern over Telnet is that passwords are sent over the network "in the clear," or unencrypted, between the two endpoints. It is not difficult to set up an application or other tool to watch every packet of information going over the network and filter the traffic for "telnet fred" and "password: whatever" pairs. ssh is intended as a secure version of rsh and may be used as a replacement for rsh and Telnet, with the addition of encryption for communication. The traditional UNIX r* commands are vulnerable to several kinds of attacks, and the X Window System also has a number of severe vulnerabilities. The ssh (Secure Shell) program allows a user these options:

- Logging into another computer over a network
- Executing commands on a remote machine
- Moving files from one machine to another

Intended as a replacement for rlogin, rsh, and rcp, ssh provides strong authentication and securer communication over insecure channels. The ssh program never sends passwords in the clear. Established $USER/.rhosts and /etc/hosts.equiv files are still usable: changing over to ssh is mostly transparent for users on these systems. If an ssh connection is attempted to a remote site that does not have an ssh server, the ssh client may fall back to use rsh.

The ssh program protects against interception of clear text passwords and other data by intermediate hosts and spoofing of several kinds—including these:

- **IP spoofing** A remote host sends out packets that pretend to come from another, trusted host.

- **DNS spoofing** An attacker forges name server records.
- **X spoofing** The system listens to X authentication data and spoofs a connection to the X11 server.

The ssh program also protects against manipulation of data by people in control of intermediate hosts between the two ends of the ssh session.

NOTE: The ssh program does have an option to use encryption of type "none." This is included only for debugging purposes, however, and is not recommended for use.

However, ssh will not help you with anything that compromises your host's security in some other way. Once an attacker has gained root privileges on a given machine, he or she can then subvert ssh use on that machine as well.

The ssh program currently runs on most flavors of UNIX and OS/2. A commercial Windows and Macintosh port has been written by Tatu Ylonen, the original author of ssh. The connection configuration screen of the Windows client is shown in Figure 15-3.

For more information, including client and server availability, the ssh FAQ website is at **http://www.ayahuasca.net/ssh/ssh-faq.html**.

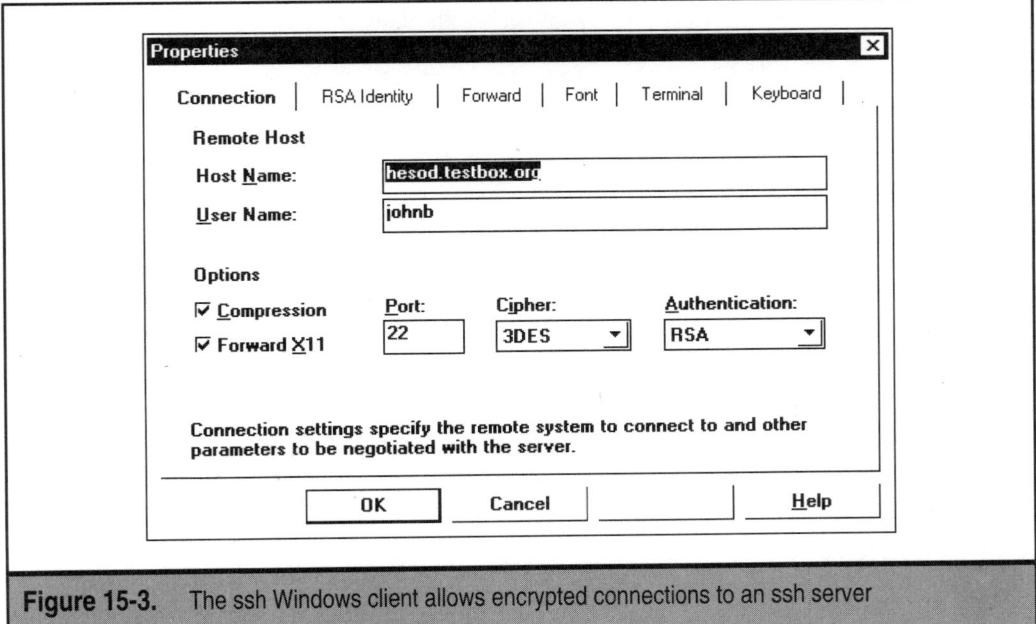

Figure 15-3. The ssh Windows client allows encrypted connections to an ssh server

TCP/IP Tools

The Exceed suite from Hummingbird Communications provides a wide assortment of X TCP/IP tools. The Inetd service is part of the Exceed TCP/IP suite. Many TCP/IP tools familiar to UNIX users are found here: a finger client, an FTP client (which supports drag and drop), a Usenet newsreader, a Telnet client (supporting VT52, VT100, and VT320 emulations), an LPR (Line Print Request, for UNIX network printing), a whois client, a Network Time Protocol client, a 3270 terminal emulator, and many others. A variation of BASIC is included for use in scripting work with Exceed applications, and in developing local X clients.

The Inetd daemon runs as a service under Windows NT and, like its UNIX counterpart, can be set to launch any application if a request is made through a particular port. Most of the tools can run in either a graphic mode or a command-line output mode. More information can be found on the Hummingbird website, at **http://www.hummingbird.com**.

SUMMARY

This chapter has presented some of the options for providing a Windows or UNIX desktop view to the other group of users without having to provide a duplicate network. For example, the main benefit of using a remote Windows server is the elimination of the need to support Windows workstations in addition to X terminals and UNIX workstations. System management costs may be reduced because there aren't 200 Windows workstations (added to the existing network of 200 UNIX workstations) to install, maintain, and upgrade; there is just one large remote Windows server. On the other hand, others argue that this trend of the centralization of remote windowing servers and using Network Computers is retrograde to the distributed trend of client/server computing, and a return to the days of the glass-house mainframe Information Systems department.

Although a centralized system may be easier to manage from one location, centralized systems have one salient disadvantage: everyone stops whenever the mainframe has a problem. Using a distributed model and locally cached files, users can continue working if a central server goes down. This absolute centralized dependence is why mainframes simply are not allowed to go down. Client/server computing has introduced an expectation that "Oh, part of the system went down again, it happens all the time." Multiprocessor servers, RAID arrays, and clustering are all attempts to provide for a zero-time failover for modern operating systems. In the meantime, users will attempt to use what they have or can acquire for their real needs, which in most cases involve the applications that run on their local desktops, rather than the server-based distributed operating systems.

CHAPTER 16

System and Network Management

System and network administration encompasses a dauntingly huge set of tasks, and it is often defined solely by example. Many computer professionals cannot give a clear and concise definition of their job, but much as with the old definition of pornography, they know it when they see it.

System and network administration covers many unrelated tasks that all tend to circle around the issue of making services available to a user's desktop computer. Sometimes the users move from workstation to workstation and need a single login distributed across a network. Sometimes the users take their workstations with them, working primarily from laptops. Whether the user is in one place or many, he or she wants a wide variety of services, which grow as the technology advances.

A DAY IN THE LIFE OF AN ADMINISTRATOR

The list of things an administrator may be asked to look after on any given day can be long and varied. Typical tasks system administrators are asked to perform include many from the following list:

- Backups/restores
- Database administration
- Desktop applications support
- Disaster recovery
- Electronic mail
- Hardware support
- OS support
- Performance tuning
- Software distribution support
- Software installation and configuration
- System analysis
- Firewall selection and administration
- Third-party hardware troubleshooting
- User training

This chapter will discuss some of the resources, possibilities, and trends available to system administrators faced with a heterogeneous UNIX and Windows environment. First, this chapter will discuss some basics of system and network administration, relevant regardless of the platform or operating system you are working with. Second, the system tools contained within Windows will be covered, followed by an explanation of the Simple Network Management Protocol. This chapter will close with coverage of two current trends: the Network Computer, and the advent of web-based extensions to system and network management applications.

BASICS

Whatever your network consists of, be it an all-Solaris network, a mixed HP-UX and Windows network, or Macintosh workstations connected to NetWare file servers, some basic concepts are appropriate wherever you are and whatever you are asked to manage.

Know What You've Got

There are a couple of subareas to knowing what you've got. First, you need to know if you have just eighty servers or a hundred and thirty Windows NT servers (don't laugh—answering that question was the first task assigned a newly hired administrator at a local company, because *no one* in the operations center knew). Knowing the network's composition provides a foundation for several of the other tasks: primarily, what operating systems to provide support for. (If ten of a hundred servers are running Solaris, but no one on staff is comfortable supporting Solaris, get someone trained or hired.)

Second, it's hard to identify improvements in performance when you don't know what performance level you started from. For example, a directive is given to improve network throughput. Where's the bottleneck? Is the network sluggish only in mid-afternoon on workdays? Can existing components of the network be reorganized to improve performance, or do large portions of the network need replacement? Or consider this possibility: your facility is a Usenet news server node. This morning you were told to calculate the expansion of your site's storage necessary to maintain a thirty-day inventory of all Usenet traffic. How do you start answering the question (after first laughing hysterically)?

Have Backups

For most organizations, their most significant investment is not in their network, or even their people—it's in the intellectual capital their people have created. To minimize productivity losses from the death of a given user's workstation (e.g., to keep the user from losing the last week's work), you can use a central file server. This allows you to set up a backup plan for that single file server, instead of providing backups for all workstations. On the other hand, it does focus your possible points of failure from many little ones to one big one. Backup data should be kept in a secure offsite location, and should be rotated as frequently as appropriate to the organization. Backups become more complicated when they must be accomplished across heterogeneous systems. (For more information regarding backups, see Chapter 4.)

Identify Points of Failure

When a portion of the network fails, what other portions does it affect? One firm had high-quality workstations, with all users operating from a central file server, and adequate network bandwidth to allow decent performance. Every workstation also had its own uninterruptible power supply (UPS). In a glaring oversight, the central file server wasn't on a UPS, so when the local power grid blanked out, the file server crashed. All the workstations survived the power outage, but they couldn't accomplish any work because their files were unavailable until the file server was restarted.

Have a Disaster Recovery Plan

In addition to helping identify performance bottlenecks, knowing what's on your network can help you recover from "unscheduled downtime incidents." Disaster recovery plans should be scaled to meet the needs of your organization. For some organizations, merely having a backup of important data is enough for them to feel secure. For others, having a complete network specification to replicate the entire information system center, and periodically rehearsing "rebuild the center from nothing," is considered necessary. For others, maintaining a complete center in another location as a backup site is necessary. This last level of disaster readiness is often found in telecommunication firms, where downtime is measured in the hundreds of thousands of dollars per minute, or in the military, where most naval vessels maintain a secondary command center in case the first one is destroyed.

For administrators, distributed access to management applications can allow faster response to perceived problems. One important trend in this area is the rapid growth of web-enabled interfaces for system management applications.

Plan for Expansion

Systems should grow and change appropriately to the needs of the users and the organization. In the case of a change (either up or down) in the number of users, procedures should be in place for adding or removing users from the system along with their access to services, files, and so on. This includes such issues as planning for easy expansion of the network by subnetting IP addresses. Several tools exist that attempt to aid administrators in user and network management and configuration.

WHAT'S IN WINDOWS 2000

Windows 2000 provides a wide range of networking and administrative services. Installing TCP/IP services from Microsoft or another vendor can greatly enhance a Windows 2000 system in a heterogeneous network. This section will discuss the server-side services or daemons, and some of the administrative tools, available for use with Windows 2000.

Windows 2000 Server-Side Services

Windows 2000 server-side services are processes that tend to be started up at boot time and do not require a user to log in and start them. These services are therefore counterparts to daemon processes under UNIX. With a default installation of Windows support for the TCP/IP package, you receive a minimal set of these low-level clients, including FTP and TFTP, Telnet (VT52 and VT100/ANSI emulation), finger, remote execute (REXEC) and remote shell (RSH), and several network-related diagnostic commands, including ping. Installing the Simple TCP/IP service in Windows NT adds a few more client tools, including the perennial message of the day command, which allows an administrator to display a message to each user when he or she logs in that day.

NOTE: Some administrators use the Message of the Day function for one of two types of messages: to announce system changes such as "The system is going down tonight at midnight for one hour," or for chatty, joking, quote-of-the-day messages. Be aware, however, that many users gloss over the message of the day, treating it much the way television watchers treat commercials: They glance at it without actually reading it.

Microsoft's TCP/IP Server-Side Services

When you install TCP/IP on a Windows server, no server-side services install by default—you have to install individual services separately. Many server-side services are included on the NT Server 4.0 installation media. The following services are discussed elsewhere in this book. Some of the TCP/IP services available include the following:

- **TCP/IP Printing** Provides an LPD (Line Printer Daemon), allowing access to and from UNIX and other systems that support TCP/IP printing (Chapter 5).
- **Internet Information Server** Provides several content-publishing protocols, including HTTP for the World Wide Web, FTP for file transfer, and Gopher (an older text file search and retrieval protocol using menus for navigation) (Chapter 11).
- **Dynamic Host Configuration Protocol** Provides dynamic IP address assignments to compatible systems (Chapter 7).
- **Domain Name Service** Provides IP names to IP address mapping, so that one can reach a server using the address **webserver.testbox.org**, for example, instead of having to remember 192.168.100.110 (Chapter 9).

Windows Administration and the Inet Daemon Server Suite

Administration of Windows workstations and servers has become a major issue with many network managers. Although Microsoft's RRAS and SMS provide a functional suite of services, their administrative power is limited when compared to that of UNIX systems. To gain control of peripherals and provide interoperable file and print services, enterprise administrators have implemented third-party TCP/IP application suites.

Enterprise system administrators can address some of the administration limitations of Windows by implementing the UNIX Inet daemon suite. Some TCP/IP products for Windows have been optimized by the incorporation of several important aspects of UNIX, such as the Inet daemon. The Inet daemon server suite was created to improve the efficiency of UNIX and TCP/IP by reducing the number of processes activated during system startup, many of which are not continuously required. *Inetd* (the InterNET service Daemon) continuously runs as an active process waiting for client connection requests.

Upon receiving the request, Inetd starts up the appropriate server daemon (telnetd, FTPd, or whatever), thereby conserving server and/or workstation resources.

Complete Inetd server suites are only provided by a few developers of TCP/IP application suites for the Windows workstation and server. A full Inet daemon server suite can give the Windows platform much of the power of a UNIX workstation, enabling the PC or server to provide client/server TCP/IP functions. This facilitates peer-to-peer connectivity among Windows workstations and workgroups.

The Inetd service can provide a valuable management utility, enabling network managers and administrators to Telnet into a Windows workstation or server and execute remote operations or scripts. The value and versatility of Inetd are often overlooked because it is a background service and is integrated into the UNIX operating system along with the TCP/IP protocol suite. Table 16-1 lists some of the services provided by Inetd.

Inetd Service	Purpose
Finger server	Responds to client inquiries as to who is logged on.
FTP server	Supports FTP client file transfer.
Gopher server	Supports Gopher client searches and menus.
LPD server	Supports PC-client, UNIX Line Printer Requests.
New Talk server	Supports (New Talk) UNIX chat facility.
Bootp server	Supports remote TCP/IP configurations.
RSH server	Supports requests to execute commands on a remote system.
Talk server	Supports (Old Talk) UNIX chat facility.
Telnet server	Services Telnet client (virtual terminal) sessions.
TFTP server	Provides file transfer for diskless workstations.
Time server	Synchronizes client time with other NFS servers.
HTTP server	Enables broadcasting of web pages.
Exec server	Provides remote execution services.
Login server	Provides remote login services.
Timed server	Provides the time of day.

Table 16-1. TCP/IP Server Suite and Functions

Windows 2000 Server's Built-in Utilities

Windows 2000 Server provides a number of basic utilities—some more functional than others—designed to simplify system administration tasks. This section will provide a short overview of some of the system management utilities included in Windows 2000 Server. These applications can be found by default in the Administrative Tools folder. If other Windows 2000 services such as DNS, RAS, or DHCP are installed, the administrative utilities for those will also be found in this folder.

Computer Management

The Computer Management utility encompasses several separate functions, grouped into three nodes:

- System Tools
- Storage
- Services

The System Tools node provides access to such subordinate administrative tools as the Event Viewer, the Performance Monitor, and the Device Manager, not to mention user and group management. The Storage functions (formerly provided by the Windows NT Disk Administrator) include disk formatting: volumes can be formatted as either FAT or NTFS, primary and extended partitions can be modified, and disk configurations can be restored. The Storage tool is also used to define disk duplexing, mirroring, and striping. Disk defragmentation also falls under Storage. The Services node provides a central point of control for services available on the Windows 2000 Server. The default list includes DNS, DHCP, Services for Macintosh, Fax, RAS, Routing, and WINS.

Remote Storage

The Windows 2000 Remote Storage utility (covered in more detail in Chapter 4) provides for backing up only NTFS volumes, either local or NFS-mounted, to a tape drive (no other media are supported, though). Backup can target an entire volume, a directory, or an individual file. It can also span backup media across multiple tapes and provides verification of the backup. Other useful concepts include logging its actions to log files and the capability to back up the local server's Windows NT Registry. The backup utility's weakest feature is in the area of scheduling. The Windows Schedule service must be used in order to perform an unattended backup.

Licensing

It is amazing how many businesses are operating with more copies of software applications than they have purchased. The Licensing administrative tool is used to enforce network compliance with software license restrictions. In addition to allowing restrictions on a per-client or per-server basis, the utility allows monitoring of usage statistics for each user. Such monitoring can reduce the expenses for software applications by determining the appropriate number of licenses needed for purchase.

Event Viewer

The Event Viewer serves as Windows 2000 Server's log file monitor. The three primary system log files you view with Event Viewer are the following:

- **System Log** Alerts and events from device drivers, processes, and services.
- **Security Log** Security-audit events such as logons, system restarts, and shutdowns.
- **Application Log** Application alerts and system messages.

The Event Viewer allows you to view the preceding logs remotely for other Windows installations on the network. A log file can be exported in plain or comma-delimited format for transporting into a database, or for saving in Event Viewer .EVT file format.

Performance

If it can't be measured, it's hard to optimize. The Performance administrative tool provides literally hundreds of measurements for system and network activities and objects. The graphical display can be customized on a per-target basis: you can specify which measurements should be displayed for each system or group of systems.

TIP: By default, Windows 2000 Professional doesn't display the Administrative Tools choice from the Programs menu. To restore the tools to the Programs menu, right-click the taskbar and select Properties, and then click the Start Menu options tab. In the Start Menu Settings pane, select the Display Administrative Tools checkbox. Click Apply, then OK.

Numerous other tools are included in the Windows 2000 administrative tool suite, such as RADIUS authentication control for virtual private networks, Terminal Services client creation and management, DHCP and DNS server management, and so on.

SNMP

The Simple Network Management Protocol (SNMP) is a protocol designed to let administrators manage computer networks remotely by setting and polling terminal values and monitoring network events. SNMP operates under the TCP/IP (Transport Control Protocol/Internet Protocol) communication stack.

SNMP Components

SNMP acquires information about a network from an MIB (Management Information Base). The MIB follows an inverted tree heirarchy; the most general information available about a network is stored at the root of the tree. As an MIB browser descends each branch of the tree, the information gets progressively more detailed into a specific network area, with the final nodes of the tree being the most specific.

Suppose, for example, that a device is a parent category in the tree, with serial and parallel devices as its children. The values of these might be set to 4, 3, and 1, respectively, in correlation with the number of devices attached (4 total devices = 3 serial + 1 parallel).

While the ISO definition of an MIB contains only a single tree structure, a point on the tree allows attachment of vendor-specific information. Figure 16-1 is a partial diagram of the MIB tree.

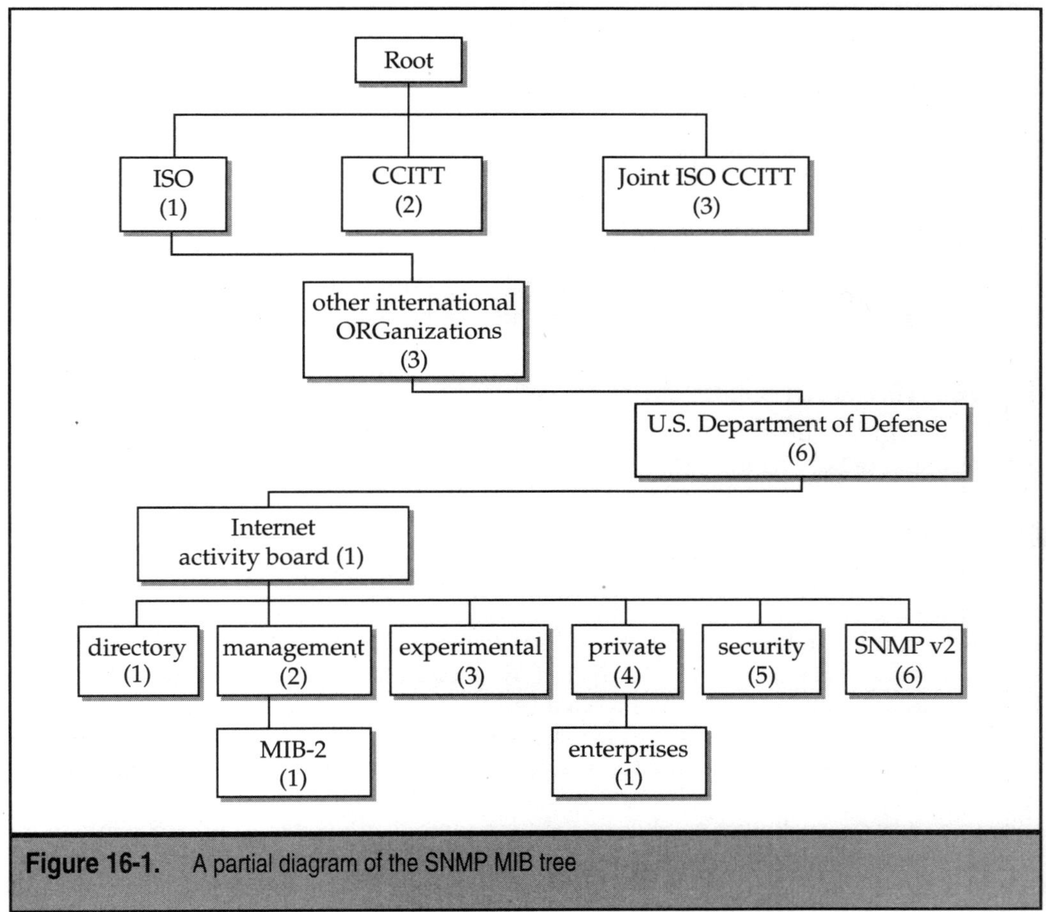

Figure 16-1. A partial diagram of the SNMP MIB tree

Not all branches are shown in this diagram. The top, also referred to as the root, is the basis from which the SNMP option paths fork. The second level contains the ISO branch (1) and two others. Below the ISO branch is the Organization branch (3), which has the U.S. Department of Defense (6) as a subordinate branch. Below that is the Internet activity board branch (1). MIB paths are written separated by periods, so the Internet branch can be described by this sequence:

```
1.3.6.1
```

or by the appropriate abbreviations of:

```
iso.org.dod.internet.
```

The two most common branches are shown in Figure 16-1. The generic branch is

```
1.3.6.1.2.1 (iso.org.dod.internet.management.mib)
```

and the enterprise-specific branch is

```
1.3.6.1.4.1 (iso.org.dod.internet.private.enterprises)
```

For a manufacturer-specific example, the MIB branch containing all IBM entries is

```
1.3.6.1.4.1.2 (iso.org.dod.internet.private.enterprises.ibm)
```

SNMP requires three components: the MIB, an agent, and a manager. The agent runs on each node on the network to collect network and terminal information. The manager is located on the host computer on the network and polls the agents for requested information.

SNMP Requests for Comment

For the most precise definitions of SNMP, Table 16-2 lists some of the most relevant Requests for Comment (RFCs) from the IETF.

SNMP Tools

A simple tool made for Windows NT to query MIB variables is the command-line program SNMPUTIL.EXE from the Microsoft Windows NT 4.0 Resource Kit. An MIB browser written in Java is available from adventnet at **http://www.adventnet.com/snmpagent**, and an SNMP-to-HTML gateway named MIBMaster is available from Equivalence at **http://www.equival.com.au/index.html**.

Sun Microsystems supplies a pair of SNMP tools, collectively called the Solstice Enterprise Agents (SEA). A master agent and a subagent, the SEA runs only under Solaris (either Sparc or Intel) 2.4 and up. In addition to SNMP, the SEA also provides the capability to work with the Desktop Management Interface (DMI). The SEA were included with Solaris 2.6 and 2.7, but if you do not have access to Sun Solaris installation

RFC	Title
RFC1089	SNMP over Ethernet
RFC1155	Structure and Identification of Management Information for TCP/IP-based internets
RFC1157	A Simple Network Management Protocol
RFC1158	Management Information Base for Network Management of TCP/IP-based internets: MIB-II
RFC1212	Concise MIB Definitions
RFC1213	Management Information Base for Network Management of TCP/IP-based internets: MIB-II
RFC1908	Coexistence between SNMPv1 and SNMPv2

Table 16-2. SNMP-Related RFCs

CD-ROMs, the SEA can also be downloaded from Sun's website at **http://www.sun.com/solstice/products/ent.agents/**.

XML: A Replacement for SNMP?

Although the SNMP management platform was supposed to facilitate sharing, administrators can too often end up with disparate administrative tools. XML (Extensible Markup Language) could be used as a common protocol to link different management applications. XML's advantage over SNMP is that it can provide a richer interchange of syntax, semantics, and presentation—the context surrounding a value. Although SNMP allows passing a 16-bit counter, that value would be more valuable if the circumstances causing that value to change were also passed with the object. XML can convey the semantics—how the information is changed and manipulated—allowing easier inclusion of new elements.

Microsoft has released SOAP (Simple Object Access Protocol), an XML-based specification for distributed applications. SOAP will replace Microsoft's Distributed Component Object Model (DCOM) architecture and will be cooked into the heart of Windows Distributed interNet Architecture (Windows DNA) 2000.

NETWORK COMPUTERS

The concept of Network Computers (NCs) was originally evangelized by Oracle and Sun as a low-cost alternative to the PC or workstation for people who didn't use the processing power of the workstation. Estimates of a single desktop PC's total purchase, installation, and support costs vary but run as high as $42,000 over a five-year period. For the purpose of our discussion, a Network Computer can be defined as almost any computing hardware that's smarter than a dumb terminal, but not as complicated or expensive as a PC. This section will discuss the initial Network Computer Reference Profile, the more detailed NetPC specification, and other issues for system managers to consider.

The Network Computer Reference Profile

The Network Computer Reference Profile is hardware-neutral, and does not impose many limitations on implementations. By being hardware-neutral, the Network Computer Reference Profile concentrates on software and protocols, such as:

- Networking protocols (TCP/IP, NFS, FTP, Telnet, SNMP, BOOTP and DHCP)
- Multimedia protocols (JPEG, GIF, WAV, and AU)
- Web-related protocols (HTTP and Java)
- Electronic mail protocols (SMTP, IMAP4, and POP3) for e-mail

In general, Network Computers are expected to work best for the following specific situations:

- Users who work with only a limited set of programs
- Users who share machines or work in different locations from day to day
- Users at remote locations (difficult to provide adequate support)
- Tasks that revolve around data stored centrally instead of local data
- As replacements for older, text-based terminals

NCs are not necessarily intended simply to save money by substituting for desktop PCs or workstations for people who need only limited features. NCs are also aimed to replace dumb, character-based terminals currently still in use. Although an NC costs more than a VT-100 terminal, an NC will have terminal emulation and will provide more capabilities, including the capability to use Windows applications and other GUI-based software.

NetPC

Like the NC, the NetPC is targeted at a class of task-oriented business users who do not require the flexibility offered by traditional PCs. In short, a NetPC is a Windows-based desktop box that runs on an Intel/PC-based architecture but is not intended as a minimally configured low-powered system. The advantages of NetPCs over traditional PCs include:

- Sealed case design (ensuring uniform components)
- Smaller desktop footprint

- No floppy drives
- Streamlining of centralized administration
- Ability to run either traditional applications or leaner, web-based applications

The NetPC definition is a specification for a low-maintenance PC system that was designed with networking in mind. Deployed in sealed boxes, NetPCs are designed so that all upgrading, software installation, and other system management functions can be deployed remotely from a server. Individual end users are not intended to reconfigure the hardware or the software.

The NetPC hardware specification includes:

- CPU: Pentium 100 MHz or equivalent
- 16MB RAM minimum
- Internal hard disk as cache
- 640 × 480 pixels at 8 bits/pixel (VGA)
- Audio device (type unspecified)
- Plug-and-Play BIOS support (32-bit PCI bus slots)
- No expansion slots
- Network interface (Ethernet, Token Ring, V.34 modem, ISDN, ATM, T1)
- Keyboard, pointing device/mouse
- Locked/sealed case
- Optional hardware additions, including an IDE floppy drive, a CD-ROM drive, PCMCIA card slots, and the Universal Serial Bus (USB) and the Firewire high-speed bus for peripherals

For software, the NetPC specification includes the following:

- Microsoft Windows operating system (either Windows 95 or NT)
- Microsoft Windows 95- and NT-standard compatible device drivers
- Machine-encoded, unique identification numbers
- Built-in network-management agent software and integration with Web-Based Enterprise Management (WBEM)
- Automatic preboot device driver configuration
- Automatic system/software scanning for policy compliance
- Diagnostic tools for monitoring and predicting component failure
- System-level trouble-ticketing software
- Remote wake utility

Microsoft is not claiming that the NetPC acquisition price will be significantly less than that of a traditional PC but, rather, sees the overall savings as coming from a reduction in support costs.

Sun's JavaStation and SunRay

Many in the computer industry want what NCs promise: heterogeneous environments where applications and data can be shared across platforms consisting of PCs, Macs, UNIX workstations, 3270 terminals, and NCs. Sun's first attempt at a kind of NetPC was the JavaStation. The JavaStation runs the JavaOS environment. JavaOS is a small operating environment that executes Java applications directly on the JavaStation hardware without requiring a separate host operating system. JavaOS consists of a small Java kernel, an embedded Java Virtual Machine (JVM), window and graphics extensions, and a suite of networking protocols. Optimized for size, JavaOS may boot and launch the HotJava browser in 2.5MB of memory. Although JavaOS is not a traditional operating system—because it does not include such traditional operating system features as a file system, virtual memory, or multiple address spaces—it includes a GUI, is multithreaded, supports a password-protected login feature, includes several device drivers, and communicates using standard network protocols.

Administrators can configure JavaOS, after a user logs in and passes authentication, to boot directly into a custom Java application. This allows the JavaStation to act as a dedicated terminal for many of the uses currently fulfilled by character-based terminals. Al ternatively, the device may launch into the HotJava Browser, the HotJava Views "Webtop," or a Windows emulation application such as Citrix's WinFrame.

The SunRay is Sun's successor to the JavaStation: Lacking the hard disk and other components, the SunRay is simply a processor packed inside a small box, connected to a monitor, a mouse, a keyboard, and the network. The processor only manages the display and the network connection. All application processing is done on the server. If this sounds like a dumb terminal, it's very close.

Will NCs Work for You?

If your company is already using centralized databases and application servers, NCs will fit well into your existing infrastructure. They may also be well-suited for IS departments that have grown up with terminal-based access to mainframe data and applications. In fact, the general concept of network computers is very similar to that of terminal networks, with the significant difference that NCs have sufficient computing power to participate as active members of client/server architectures. For terminal-based users, NCs offer the same features as IBM3270, IBM5250, VT100, and other types of terminals, but they provide more options for future expansion. On the other hand, terminal-based users may resist having to go through a GUI to get to their familiar terminal interface.

NCs are fine alternatives for users who work with only a few applications, who share machines, or who work at remote locations where technical support is not readily available. NCs are also well-suited to tasks that revolve around central data stores, because they act as upgrades to older, character-based terminals that were never designed to function in today's growing number of intranet environments.

NOTE: NCs are not designed for the needs of power users, so don't force a technically savvy employee to use an NC. It's better to let your more knowledgeable users have workstations adequate to their assigned tasks, since they will often perform their own technical support anyway. (Admittedly, however, this can be a mixed blessing for the official system support groups, as a power user trying to fix something may occasionally cause significant havoc.)

THE WEB EATS THE NETWORK

The World Wide Web has experienced explosive growth since its beginnings in 1992, with millions of people now using it for a seemingly infinite variety of tasks and activities. Part of the web's growth has come from its expanding to encompass some of the older formats of information on the Internet, such as Usenet newsgroups, and from the capability of most web browsers to act as FTP clients as well. Other areas of the web's growth have arisen from the fact that HTML forms are a simple and highly platform-independent way of creating a distributed client/server application. Given this dynamic history, it is not surprising that numbers of system and network administration tools have appeared to allow access to administrative functions via web browsers. The addition of Java as an Internet standard language and platform has merely increased this trend, especially with Sun's introduction of JMAPI (Java Management API). This section will deal with some of the web-based management approaches that have appeared or are expected to appear in the near future.

Before beginning this section, it is necessary to define what web-based management is and is not, in order to reduce confusion. Web-based management is the use of server and browser technology for viewing, identifying, and reporting enterprise-scale network and systems management data. Web-based management technology can be used to monitor and sometimes configure the following types of network parameters: LAN traffic, UNIX host IP addresses, router congestion, or mainframe network throughput, to name a few examples. Web management, however, refers to a different problem space: the tools and functions required to manage web servers, firewalls, and related content and subsystems.

This section will begin by discussing the beginnings of this trend in developing browser interfaces for viewing systems and network status. It will then move into a discussion of new standards such as Sun's Java Management API and the Web-Based Enterprise Management standard.

The Browser Interface

A widespread development among network management application vendors has been the addition of web browser interfaces as an alternative access method to their existing management strategies. Most network management platforms, such as HP OpenView,

SunNet Manager, and IBM's NetView for AIX, were designed primarily to be used by network engineers and administrators.

Other members of the business now want access to the information available from the enterprise's network management applications. A remote administrator needs to identify points of failure rapidly, without physically traveling about the corporate network. A user wants to identify the source of a delay, whether it is a temporary or systemic bottleneck. Senior management personnel want to know the network's status because of its effect on the business's financial status. For many of these users, full administrator access is unnecessary, if not an actual danger: Having a control in reach increases the odds that that control will be triggered, either by intention, ignorance, or accident.

Corporate savings arise from the reduction of calls or other contacts users make to the help desk or call center. Instead of calling technical support when the network is perceived as being slow, users can investigate network delays on their own and not interrupt the support staff in the middle of trying to solve the failure. To satisfy many of these users, system and network administrators want to offer viewer access to some subgroup of the information available in their network management applications. As a well-known and widespread user interface, a web browser is an appropriate choice for providing a monitoring window on the network's status. The view-only browsing nature of the Hypertext Transport Protocol behavior also provides a "look, but don't touch" one-way window into the network. Some users, such as the remote LAN administrator, may need to interact with the network or system components in order to manage those components.

Tribe, a router manufacturer, produced one of the earliest examples of web-based management utilities, providing a tool for viewing and configuring its routers, built from web forms, as early as 1995. With their tool WebManage, administrators could configure ports, protocols, and users, as well as get a snapshot of current router activity. Unlike when logging into the router through Telnet, passwords were transmitted in encrypted form. As a device connected to the Internet almost by definition, WebManage also provided direct links to Tribe's online manuals, technical support, and FTP server. The WebManage tool became the primary product of the company, such that Tribe changed its name to WebManage. For more information, please see their website at **http://www.webmanage.com**.

Other network management software vendors are now adding browser interfaces to many of their products, from management frameworks to routers. Hewlett-Packard ships a free web viewer for the main component of Hewlett-Packard's OpenView. Cisco includes a web server with its operating system for Cisco routers, allowing users to view and configure the status of routers and switches from a browser.

Turner View

One early and successful example of this trend was provided by Turner Broadcasting Systems. TBS created a web browser interface for its network management application, allowing its information support staff to view status information without requiring the expense of an X terminal or workstation.

Named Turner View, their assembled solution consisted of Hewlett-Packard Co.'s OpenView management framework, Seagate Software's NerveCenter for event management and filtering, and several internally developed applications correlating the pieces. Administrators use a web browser to view an OpenView log to identify the status of a single node or larger portions of the network.

What'sUp

IPSwitch's What'sUp is a scalable network monitor that runs on Windows servers and can be used to monitor a wide variety of components of the network. In addition, the What'sUp Gold version incorporates a small, self-contained web server that allows remote monitoring of network data from anywhere that can reach the What'sUp server. For more information, visit IPSwitch's website at **http://www.ipswitch.com**.

Web Administration for Microsoft Windows NT Server

The Web Administration package for Microsoft Windows NT Server allows remote administration of Microsoft Windows NT Server using existing web browsers. The package does not allow control identical to that of working at a Windows NT computer, in that it doesn't support the complete range of administrative tools described in the "Windows 2000 Server's Built-in Utilities" section of this chapter. Still, the package does allow several tasks to be performed from non–Windows NT workstations. The Web Administration package can be installed on a server running Windows NT Server and Microsoft Internet Information Server. Servers must support Basic Authentication or Windows NT Challenge Response security. If the browser you use supports Secure Sockets Layer (SSL) encryption of a session, the server side of the Web Administration process also supports SSL.

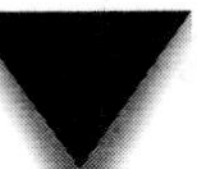

NOTE: Although both the major web browsers (Microsoft Internet Explorer and Netscape Navigator/Communicator) support SSL, Windows Challenge Response is only supported in Internet Explorer.

You can install the Web Administration software on any server that runs Windows NT Server 4.0 and Microsoft Internet Information Server (IIS). IIS is required because the Web Administration tool is an ISAPI.DLL, and the IIS service is required to make the API calls into ISAPI.DLL (other web servers do not support the ISAPI.DLLs). Installing the Web Administration software on the server causes the server to publish web pages that include forms you can use to administer that particular server. Accessing the Web Ad ministration pages is accomplished by entering the URL **http://*your_server_name*/ntadmin/ntadmin.htm** and beginning your work.

The administrative interface is a set of HTML pages designed to resemble the normal look of the Windows NT administrative tools. Some of the sections of the web interface include the following:

- The Account Management section allows you to view, create, disable, edit, and delete user accounts and properties, as well as change user passwords.

You can also view, create, edit, and delete groups, and you can add workstations to that domain.

- The Share Management section gives an administrator the ability to view, create, and change permissions for shares for all installed file services.
- The Session Management section allows administrators to view and delete current sessions, and to send pop-up broadcast messages to currently logged-in users.
- The Server Management section allows remote administrators to shut down the server and view and change server services and driver configuration. The system, application, and security log event files can be viewed, and the current server configuration can be viewed and saved to a file.
- The Printer Management section allows administrators to view print queues and their current jobs, and to pause or delete entire print queues or specific print jobs.

For more information, including downloading of this package, see Microsoft's website at **http://www.microsoft.com/ntserver/management/exec/feature/WebAdmin.asp**.

Web-Related Initiatives

As described in "The Browser Interface" section of this chapter, web browsers and web forms are used primarily for viewing system and network status, with limited control capabilities. Many management applications have interfaces, methods of information gathering, and report formats that are radically different from each other. This inconsistency causes administrators to have to launch separate applications for different components of the system and network. Although these low-level applications or agents don't communicate with each other, they can often report information to a framework. A *framework* is a larger management application that is traditionally used to see an overview of a network's status. There are two industry initiatives intended to aid integration of system and network monitoring and management tools: Sun's Java Management API, and the Web-Based Enterprise Management consortium. This section will discuss these two evolving initiatives.

Sun's Java Management API

Sun's Java Management API (JMAPI) is part of Sun's Java Standard Extension API framework, providing a set of extensible objects and methods for building applets that can manage a network. JMAPI uses remote method invocation (RMI) as its remote communication mechanism. For a loose analogy, RMI can be categorized as the Java version of remote procedure calls (RPCs).

Backed by a wide range of networking and management companies, JMAPI is intended to assist developers in writing applets, or small Java applications, that can be downloaded across Internet links. This dynamic loading of code as required allows administrators to perform diagnostic functions from any device, even if that device is not attached to an SNMP management workstation. With the object-oriented nature of Java, the applets will aid in establishing relationship links between management applications and network components to more rapidly identify the true cause of a system or network failure.

Sun's engineers have used the JMAPI to build a web interface for Solaris' JumpStart automatic configuration technology. The web-enabled software includes different APIs for installation, configuration, registration, and licensing, and it can also perform uninstalls, reinstalls, or upgrades. Sun has stated that the long-term plan is to Java-enable the entire suite of Solstice Solaris administration tools, although it has been confirmed that a command-line interface will remain part of Solaris.

Other companies are developing Java applications for other management uses. Applets have been developed that allow remote administrators with a web browser to view all applications running on a server. The applet dynamically updates, and it allows administrators to find state information and shut down or pause an application as needed. Other Java applets can be used to display a real-time graph of transaction processing rates. More information on JMAPI is available at **http://java.sun.com/APIext/JMAPI**.

WBEM

The Web-Based Enterprise Management (WBEM) industry initiative establishes an architecture that supports the management of an enterprise across a network. The WBEM architecture is intended to define the structures and conventions required to access information about objects being managed, and to centralize information for analysis and support, as well as to provide location-transparent access to managed objects for remote administrators' control. The WBEM group intends to define an umbrella set of standards that merges DMI, HTTP, and SNMP into an architecture that can be viewed and modified by any standard web browser. WBEM was designed to be compatible with major existing management protocols, including SNMP, DMI, and CMIP. A wide range of companies, including Cisco, Compaq, Intel, and Microsoft, are participating in the WBEM initiative, and many of them are also working with JMAPI. WBEM also defines a new protocol for access of management information, in order to allow management solutions to be platform independent and physically distributed across the enterprise. This protocol is known as the HyperMedia Management Protocol (HMMP).

HMMP HMMP provides management services across platform boundaries by defining a common network access model, schema, and security model. HMMP is a transport-independent protocol that uses a request-response paradigm to represent management activities. In a familiar client/server model, a client makes requests concerning a management task. An HMMP server processes the requested task and returns the appropriate response. An HMMP server may act as a client of yet another server in order to complete the task the first client requested of it.

HMOM AND HMMS HyperMedia Object Manager (HMOM) is a software development technology that enables WBEM-compliant applications to manage network elements as objects. HyperMedia Management Schema (HMMS) was designed as an extensible data model of the managed network environment. The HMMS portion of WBEM was rejected by the Desktop Management Task Force, and its inclusion in WBEM is currently in limbo. More information on the WBEM initiative is available on the web at **http://www.dmtf.org/wbem/**.

Web-Based Management Tradeoffs

As shown, web-based management strategies are becoming common. Some of the advantages of such an approach are presented here:

- **Universal viewing of management applications** Administrators do not have to use an X terminal or a UNIX workstation to view a management framework application.
- **Low cost** A PC or Macintosh desktop equipped with a browser costs much less than a typical X terminal or UNIX workstation configured to run a management framework. Also, with many current management products adding a web interface, any current investment in hardware or applications licenses and training is not wasted.
- **Ease of use** Administrators will require less training because the browser metaphor is familiar to most people. The ease of use translates to a shorter learning curve before an administrator becomes productive.
- **Reduced external technical support costs** Management applications can often require extensive training and experience before an administrator becomes productive. Management applications themselves also may require significant configuration and support costs.
- **Reduced external technical support costs** Users can check the state of the network themselves. This can reduce call volume to the organization's help desk.
- **Better interoperability** An administrator can use a browser to switch between multiple management applications at various levels. A browser can also access vendors' help sites on the Internet, allowing the vendor to update and correct the documentation quickly.

However, some people perceive problems with web-based management:

- Decreased security
- Inconsistency between Java Virtual Machines (JVMs), causing applets to work differently or not at all on different platforms
- The fact that proliferation of Java applets on networks will create other management concerns besides security, such as bandwidth and version-management issues

For example, users may tire of downloading Java applets. Caching Java applets on a local machine can reduce this problem, but the JVM environments do not currently include a method of controlling the versions of the Java applets cached on the local machine. Many feel that the security issues with browser-based management are no worse than traditional approaches, given that much current system management occurs over a Telnet session, with logins and passwords passed in unencrypted ASCII format over the network.

SUMMARY

System and network management is becoming more difficult all the time. With the rapid growth of networks, administrators are constantly asked to make different computer systems communicate with each other—preferably seamlessly, transparently to the user, reliably, inexpensively, and "get it done today." Various attempts have been made to extend portions of networks outward, with varying degrees of success and general acceptance. Initiatives to use NFS for file services, TCP/IP for printing (or for all network services), the distributed login capability offered earlier by the Open Software Foundation's Distributed Computing Environment (and more recently offered to an extent by Windows 2000), the Common Desktop Environment GUI offered for most versions of UNIX and Windows, and so on, are all becoming more common. As networks grow in complexity, standardizing on some points simplifies administration. Some of these solutions are even free or inexpensive, as in the case of Samba for file and print services.

The original initiative of Network Computers arose from a current trend designed to reduce the high cost of information systems support. By being standardized and minimally configurable, NCs are supposed to be easier to manage than normal UNIX or PC workstations. However, Network Computers are not for everyone: few business facilities have completely replaced their workstations with Network Computers. Network Computers may provide less savings than predicted, as many businesses already have standardized their workstation configurations by job level and expected use, in order to realize quantity savings on bulk ordering as well as making the administrators' jobs easier. Although Network Computers may be even easier than standardized PC workstations to set up and maintain, they may not yield the drastic savings predicted for all customers. The thin-client model can lower the total cost of ownership, as shown by Citrix's MetaFrame and Microsoft's Terminal Server.

Central administrative platforms such as CA's Unicenter-TNG and Tivoli's TME-10 are attempting to evolve view and control capabilities for all components in a heterogeneous network. Although in many ways such attempts have succeeded, implementation and deployment of such overarching control platforms is still nontrivial. IT departments may wish to examine their need for such an encompassing control platform, and consider whether smaller, more focused point management solutions for subsets of the network can provide more efficient and realistic solutions.

One of the true enemies of system administration is time: no time to keep up with system security notices, to perform routine tasks, and to solve problems before they become critical nightmares. Since distance takes time to traverse, good distributed system and network management tools save the travel time by allowing fast remote diagnosis and reconfiguration or repair without having to physically travel from a given location—that is, if the travel time saved is not outweighed by the time spent on evaluating, acquiring, installing, and learning the distributed management tool. Some of the higher-end distributed system management tools are reported to have a horrifically steep learning curve before competence is attained. There is also a tradeoff of simplicity versus detail, in that if a picture is clear and simple enough to take in at a glance, it's likely that important information has been filtered out along with the noise. However, distributed management tools will continue to evolve and improve.

APPENDIX A

Common Desktop Environment (CDE) Frequently Asked Questions

(Reprinted with permission.)

Maintained by: Aditya Talwar and Vivek Arora (**cosc4hf@bayou.uh.edu**) at **http://www.laxmi.net/cde.htm**.

Objective: This FAQ will attempt to provide answers to overcome day-to-day snags encountered in using CDE desktop.

The author of the FAQ is grateful to Mr. Steven Burnett for hosting the site since inception. And forwarding comments to improve the site!

The following is a list of questions that are frequently asked about CDE (Common Desktop Environment) in the **comp.unix.cde** newsgroup. You can help make it even better-quality FAQ by writing a succinct contribution or update it by sending an *email* to me at **cosc4hf@bayou.uh.edu**. The FAQs are updated on a daily basis and the latest version can be found at **www.laxmi.net/cde.htm**.

My employer/account is *not* responsible for the contents of this FAQ. Since CDE is a joint venture between several UNIX vendors, this document may not contain the latest or most accurate information on all platforms and versions at all times. Whenever time permits I'll try my level best to keep the information in this document updated.

To get the initial structure of the CDE FAQ going, I have added some questions; please send me what you think should be useful over here. I'll try my best to keep this FAQ updated and post it on a weekly schedule initially, and then lengthen the interval later. Thanks for your help in advance! (Please bear in mind this is still in primitive form.)

The indexed, HTML, WWW version of this FAQ is available at **http://www.laxmi.net/cde.htm**

+ added questions

* updated answers

1. GENERAL

*1.1) What is CDE? Why should I use CDE?

+ 1.2) What are the current platforms and versions of CDE?

2. MORE INFO

*2.1) What WWW/FTP sites contain CDE information?

*2.2) What books should I read for CDE?

2.3) Where can I look for more information for setting up my desktop?

3. DESKTOP SETUP

3.1) How can I change my default window manager in CDE?

3.2) How can I change my keyboard settings in CDE?

3.3) Is there a .mailcap/.mime types file for dtmail? Where can I find it?

3.4) What if I have login problems? How can I see the errors?

3.5) Why can't some applications like Netscape, etc., start up in workspaces other than my login workspace?

3.6) Would someone please tell me how to access a floppy while in CDE 1.0.2?

3.7) One question I see a lot is "How do I deal with multiple heads?"

3.8) How do I change the keyboard repeat rate?

3.9) I'm new to CDE. I'm running it on a Sun with Solaris 2.5. The lock icon on the Control Panel doesn't work.

3.10) How do I use arrow keys to switch between workspaces?

3.11) How do I use xv under CDE to create smaller icons?

3.12) I have recently installed CDE on my Solaris 2.5.1 server. I would like to have CDE throw up the login screen at boot time on my console, but miss the console messages that are normally displayed there.

3.13) Does anyone know how to switch between desktops without having to use the TAB key?

3.14) When I log on to CDE in HP-UX, I want certain applications automatically started, like a dtterm running a certain script, etc. How can this be done?

3.15) Why does xsetroot not work?

3.16) How do I disable "Open Terminal" on the File Manager?

3.17) How do I replace the clock on the front panel with a digital clock?

3.18) Where are all of the f.<functions> in dtwm documented? If you say the dtwm man page, I will ask you to find f.goto_workspace, f.next_workspace, etc. I can't find any reference to them in the dtwm man pages.

3.19) How do I get an application to appear in a particular workspace? For example: xterm –xrm "???". What goes inside the quotes?

3.20) What is dtsmcmd, and where can I find documentation on it? Is it an undocumented function of CDE? A find was unable to find the binary, and a search through the man pages was fruitless as well.

3.21) Is there an equivalent .xinitrc file in CDE which can be edited so apps get launched on startup?

3.22) Maybe we're backward or something, but our Sun with Solaris is not configured to give users access to /usr. All docs talk about is copying some file from /etc/dt to /usr/dt and modifying it, which doesn't work in our environment.

3.23) What are the advantages of dtterm over xterm? The only one I can think of is that it is already installed as the default. Apart from that, cut-and-paste requires more effort than with xterm, and it is not identified as VT100 compatible when logging in to remote systems (I'm getting tired of typing export TERM=vt100 and SET/TERM=vt100). Before I give up on it, are there some features I'm overlooking?

*3.24) How do I set up a replacement "switch" for the front panel and work around the "only 1 front panel" problem on multiscreen servers?

3.25) I'm having a problem in that /etc/profile doesn't seem to be read when I log in on the CDE environment. I put some environment stuff in there (path and others) but nothing seems to be set. I know about $HOME/.dtprofile and DTSOURCEPROFILE=true, but that doesn't help for /etc/profile. Is there a /etc/profile.dt that should exist or a similar file for CDE?

3.26) I am trying to find out if it's possible to toggle between two different actions in one space on the subpanel. For example, if you had an option on a subpanel that was titled "printer enable," as soon as you clicked on that action the next time that subpanel were brought up it would read "printer disable."

3.27) How do I disable the CDE front panel entirely?

3.28) I'm using Solaris 2.7 under CDE. When I try to put the image on the root by the command

```
xv  -rmode 2  .Images/grass.gif&
```

a xv control window pops up. There is no picture appearing on the background. But when I log out, I can see the picture for a very short time. This is not what I expect. It seems that the root hides behind the background.

3.29) I'm looking for a way to configure my front panel. (In particular, I would like to remove the mail icon, or to replace its action by one that I define.) Which is easier to do?

4. APPLICATION DEVELOPMENT

4.1) What are actions and datatypes in CDE?

4.2) How can I reload new actions and datatypes in CDE?

5. TROUBLESHOOTING

5.1) What directories/files can I look at to check for errors?

+5.2) The lock button doesn't work, and .dt/errorlog shows "dtsession: Unable to lock display due to security restrictions."

*5.3) We are trying to get some older DEC X terminals to start up IP X sessions through dtlogin. I think I have the configuration right, but very little happens, and the dtlogin freezes up. The X-terminal sends its request, and I get the CDE hourglass on the display, then *POOF* nothing on the X-term, and a dead dtlogin. I'm using CDE 1.0.1 on an Ultra-1 with Solaris 2.5.

6. BUGS AND PATCHES

6.1) Solaris™ versions: 2.6, 2.6_x86, 2.5.1, 2.5.1_x86, 2.5, 2.5_x86, 2.4, and 2.4_x86 running CDE if exploited, all these vulnerabilities could lead to root access or allow arbitrary files to be overwritten.

7. ACKNOWLEDGMENTS

1. GENERAL

*1.1) What is CDE? Why should I use CDE?

The Common Desktop Environment is a standard desktop for UNIX, providing services to end-users, systems administrators, and application developers consistently across many platforms.

CDE was originally developed under the COSE (Common Open Software Environment) initiative by Hewlett-Packard, IBM, Novell and SunSoft. Those companies were joined by Digital, Fujitsu, and Hitachi as sponsors of the CDE-Motif PST under the auspices of the Open Software Foundation (OSF). That project is developing the successors to CDE 1.0 and Motif 2.0, along with enhancements to X11R6 that will be included in the Broadway Release. The X Consortium is the Prime Contractor for the PST.

*1.2) What are the current platforms and versions of CDE?

All of the companies in 1.1 offer CDE in some form. In addition, TriTeal offers the TriTeal Enhanced Desktop (TED), their CDE implementation, on several other platforms.

X Inside has just recently released a port of CDE for Linux and FreeBSD. WGS (Work Group Solutions) are selling it bundled with X Inside's Accelerated X server (which is needed for their CDE kit).

Each company produces CDE in its own way, including defect repairs, platform-specific hardware/software support and value-added features onto the common software base that is available to sponsors of the technology and licensees. This is similar to what has happened in the past with Motif and X11.

OSF licenses the common source base without modifications. The original COSE source was version 1.0.0; the CDE Maintenance Release was 1.0.10 (to avoid conflicts with sponsor-specific version numbers, e.g., 1.0.2 from Sun that comes with Solaris 2.5.1, the source base produced by the CDE-Motif CST will be version 2.1.0 and will include Motif 2.1.0 so that the numbering schemes for CDE and Motif can be unified).

Therefore, it is very important for people to provide not only the version number but also the vendor when identifying the version of CDE that they are using.

Here is a short list of CDE versions with the various platforms:

- Sun Solaris 2.6:

  CDE 1.2.1 + Motif 1.2.6 + X11R5
- Sun Solaris 2.6 + Solaris Desktop Extensions (SDX):

  CDE 1.2/1.3 + Motif 1.2.6 + X11R5
- Sun Solaris 7:

  CDE 1.3 + Motif 2.1.0 + X11R6
- HP-UX 10.20:

  CDE 1.0 + Motif 1.2.6 + X11R5+ and X11R6+
- HP-UX 11.00:

  CDE 2.1 + Motif 2.1.0 + X11R6+

Gurus: If anyone has come across any findings which could be included in the FAQ, please e-mail them to me.

2. MORE INFO

*2.1) What WWW/FTP sites contain CDE information?

Action-definitions and the icons can be found at:

http://www.tm.bi.ruhr-uni-bochum.de/dt/

ftp://ftp.tm.bi.ruhr-uni-bochum.de/pub/dt

These directories are mirrors of our /etc/dt/appconfig.

Does anybody know another resource of this kind on the web or did anybody do the same work as we did?

***ftp://ftp.frontec.se/pub/cde** is a great site for actions and icons which can be placed in /etc/dt.

Any mail or upload in **ftp://ftp.tm.bi.ruhr-uni-bochum.de/incoming/dt** would be greatly appreciated.

http://www.kfa-juelich.de/zam/docs/tki/tki_html/t0289/t0289cde.html
http://www.austin.ibm.com/cgi-bin/CDE/faqtop - AIX flavored FAQ
http://docs.hp.com
http://docs.hp.com/dynaweb/hpux11/dtdcen1a/
http://www.hp.com/wsg/ssa/cde.html
http://www.hp.com/xwindow/windowmgrs/cde.html

is the main descriptive page about HP-CDE. Use the site-specific search engine to look for "CDE." My last search turned up 154 documents that reference it on the HP website.

http://www.partner.digital.com/www-swdev/pages/Home/TECH/CDE/cdedocs.html

This seems to have a complete list of manuals for various CDE tasks as system administration, programming, etc. in HTML format.

http://www.iac.net/~hollende/manual/hd_cde.html

is the top of an elaborate description of how Hale & Dorr, a prestigious Boston law firm, has adapted CDE for use in their environment.

http://www.triteal.com/cde.html

has the information about TED.

http://www.sun.com/cde/index.html

has the description of the current CDE offering for Solaris from Sun.

The complete Solaris documentation, including CDE manuals, can be found at

http://docs.sun.com
http://docs.sun.com/ab2/coll.8.40/@Ab2CollToc
http://docs.sun.com/ab2/coll.72.3/@Ab2CollToc
http://www.unix.digital.com
http://www.unix.digital.com/faqs/publications/pub_page/V40D_DOCS.HTM
http://www.openvms.digital.com/openvms/doc-sets/cde/index.html

have the necessary documentation for CDE under the HTML and PDF format.

http://www.osf.org/motif/CDE/cde.html

contains information about licensing from OSF, the CDE Maintenance Release that was produced by the CDE-Motif PST.

http://www.lib.ox.ac.uk/internet/news/faq/archive/cde-cose-faq.html

is on old FAQ about CDE from the COSE days.

http://www.xinside.com/

is the X Inside, Inc. website—we also have some screen shots up of CDE as well. Other versions floating around? Please let me know.

*2.2) What books should I read for CDE?

A series of official documentation is available from Addison Wesley:

http://www.aw.com/devpress/series/cde.html

I found the Advanced Users and System Administrators guide most useful to get jump-started.

Can you recommend any books/websites where I can get some good information on: personalizing CDE? Basic configuration?

See: **http://www.opengroup.org/public/pubs/catalog/mo.htm.**

I have another book about CDE, not listed in the FAQs: (It is in German, so only for a few people of interest, but ...); Hanser Verlag: Eickemeyer / Koslowski; Der UNIX=AE Common Desktop, 205 Seiten, 102 Bilder. 1996. Kartoniert. ISBN 3-446-18342-6. See:

http://www.hanser.de/computer/buecher/ei18342.htm

or

http://www.hanser.de/computer/index.htm

2.3) Where can I look for more information for setting up my desktop?

Make sure /usr/dt/man is added to your $MANPATH. Section 4 of /usr/dt/man contains useful setup information, e.g., dtfpfile, dtactionfile, dtdtfile, etc.

3. DESKTOP SETUP

3.1) How can I change my default window manager in CDE?

I asked if it were possible to add other window managers such as twm or fvwm to the CDE login. I did get a few responses saying that it could be done, but unfortunately no one knew how. I'm running fvwm right now. All I had to do was put: Dtsession*wmStartupCommand: /home/orb/bin/sunos5/fvwm in my .Xdefaults file; just change the path to wherever you put fvwm.

3.2) How can I change my keyboard settings in CDE?

Try putting something like this in your .dt/dtwmrc:

```
Keys DtKeyBindings

{
    Meta<Key>space                 icon|window             f.post_wmenu
    Meta<Key>Tab                   root|icon|window        f.next_key
    Meta Shift<Key>Tab             root|icon|window        f.prev_key
    Meta<Key>Prior                 root|icon|window        f.next_key
    Meta<Key>Next                  root|icon|window        f.prev_key
    Meta<Key>Down                  root|icon|window        f.circle_down
    Meta<Key>Up                    root|icon|window        f.circle_up
    Meta Ctrl Shift<Key>exclam     root|icon|window        f.set_behavior
    Meta<Key>F6                    window                  f.next_key transient
    <Key>F11                       root|icon|window        f.next_workspace
    Shift<Key>F11                  root|icon|window        f.prev_workspace
}
```

You might need to change the key names—this is based on an HP keyboard. Under this config, F11 will switch workspaces, and SHIFT F11 will switch backwards.

3.3) Is there a .mailcap/.mime types file for dtmail? Where can I find it?

DtMail, like most other CDE applications uses the CDE database to figure out the MIME types. Look at the *Advanced User's and System Administrator's Guide* that comes with CDE in the sections on Actions and DataTypes.

These Actions and DataTypes allow you to do a lot more than just a MIME file and are not all that hard to work with. Just remember to reload the actions and restart the applications you are testing with.

3.4) Wht if I have login problems? How can I see the errors?

If you cannot log in, from the login session interface, choose the Options menu, then choose Failsafe login selection. Then log in. If there is an error, you can log into the following location and fix the problem:

$HOME/.dt/errorlog, $HOME/.dt/startlog, and /var/dt/Xerrors, etc.

3.5) Why can't some applications like Netscape, etc., start up in workspaces other than my login workspace?

Some applications, like Netscape, are non-ICCCM compliant, i.e., they don't write their command line to the WM_COMMAND property. This means they don't follow the –xrm resource setting and can't open in the workspace you want. I believe it will take some time for vendors to make their applications ICCCM/CDE compliant.

3.6) Would someone please tell me how to access a floppy while in CDE 1.0.2?

You can still use /usr/openwin/bin/filemgr to manage floppies and CD-ROMs. Or you can use the volcheck(1) command and then do

```
dtaction Open /floppy/floppy0
```

Full support for removable media will be in CDE 1.1.

3.7) One question I see a lot is, "How to deal with multiple heads?"

mrz@nimba.NSD.3Com.COM (Matthew Zeier) writes: I have CDE configured to use two screens. The only problem is that I cannot get CDE to display a second toolbar on my other screen. Without that, I don't quite know how to easily switch workspaces nor do I know how to change backdrops.

Running a second toolbar would require having a second dtwm running; I've never tried this, but I've talked to people who have. Some had problems, some seemed to work just fine. I've never bothered to try myself, since the following hacks are good enough for me.

- Customize dtwm keystrokes to change workspaces. In ~/.dt/dtwmrc I have key bindings including the following:

```
Keys DtKeyBindings
{
    Meta<Key>Right         root|icon|window  f.next_workspace
    Meta<Key>Left          root|icon|window  f.prev_workspace
}
```

I then use meta and the left/right arrows to bang around the workspaces. This works on both screens.

- Put the programs I use most often on the second screen in the dtwm root menu:

```
Menu DtRootMenu
{
```

```
        "Workspace Menu"                  f.title
        "Xemacs"                          f.exec "xemacs"
        "Cmdtool"                         f.exec "/usr/openwin/bin/cmdtool"
        "Dtterm"                          f.exec "/usr/dt/bin/dtterm"
         no-label                         f.separator
        "Refresh"                         f.refresh
        "Minimize/Restore Front Panel"    f.toggle_frontpanel
        "Next workspace"                  f.next_workspace
         no-label                         f.separator
        "Restart Workspace Manager..."    f.restart
        "Log out..."                      f.action ExitSession
}
```

This gives me a way to launch these apps on the second screen, since dtwm sets DISPLAY according to which screen you're on when you pick an app off the root menu. (You'll note this includes a dtterm, so I can always launch other applications via the shell.)

- To set backdrops, just run dtstyle on the other screen, e.g., $ dtstyle -display :0.1. This gets the style manager running on the other screen; you can now set backdrops as normal. For those who really want a GUI gadget for changing the workspaces, check out the sample script in /usr/dt/examples/dtksh/DtWsTest1. This is a dtksh script that uses the workspace management APIs to change the workspaces when buttons are clicked. It's just a sample, and a little rough, but it works. (I'd love to see somebody come up with a polished-up version of this.) Note the sample scripts in /usr/dt/examples are only loaded if you installed the "developer's" version of CDE on Solaris; I don't know about the other platforms.

3.8) How do I change the keyboard repeat rate?

To turn the autorepeat feature on or off, open the workspace menu, bring up the style manager, click on the kbd icon, and change the repeat rate. You can also do this from within a dtterm window: Options=>Global BlinkingCursor (Disabled | Enabled).

To change the keyboard repeat rate you need to pass some options to the X server (Xsun is the default for CDE). dtlogin will start the X server by first looking at /etc/dt/config/Xservers. If it does not exist it will use /usr/dt/config/Xservers. See dtlogin(1X) for more information. Copy /usr/dt/config/Xservers to /etc/dt/config/Xservers and add your preferences there. Then you must restart the X server for changes to take effect. The line to start the server should look something like this:

```
:0   Local local_uid@console root /usr/openwin/bin/Xsun :0 -nobanner -ar1 350 -ar2 30
 # /etc/rc2.d/S99dtlogin stop
 # /etc/rc2.d/S99dtlogin start
```

from Xsun man page ...

```
-ar1 milliseconds
```

Specify amount of time in milliseconds before a pressed key begins to autorepeat. The default is 500 milliseconds.

```
-ar2 milliseconds
```

Specify the interval in milliseconds between autorepeats of pressed keys. The default is 50 milliseconds.

3.9) I'm new to CDE. I'm running it on a Sun with Solaris 2.5. The lock icon on the Control Panel doesn't work.

This is a known problem with CDE and is being investigated. This is known to happen in an NIS+ environment.

3.10) How do I use arrow keys to switch between workspaces?

Take the following lines and add them to the Keys DtKeyBindings section of your $HOME/.dt/dtwmrc file:

```
<Key>F20                root|window|icon        f.next_workspace
<Key>F19                root|window|icon        f.prev_workspace
```

or something similar.

3.11) How do I use xv under CDE to create smaller icons?

For the trivia file: The problem is caused by xv refusing to force itself to be drawn smaller than the window manager-recommended minimum size. To defeat that, add this to .Xdefaults:

```
Dtwm*xv*clientDecoration: none
```

This makes the main xv window borderless, but you can still move it in CDE's dtwm (by default, anyway) with ALT+mouse1drag.

3.12) I have recently installed CDE on my Solaris 2.5.1 server. I would like to have CDE throw up the login screen at boot time on my console, but miss the console messages that are normally displayed there.

A. Add the following to /etc/dt/config/Xconfig:

```
Dtlogin._0.setup:       Xsetup_0
Dtlogin*grabServer:     False
```

B. Copy /usr/dt/config/Xsetup to /etc/dt/config/Xsetup_0 and add to the following line at the bottom:

```
( sleep 2; /usr/openwin/bin/xconsole -geometry 480x130-0-0
-daemon -notify
-verbose -fn fixed -exitOnFail )&
```

Then restart dtlogin.

3.13) Does anyone know how to switch between desktops without having to use the TAB key?

The neat way to do this is to edit your $HOME/.dt/dtwmrc file and add the following lines in the Keys DtKeyBindings section:

```
<Key>F5        root|icon|window                f.goto_workspace ws0
<Key>F6        root|icon|window                f.goto_workspace ws1
<Key>F7        root|icon|window                f.goto_workspace ws2
<Key>F8        root|icon|window                f.goto_workspace ws3
```

If you don't have a dtwmrc file in this directory, then copy the /usr/dt /config/C/sys.dtwmrc to $HOME/.dt/dtwmrc.

3.14) When I log on to CDE in HP-UX, I want certain applications automatically started, like a dtterm running a certain script, etc. How can this be done?

You can create a script in ~/.dt/sessions called sessionetc. The script is executed at CDE startup, and in it, you can start up all those cde-unaware apps that cde can't start up itself. If necessary, you can also use ~/.dt/sessions/sessionexit to execute commands at CDE exit time.

3.15) Why does xsetroot not work?

Change backdrop to Transparent.

3.16) How do I disable "Open Terminal" on the File Manager?

Create ACTION Terminal {EXEC_STRING dterror.ds "Unavailable"}, etc.

3.17) How do I replace the clock on the front panel with a digital clock?

Anybody knows this ... forward me the answer!

3.18) Where are all of the f.<functions> in dtwm documented? If you say the dtwm man page, I will ask you to find f.goto_workspace, f.next_workspace, etc. I can't find any reference to them in the dtwm man pages.

The dtwmrc man page has all this information: dtwmrc(4), to be precise. From the man page:

```
f.goto_workspace workspace
```

This function causes the workspace manager to switch to the workspace named by workspace. If no workspace exists by the specified name, then no action occurs. Note that adding and deleting workspaces dynamically can affect this function.

```
f.next_workspace
```

This function causes the workspace manager to switch to the next workspace. If the last workspace is currently active, then this function will switch to the first workspace. Etc., etc., etc.

3.19) How do I get an application to appear in a particular workspace? For example: xterm –xrm "*???*". What goes inside the quotes?

```
xterm -xrm "*workspaceList: ws0 ws1"
```

1. The workspace names can be either ws0, ws1, etc., or the Names entered in the labels on the front panel workspace switch. The application must copy the –xrm option to a WM_COMMAND property on the application's top level window. You can usually check whether an application does that by running xprop WM_COMMAND and clicking on the application's window. (The dtterm command is aware of workspaces and will obey the resource but does not have any WM_COMMAND property before the session manager asks it to update one.)

3.20) What is dtsmcmd, and where can I find documentation on it? Is it an undocumented function of CDE? A find was unable to find the binary, and a search through the man pages was fruitless as well.

It is an undocumented internal mechanism of the session manager.

3.21) Is there an equivalent .xinitrc file in CDE that can be edited so apps get launched on startup?

Explore $HOME/.dt~—you'll find a bunch of stuff in there. But the equivalent to .xinitrc for the home session would be $HOME/.dt/sessions/home/dt.session. You can, however, have more than one session, so you'll have to edit each one separately.

3.22) Maybe we're backward or something, but our Sun with Solaris is not configured to give users access to /usr. All docs talk about is copying some file from /etc/dt to /usr/dt and modifying it, which doesn't work in our environment.

1. This is for system-wide configuration only! It affects all CDE users on that system. And it's not from /etc/dt to /usr/dt, but probably the other way around—original copies are stored in /usr/dt, but if you plan to modify them, copy them to /etc/dt, so that an upgrade of CDE which would overwrite the files in /usr/dt would not wipe out your customizations.
2. For user customizations, I assume we can make these types of /usr/dt changes in $HOME/.dt?
3. That's correct. Individuals who want to modify the behavior of CDE for their use only, should do it in $HOME/.dt.

3.23) What are the advantages of dtterm over xterm?

The only one I can think of is that it is already installed as the default. Apart from that, cut-and-paste requires more effort than with xterm, and it is not identified as VT100 compatible when logging in to remote systems (I'm getting tired of typing export TERM=vt100 and SET/TERM=vt100). Before I give up on it, are there some features I'm overlooking?

You can use the middle mouse button (if you have one) for pasting a selection. Putting the following line in ~/app-defaults/Dtterm causes dtterm to set the TERM environment variable to vt100:

```
Dtterm*termName: vt100
```

Other examples of resources that I find useful are

```
Dtterm*kshMode: True
Dtterm*autoWrap: True
Dtterm*userFont: -*-lucida sans typewriter-medium-*-*-*-*-120-*
Dtterm*sunFunctionKeys: True       - if you are using a Sun machine
Dtterm*saveLines: 100s
Dtterm*loginShell: True
```

*3.24) How do I set up a replacement switch for the Front Panel and work around the "only 1 front panel" problem on multiscreen servers?

Chuck Campbell wrote: Is it possible to have the workspaces buttons change both screens at once, or is it possible to have two front panels, one on each head, to achieve this?

Workspaces are managed on a per-screen basis. The defaults are 4 workspaces for screen 0, and 1 for any others. It is possible to have several workspaces on other screens by modifying dtwm resources (see /usr/dt/app-defaults/C/Dtwm). The CDE front panel is part of the window manager and it is NOT possible to have 2 front panels. (It is possible to run 2 copies of dtwm, 1 per display, but they won't behave as expected.)

The next question then is "How do I switch workspaces on display 1 without a front panel?" One option is to add "f.next_workspace and f.prev_workspace" to your dtwmrc root menu windows. Another option is to write a stand-alone workspace switch client using the CDE API.

```
Content-Disposition: inline; filename="switch.c"
author: Chuck Slivkoff

A
#include
#include
#include
#include

Widget shell;

static void SetWorkspaceCB(Widget w, XtPointer client_data, XtPointer call_data)
{
    DtWsmSetCurrentWorkspace(shell,(Atom)client_data);
    return;
```

```
    } /* SetWorkspaceCB */

A
static void WsCB(Widget w,Atom aWorkspace,XtPointer client_data) {
    return;
    }

int main ( int argc, char **argv )
{
    Display *dpy;
    Window root;
    Widget       rc, pb;
    XtAppContext app;
    XmString     xmstr;
    Atom *aWs;
    int wscount,i;
    DtWsmWorkspaceInfo *pWsInfo;
    String wsname;

    shell = XtAppInitialize ( &app, "Switch", NULL, 0,
                              &argc, argv, NULL, NULL, 0 );

    dpy = XtDisplay(shell);
    root = XDefaultRootWindow(dpy);

    rc = XtVaCreateManagedWidget("rc",
                                 xmRowColumnWidgetClass,
                                 shell,
                                 XmNorientation,XmHORIZONTAL,
                                 XmNnumColumns,2,
                                 XmNpacking,XmPACK_COLUMN,
                                 NULL);
    if (DtWsmGetWorkspaceList(dpy,root,&aWs,&wscount) == Success) {
       for (i=0;ipchTitle,XmFONTLIST_DEFAULT_TAG);
pb=XtVaCreateManagedWidget(wsname,
                                    xmPushButtonWidgetClass,
                                    rc,
                                    XmNlabelString,xmstr,
                                    XmNshadowThickness,3,
                                    XmNbackground,pWsInfo->fg,
                                    NULL);
```

```
XtAddCallback(pb,XmNactivateCallback,SetWorkspaceCB,(XtPointer)aWs[i]);
              DtWsmFreeWorkspaceInfo(pWsInfo);
              XtFree(wsname);
              XmStringFree(xmstr);
              } /* for */
           } /* if */
else {
         printf("Error: can't get workspace info. Exiting\n");
         exit(-1);
      }


DtWsmAddCurrentWorkspaceCallback(shell,(DtWsmWsChangeProc)WsCB,NULL);

      XtRealizeWidget ( shell );
      DtWsmOccupyAllWorkspaces(dpy,XtWindow(shell));
      XtAppMainLoop ( app );
}
```

-chuck
Chuck Slivkoff

3.25) I'm having a problem in that /etc/profile doesn't seem to be read when I log in on the CDE environment. I put some environment stuff in there (path and others) but nothing seems to be set. I know about $HOME/.dtprofile and DTSOURCEPROFILE=true, but that doesn't help for /etc/profile. Is there a /etc/profile.dt that should exist or a similar file for CDE?

Xsession can source a user's traditional HomeDir/.profile or .login script. By default this capability is disabled. To tell the Xsession to source the .profile or the .login script, we set the DTSOURCEPROFILE to true.

To change the DTSOURCEPROFILE for all users or other variables for all users, create an /etc/dt/config/Xsession.d script that sets the new values. For example create, an executable ksh script, /etc/dt/config/Xsession.d/test containing export MYVAR="*value*". This should work in place of /etc/profile.

3.26) I am trying to find out if it's possible to toggle between two different actions in one space on the subpanel. For example, if you had an option on a subpanel that was titled "printer enable," as soon as you clicked on that action the next time that subpanel were brought up it would read "printer disable."

I know that by restarting the workspace manager the screen will get redrawn, but we can't use that. We need to have no interface with the user.

Here is the script. I have to admit it's like I'm cheating but it works. Basically you just have to find a unique difference in the window you're trying to capture, then look for its id and take a capture on that id.

Here it is:

```
#! /bin/ksh
############################################################################
#
#  This script will take a capture of the top-most window on the desktop.
#
#  The action will come from the user's right-click on the background of the
#
#  common desktop environment (CDE).
############################################################################
set -x
touch /tmp/window.xwd

sleep 5

id=`/usr/openwin/bin/xlswins | grep : | /bin/tail -1 | /bin/awk '{print
$1}'`

xwd -id $id -out /tmp/window.xwd

sleep 3

xpr -output /tmp/window.gif /tmp/window.xwd

lp window.gif

rm /tmp/window.xwd
rm /tmp/window.gif
```

3.27) How do I disable the CDE front panel entirely?

For those who are feeling nostalgic for mwm or have no use for the CDE front panel, it's possible to disable the front panel entirely by setting:

```
Dtwm*useFrontPanel:      false
```

in your .Xdefaults file.

3.28) I'm using Solaris 2.7 under CDE. When I try to put the image on the root by the command xv –rmode 2 .Images/ grass.gif&, a xv control window pops up. There is no picture appearing on the background. But when I log out, I can see the picture for a very short time. This is not what I expect. It seems that the root hides behind the background.

You need to set the backdrop to item NoBackdrop.

3.29) I'm looking for a way to configure my front panel. (In particular, I would like to remove the mail icon, or to replace its action by one that I defined.) Which is easier to do?

There is no direct way to delete a main control from the front panel. Simply copying dtwm.fp to ~/.dt/types or ~/.dt/types/$LANG and modifying it there does NOT work, at least not in 1.0. dtwm builds the front panel by reading /usr/dt/appconfig/types/C/dtwm.fp and then applying incremental changes by what it finds in ~/.dt/types.

To remove a control, such as Mail, one has to *create* a new file (in our example: DelMail.fp) looking like this:

```
CONTROL Mail
{
   CONTAINER_NAME         Top
      CONTAINER_TYPE      BOX
         DELETE           True
}
```

To *replace* a control by an action that I created on my own, I used the following method. (I did not look for simpler ones, since this worked fine):

1. Using the right mouse button, create a subpanel.

2. Put the action into the subpanel by dragging it from the file manager to the open subpanel.
3. Using the right mouse button on the open subpanel, select "copy to the main panel."

   Now we have the new action in the main control, the old one still in the subpanel.
4. Using the right mouse button on the old control in the open subpanel, select Delete.

4. APPLICATION DEVELOPMENT

4.1) What are actions and datatypes in CDE?

Actions are modular programming methods by which CDE can automate desktop tasks like running applications or manipulating data files. You can create your own actions, datatypes, and icons for your local environment. If you are new to CDE, the following link is a good site and contains good examples, which are installed in /etc/dt of your machine: The complete thing is now accessible as **ftp://ftp.frontec.se/pub/cde**, just to point it out.

And now, we want to see more! There just MUST be other people sitting on resources like this! Maybe you should make an explicit request for such resources in **comp.unix.cde**?

—Michael
datatype (can someone give me a good definition?)

4.2) How can I reload new actions and datatypes in CDE?

There are two ways: /usr/dt/bin/dtaction ReloadActions, or click on the Reload_Actions icon under the Desktop_Tools folder.

5. TROUBLESHOOTING

5.1) What directories/files can I look at to check for errors?

$HOME/.dt/errorlog

$HOME/.dt/startlog

/var/dt/Xerrors

+5.2) The lock button doesn't work, and .dt/errorlog shows "dtsession: unable to lock display due to security restrictions."

Kevin Davidson, **tkld@cogsci.ed.ac.uk**, suggests creating Xlock.dt in ~/.dt/types or /etc/dt/ appconfig/types/C, containing

```
## Replace broken LockDisplay action
## Built in one claims it cannot lock the screen...
ACTION LockDisplay
{
        LABEL   LockDisplay
        TYPE    COMMAND
        EXEC_STRING     xlock -remote
        WINDOW_TYPE     NO_STDIO
        DESCRIPTION     The LockDisplay action locks the workstation. \
                        You must know the user's or root password to \
                        unlock the workstation.
}
```

*5.3) We are trying to get some older DEC X terminals to start up IP X sessions through dtlogin. I think I have the configuration right, but very little happens, and the dtlogin freezes up. The X terminal sends its request, and I get the CDE hourglass on the display, then *POOF* nothing on the X term, and a dead dtlogin. I'm using CDE 1.0.1 on an Ultra-1 with Solaris 2.5.

Your X terminal probably doesn't know about the CDE font aliases. I've seen this problem several times when X terminals or non-CDE-aware machines try to start up a CDE session through XDMCP. How far you get into the session before it dies is platform specific. (You can get all the way in on AIX, but the fonts are weird. You can't even get the dtlogin screen on HPUX. Sun dies when dthello(1) tries to run midway through the login sequence.)

CDE tries to fix the font path in /usr/dt/config/Xsetup, but the code won't work unless the X terminal has NFS or tftp access to the font directories in /usr/dt/config/xfonts.

You can typically make an X terminal CDE aware by booting it from a CDE-aware host.

My favorite solution is to run a fontserver fs(1) or xfs(1) on the machine that accepts X terminal logins. Then copy /usr/dt/config/Xsetup to /etc/dt/config/Xsetup and change the X terminal case to install your font server in the font path. Before configuring a font server yourself, check your sysadmin tools. The turn-key font server on HPUX turned out to be exactly the one required, but I still had to fix Xsetup.

—Roger Droz

6. BUGS AND PATCHES

6.1) Solaris™ versions: 2.6, 2.6_x86, 2.5.1, 2.5.1_x86, 2.5, 2.5_x86, 2.4, and 2.4_x86 running CDE if exploited, all these vulnerabilities could lead to root access or allow arbitrary files to be overwritten.

Apply the following patches:

CDE Version	Patch ID
1.3	107022-01
1.3_x86	107023-01
1.2	105566-06
1.2_x86	105567-07
1.0.2	103670-06
1.0.2_x86	103717-06
1.0.1	103671-06
1.0.1_x86	103718-06

7. ACKNOWLEDGMENTS

This is a rudimentary set of initial questions I have come up with to help the new user or the guru to look for common problems and answers. Your contributions to enhance this document will be much appreciated.

I have written some material in this document and shamelessly copied some of your Usenet postings from the CDE newsgroup.

Acknowledgements for contributions go to:

Rich McAllister: **rfm@eng.sun.com**
Claus Oberste-Brandenburg: **cob@tm.bi.ruhr-uni-bochum.de**
Andrew Page: **page@cv.hp.com**
Brian Holtz: **holtz@netcord.Eng.Sun.COM**
Scott Raney: **raney@metacard.com**
Rick Beldin: **rbeldin@atl.hp.com**
Chris O'Regan: **chris@ECE.Concordia.CA**
Steven F. Burnett: **burnett@pobox.com**
Michael Kolmodin: **Michael.Kolmodin@lule.frontec.se**
Amit Paul: **akpaul@leland.Stanford.EDU**
Ola Andersson: **mailto:rand@ling.umu.se**
Himanshu Gohel: **gohel@rad.usf.edu**
Mike Stroyan: **mike_stroyan@fc.hp.com**
Andy Warburton: **andyw@parallax.co.uk**
Roger Droz: **Roger.Droz@Seaslug.ORG**
Aditya Talwar and Vivek Arora: **cosc4hf@bayou.uh.edu**

APPENDIX B

SMB How To

David Wood, **dwood@plugged.net.au**
v1.1.1, 25 June 1999

This is the SMB HOWTO. This document describes how to use the Server Message Block (SMB) protocol, also called the Session Message Block, NetBIOS or LanManager protocol, with Linux. Although this document is Linux-centric, Samba runs on most UNIX-like operating systems.

1. INTRODUCTION

This document is maintained by David Wood (**dwood@plugged.net.au**). Additions, modifications or corrections may be mailed there for inclusion in the next release.

Much more Samba documentation is available at the Samba website, located at **http://www.samba.org/**. You also might try the **comp.protocols.smb** newsgroup.

The SMB protocol is used by Microsoft Windows 3.11, NT and 95/98 to share disks and printers. Using the Samba suite of tools by Andrew Tridgell (**Andrew.Tridgell@anu.edu.au**), UNIX (including Linux) machines can share disk and printers with Windows hosts. The smbfs tools by Paal-Kr. Engstad (**engstad@intermetrics.com**) and Volker Lendecke (**lendecke@namu01.gwdg.de**) enable UNIX machines to mount SMB shares from Windows or Samba hosts.

There are four things that one can do with Samba:

1. Share a Linux drive with Windows machines.
2. Share a Windows drive with Linux machines.
3. Share a Linux printer with Windows machines.
4. Share a Windows printer with Linux machines.

All of these are covered in this document.

Disclaimer: The procedures and scripts either work for the author or have been reported to work by the people that provided them. Different configurations may not work with the information given here. If you encounter such a situation, you may e-mail the author with suggestions for improvement in this document, but the author guarantees nothing. What did you expect? The author is, after all, a consultant....

Please note that for Windows 3.*x* machines to access SMB shares, they must have a TCP/IP stack and the Win32s DLLs. Both of these are available on Microsoft's website (**http://www.microsoft.com**).

2. FURTHER INFORMATION

This HOWTO attempts to explain how to configure basic SMB file and print services on a Linux machine. Samba is a very complex and complete package. There would be no point in attempting to duplicate all of the documentation for Samba here.

For further information, please see the following documents:

- The Samba documentation, available as part of the Samba distribution. The distribution is available at: **ftp://ftp.samba.org/**.
- The Linux Printing HOWTO
- The Print2Win Mini-HOWTO
- Protocol Standard for a NetBIOS Service On A TCP/UDP Transport
- RFC1001
  Concepts and Methods
- RFC1002
  Detailed Specifications

3. INSTALLATION

First, in order to use Samba, your machines must be on a single ethernet LAN segment using the TCP/IP protocol. Samba will not work using other network protocols. This is generally easy since Linux and Windows 95/98/NT ship with TCP/IP support. However, if you are using Windows 3.*x* machines, TCP/IP support will need to be added.

SMB services cannot be used across routers. If you want to do something like that, you would need to set up an IP tunnel, which is beyond the scope of this document.

To get the latest source version of Samba, go to this URL and pick the closest mirror site to you: **ftp://ftp.samba.org/**.

However, if you have installed the Red Hat distribution of Linux, you have the option of installing it as a package. Some other distributions also include the Samba binaries.

The following two daemons are required for the Samba package. They are typically installed in /usr/sbin and run either on boot from the systems startup scripts or from inetd. Example scripts are shown in Running the Daemons.

- **smbd** The SMB daemon
- **nmbd** Provides NetBIOS nameserver support to clients

Please note that the name service provided by the nmbd daemon is different from the name service provided by the Domain Name Service (DNS). NetBIOS name service is a "Windows-style"name service used for SMB. In other words, having DNS name service tells you nothing about the state of the ability for Samba to resolve host names.

Typically, the following Samba binaries are installed in /usr/bin or /usr/local/samba/bin, although the location is optional.

- **smbclient** An SMB client for UNIX machines.
- **smbprint** A script to print to a printer on an SMB host.
- **smbprint.sysv** As foregoing, but for SVR4 UNIX machines.
- **smbstatus** Lists the current SMB connections for the local host.
- **smbrun** A "glue" script to facilitate running applications on SMB hosts.

The binaries for smbfs file system support are discussed later in this document.

Additionally, a script called "print" is included with this HOWTO, which serves as a useful front end to the smbprint script.

The Samba package is simple to install. Simply retrieve the source from the location mentioned earlier, and read the file README in the distribution. There is also a file called docs/INSTALL.txt in the distribution that provides a simple step-by-step set of instructions.

Following installation, place the daemons in /usr/sbin and the binaries in /usr/bin. Install the man pages in /usr/local/man.

When you made the Samba package, you would have specified in the Makefile the location for the configuration file, smb.conf. This is generally in /etc, but you can put it anywhere you like. For these directions, we will presume that you specified the location of the configuration file as /etc/smb.conf, the log file location as log file = /var/log/samba-log.%m and the lock directory as lock directory = /var/lock/samba.

Install the configuration file, smb.conf. Go to the directory where Samba was built. Look in the subdirectory examples/simple and read the file README. Copy the file smb.conf found in that directory to /etc. BE CAREFUL! If you have a Linux distribution that already has Samba installed, you may already have a Samba configuration file in /etc. You should probably start with that one.

If you don't want to have your configuration file in /etc, put it wherever you want to, then put a symlink in /etc:

```
ln -s /path/to/smb.conf /etc/smb.conf
```

4. RUNNING THE DAEMONS

The two SMB daemons are /usr/sbin/smbd and /usr/sbin/nmbd.

You can run the Samba daemons from inetd or as stand-alone processes. Samba will respond slightly faster as a stand-alone daemon than running from inetd.

In either case, you should check the file /etc/services for lines that look like this:

```
netbios-ns      137/tcp         nbns
netbios-ns      137/udp         nbns
netbios-dgm     138/tcp         nbdgm
netbios-dgm     138/udp         nbdgm
netbios-ssn     139/tcp         nbssn
```

Make sure they are all uncommented. Depending on your distribution, you may even need to add them. Samba will not be able to bind to the appropriate ports unless /etc/services has these entries.

To run the daemons from inetd, place the following lines in the inetd configuration file, /etc/inetd.conf:

```
# SAMBA NetBIOS services (for PC file and print sharing)
netbios-ssn stream tcp nowait root /usr/sbin/smbd smbd
netbios-ns dgram udp wait root /usr/sbin/nmbd nmbd
```

Then restart the inetd daemon by running the command:

```
kill -HUP `cat /var/run/inetd.pid`
```

To run the daemons from the system startup scripts, put the following script in the file called /etc/rc.d/init.d/smb (for a Red Hat distribution) and symbolically link it to the files specified in the comments:

```
#!/bin/sh
#
# /etc/rc.d/init.d/smb - starts and stops SMB services.
#
# The following files should be symbolic links to this file:
# symlinks: /etc/rc.d/rc1.d/K35smb  (Kills SMB services on shutdown)
#           /etc/rc.d/rc3.d/S91smb  (Starts SMB services in multiuser mode)
#           /etc/rc.d/rc6.d/K35smb  (Kills SMB services on reboot)
#
```

```
# Source function library.
. /etc/rc.d/init.d/functions
# Source networking configuration.
. /etc/sysconfig/network
# Check that networking is up.
[ ${NETWORKING} = "no" ] && exit 0
# See how we were called.
case "$1" in
  start)
    echo -n "Starting SMB services: "
    daemon smbd -D
    daemon nmbd -D
    echo
    touch /var/lock/subsys/smb
    ;;
  stop)
    echo -n "Shutting down SMB services: "
    killproc smbd
    killproc nmbd
    rm -f /var/lock/subsys/smb
    echo ""
    ;;
  *)
    echo "Usage: smb {start|stop}"
    exit 1
esac
```

If when starting Samba you get an error that says something about the daemon failing to bind to port 139, then you probably have another Samba process already running that hasn't yet shut down. Check a process list (with "ps auxww | grep mbd") to determine if another Samba service is running.

5. GENERAL CONFIGURATION (/ETC/SMB.CONF)

Samba configuration on a Linux (or other UNIX machine) is controlled by a single file, /etc/smb.conf. This file determines which system resources you want to share with the outside world and what restrictions you wish to place on them.

Since the following sections will address sharing Linux drives and printers with Windows machines, the smb.conf file shown in this section is as simple as you can get, just for introductory purposes.

Don't worry about the details, yet. Later sections will introduce the major concepts.

Each section of the file starts with a section header such as [global], [homes], [printers], etc.

The [global] section defines a few variables that Samba will use to define sharing for all resources.

The [homes] section allow remote users to access their (and only their) home directory on the local (Linux) machine. That is, users trying to connect to this share from Windows machines, will be connected to their personal home directories. Note that to do this, they must have an account on the Linux box.

The following sample smb.conf file allows remote users to get to their home directories on the local machine and to write to a temporary directory. For a Windows user to see these shares, the Linux box has to be on the local network. Then the user simply connects a network drive from the Windows File Manager or Windows Explorer.

Note that in the following sections, additional entries for this file will be given to allow more resources to be shared.

```
; /etc/smb.conf
;
; Make sure and restart the server after making changes to this file, ex:
; /etc/rc.d/init.d/smb stop
; /etc/rc.d/init.d/smb start
[global]
; Uncomment this if you want a guest account
; guest account = nobody
   log file = /var/log/samba-log.%m
   lock directory = /var/lock/samba
   share modes = yes
[homes]
   comment = Home Directories
   browseable = no
   read only = no
   create mode = 0750
[tmp]
   comment = Temporary file space
   path = /tmp
   read only = no
   public = yes
```

Having written a new smb.conf, it is useful to test it to verify its correctness. You can test the correctness of a smb.conf file, using the 'testparm' utility (man page: testparm); if testparm reports no problems, smbd will correctly load the configuration file.

Here's a good trick: If your Samba server has more than one ethernet interface, the smbd may bind to the wrong one. If so, you can force it to bind to the intended one by adding a line that looks like this to the [global] section of /etc/smb.conf:

```
interfaces = 192.168.1.1/24
```

where you replace the IP address with the one that is assigned to the correct ethernet interface. The "24" is correct for a Class C network, but may have to be recalculated if you have subnetted the network. The number relates to the netmask. Numbers for other classes of networks are given in the IP-Masquerade mini-HOWTO.

There is now a GUI configuration tool for Samba: GtkSamba. See **http://www.open-systems.com/gtksamba.html**.

6. SHARING A LINUX DRIVE WITH WINDOWS MACHINES

As shown in the previous simple smb.conf, sharing Linux drives with Windows users is easy. However, like everything else with Samba, you can control things to a large degree. Here are some examples:

To share a directory with the public, create a clone of the earlier [tmp] section by adding something like this to smb.conf:

```
[public]
       comment = Public Stuff
       path = /home/public
       public = yes
       writable = yes
       printable = no
```

To make this directory readable by the public, but only writable by people in group staff, modify the entry like this:

```
[public]
       comment = Public Stuff
       path = /home/public
       public = yes
       writable = yes
       printable = no
       write list = @staff
```

It used to be that easy; you would now be able to start Samba and browse the shares from a Windows PC. However, Microsoft has recently made life slightly more difficult for those using Samba. Windows 98, Windows NT (service pack 3 or higher) and later builds of Windows 95 now use encrypted passwords by default. Samba uses unencrypted passwords by default. You can't browse servers when either the client or server is using encrypted passwords, because a connection cannot be made anonymously.

You can tell if you have a password type mismatch between client and server if when you try to connect to a share you see a dialog box which reads something like "You are not authorized to access that account from this machine."

You can either configure your Samba server to use encrypted passwords, or configure the Windows machines to use unencrypted passwords.

To get Windows to work with encrypted SMB passwords:

Windows 95/98 =============

Using the registry editor (regedit), create the registry setting HKEY_LOCAL_MACHINE\System\CurrentControlSet\Services\VxD\VNETSUP Add a new DWORD value: Value Name: EnablePlainTextPassword Data: 0x01.

Windows NT ==========

Using the registry editor (regedit), create the registry setting HKEY_LOCAL_MACHINE\System\CurrentControlSet\Services\Rdr\Parameters Add a new DWORD value: Value Name: EnablePlainTextPassword Data: 0x01.

Once these registry changes have been made, reboot the Windows machine and try to map a network drive on the Samba server again. It should work as long as the Samba server is using plain text passwords.

To configure Samba to use encrypted passwords:

In the [global] section of /etc/smb.conf, add the following lines:

```
encrypt passwords = yes
smb passwd file = /etc/smbpasswd
```

You are highly encouraged to read the files ENCRYPTION.txt, Win95.txt and WinNT.txt in the Samba documentation before doing this!

If your clients and server are using encrypted passwords, you will not be able to browse the available shares on the server until an initial connection has been made with the appropriate authentication. To get the initial connection, enter the share name manually in the Windows File Manager or Explorer dialog box, in the form \\<hostname>\<sharename>. Log onto the server with a username and password that is valid on the server!

If you suspect that your NetBIOS name service is not correctly configured (perhaps because you get "host not found" errors when trying to connect), try using just the IP address of the server: \\<host ip address>\<sharename>.

In order to get filenames to appear correctly, you may also need to set some options in the appropriate share section. These work for Windows 95/98/NT clients, but may need to be modified if you have Windows 3.*x* clients:

```
; Mangle case = yes seems to give the correct filenames
; for Win95/98/NT.
mangle case = yes
; If samba is case sensitive when looking for files
case sensitive = no
; Default case of files that are created
default case = lower
; Preserve case for all filenames
preserve case = yes
; Preserve case for dos (8.3) filenames
short preserve case = no
```

For other tricks to play with drive shares, see the Samba documentation or man pages.

```
interfaces = 192.168.1.1/24
```

Note: The bit after the / is a reference to the subnet mask. "24" is the value to use for an unsegmented Class C network. For more information on subnet calculations, you might want to see **http://www.ziplink.net/~ralphb/IPSubnet/index.html**.

There is a lot more to Samba configuration than this, but this will get you started. If you want to do something more advanced, I refer you to the Samba website mentioned earlier.

7. SHARING A WINDOWS DRIVE WITH LINUX MACHINES

An SMB client program for UNIX machines is included with the Samba distribution. It provides an ftp-like interface on the command line. You can use this utility to transfer files between a Windows "server" and a Linux client.

To see which shares are available on a given host, run:

```
/usr/sbin/smbclient -L host
```

where "host" is the name of the machine that you wish to view. This will return a list of "service" names—that is, names of drives or printers that it can share with you. Unless the SMB server has no security configured, it will ask you for a password. Get the password for the "guest" account or for your personal account on that machine.

For example:

```
smbclient -L zimmerman
```

The output of this command should look something like this:

```
Server time is Sat Aug 10 15:58:27 1996
Timezone is UTC+10.0
Password:
Domain=[WORKGROUP] OS=[Windows NT 3.51] Server=[NT LAN Manager 3.51]
Server=[ZIMMERMAN] User=[] Workgroup=[WORKGROUP] Domain=[]
        Sharename      Type      Comment
        ---------      ----      -------
        ADMIN$         Disk      Remote Admin
        public         Disk      Public
        C$             Disk      Default share
        IPC$           IPC       Remote IPC
        OReilly        Printer   OReilly
        print$         Disk      Printer Drivers
This machine has a browse list:
        Server              Comment
        ---------           -------
        HOPPER              Samba 1.9.15p8
```

```
KERNIGAN                Samba 1.9.15p8
LOVELACE                Samba 1.9.15p8
RITCHIE                 Samba 1.9.15p8
ZIMMERMAN
```

The browse list shows other SMB servers with resources to share on the network. To use the client, run:

```
/usr/sbin/smbclient service <password>
```

where "service" is a machine and share name. For example, if you are trying to reach a directory that has been shared as "public" on a machine called zimmerman, the service would be called \\zimmerman\public. However, due to shell restrictions, you will need to escape the backslashes, so you end up with something like this:

```
/usr/sbin/smbclient \\\\zimmerman\\public mypasswd
```

where "mypasswd" is the literal string of your password. You will get the smbclient prompt:

```
Server time is Sat Aug 10 15:58:44 1996
Timezone is UTC+10.0
Domain=[WORKGROUP] OS=[Windows NT 3.51] Server=[NT LAN Manager 3.51]
smb: \>
```

Type "h" to get help using smbclient:

```
smb: \> h
ls          dir         lcd         cd          pwd
get         mget        put         mput        rename
more        mask        del         rm          mkdir
md          rmdir       rd          prompt      recurse
translate   lowercase   print       printmode   queue
cancel      stat        quit        q           exit
newer       archive     tar         blocksize   tarmode
setmode     help        ?           !
smb: \>
```

If you can use ftp, you shouldn't need the man pages for smbclient. Although you can use smbclient for testing, you will soon tire of it for real work. For that you will probably want to use the smbfs package. Smbfs comes with two simple utilties, smbmount and smbumount. They work just like mount and umount for SMB shares.

The smbfs package is now included in most Linux distributions. One important thing to note: You must have smbfs support compiled into your kernel to use these utilities!

8. SHARING A LINUX PRINTER WITH WINDOWS MACHINES

To share a Linux printer with Windows machines, you need to make certain that your printer is set up to work under Linux. If you can print from Linux, setting up an SMB share of the printer is straightforward.

See the Printing HOWTO to set up local printing.

Since the author used a printer connected to a Windows NT machine (a long time ago—before converting our network nearly totally to Linux), this section should not be taken as definitive, but merely a suggestion. Anyone with details to share, please send them to **dwood@plugged.net.au** so this section can be completed.

Add printing configuration to your smb.conf:

```
[global]
   printing = bsd
   printcap name = /etc/printcap
   load printers = yes
   log file = /var/log/samba-log.%m
   lock directory = /var/lock/samba
[printers]
   comment = All Printers
   security = server
   path = /var/spool/lpd/lp
   browseable = no
   printable = yes
   public = yes
   writable = no
   create mode = 0700
[ljet]
   security = server
   path = /var/spool/lpd/lp
   printer name = lp
   writable = yes
   public = yes
   printable = yes
   print command = lpr -r -h -P %p %s
```

Make certain that the printer path (in this case under [ljet]) matches the spool directory in /etc/printcap!

The lines:

```
printcap name = /etc/printcap
load printers = yes
```

controls whether all the printers in /etc/printcap should be loaded by default. If you do this, there is no reason to set up printers individually. The section [printers] specifies options for the printers that you wish to explicitly define. If the printing subsystem you are using doesn't work this way (BSD), you need to set up a fake printcap file (or to use the "print command" technique, see the following). For more information on the printcap system see the Printing HOWTO.

A useful technique to test the network connection is to change the print command to:

```
print command = cp %S /tmp/print.%P.%S
```

The resulting file can then be analyzed.

Note: There are some problems sharing printers on UNIX boxes with Windows NT machines using Samba. One problem is with NT seeing the shared printer properly. To fix this, see the notes in the Samba distribution in the file docs/WinNT.txt. The other deals with password problems. See the comments in the same file for an annoying gain of understanding and failure to fix the problem.

Oleg L. Machulskiy (**machulsk@shade.msu.ru**) suggests that a better print command to use in the preceding example would be:

```
print command = smb2ps %s | lpr -r -h -P %p
```

where "smb2ps" is a script which transforms the spool file received from Windows into a usable Postscript file. It must cut off the first 3 lines and last 2 lines, because these lines contain some PJL or PCL codes.

That approach is only needed if your Windows machine is printing PCL and not real Postscript. I have found that Windows 95/98/NT don't have a generic Postscript driver per se, but the "Digital turbo Printserver 20" driver acts as a good general Postscript driver for most setups. I have also heard that the "Apple LaserWriter II NTX" driver works for this purpose.

Jeff Stern (**jstern@eclectic.ss.uci.edu**) reported the following that may be of help to some of you:

The problem I was having was that I could print via lpd/lpr to my Linux printer from the Linux box itself. But I couldn't get it to print from a remote Win95 machine. When I tried

```
smbclient \\eclectic\belen -P
```

```
to print myfile
```

I got errors about access denied. So I reset the permissions on my /var/spool/lpd/lp1 directory to 777. I'm sorry, but that's what I had to do. I suppose alternatively I could have a message putting everyone on the Linux box in the "lp" group, or made the directory owned by the group "users", etc. But for now, this works (with ownership root:lp).

Finally, the other thing administrators should know is that the name of the account on the Windows machine (which is trying to use the Linux printer via Samba) should have an equivalently-named account on the Linux box. Thus, if there is a user named joe on the Windows machine, mywinbox, trying to print to the printer belen on the Linux machine, eclectic (\\eclectic\belen), then there should be a user named 'joe' on the Linux box.

Then joe's login password will be the password to access eclectic's belen printer. This password will be asked for on the Windows machine when setting up the printer on the Windows box with Printers | Add Printer.

I kind of thought maybe this wouldn't be the case, since I have set up my printer to be "public" in the smb.conf. But apparently it still asks for a password. The windows box unfortunately doesn't give you the opportunity to supply a different username to the remote (Linux) printer. It just uses your local username which you signed in as when you started up Win95.

Dr. Michael Langner (**langner@fiz-chemie.de**) points out that write permission problems on the /var/spool/lpd/ tree could be avoided by using something like "path = /tmp" and "print command = lpr -r -P%p %s" instead.

Sometimes, a Postscript parsing error will occur with Postscript printing from Windows machines that causes an extra page to be printed at the end of every print job. The last page will always have "%%[Lastpage]%%" at the top of it. This seems to happen with Windows 95 and 98 only and is because the Postscript is malformed.

One way to handle that is to use a script to remove that bit of bad Postscript from the spooled jobs. Another way is to try to find a better Windows Postscript driver. Probably the best way is to use LPRng instead of Postscript to print to a Samba server.

Erik Ratcliffe (**erik@caldera.com**) from Caldera tells me that using LPRng means that any printer driver can be used from Windows machines. On the Samba server, they used an /etc/printcap entry that looked like this:

```
raw:\
:rw:sh:
:lp=/dev/lp1
:sd=/var/spool/lpd/raw
:fx=flp
```

LPRng doesn't require :\ at the end of every line. A printer entry will still need to be made in /etc/smb.conf for the physical printer. The print command line needs to use the "raw" entry in /etc/printcap and data must be sent to the printer in binary form. Try a print command line like this:

```
print command = lpr -b -Praw %s
```

You may also need to set the spooling on the Windows 95 end to print directly to the printer instead of spooling.

9. SHARING A WINDOWS PRINTER WITH LINUX MACHINES

To share a printer on a Windows machine, you must do the following:

1. You must have the proper entries in /etc/printcap and they must correspond to the local directory structure (for the spool directory, etc.).
2. You must have the script /usr/bin/smbprint. This comes with the Samba source, but not with all Samba binary distributions. A slightly modifed copy is discussed soon.
3. If you want to convert ASCII files to Postscript, you must have nenscript, or its equivalent. nenscript is a Postscript converter and is generally installed in /usr/bin.
4. You may wish to make Samba printing easier by having an easy-to-use front end. A simple Perl script to handle ASCII, Postscript or created Postscript is given shortly.
5. You could also use MagicFilter to do the foregoing. The details on setting up MagicFilter are given after the Perl script. MagicFilter has advantages because it knows how to automatically convert a lot of file formats.
6. The following /etc/printcap entry is for an HP 5MP printer on a Windows NT host. The entries are as follows:

   ```
   cm - comment
   lp - device name to open for output
   sd - the printer's spool directory (on the local machine)
   af - the accounting file
   mx - the maximum file size (zero is unlimited)
   if - name of the input filter (script)
   ```

   For more information, see the Printing HOWTO or the man page for printcap.

```
                # /etc/printcap
                #
                # //zimmerman/oreilly via smbprint
                #
                lp:\
:cm=HP 5MP Postscript OReilly on zimmerman:\
:lp=/dev/lp1:\
:sd=/var/spool/lpd/lp:\
:af=/var/spool/lpd/lp/acct:\
:mx#0:\
:if=/usr/bin/smbprint:
```

Make certain that the spool and accounting directories exist and are writable. Ensure that the "f" line holds the proper path to the smbprint script (given next) and make sure that the proper device is pointed to (the /dev special file). Next is the smbprint script itself.

It is usually placed in /usr/bin and is attributable to Andrew Tridgell, the person who created Samba as far as I know. It comes with the Samba source distribution, but is absent from some binary distributions, so I have re-created it here. You may wish to look at this carefully. There are some minor alterations that have shown themselves to be useful.

```
#!/bin/sh -x
# This script is an input filter for printcap printing on a unix machine. It
# uses the smbclient program to print the file to the specified smb-based

# server and service.
# For example you could have a printcap entry like this
#
# smb:lp=/dev/null:sd=/usr/spool/smb:sh:if=/usr/local/samba/smbprint

#
# which would create a unix printer called "smb" that will print via this
# script. You will need to create the spool directory /usr/spool/smb with
# appropriate permissions and ownerships for your system.
# Set these to the server and service you wish to print to
# In this example I have a WfWg PC called "lapland" that has a printer
# exported called "printer" with no password.
#
# Script further altered by hamiltom@ecnz.co.nz (Michael Hamilton)
# so that the server, service, and password can be read from
# a /usr/var/spool/lpd/PRINTNAME/.config file.
#
# In order for this to work the /etc/printcap entry must include an
# accounting file (af=...):
#
#   cdcolour:\
#        :cm=CD IBM Colorjet on 6th:\
#        :sd=/var/spool/lpd/cdcolour:\
#        :af=/var/spool/lpd/cdcolour/acct:\
#        :if=/usr/local/etc/smbprint:\
#        :mx=0:\
#        :lp=/dev/null:
#
               # The /usr/var/spool/lpd/PRINTNAME/.config file should contain:
#   server=PC_SERVER
#   service=PR_SHARENAME
#   password="password"
#
```

```
# E.g.
#   server=PAULS_PC
#   service=CJET_371
#   password=""
#
# Debugging log file, change to /dev/null if you like.
#
logfile=/tmp/smb-print.log
# logfile=/dev/null
#
# The last parameter to the filter is the accounting file name.
#
spool_dir=/var/spool/lpd/lp
config_file=$spool_dir/.config
# Should read the following variables set in the config file:
#   server
#   service
#   password
#   user
eval `cat $config_file`
#
# Some debugging help, change the >> to > if you want the same space.
#
echo "server $server, service $service" >> $logfile
(
# NOTE You may wish to add the line `echo translate' if you want automatic
# CR/LF translation when printing.
echo translate
echo "print -"
cat
) | /usr/bin/smbclient "\\\\$server\\$service" $password -U $user -N -P >> $logfile
-------------------------------------------------------------
```

Most Linux distributions come with nenscript for converting ASCII documents to Postscript. The following Perl script makes life easier by providing a simple interface to Linux printing via smbprint.

```
Usage: print [-a|c|p] <filename>
       -a prints <filename> as ASCII
       -c prints <filename> formatted as source code
       -p prints <filename> as Postscript
```

```
If no switch is given, print attempts to
guess the file type and print appropriately.
```

Using smbprint to print ASCII files tends to truncate long lines. This script breaks long lines on whitespace (instead of in the middle of a word), if possible. The source code formatting is done with nenscript. It takes an ASCII file and foramts it in two columns with a fancy header (date, filename, etc.). It also numbers the lines. Using this as an example, other types of formatting can be accomplished. Postscript documents are already properly formatted, so they pass through directly.

```
#!/usr/bin/perl
# Script:   print
# Authors:  Brad Marshall, David Wood
#           Plugged In Communications
# Date:     960808
#
# Script to print to a Postscript printer via Samba.
# Purpose:  Takes files of various types as arguments and
# processes them appropriately for piping to a Samba print script.
#
# Currently supported file types:
#
# ASCII      - ensures that lines longer than $line_length characters wrap on
#              whitespace.
# Postscript - Takes no action.
# Code       - Formats in Postscript (using nenscript) to display
#              properly (landscape, font, etc.).
#
# Set the maximum allowable length for each line of ASCII text.
$line_length = 76;


# Set the path and name of the Samba print script
$print_prog = "/usr/bin/smbprint";


# Set the path and name to nenscript (the ASCII-->Postscript converter)
```

```
$nenscript = "/usr/bin/nenscript";


unless ( -f $print_prog ) {
die "Can't find $print_prog!";
}
unless ( -f $nenscript ) {
die "Can't find $nenscript!";
}


&ParseCmdLine(@ARGV);


# DBG
print "filetype is $filetype\n";


if ($filetype eq "ASCII") {
&wrap($line_length);
} elsif ($filetype eq "code") {
&codeformat;
} elsif ($filetype eq "ps") {
&createarray;
} else {
print "Sorry..no known file type.\n";
exit 0;
}
# Pipe the array to smbprint
open(PRINTER, "|$print_prog") || die "Can't open $print_prog: $!\n";
foreach $line (@newlines) {
print PRINTER $line;
}
# Send an extra linefeed in case a file has an incomplete last line.
print PRINTER "\n";
close(PRINTER);
print "Completed\n";
exit 0;


# -------------------------------------------------- #
#         Everything below here is a subroutine        #
# -------------------------------------------------- #
```

```
sub ParseCmdLine {
# Parses the command line, finding out what file type the file is


# Gets $arg and $file to be the arguments (if they exist)
# and the filename
if ($#_ < 0) {
&usage;
}
# DBG
#       foreach $element (@_) {
#               print "*$element* \n";
#       }


$arg = shift(@_);
if ($arg =~ /\-./) {
$cmd = $arg;
# DBG
#       print "\$cmd found.\n";


$file = shift(@_);
} else {
$file = $arg;
}


# Defining the file type
unless ($cmd) {
# We have no arguments


if ($file =~ /\.ps$/) {
$filetype = "ps";
} elsif ($file =~
/\.java$|\.c$|\.h$|\.pl$|\.sh$|\.csh$|\.m4$|\.inc$|\.html$|\.htm$/) {
$filetype = "code";
} else {
$filetype = "ASCII";
}


# Process $file for what type it is and return $filetype
} else {
```

```
# We have what type it is in $arg
if ($cmd =~ /^-p$/) {
$filetype = "ps";
} elsif ($cmd =~ /^-c$/) {
$filetype = "code";
} elsif ($cmd =~ /^-a$/) {
$filetype = "ASCII"
}
}
}


sub usage {
print "
Usage: print [-a|c|p] <filename>
-a prints <filename> as ASCII
-c prints <filename> formatted as source code
-p prints <filename> as Postscript
If no switch is given, print attempts to
guess the file type and print appropriately.\n
";
exit(0);
}


sub wrap {
# Create an array of file lines, where each line is < the
# number of characters specified, and wrapped only on whitespace


# Get the number of characters to limit the line to.
$limit = pop(@_);


# DBG
#print "Entering subroutine wrap\n";
#print "The line length limit is $limit\n";
# Read in the file, parse and put into an array.
open(FILE, "<$file") || die "Can't open $file: $!\n";
while(<FILE>) {
$line = $_;


# DBG
#print "The line is:\n$line\n";
```

```
# Wrap the line if it is over the limit.
while ( length($line) > $limit ) {

# DBG
#print "Wrapping...";

# Get the first $limit +1 characters.
$part = substr($line,0,$limit +1);

# DBG
#print "The partial line is:\n$part\n";

# Check to see if the last character is a space.
$last_char = substr($part,-1, 1);
if ( " " eq $last_char ) {
# If it is, print the rest.

# DBG
#print "The last character was a space\n";

substr($line,0,$limit + 1) = "";
substr($part,-1,1) = "";
push(@newlines,"$part\n");
} else {
# If it is not, find the last space in the
# sub-line and print up to there.

# DBG
#print "The last character was not a space\n";

# Remove the character past $limit
substr($part,-1,1) = "";
# Reverse the line to make it easy to find
# the last space.
$revpart = reverse($part);
$index = index($revpart," ");
if ( $index > 0 ) {
substr($line,0,$limit-$index) = "";
```

```
push(@newlines,substr($part,0,$limit-$index)
. "\n");
} else {
# There was no space in the line, so
# print it up to $limit.
substr($line,0,$limit) = "";
push(@newlines,substr($part,0,$limit)
. "\n");
}
}
}
push(@newlines,$line);
}
close(FILE);
}


sub codeformat {
# Call subroutine wrap then filter through nenscript
&wrap($line_length);


# Pipe the results through nenscript to create a Postscript
# file that adheres to some decent format for printing
# source code (landscape, Courier font, line numbers).
# Print this to a temporary file first.
$tmpfile = "/tmp/nenscript$$";
open(FILE, "|$nenscript -2G -i$file -N -p$tmpfile -r") ||
die "Can't open nenscript: $!\n";
foreach $line (@newlines) {
print FILE $line;
}
close(FILE);


# Read the temporary file back into an array so it can be
# passed to the Samba print script.
@newlines = ("");
open(FILE, "<$tmpfile") || die "Can't open $file: $!\n";
while(<FILE>) {
push(@newlines,$_);
}
close(FILE);
system("rm $tmpfile");
}
```

```
sub createarray {
# Create the array for postscript
open(FILE, "<$file") || die "Can't open $file: $!\n";
while(<FILE>) {
push(@newlines,$_);
}
close(FILE);
}
```

Now the MagicFilter way. Thanks to Alberto Menegazzi (**flash.egon@iol.it**) for this information. Alberto says:

Install MagicFilter with the filter for the printers you need in /usr/bin/local but DON'T fill /etc/printcap with the suggestion given by the documentation from MagicFilter. 2) Write the /etc/printcap this way (it's done for my LaserJet 4L): lp | ljet4l:\ :cm=HP LaserJet 4L:\ :lp=/dev/null:\ # or /dev/lp1 :sd=/var/spool/lpd/ljet4l:\ :af=/var/spool/lpd/ljet4l/acct:\ :sh:mx#0:\ :if=/usr/local/bin/main-filter. You should explain that the lp=/dev/... is opened for locking so "virtual" devices, one for every remote printer, should be used. Example creating with: touch /dev/ljet4l. 3) Write the filter /usr/local/bin/main-filter the same as you suggest using the ljet4l-filter instead of cat. Here's mine: #! /bin/sh logfile=/var/log/smb-print.log spool_dir=/var/spool/lpd/ljet4l (echo "print -" /usr/local/bin/ljet4l-filter) | /usr/bin/smbclient "\\\\SHIR\\HPLJ4" -N -P >> $logfile P.S. Here is the quote from the Print2Win mini-HOWTO about locking and why create virtual printers. Hint from Rick Bressler: Good tip sheet. I use something very similar. One helpful tip, this is not a particularly good idea; :lp=/dev/null:\ lpr does an "exclusive" open on the file you specify as lp=. It does this in order to prevent multiple processes from trying to print to the same printer at the same time. The side effect of this is that in your case, eng and colour can't print at the same time (usually more or less transparent since they probably print quickly, and since they queue, you probably don't notice) but any other process that tries to write to /dev/null will break! On a single user system, probably not a big problem. I have a system with over 50 printers. It would be a problem there. The solution is to create a dummy printer for each. Example: touch /dev/eng. I have modified the lp entries in the earlier printcap file to take into account Rick's suggestion. I did the following: #touch /dev/eng #touch /dev/colour.

10. BACKING UP WINDOWS MACHINES TO A LINUX HOST

Adam Neat (**adamneat@ipax.com.au**) kindly contributed the following script to back up Windows machines to a Linux host, using the smbclient utility. Adam says that it is used to back up Windows 3.*x* and NT machines to a Linux-based DAT SCSI drive.

Adam is not proud of the coding style used here, but it works. As I like to say, "If it works and it's stupid, then it is not stupid."

In this script, the string "agneal" is the username on the Linux machine that does the backups.

```
#!/bin/bash
clear
echo Initialising ...
checkdate=`date | awk '{print $1}'`
if [ -f "~agneal/backup-dir/backup-data" ]; then
        echo "ERROR: No config file for today!"
        echo "FATAL!"
        exit 1
fi
if [ -d "~agneal/backup-dir/temp" ]; then
        echo "ERROR: No tempoary directory found!"
        echo
        echo "Attempting to create"
        cd ~agneal
        cd backup-dir
        mkdir temp
        echo "Directory Made - temp"
fi
if [ "$1" = "" ]; then
        echo "ERROR: enter in a machine name (ie: cdwriter)"
        exit 1
fi
if [ "$2" = "" ]; then
        echo "ERROR: enter in a SMB (Lan Manager) Resource (ie: work)"
        exit 1
fi
if [ "$3" = "" ]; then


        echo "ERROR: enter in an IP address for $1 (ie:
        130.xxx.xxx.52)" exit 1
fi


################################################################################
# Main Section
#
################################################################################


cd ~agneal/backup-dir/temp
rm -r ~agneal/backup-dir/temp/*
cd ~agneal/backup-dir/


case "$checkdate"
in
        Mon)
```

```
  echo "Backuping for Monday"
  cat backup-data | /usr/local/samba/bin/smbclient
  \\\\$1\\$2 -I$3 -N echo "Complete"


          if [ -d "~agnea1/backup-dir/Monday" ]; then
echo "Directory Monday Not found ...
making" mkdir
~agnea1/backup-dir/Monday
          fi


  echo "Archiving ..."
  cd ~agnea1/backup-dir/temp
  tar -cf monday.tar *                echo "done ..."
  rm ~agnea1/backup-dir/Monday/monday.tar
  mv monday.tar ~agnea1/backup-dir/Monday
  ;;


            Tue)
  echo "Backuping for Tuesday"
  cat backup-data | /usr/local/samba/bin/smbclient
  \\\\$1\\$2 -I$3 -N echo "Complete"


          if [ -d "~agnea1/backup-dir/Tuesday" ]; then
echo "Directory Tuesday Not found ...
making" mkdir
~agnea1/backup-dir/Tuesday
          fi
  echo "Archiving ..."
  cd ~agnea1/backup-dir/temp
  tar -cf tuesday.tar *
  echo "done ..."
  rm ~agnea1/backup-dir/Tuesday/tuesday.tar
  mv tuesday.tar ~agnea1/backup-dir/Tuesday
  ;;


            Wed)
  echo "Backuping for Wednesday"
  cat backup-data | /usr/local/samba/bin/smbclient
  \\\\$1\\$2 -I$3 -N echo "Complete"


          if [ -d "~agnea1/backup-dir/Wednesday" ]; then
echo "Directory Wednesday Not found ...
making" mkdir
```

```
 ~agneal/backup-dir/Wednesday
           fi
   echo "Archiving ..."
   cd ~agneal/backup-dir/temp
   tar -cf wednesday.tar *
   echo "done ..."
rm ~agneal/backup-dir/Wednesday/wednesday.tar
   mv wednesday.tar ~agneal/backup-dir/Wednesday
   ;;


            Thu)
   echo "Backuping for Thrusday"
   cat backup-data | /usr/local/samba/bin/smbclient
   \\\\$1\\$2 -I$3 -N echo "Complete"


           if [ -d "~agneal/backup-dir/Thursday" ]; then
 echo "Directory Thrusday Not found ...
 making" mkdir
 ~agneal/backup-dir/Thursday
           fi
   echo "Archiving ..."
   cd ~agneal/backup-dir/temp
   tar -cf thursday.tar *
   echo "done ..."
   rm ~agneal/backup-dir/Thursday/thursday.tar
   mv thursday.tar ~agneal/backup-dir/Thursday
   ;;


            Fri)
   echo "Backuping for Friday"
   cat backup-data | /usr/local/samba/bin/smbclient
   \\\\$1\\$2 -I$3 -N echo "Complete"


           if [ -d "~agneal/backup-dir/Friday" ]; then
 echo "Directory Friday Not found ...
 making" mkdir
 ~agneal/backup-dir/Friday
           fi
   echo "Archiving ..."
   cd ~agneal/backup-dir/temp
   tar -cf friday.tar *
   echo "done ..."
   rm ~agneal/backup-dir/Friday/friday.tar
   mv friday.tar ~agneal/backup-dir/Friday
   ;;
```

```
            *)
echo "FATAL ERROR: Unknown variable passed for day"
exit 1;;


  esac
  ###########
```

11. COPYRIGHT

12. ACKNOWLEDGMENTS

Brad Marshall (**bmarshall@plugged.net.au**) and Jason Parker (**jparker@plugged.net.au**) contributed time, patience, scripting, and research.

Adam Neat (**adamneat@ipax.com.au**) contributed the bash script used to back up Windows machines to a Linux host.

Matthew Flint told me about the use of the "nterfaces"option in smb.conf.

Oleg L. Machulskiy (**machulsk@shade.msu.ru**), Jeff Stern (**jstern@eclectic.ss.uci.edu**), Dr. Michael Langner (**langner@fiz-chemie.de**) and Erik Ratcliffe (**erik@caldera.com**) suggested modifications to the section "Sharing a Linux Printer with Windows Machines."

Alberto Menegazzi (**flash.egon@iol.it**) contributed the MagicFilter setup to enable a Linux machine to share a Windows printer.

Andrea Girotto (**icarus@inca.dei.unipd.it**) contributed a number of valuable suggestions throughout the document.

Thanks, also, to all of the international translators that have brought this HOWTO to the non-English speaking world: Takeo Nakano (**nakano@apm.seikei.ac.jp**), Klaus-Dieter Schumacher (**Klaus-Dieter.Schumacher@fernuni-hagen.de**), Andrea Girotto (**icarus@ inca. dei.unipd.it**), and many others for whom I don't have contact details.

APPENDIX C

sendmail Frequently Asked Questions (FAQ)

Sendmail, Inc. delivers the ubiquitous Internet Mail platform for e-communications, applications, and services. sendmail provides standards-based Internet Mail solutions, products, and support to businesses and Internet service providers for whom e-mail is mission-critical.

Sendmail, Inc. is the leading provider of the standards-based Internet Mail platform responsible for powering over 75 percent of the Internet's mail servers. We provide complete solutions for mail routing and mail hosting to service providers and corporations for whom e-mail is mission critical. Our solutions are scalable, reliable, and secure, and include graphical tools to simplify deployment, administration, and spam control. sendmail's cost-effective, commercially packaged solutions are also fully supported by the same people who created Open Source *sendmail*, the world's first Internet e-mail program, in 1979. The sendmail website is located at **www.sendmail.com**.

SENDMAIL'S PARTNERSHIP WITH THE OPEN SOURCE COMMUNITY

- ▼ **sendmail.com** sendmail, Inc. has a long tradition of working with the Open Source community to drive Internet standards. It's the source of our innovation and enables us to provide customers with a technology advantage.
- ■ **sendmail.net** To support our collaboration approach, sendmail has developed sendmail.net, a destination site for the Internet Mail and Open Source community. sendmail.net brings together the technologists, ideas, and information needed to evolve Internet mail. The site provides sendmail users with access to thought leaders, shared knowledge via forums and chats, and the opportunity to evolve the site based on their own unique requirements. sendmail.net is a key component for growing the Internet Mail platform.
- ▲ **sendmail.org** In addition, sendmail is the exclusive sponsor of sendmail.org, the repository for sendmail technical content, source code, FAQs, and more. sendmail also supports many of the Open Source conferences, including FreeBSD, LinuxWorld, O'Reilly Open Source Convention, and USENIX.

SENDMAIL FAQ ON SENDMAIL PRODUCTS AND WINDOWS 2000

Table of Contents

1. SENDMAIL PRODUCTS FOR WINDOWS

1.1) What sendmail hosting solutions are available for Windows?

sendmail for NT Mail Hosting is a complete mail solution for companies running on or migrating to the Windows NT platform, meeting the market's increasing demand for scalable and secure Internet communications.

Designed for small enterprises and small- to medium-sized ISPs, sendmail for NT Mail Hosting offers you the reliable performance of sendmail technology integrated with NT's administration and management toolset.

sendmail for NT Mail Hosting includes the sendmail mail transfer agent (MTA), a messages store, and a POP3 server with standard NT integration and services. You can also benefit from sendmail's commercial service and support, to ensure your success.

sendmail for NT Mail Hosting offers:

- Proven *sendmail* 8.9.3 MTA
- Fast installation
- Graphical configuration tools
- Day-to-day management tools
- Anti-spam tools
- Commercial packaging and documentation
- Supported systems: Windows NT 4.0 with TCP/IP networking installed

Find out more about sendmail Hosting Solutions at **www2.sendmail.com/solutions/products.**

1.2) What sendmail Routing Solutions Are Available for Windows?

The sendmail for NT Mail Routing option provides a high performance, rapidly scalable solution to route Internet Mail between disparate systems and across the Internet.

Designed for corporations and Internet service providers, sendmail for NT Mail Routing provides a layer of enhanced security and performance when you expose your mail system to the public Internet.

sendmail for NT Mail Routing gives corporations and ISPs the confidence of having enterprise-tested software for Internet Mail relay, backed by sendmail's commercial service and support.

sendmail for NT Mail Routing Edition offers:

- Proven sendmail 8.9.3 MTA
- Fast installation
- Graphical configuration tools
- Day-to-day management tools
- Anti-spam tools
- Commercial packaging and documentation
- Supported systems: Windows NT 4.0 with TCP/IP networking installed

Find out more about sendmail Routing Solutions at **www2.sendmail.com/solutions/products**.

1.3) Does sendmail for NT support Windows 2000?

Sendmail does have future plans to produce products for Windows 2000, beginning with sendmail Switch products. However, at the time of the writing of this book in March 2000, sendmail for NT solutions DO NOT support Windows 2000. This also applies to the trial version of sendmail for NT included in this publication.

Find out more about sendmail support for Windows 2000 at **www2.sendmail.com/Win2000**.

1.4) How Do sendmail products for Windows work with Linux?

For those who enjoy the ease of use of Windows, sendmail products for Windows work very well with Linux. With the extensive Open Source history of sendmail development as a de facto implementation standard for Internet mail, sendmail products have exceptional interoperability. In most cases sendmail for NT Routing Solutions can be used well with the available Linux hosting solutions and vice versa.

2. SENDMAIL FOR NT FEATURES

2.1) What are key features of sendmail for NT hosting solutions?

Building on the solid, tested sendmail foundation, sendmail for NT Mail Hosting Edition offers corporations and ISPs a full mail hosting server with the proven performance of sendmail integrated with NT's administration and management tools.

sendmail for NT is designed for small enterprises and small-to mid-size ISPs who need the proven reliability, robustness, and interoperability of Open Source sendmail integrated with standard NT administration tools and services for hosting mailboxes. sendmail for NT delivers a complete mail solution that includes the sendmail mail transfer agent (MTA), a message store, mailing list server and POP3 server, and is backed by commercial service and support from sendmail, Inc., the company that offers the Internet's most widely used mail delivery software.

sendmail for NT now empowers NT users with the sendmail platform's e-communication capabilities, until recently only available to UNIX users.

Fast Installation

Installing sendmail for NT is quick and easy. An installation wizard guides administrators through the process, so the mail server is up and running in minutes.

- ▼ Intelligent installation options test the server's DNS configuration and other critical parameters to ensure successful installation.
- ▲ Silent Install option enables servers to be installed and configured using Systems Management Server tools.

Graphical Configuration Tools

sendmail for NT provides system administrators the ability to easily manage their mail system configuration. Administrators will save hours in configuring sendmail because sendmail for NT:

- ▼ Manages users and configuration parameters for built-in high-performance POP3 server.
- ▲ Automatically generates and installs configuration files with the click of a button.

Day-to-Day Management Tools

sendmail for NT enables administrators to manage the sendmail MTA and POP3 server from both a remote web interface and via a traditional NT Control Panel applet.

- ▼ **Installing new configuration files** Administrators can stop and start the sendmail service with a few mouse clicks, reducing mail system downtime.

- **Modifying databases** Mail administrators can edit aliases, user accounts, access records, mailers, and other tables using intuitive graphical tools.
- **Managing the message queue** The queue is viewed and run using a graphical interface.
- **Analyzing e-mail traffic** sendmail for NT publishes NT performance monitor counters, helping administrators to use standard NT administration tools to predict peak load or know when to perform routine maintenance.

Anti-Spam Tools

sendmail for NT documents and provides access to the Anti-Spam tools included in sendmail 8.9.3. Some of these features include:

- Relay control options to specify what hosts or domains are allowed to use the sendmail server as a mail relay.
- The Access database file specifies domains, users, or IP ranges that are allowed or rejected entry into sendmail.
- The Mail Abuse Prevention System's Realtime Blackhole List (MAPS RBL) is a third party database of known domains and IP addresses where spam has originated.
- Per message sizing and recipient limits to reduce MTA processing volumes.

Robust POP Server and Message Store

sendmail for NT provides a robust POP3 server and message store combination to create mailbox accounts tuned to handle hundreds of messages per second.

- Account tools provide a table for adding and editing user accounts. This table has three columns: POP3 Account Name, Full Name, and Domain.
- Full compliance with standards protocol RFC1939 optimizes performance and compatibility with a wide range of mail clients.
- Enhancements for Dial-Up and slower networks avoid timeouts during mail delivery.

Powerful List Server

sendmail for NT provides a powerful mailing list tool to effectively manage mailings to multiple recipients.

- The List Server interface makes it easy to create lists, add users to a list and write prologue and epilogue messages to include in mass mailings.
- Management tools allow administrators to limit message size, view number of posts and bounced e-mail per subscriber, control whether users receive digest or normal delivery, add or remove moderators.

- Automatic pruning of e-mail addresses allows administrators to say, "after 'x' number of tries to send an e-mail, the address is automatically deleted."
- Subscribe/Unsubscribe facilities allow administrators to provide a single address to post mail and subscribe or unsubscribe list members.

Dynamic AutoResponder

The perfect tool for sales departments, help desks, system administrators, or anyone who needs to quickly respond to incoming product and service inquiries, sendmail for NT provides an AutoResponder to dynamically reply to Internet Mail.

- Editing tools to customize AutoResponder messages by subject or body text and attach specific files to outgoing messages
- Scheduling tools to send messages at specific time intervals—send a reminder that an evaluation or warranty period will end in 'x' number of days

Commercial Packaging and Documentation

sendmail for NT's new packaging provides documentation and online help to reduce setup costs and shorten the sendmail learning curve.

- Documentation familiarizes the user with sendmail for NT, and provides advice for troubleshooting and advanced configuration options.
- Context-sensitive online help within sendmail for NT answers most administrators' questions regarding sendmail configuration alternatives.
- HTML online help is available even when performing remote administration tasks.

Sendmail for NT Technical Support

A full complement of services is available from sendmail for ISPs and corporate customers, large or small.

2.2) What are key features of sendmail for NT routing solutions?

The sendmail for NT Mail Routing Edition is designed for corporations and ISPs looking to add security and boost the performance of an existing mail system or to integrate a multi-platform environment. The sendmail for NT Mail Routing Edition works seamlessly with installed hosting resources, such as POP3 or IMAP4 servers, message stores or groupware systems that support standards-based protocols.

Because sendmail powers over 75 percent of the Internet's mail servers, sendmail for NT delivers corporations the confidence of enterprise-tested software that you can rely on for Internet Mail relay, backed by commercial service and support from sendmail.

The Routing Edition works to relay Internet Mail between networks and across the Internet by providing the proven reliability, robustness and interoperability of Open Source sendmail combined with commercial ease-of-use features, services, and accountability. Backed by decades of use and improvement on the Internet, the Routing Edition provides the scalability and security necessary for your mail interface to the public Internet.

A Dedicated Relay

The sendmail for NT Mail Routing Edition provides a high performance, highly scalable solution to relay Internet Mail between servers and across the Internet.

- A firm foundation to scale your groupware application to handle large volumes of Internet Mail
- Alias file capability to reliably forward all incoming mail to groupware and hosting servers
- Extensive compatibility to handle a wide variety of mail clients and address conventions
- Unmatched security to defend against malicious attacks that attempt to compromise a system's integrity
- A high reliability interface to the public Internet to keep your system up and running

Graphical Configuration Tools

The sendmail for NT Mail Routing Edition provides system administrators the ability to easily manage their mail system configuration and save them hours in configuring sendmail.

- Step-by-step configuration wizard guides you through options such as masquerading, routing and common SMTP settings, putting all of sendmail for NT's most important features within easy reach.
- Advanced configuration helps you bolster security, set detailed anti-spam rules, and customize your routing and queue options to fit your individual needs.

Day-to-Day Management Tools

The sendmail for NT Mail Routing Edition enables administrators to manage the sendmail MTA from both a remote web interface and via a traditional NT Control Panel applet.

- Message queue management tools to view and run your queues using a graphical interface
- Performance monitoring tools for administrators to analyze e-mail traffic, predict peak load, or know when to perform routine maintenance

- Service controls to stop and start the sendmail service with a few mouse clicks, reducing mail system downtime

Anti-Spam Tools

The sendmail for NT Mail Routing Edition documents and provides access to the Anti-Spam tools included in sendmail 8.9.3.

- Relay control options to specify what hosts or domains are allowed to use the sendmail server as a mail relay.
- The Access database file specifies domains, users, or IP ranges that are allowed or rejected entry into sendmail.
- The Mail Abuse Prevention System's Realtime Blackhole List (MAPS RBL) is a third party database of known domains and IP addresses where spam has originated.
- Per message sizing and recipient limits to reduce MTA processing volumes.

Fast Installation

Installing the sendmail for NT Mail Routing Edition is quick and easy. An installation wizard that is specifically tuned to set up sendmail as a dedicated relay guides you through the process, so your Internet Mail Relay server is up and running in minutes.

- Intelligent installation options test the server's DNS configuration and other critical parameters to ensure successful installation.
- Silent Install option enables servers to be installed and configured using Systems Management Server tools.

Commercial Packaging and Documentation

The new packaging for the sendmail for NT Mail Routing Edition provides documentation and online help to reduce setup costs and shorten the sendmail learning curve.

- Documentation familiarizes the user with sendmail for NT, and provides advice for troubleshooting and advanced configuration options.
- Context-sensitive online help within sendmail for NT answers most administrators' questions regarding sendmail configuration alternatives.
- HTML online help is available even when performing remote administration tasks.

Sendmail for NT Technical Support

A full complement of services is available from sendmail for ISPs and corporate customers, large or small.

3. USING SENDMAIL LINUX PRODUCTS WITH WINDOWS

3.1) What sendmail products are available for Linux?

Sendmail Switch products are available on Linux.

Find out more about sendmail Switch solutions at **www2.sendmail.com/solutions/products**.

3.2) What Is sendmail Switch?

sendmail Switch is the new product line built on Open Source sendmail 8.10 to take control of your Internet Mail environment.

Building on a solid foundation of cost-effective, commercial Internet Mail software and services, sendmail now offers a comprehensive set of mail routing solutions for corporations and service providers seeking greater control of their environment.

The sendmail Switch product line combines a graphical administration console for greater manageability with enhanced security on top of the latest release of the Internet's ubiquitous SMTP implementation, sendmail 8.10 to give your business an advantage.

- **Simplified administration** Ensure smooth, continuous operations of incoming and outgoing Internet Mail.
- **Unmatched control** Manage your entire mail routing environment as a unified network.
- **Rapid scalability** Support your organization's growth and enable universal Internet Mail delivery.
- **Advanced security** Protect your mail servers from intrusion and abuse, and ensure message integrity.

The sendmail Switch product line offers three packaged solutions to meet your needs:

sendmail Single Switch

Take command of sendmail and gain greater control, security, and scalability.

sendmail Secure Switch

Secure your mail server's connection to the Internet.

sendmail Multi Switch

Manage and administer your enterprise mail system as a unified network.

3.3) How do sendmail Linux products work with windows?

For those who enjoy the ease of use of Windows, sendmail Routing Solutions for Linux work very well with most Windows Hosting solutions. With the extensive Open Source history of sendmail development as a de facto implementation standard for Internet Mail, sendmail products have exceptional interoperability. The high performance afforded by Linux operating systems makes use of Linux-based sendmail Routing Solutions particularly popular in combination with Windows groupware solutions.

FAQS

Last updated January 25, 1999.
(*Reprinted with permission.*)

Latest update can be found at **www.sendmail.org**.

Comments and questions on this FAQ should be directed to **sendmail+faq@sendmail.org**.

General questions about sendmail should be directed to **sendmail-questions@sendmail.org**.

Bug reports should be directed to **sendmail-bugs@sendmail.org**.

Questions and comments about this website should be directed to **sendmail-www@sendmail.org**.

If you post a message to **comp.mail.sendmail** and send it to one of the preceding addresses, please clearly indicate so at the top of your message.

Top 5—The Most Frequently Asked Questions About sendmail

1. Local config error: see 4.5.
2. Y2K: see 4.11.
3. Relaying denied: see 3.27.
4. Directory permissions: see 3.33.
5. Virtual hosting: see 3.7 and 3.28.

Table of Contents

+ 2.5 Where can I ask e-mail-related DNS questions?

+ 2.6 How can I subscribe to these newsgroups?

+ 2.7 Which version of sendmail should I run?

+ 2.8 What is the latest release of sendmail?

+ 2.9 Where can I find it?

+ 2.10 What are the differences between version 8 and other versions?

+ 2.11 What's the best platform for running sendmail?

+ 2.12 What is BIND and where can I get the latest version?

+ 2.13 What is smrsh and where can I get it?

+ 2.14 What is smap and where can I get it?

+ 2.15 What is TCP-Wrappers and where can I get it?

+ 2.16 Why won't DB 1.85 build on my machine?

+ 2.17 What is makemap and where can I get it?

*** 3. VERSION 8- SPECIFIC ISSUES**

+ 3.1 How do I make all my addresses appear to be from a single host?

+ 3.2 How do I rewrite my From: lines to read First_Last@My.Domain

+ 3.3 But what about fully-qualified addresses, such as those from Pine or FEATURE(always_add_domain)?

+ 3.4 So what was the user database feature intended for?

+ 3.5 Why the hostility toward using full names for e-mail addresses?

+ 3.6 has been deprecated

+ 3.7 How do I manage several (virtual) domains?

+ 3.8 There are four UUCP mailers listed in the configuration files. Which one should I use?

+ 3.9 How do I fix "undefined symbol inet_aton" and "undefined symbol_strerror" messages?

+ 3.10 How do I solve "collect: I/O error on connection"

+ 3.11 Why can't my users forward their mail to a program?

+ 3.12 Why do connections to the SMTP port take such a long time?

+ 3.13 Why do I get "unknown mailer error 5—mail: options MUST PRECEDE recipients" errors?

+ 3.14 Why does version 8 sendmail panic my SunOS box?

+ 3.15 Why does the UNIX "From" header get mysteriously munged when I send to an alias?

+ 3.16 Why doesn't MASQUERADE_AS (or the user database) work for envelope addresses as well as header addresses?

+ 3.17 How do I run version 8 sendmail and support the MAIL11V3 protocol?

+ 3.18 Why do messages disappear from my queue unsent?

+ 3.19 When is sendmail going to support RFC1522 MIME header encoding?

+ 3.20 Why can't I get mail to some places, but instead always get the error "reply:read error from name.of.remote.host"?

+ 3.21 Why doesn't "FEATURE(xxx)" work?

+ 3.22 How do I configure sendmail not to use DNS?

+ 3.23 How do I get all my queued mail delivered to my UNIX box from my ISP?

+ 3.24 Why do I get the error message unable to write /etc/mail/sendmail.pid?

+ 3.25 Why can't I compile sendmail with Berkeley DB 2.X?

+ 3.26 What operating systems has Berkeley sendmail been ported to?

+ 3.27 How do I prevent relaying denied errors for my clients?

+ 3.28 Why isn't virtual hosting working, even after I added a Kvirtuser line to sendmail.cf ?

+ 3.29 How can I add a header specifying the actual recipient when having multiple users in a virtual domain go to a single mailbox?

+ 3.30 What do I do when Build fails because groff was not found?

+ 3.31 What does "class hash not available" mean?

+ 3.32 How do I configure Majordomo with sendmail 8.9 without relaxing the DontBlamesendmail option?

+ 3.33 How do I configure my system in general with sendmail 8.9?

+ 3.34 What does "foo not available for sendmail programs" mean?

*** 4. GENERAL SENDMAIL ISSUES**

+ 4.1 Should I use a wildcard MX for my domain?

+ 4.2 How can I set up an auto-responder?

+ 4.3 How can I get sendmail to deliver local mail to $HOME/.mail instead of into /usr/spool/mail (or /usr/mail)?

+ 4.4 Why does it deliver the mail interactively when I'm trying to get it to go into queue-only mode?

+ 4.5 How can I solve "MX list for hostname points back to hostname" and "config error: mail loops back to myself" messages?

+ 4.6 Why does my sendmail process sometimes hang when connecting over a SLIP/PPP link?

+ 4.7 How can I summarize the statistics generated by sendmail in the syslog?

+ 4.8 How can I check my sendmail.cf to ensure that it's re-writing addresses correctly?

+ 4.9 What is procmail, and where can I get it?

+ 4.10 How can I solve "cannot alias non-local names" errors?

+ 4.11 Is sendmail Year 2000 (Y2K) compliant?

+ 4.12 How can I batch remote mail to be sent using my ISP while delivering local mail immediately?

+ 4.13 What does "unknown mailer error 1" mean?

+ 4.14 How do I queue mail for another domain?

+ 4.15 How do I create attachments with sendmail?

+ 4.16 How do I find sendmail's version number?

+ 4.17 How do I handle usernames with uppercase characters?

1. COPYRIGHT NOTICE/REDISTRIBUTION REQUIREMENTS

This document may be freely distributed for non-profit purposes (including, but not limited to: posting to mailing lists, Usenet newsgroups, and World Wide Web pages; inclusion on CD-ROM or other distribution media; and insertion into text retrieval systems), so long as it is the latest version available at the time, all parts are distributed together, and it is kept completely intact without editing, changes, deletions, or additions. Non-profit redistribution in accordance with these guidelines does not require contact with or approval from the copyright holder.

Redistribution of this document for profit without express prior permission is not allowed. At the very least, expect to provide the copyright holder a free copy of the product (exactly as it would be sold to customers, all distribution media intact), or a percentage of the gross revenue from said product and sufficient proof that the integrity and completeness requirements set for non-profit distribution will be met.

In the event that the copyright holder discovers a redistributed version that is not in compliance with these requirements, he will make a good-faith effort to get it corrected or removed, and failing that, at least note its deprecated status in a new version. Legal action will likely be taken against redistribution for profit that is not in compliance with these requirements.

2. INTRODUCTION/MISCELLANEOUS

2.1) What is this newsgroup?

Date: May 28, 1996

The Usenet newsgroup **comp.mail.sendmail** is dedicated to the discussion of the program named "sendmail" in all its various forms. It is most commonly found on computers running a flavor of the Operating System known as UNIX, or derived from UNIX.

This program has been ported to other OSes, but those versions have typically been ported by a particular vendor and are considered proprietary. There are many versions of sendmail, but the original author (Eric Allman) is continuing development on a particular version typically referred to as "Version Eight" or sometimes just V8. This is considered by many to be the One True Version. This is also the version that this FAQ is centered around.

If you have a question that amounts to "How do I send mail to my friend?", then you're in the wrong newsgroup. You should first check with your System or E-Mail Administrator(s), BBS SysOp(s), etc., before you post your question publicly, since the answer will likely be very highly dependent on what software and hardware you have. You also don't want to embarrass yourself publicly, nor do you want to annoy the kinds of people who are likely to be the counterparts of your System or E-Mail Administrator(s), BBS SysOp(s), etc. If asking them doesn't do you any good, make sure you read this FAQ and the other mail-related FAQs at the archive sites listed below.

If you have a question about another program similar to sendmail (technically referred to as an "SMTP MTA"), an SMTP Gateway package, or a LAN e-mail package, then you should see if there is another group in the **comp.mail** hierarchy that more closely matches the particular program you want to ask a question about. For example, the SMTP MTA known as Smail has **comp.mail.smail** dedicated to it. The mail user agent (MUA) Eudora has two newsgroups dedicated to it (**comp.mail.eudora.mac** and **comp.mail.eudora.ms-windows**), depending on which hardware platform you use. If there isn't a more appropriate newsgroup, try **comp.mail.misc**. Again, make sure your question isn't already addressed in one of the mail-related FAQs or other available documentation. See the IMC website (more information to come) for a good list of mail-related FAQs.

If you have a question about an older or vendor-proprietary version of sendmail, be prepared for a lot of answers that amount to "Get V8." Version 8 isn't a panacea, but it does solve many problems known to plague previous versions, as well as having many new features that make it much easier to administer large or complex sites. In many cases, it makes at least possible what was previously virtually impossible, and relatively easy the previously difficult.

There are, of course, many alternative programs that have sprung up in an attempt to answer one or another weakness or perceived fault of sendmail, but so far, none of them have had the kind of success it would require to unseat it as the de facto standard program for sending Internet mail. Obviously, this forum should not be used to discuss the merits of any of the alternative programs versus sendmail. These kinds of discussions should be taken to **comp.mail.misc**, or you should agitate to get a new newsgroup or newsgroup hierarchy created where that sort of thing is acceptable (or even the norm, such as a **comp.mail.advocacy** or **news:comp.mail.mta.advocacy newsgroup)**.

2.2) What is the scope of this FAQ?

Date: April 9, 1997

This FAQ is strongly centered around version 8 sendmail, for many reasons. First and foremost, this is the area of most interest on the part of the maintainers of this FAQ. Secondly, version 8 is where most of the additional development is being concentrated. Version 8 sendmail is also the best documented of all SMTP MTAs, by virtue of the book by Bryan Costales (see entry sendmail-faq//book/ISBN/1-56592-222-0 in 6.1).

Other versions of sendmail get mentioned in passing, and some interesting interactions between version 8 and various OSes is also covered.

This FAQ is aimed primarily at the experienced UNIX System Administrator/Postmaster/DNS Domain Administrator. If you're looking for introductory texts, see the references in 6.1.

2.3) Where can I find the latest version of this FAQ?

Date: February 20, 1998

We post changes as they occur to the sendmail FAQ support page at **http://www.sendmail.org/faq/**.

2.4) How do I access comp.mail.sendmail by e-mail?

Date: November 24, 1996

Send e-mail to **mxt@dl.ac.uk** with the command "sub comp-news.comp.mail.sendmail full-US-ordered-email-address" as the body of the message (with your correct address in place of the "full-US-ordered-email-address,"and omitting the double quotes in all cases of this example).

E-mail you want posted on **comp.mail.sendmail** should be sent to **comp-mail-sendmail@dl.ac.uk**.

2.5) Where can I ask e-mail-related DNS questions?

Date: March 23, 1996

Depending on how deeply they get into the DNS, they can be asked here. However, you'll probably be told that you should send them to the Usenet newsgroup **comp.protocols.tcp-ip.domains** (DNS in general) or to the Info-BIND mailing list (if the question is specific to that program).

2.6) How can I subscribe to these newsgroups?

Date: June 19, 1997

For **comp.protocols.tcp-ip.domains**, you have to be on Usenet. They don't have a news-to-mail gateway yet (I'm working on this), but they do have a FAQ.

Questions from all levels of experience can be found on this newsgroup (as well as people to answer them), so don't be shy about asking a question you think may be too simple.

Some more information from the BIND 8.1 src/README file:

▼ CAPTION: Kits, Questions, Comments, and Bug Reports

- URL Purpose
- **ftp.isc.org/isc/bind/src/cur** current non-test release
- **ftp.isc.org/isc/bind/src/testing** latest public test kit
- **comp.protocols.dns.bind** using BIND
- **comp.protocols.dns.ops** DNS operations in general
- **comp.protocols.dns.std** DNS standards in general
- **bind-users-request@vix.com** gw'd to c.p.d.bind
- **namedroppers-request@internic.net** gw'd to c.p.d.std
- **bind-workers-request@vix.com** code warriors only please

- **www.isc.org/bind.html** the BIND home page
- **bind-bugs@isc.org bug reports**

2.7) Which version of sendmail should I run?

Date: April 8, 1997
Updated: October 8, 1998

If you're concerned at all about the security of your machines, you should make sure you're at least running a recent release of version 8 sendmail (either from your vendor or the public version detailed in Q2.8).

Check the CERT Alerts and Summaries to make sure that you're running a version that is free of known security holes. Just because the sendmail program provided by your vendor isn't listed doesn't mean that you're not vulnerable, however. If your particular vendor or version isn't listed, check with your vendor and on the appropriate Internet mailing lists and Usenet newsgroups to verify.

If nothing else, the most recent public version is usually a pretty good bet, although you should check **comp.mail.sendmail** to see if anyone has posted recent comments that haven't yet been folded into a new release.

That said, you need to look at what the primary function is for the machine. If its primary function is to run some CAD/CAM package on the desk of an engineer, then there's probably not much sense in replacing the vendor-supplied version of sendmail (assuming it's secure, according to the CERT Alerts and Summaries). Just set the machine up to forward all outbound mail to a central mail relay, and then worry about making that central mail relay the best it can be. Also arrange to have all their inbound mail pass through a central Mail eXchanger (probably the same machine as the central Mail Relay), for the same reasons.

If the primary function for a machine is to act as that central Mail Relay/Mail eXchanger, then we *strongly* recommend the best version of sendmail you can get, and in our opinion that is the latest release of version 8. IDA sendmail is also pretty good, but virtually everything it does, version 8 does better, and version 8 has the additional advantage of having continued development as well.

If fighting spam is a concern, then by all means upgrade to 8.9.X. 8.8.X has some good anti-spam features, but 8.9.X has more features, and the anti-spam ones are far easier to configure than those in 8.8.X.

However, keep in mind that version 8 still hasn't been ported (so far as we know) to some of the older (and perhaps more esoteric) platforms, and if you're stuck using one of them, you may not have much choice.

Some vendors have started shipping (or announced that they will soon ship) version 8 sendmail pre-configured for their machines. Unfortunately, in most cases this means you get a pre-compiled binary and a sendmail.cf file (that may need a bit of tweaking), but not much else of the "standard" version 8 sendmail installation kit. Silicon Graphics (SGI) and Hewlett-Packard are known to already be shipping version 8 sendmail in this fashion.

Sun Microsystems did the same with SunOS 5.5, 5.5.1 and 5.6, shipping a version based on 8.6 with their own proprietary config files. Recent patches for 5.5.1 and 5.6, however, upgrade to a version based on 8.8.8 with a sendmail.cf that is only slightly tweaked. More importantly, a cf hierarchy is available under /usr/lib/mail/. More details are available at the Sun migration page.

2.8) What is the latest release of sendmail?

Date: October 24, 1997
Updated: February 4, 1999

For version 8 sendmail, there are four release trees.

For those people who, for whatever reason, are unable or unwilling to upgrade to version 8.8.z, releases of version 8.6 and 8.7 sendmail are still available. As of this writing, the most recent release of version 8.6 sendmail is 8.6.13, and the most recent release of version 8.7 sendmail is 8.7.6.

For the most recent releases of 8.6 and 8.7 sendmail, there is a version number difference between the sendmail program itself and the associated configuration files. This is okay. The security-related bug fixes that were made only required changes to the sendmail program itself and not the configuration files, so only the version number of the sendmail program itself was incremented.

Version 8.9.3 was released on February 4, 1999.

Version 8.9.2 was released on December 31, 1998.

Version 8.9.1 was released on July 2, 1998.

Version 8.9.0 was released on May 20, 1998.

On machines exposed directly to the Internet, you should either already be running sendmail 8.9.3 or plan on upgrading to it in the immediate future. 8.9.3 is considered "stable,"has security fixes included that will not be found in any previous release, and therefore supercedes all previous releases.

There is no further support for previous releases of sendmail.

2.9) Where can I find it?

Date: January 21, 1997

By anonymous FTP from **ftp.sendmail.org** in /pub/sendmail, or (in URL form) via **ftp://ftp.sendmail.org/pub/sendmail/**. If you care, there should be files in this directory that end with the extension ".sig" which you can check with PGP to make sure that corresponding archives haven't been modified. You'll need to have the PGP key of Eric Allman on your public keyring to be able to verify these archives with their associated .sig files.

There are no other known official version 8 sendmail mirrors.

Check the sendmail home page at **http://www.sendmail.org/** for late-breaking updates and other useful information.

If you want to be notified regarding future updates to sendmail and other items of potential interest, you may want to subscribe to the sendmail-announce mailing list. Address your subscription requests to **"majordomo@lists.sendmail.org"** with "subscribe sendmail-announce" as the body of the message.

2.10) What are the differences between Version 8 and other versions?

Date: March 23, 1996

See doc/changes/changes.{me,ps} in the distribution. See also RELEASE_NOTES at the top level.

2.11) What's the best platform for running sendmail?

Date: April 8, 1997

Generally speaking, I adhere to the old axiom that you should choose what software you want to run first, then choose the platform (hardware and OS) that best runs this software. By this token, if sendmail is the software, then a recent version of BSD UNIX would probably be best, since sendmail was developed at UC Berkeley on BSD UNIX. FreeBSD and BSD/OS are two known implementations of BSD UNIX for Intel-based PCs (among other hardware platforms), and this would make them the most "native" OSes for sendmail. FreeBSD is freely available by anonymous ftp or on CD-ROM, and BSD/OS is a commercial product.

However, not everyone has this kind of "luxury." If you're on a homogeneous network (i.e., completely composed of only one type of hardware and OS), then you should probably be running the same OS as the rest of the machines on the network, regardless of the axiom just stated. You may have other problems, but you should at least be able to get some local support on the OS for your machine.

Either way, if the primary function of the machine is to handle "large" quantities of mail (for whatever value you define "large" to be), I strongly recommend getting the latest stable release of version 8 sendmail.

You may be surprised to find that it is easier for you to support only one version of sendmail across all the various platforms than it is to try to support multiple versions of sendmail, each unique for their particular platform. In that case, the easy solution is to put version 8 sendmail everywhere, and not have to worry about vendor-specific problems with older versions.

For more information on BSD UNIX in general, see the Usenet newsgroups under **comp.unix.bsd**, **comp.bugs.4bsd**, **comp.os.386bsd**. For more information on BSD/OS, see the BSD newsgroups mentioned here, or the BSD/OS Home Page at **http://www.bsdi.com/**. For more information on FreeBSD, see the Usenet newsgroups under **news:comp.unix.bsd.freebsd**, or the FreeBSD Home Page at **http://www.freebsd.org/**.

2.12) What is BIND and where can I get the latest version?

Date: June 24, 1997

BIND stands for "Berkeley Internet Name Daemon," and is the Internet de-facto standard program for turning host names into IP addresses.

The BIND Home Page is at **http://www.isc.org/bind.html**, which provides pointers to the most recent release of BIND. In May of 1997, the first production version of BIND-8 was released. The ISC has deprecated BIND-4 other than for security related patches. No new features or portability changes will be added to BIND-4. You should be using BIND-8.

Note that there are bugs in older resolver libraries, which can cause problems getting to large sites (that list more than five IP addresses for a particular name), or represent a huge security hole as they do not check the returned data to see if it will fit in the amount of space pre-allocated for it.

If at all possible, you should get the most recent "release" version of BIND and make a serious attempt to integrate it into your configuration, since virtually all vendor-provided resolver libraries are woefully out of date.

Note that since the release of BIND version 8.1, many people building sendmail have experienced problems compiling and linking with the new BIND including files and libraries under /usr/local/. A section in our Compiling sendmail page explains this.

2.13) What is smrsh and where can I get it?

Date: July 9, 1996

From **ftp://info.cert.org/pub/tools/smrsh/README**:

- smrsh is a restricted shell utility that provides the ability to specify, through a configuration, an explicit list of executable programs. When used in conjunction with sendmail, smrsh effectively limits sendmail's scope of program execution to only those programs specified in smrsh's configuration.
- smrsh has been written with portability in mind, and uses traditional UNIX library utilities. As such, smrsh should compile on most UNIX C compilers.

The purpose for restricting the list of programs that can be executed in this manner is to keep mail messages (either through an alias or the .forward file in a user's home directory) from being sent to arbitrary programs which are not necessarily known to be sufficiently paranoid in checking their input, and can therefore be easily subverted (this is related to, but different from, the /etc/shells feature discussed in Q3.11).

More information regarding the CERT-CC can be found at their website, **http://www.cert.org.** For more information on CERT Alerts and CERT Summaries, see their advisories and summaries, respectively.

You can find smrsh in the most recent sendmail source archive, as well as **ftp://info.cert.org/pub/tools/smrsh/**. Other very useful programs can be found in **ftp://info.cert.org/pub/tools/**.

2.14) What is smap and where can I get it?

Date: July 5, 1996

Smap (and smapd) are tools out of the Trusted Information Systems (TIS) Firewall Toolkit (fwtk). They were originally written by firewall expert Marcus Ranum under contract to TIS, and TIS is continuing what maintenance there is. The toolkit may be found here. Support questions regarding the toolkit may be sent to **fwall-support@tis.com**, while you may join their mailing list **fwall-users@tis.com** by sending electronic mail to **fwall-users-request@tis.com**.

The concept of smap and smapd is that sendmail is a huge, monolithic setuid root program that is virtually impossible to verify as being "correct" and free from bugs (historically, sendmail has been rather buggy and an easy mark for system crackers to exploit, although with the advent of version 8 sendmail, this becomes much more difficult). In contrast, smap and smapd are very small (only a few hundred lines long), and relatively easy to verify as being correct and functioning as designed (however, as you will see later, we can question their design). According to the theory, it is therefore safer and "better" to run smap and smapd as "wrappers" around sendmail, which would no longer need to be run setuid root.

Unfortunately, smap and smapd have a few problems of their own, and don't appear to have been updated since late March 1996. There have been conflicting reports of incompatibilities between smapd and sendmail 8.7.y (both cannot be run on the same machine, although if you're running sendmail 8.6.x and smap/smapd on the local machine, people on the outside can still use sendmail 8.7.y to talk to you).

For further information on smap and smapd, see the documentation that comes with the TIS Firewall Toolkit.

For more information on firewalls, see the Firewalls FAQ at **http://www.interhack.net/pubs/fwfaq/**.

2.15) What is TCP-Wrappers and where can I get it?

Date: April 8, 1997
Updated: December 6, 1999

TCP-Wrappers is another security enhancement package. The theory is that you take programs being run under inetd (see /etc/inetd.conf) and before you run the program to do the real work (ftpd, telnetd, etc.), you first run the connection attempt through a package that checks to see if the IP address of the source packet is coming from a host known to be either good or bad (you may filter connection attempts by source host name, domain name, raw IP address, port they are attempting to connect to; and either allow known good connections through thus refusing unknown connections, or accept all connections except those known to be bad).

The practice of TCP-Wrappers actually follows the theory quite well. It is a very useful and important tool in the System Administrator's Bag of Things to Help You Secure Your Machine from Crackers, Spammers, Junkmailers, and Other Undesirables. However, it only works for programs that communicate via TCP packets (not UDP, such as NFS) started up out of inetd. It does not work for RPC-based services, and programs that start up a daemon outside of inetd and just leave it running obviously don't benefit beyond the initial connection that gets the daemon started (however, see the following FTP URL for other packages that can help secure RPC and portmapper-based services).

However, most sendmail installations tend to start up a daemon and leave it running at all times. If you did run sendmail out of inetd, you'd lose the benefit of the load average checking code that is executed only in daemon mode, and for systems that handle a lot of mail, this is vitally important.

You can get TCP-Wrappers from **ftp://ftp.win.tue.nl/pub/security/**, a site that has a whole host of other useful security tools, such as securelib, portmap, satan, cops, crack, etc. You can also find pointers to many other useful security tools at **http://ciac.llnl.gov/ciac/SecurityTools.html**, and the COAST Archive at **http://www.cerias.purdue.edu/coast/** is a veritable cornucopia of all things security related.

For the adventurous, you can get a source patch for version 8 sendmail (created for 8.7.6, but, with work, applicable to older releases) that will take the core TCP-Wrappers code and integrate it into the daemon, so that you get the best of both worlds. However, this isn't as smoothly integrated as it should be, is not for the faint-of-heart, and is certainly not officially supported by the original author of sendmail (Eric Allman). This functionality is integrated in a different fashion into version 8.8.5 sendmail.

You should be able to find the unsupported patch at **ftp://ftp.win.tue.nl/pub/security/sendmail-tcpd.patch**.

2.16) Why won't DB 1.85 build on my machine?

Date: April 8, 1997
Updated: May 20, 1997
URL Updated: July 27, 1999

As of release 8.9.X of sendmail, DB 1.85 is no longer needed, as support for DB 2.X is included (starting with 2.3.16). More details are given at Q3.25. The rest of this answer only applies if you have not yet upgraded to 8.9.X.

The DB 1.85 package as available from **http://www.sleepycat.com/register.html** provides Irix support up to Irix 4.05F, but 5.{2,3} need a slightly patched version, as does HP-UX 10.20. Some vendors also provide DB standard with their OS (DEC UNIX 4.0, for example).

A tarball incorporating these changes for Irix 5.x is available at **ftp://ftp.his.com/pub/brad/sendmail/irix5.tar.gz**. This will extract into ./db.1.85/PORT/irix.5.2, with a symbolic link created from ./db.1.85/PORT/irix.5.3 to this same directory. Make sure you extract this archive into the same directory where you extracted the DB 1.85 archive as available from **ftp.cs.berkeley.edu.** (see Q3.5 for more information on getting the DB 1.85 package). An ASCII context diff of this same patch is at **ftp://ftp.his.com/pub/brad/sendmail/irix4-5.diff**.

A version of DB 1.85 that has supposedly been patched to compile under Irix 6.2 has been made available at **http://reality.sgi.com/ariel/freeware/#db**, but I haven't had a chance to download and check it out yet.

The context diffs required to get DB 1.85 working under HP-UX 10.20 are available at ftp://ftp.his.com/pub/brad/sendmail/hpux.10.20.diff. A tarball incorporating these changes is available at **ftp://ftp.his.com/pub/brad/sendmail/hp-ux.10.20.tar.gz**. This will extract into ./db.1.85/PORT/hpux.10.20, so make sure you extract this archive into the same directory where you extracted the DB 1.85 archive as available from **ftp.cs.berkeley.edu**.

2.17) What is makemap and where can I get it?

Date: August 30, 1996

The program "makemap" is used to build the databases used by version 8 sendmail, for things like the UserDB, mailertables, etc.

It is distributed as part of the basic operating system from some vendors, but source code for it is also included at the root level of the sendmail archive (at least, it is for sendmail 8.6.12 and 8.7.5, and presumably will continue to be as newer releases come out). However, it is not considered a "supported" part of version 8 sendmail. Just like the other source provided in the archive, the Makefile will likely need some tweaking for your specific site.

It turns out that Irix 5.3 doesn't appear to have the dbm or ndbm libraries, but to compile makemap.c, you need to have -DNDBM on the "DBMDEF=" line (some necessary things are defined only in /usr/include/ndbm.h). Try just leaving off "-lndbm" from the "LIBS=" line in the Makefile for makemap.

If you plan on using makemap with DB 1.85 on an SGI machine running a version of Irix later than 4.x, see Q2.16 for some additional steps to get DB 1.85 compiled on your machine.

3. VERSION 8- SPECIFIC ISSUES

3.1) How do I make all my addresses appear to be from a single host?

This question is answered in detail at the configuration Masquerading and Relaying page.

3.2) How do I rewrite my from: Lines to Read "*First_Last@ My.Domain*"?

Date: September 23, 1997
Updated: November 8, 1999

Use the generics table, as described in steps 6 and 7 of the Virtual Hosting page.

3.3) But what about fully-qualified addresses, such as those from pine or FEATURE(always_add_domain)?

Date: July 19, 1996
Updated: November 8, 1999
Updated: January 25, 2000

NOTE: This question used to be "How do I get the user database to work with Pine or with FEATURE(always_add_domain)?" But the user database is no longer the recommended solution for this problem, so the question has been clarified appropriately.

The proper solution is to use the generics table, as described in steps 6 and 7 of the Virtual Hosting page. The important thing to note is that the host/domain part of the fully-qualified address must be specified via GENERICS_DOMAIN() or GENERICS_DOMAIN_FILE().

3.4) So what was the User Database feature intended for?

Date: May 12, 1997

The intent was to have all information for a given user (where the user is the unique login name, not an inherently non-unique full name) in one place. This would include phone numbers, addresses, and so forth. The "maildrop" feature is because Berkeley does not use a centralized mail server (there are a number of reasons for this that are mostly historic), and so we need to know where each user gets his or her mail delivered—i.e., the mail drop.

UC Berkeley is (was) in the process of setting up their environment so that mail sent to an unqualified "name" goes to that person's preferred maildrop; mail sent to *name@host* goes to that host. The purpose of "FEATURE(notsticky)" is to cause *name@host* to be looked up in the user database for delivery to the maildrop.

3.5) Why the hostility toward using full names for e-mail addresses?

Date: May 12, 1997

Because full names are not unique. For example, the computer community has two Peter Deutsches. At one time, Bell Labs had two Stephen R. Bournes with offices a few doors apart. You can create alternative addresses (e.g., Stephen_R_Bourne_2), but that's even worse — which one of them has to have their name desecrated in this way? And you can bet that one of them will get most of the other person's e-mail.

So called "full names" are just an attempt to create longer versions of unique names. Rather than lulling people into a sense of security, I'd rather that it be clear that these handles are arbitrary. People should use good user agents that have alias mappings so that they can attach arbitrary names for their personal use to those with whom they correspond (such as the MH alias file).

The problem is even worse outside of America, where non-ASCII characters (e.g., characters with umlauts or the Norwegian ÿ) are used in names. Since non-ASCII characters cannot be used in the SMTP envelope or e-mail headers, the full names are mangled anyway.

Even worse is fuzzy matching in e-mail-this can make good addresses turn bad. For example, Eric Allman is currently (to the best of our knowledge) the only "Allman" at Berkeley, so mail sent to **<Allman@Berkeley.EDU>** should get to him. But if another Allman ever appears, this address could suddenly become ambiguous. He's been the only Allman at Berkeley for over fifteen years—to suddenly have this "good address" bounce mail because it is ambiguous would be a heinous wrong.

Directory services should be as fuzzy as possible (within reason, of course). Mail services should be unique.

3.6) Has been deprecated

3.7) How do I manage several (virtual) domains?

This question is answered in detail at the Virtual Hosting page.

3.8) There are four UUCP mailers listed in the configuration files. which one should I use?

This question is answered in detail at the configuration Using UUCP Mailers page.

3.9) How do I fix "undefined symbol inet_aton" and "undefined symbol_strerror" messages?

This question is answered in detail within the Compiling sendmail page.

3.10) How do I solve "collect: I/O error on connection" errors?

Date: April 8, 1997
Updated: June 4, 1998

There is nothing wrong. This is just a diagnosis of a condition that had not been diagnosed before. If you are getting a lot of these from a single host, there is probably some incompatibility between 8.X and that host. If you get a lot of them in general, you may have network problems that are causing connections to get reset.

Note that this problem is sometimes caused by incompatible values of the MTU (Maximum Transmission Unit) size on a SLIP or PPP connection. Be sure that your MTU size is configured to be the same value as what your ISP has configured for your connection. If you are still having problems, then have your ISP configure your MTU size for 1500 (the maximum value), and you configure your MTU size similarly.

Although it seems like a problem of this sort would affect all of your connections, that is not the case. You may encounter this problem with only a small number of sites with which you exchange mail, and it may even affect only certain size messages.

3.11) Why can't my users forward their mail to a program?

Date: July 9, 1996
Updated: November 19, 1999

I just upgraded to version 8 sendmail and now when my users try to forward their mail to a program they get an "illegal shell" or "cannot mail to programs" message and their mail is not delivered. What's wrong?

In order for people to be able to run a program from their .forward file, version 8 sendmail insists that their shell (that is, the shell listed for that user in the passwd entry) be a "valid" shell, meaning a shell listed in /etc/shells. If /etc/shells does not exist, a default list is used, typically consisting of /bin/sh and /bin/csh.

This is to support environments that may have NFS-shared directories mounted on machines on which users do not have login permission. For example, many people make their file server inaccessible for performance or security reasons; although users have directories, their shell on the server is /usr/local/etc/nologin or some such. If you allowed them to run programs anyway you might as well let them log in.

If you are willing to let users run programs from their .forward file even though they cannot telnet or rsh in (as might be reasonable if you run smrsh to control the list of programs they can run) then add the line:

```
/sendmail/ANY/SHELL/
```

to /etc/shells. This must be typed exactly as indicated, in caps, with the trailing slash.

NOTA BENE: DO NOT list /usr/local/etc/nologin in /etc/shells—this will open up other security problems.

IBM AIX does not use /etc/shells—a list of allowable login shells is contained, along with many other login parameters, in /etc/security/login.cfg. You can copy the information in the "shells=" stanza into /etc/shells on your system so sendmail will have something to use. Do NOT add "/usr/lib/uucp/uucico" or any other non-login shell into /etc/shells.

Also note that there are some weird things that AFS throws into the mix, and these can keep a program from running or running correctly out of .forward files or the system-wide aliases.

See also "smrsh" in Q2.13 and Q3.34, and "directory permissions" in Q3.33.

3.12) Why do connections to the SMTP port take such a long time?

Date: November 24, 1996

I just upgraded to version 8 sendmail and suddenly connections to the SMTP port take a long time. What is going wrong?

It's probably something weird in your TCP implementation that makes the IDENT code act oddly. On most systems version 8 sendmail tries to do a "callback" to the connecting host to get a validated username (see RFC1413 for details). If the connecting host does not support such a service it will normally fail quickly with "Connection refused," but certain kinds of packet filters and certain TCP implementations just time out.

To test this (pre-8.7.y sendmail), set the IDENT timeout to zero using:

```
define(`confREAD_TIMEOUT',`Ident=0')dnl
```

in the .mc file used by m4 to generate your sendmail.cf file.

Alternatively, if you don't use m4, you can put "OrIdent=0" in the configuration file (we recommend the m4 solution, since that makes maintenance much easier for people who don't understand sendmail re-write rules, or after you've been away from it for a while). Either way, this will completely disable all use of the IDENT protocol.

For version 8.7.y sendmail (and above), you should instead use:

```
define(`confTO_IDENT',`0s')dnl
```

Another possible problem is that you have your name server and/or resolver configured improperly. Make sure that all "nameserver" entries in /etc/resolv.conf point to functional servers. If you are running your own server, make certain that all the servers listed in your root cache are up to date (this file is usually called something like "/var/namedb/root.cache;" see your /etc/named.boot file to get your value). Either of these can cause long delays.

3.13) Why do I get "unknown mailer error 5—mail: options MUST PRECEDE recipients" errors?

Date: March 23, 1996

I just upgraded to version 8 sendmail and suddenly I get errors such as "unknown mailer error 5—mail: options MUST PRECEDE recipients." What is going wrong?

You need OSTYPE(systype) in your .mc file, where "systype" is set correctly for your hardware and OS combination—otherwise the configurations use a default that probably disagrees with your local mail system. See the configuration OSTYPE page for details.

If this is on a Sun workstation, you might also want to take a look at the local mailer flags in the Sun-supplied sendmail.cf and compare them to the local mailer flags generated for your version 8 sendmail.cf. If they differ, you might try changing the V8 flags to match the Sun flags.

3.14) Why does Version 8 sendmail panic my SunOS Box?

Date: March 24, 1996
Updated: November 4, 1997

Sendmail 8.7.y panics SunOS 4.1.3_U1 (at least for 1 <= y <= 3) and SunOS 4.1.3, and sendmail 8.6.X seems fine on both machines (at least for 9 <= x <= 12).

The problem is that a kernel patch is missing, specifically 100584-08 (4.1.3), 102010-05 (4.1.3_U1), or 102517 (4.1.4). This should be available from your hardware vendor through your support contract or their online support facilities (including being available on the SunSolve CD).

3.15) Why does the unix "from" header get mysteriously munged when I send to an alias?

Date: December 3, 1997

"It's not a bug, it's a feature." This happens when you have an owner-list alias and you send to list. V8 propagates the owner information into the SMTP envelope sender field (which appears as the UNIX From line [sometimes incorrectly referred to as the From-space "header"] on UNIX mail or as the Return-Path: header) so that downstream errors are properly returned to the mailing list owner instead of to the sender. In order to make this appear as sensible as possible to end users, I recommend making the owner point to a "request" address—for example:

```
list:           :include:/path/name/list.list
owner-list:     list-request
list-request:   eric
```

This will make message sent to list come out as being "From list-request" instead of "From eric."

3.16) Why doesn't MASQUERADE_AS (or the user database) work for envelope addresses as well as header addresses?

Date: November 24, 1996

Believe it or not, this is intentional. The interpretation of the standards by the version 8 sendmail development group was that this was an inappropriate rewriting, and that if the rewriting were incorrect at least the envelope would contain a valid return address.

If you're using version 8.7.y sendmail (or later), you can use

```
FEATURE(masquerade_envelope)
```

in your sendmail.mc file to change this behavior. This is discussed in greater detail at the configuration Masquerading and Relaying page.

3.17) How do I run version 8 sendmail and support the MAIL11V3 protocol?

Date: March 23, 1996

Get the reimplementation of the mail11 protocol by Keith Moore from **ftp://gatekeeper.dec.com/pub/DEC/gwtools/** (with contributions from Paul Vixie).

3.18) Why do messages disappear from my queue unsent?

Date: March 23, 1996

When I look in the queue directory I see that qf* files have been renamed to Qf*, and sendmail doesn't see these. What's wrong?

If you look closely you should find that the Qf files are owned by users other than root. Since sendmail runs as root it refuses to believe information in non-root-owned qf files, and it renames them to Qf to get them out of the way and make it easy for you to find. The usual cause of this is twofold: first, you have the queue directory world writable (which is probably a mistake—this opens up other security problems) and someone is calling sendmail with an "unsafe" flag, usually a -o flag that sets an option that could compromise security. When sendmail sees this it gives up setuid root permissions.

The usual solution is to not use the problematic flags. If you must use them, you have to write a special queue directory and have them processed by the same uid that submitted the job in the first place.

3.19) When is sendmail going to support RFC1522 MIME header encoding?

Date: March 23, 1996
Updated: September 5, 1999

This is considered to be a MUA issue rather than an MTA issue.
Quoth Eric Allman:

The primary reason is that the information necessary to do the encoding (that is, 8->7 bit) is unknown to the MTA. In specific, the character set used to encode names in headers is _NOT_ necessarily the same as used to encode the body (which is already encoded in MIME in the charset parameter of the Content-Type: header). Furthermore, it is perfectly reasonable for, say, a Swede to be living and working in Korea, or a Russian living and working in Germany, and want their name to be encoded in their native character set; it could even be that the sender was Japanese, the recipient Russian, and the body encoded in ISO 8859-1. If all I have are 8-bit characters, I can't choose the charset properly. Similarly, when doing 7->8 bit conversions, I don't want to throw away this information, as it is necessary for proper presentation to the end user.

3.20) Why can't I get mail to some places, but instead always get the error "reply: read error from name.of.remote.host"?

Date: January 17, 1997

This is usually caused by a bug in the remote host's mail server, or mail transport Agent (MTA). The "EHLO" command of ESMTP causes the remote server to drop the SMTP connection. There are several MTAs that have this problem, but one of the most common server implementations can be identified by the "220 All set, fire away" greeting it gives when you telnet to its SMTP port.

To work around this problem, you can configure sendmail to use a mailertable with an entry telling sendmail to use plain SMTP when talking to that host:

name.of.remote.host smtp:*name.of.remote.host*

Sites which must run a host with this broken SMTP implementation should do so by having a site running sendmail or some other reliable (and reasonably modern) SMTP MTA act as an MX server for the problem host.

There is also a problem wherein some TCP/IP implementations are broken, and if any connection attempt to a remote end gets a "connection refused," then *all* connections to that site will get closed. Of course, if you try to use the IDENT protocol across a firewall (at either end), this is highly likely to result in the same apparent kind of "read error."

The fix is simple—on those machines with broken TCP/IP implementations, do not attempt to use IDENT. When compiling newer releases of version 8 sendmail, the compiler should automatically detect whether you're on a machine that is known to have this kind of TCP/IP networking problem, and make sure that sendmail does not attempt to use IDENT. If you've since patched your machine so that it no longer has this problem, you'll need to go back in and explicitly configure sendmail for support of IDENT, if you want that feature.

3.21) Why doesn't "FEATURE(xxx)" work?

Date: January 17, 1996

When creating m4 Master Config (".mc") files for version 8 sendmail, many FEATURE() macros simply change the definition of internal variables that are referenced in the MAILER() definitions.

To make sure that everything works as desired, you need to make sure that OSTYPE() macros are put at the very beginning of the file, followed by FEATURE() and HACK() macros, local definitions, and at the very bottom, the MAILER() definitions. See the configuration Introduction and Example page for more details.

3.22) How do I configure sendmail not to use DNS?

Date: March 24, 1997

In situations where you're behind a firewall, or across a dial-up line, there are times when you need to make sure that programs (such as sendmail) do not use the DNS at all.

With version 8.8, you change the service switch file to omit "DNS" and use only NIS, files, and other map types as appropriate.

With previous releases of version 8 sendmail, you need to recompile the binary and make sure that "NAMED_BIND" is turned off in src/conf.h.

Note that you'll need to forward all your outbound mail to another machine as a "relay" (one that does use DNS, and understands how to properly use MX records, etc.), otherwise you won't be able to get mail to any site(s) other than the one(s) you configure in your /etc/hosts file (or whatever).

3.23) How do I get all my queued mail delivered to my UNIX box from my ISP?

Date: June 6, 1997
Updated: October 8, 1998

In the contrib directory of the sendmail distribution is a Perl script called etrn.pl. Assuming you're running sendmail or some other SMTP MTA on some sort of a UNIX host, and your ISP uses version 8.8 sendmail and they queue all mail for your domain (as opposed to stuffing it all in one file that you need to download via POP3 or some such), the command

```
etrn.pl mail.myisp.com mydomain.com
```

will do the trick. You can learn about Perl at the Perl Language Home Page. The O'Reilly book is also very helpful.

If you don't have Perl, something like the following script should do the trick:

```
#!/bin/sh
telnet mail.myisp.com. 25 << __EOF__
EHLO me.mydomain.com
ETRN mydomain.com
QUIT

__EOF__
```

Note that this is indented for readability, and the real script would have column position #1 of the file be the first printable character in each line.

Of course, you'll have to fill in the appropriate details for "mail.myisp.com," "mydomain.com," etc.

If your ISP doesn't use version 8.8 sendmail, you may have to cobble together alternative solutions. They may have a "ppplogin" script that is executed every time your machine dials them up, and if so, you may be able to have them modify this script so as to put a "sendmail -qRmydomain.com" in it (which is effectively what the "ETRN" command does, but in a safer fashion).

Alternatively, they may have a hacked finger daemon, so that you'd put "finger mydomain.com@theirhost.theirdomain.com" in your script. Or, they may have some other solution for you. However, only they would be able to answer what solutions they have available to them.

Obviously, the easiest and most "standard" solution is to have them upgrade their system to the most recent stable release of version 8 sendmail. See Q2.8 to find out what exact version this is.

3.24) Why do I get the error message, "unable to write /etc/mail/sendmail.pid"?

Date: August 6, 1997

Sendmail checks if it has write access to the directory in which it wants to create a file without granting special privileges to 'root'. To have sendmail run properly, the directories /etc, /etc/mail, and/or /var/run should be owned by root and be writable by its owner.

3.25) Why can't I compile sendmail with Berkeley DB 2.*x*?

Date: August 12, 1997
Updated: May 20, 1998

Sendmail 8.8 only supports Berkeley DB 1.85. It will not work with newer Berkeley DB versions, even in compatibility mode. sendmail 8.9, however, does include support for Berkeley DB 2.*x*, starting with 2.3.16.

3.26) What operating systems has Berkeley sendmail been ported to?

Date: December 18, 1997
Updated: September 9, 1999

Berkeley sendmail 8.9.3 supports most known flavors of UNIX, including:

386BSD	A-UX	AIX	Altos
BSD-OS	BSD43	CLIX	CSOS
ConvexOS	Dell	DomainOS	Dynix
EWS-UX_V	FreeBSD	HP-UX	IRIX
ISC	KSR	LUNA	Linux
Mach386	NCR.MP-RAS	NEWS-OS	NeXT
NetBSD	NonStop-UX	OSF1	OpenBSD
PTX	Paragon	PowerUX	RISCos
SCO	SINIX	SMP_DC. OSx. NILE	Solaris
SunOs	SVR4	Titan	ULTRIX
UMAX	UNICOS	UNIX_SV.4.x.i386	Utah
uts.systemV	UX4800	UXPDS	dgux
maxion			

Also, a Windows NT version is available from sendmail, Inc.

3.27) How do I prevent relaying denied errors for my clients?

Date: April 12, 1998
Last updated: August 9, 1998

You need to add the fully-qualified host name and/or IP address of each client to class R, the set of relay-allowed domains. For version 8.8.X, this is typically defined by the file /etc/sendmail.cR; for 8.9.X, it is typically /etc/mail/relay-domains. Note: if your DNS is problematic, you may need to list the IP address in square brackets (e.g., [1.2.3.4]) to get the ${client_name} macro to work properly; in general, however, this should not be necessary.

Once you've updated the appropriate file, SIGHUP your sendmail daemon and you should be OK.

Further details are available on our allowing controlled SMTP relaying in sendmail 8.9 page.

3.28) Why isn't virtual hosting working, even after I added a Kvirtuser line to sendmail.cf?

Date: April 12, 1998

Just adding the proper Kvirtuser line to sendmail.cf is not enough to enable the virtual user table feature, a key ingredient for virtual hosting. You need to use the m4 technique FEATURE(virtusertable); detailed instructions are provided at our Virtual Hosting with Sendmail page.

3.29) How can I add a header specifying the actual recipient when having multiple users in a virtual domain go to a single Mailbox?

Stuffing multiple user's mail into a single mail box is not a good method of distributing user mail but if you must do this, the following solution should allow a tool like fetchmail to separate the messages for individual users.

1. Use FEATURE(local_procmail) in your .mc file so procmail (which you must install separately) will deliver mail to the mailbox.
2. Use FEATURE(virtusertable) to create a virtual user table entry for the domain as follows:

   ```
   @domain.com     domuser+%1
   ```

   where domuser is the username of the mailbox you will be using.

3. Put this in the respective domuser's $HOME/.procmailrc:

   ```
   DOMAIN=domain.com
   ENV_TO=$1
   :0f
   * ENV_TO ?? .
   | formail -i "X-Envelope-To: "$ENV_TO@$DOMAIN
   :0fE
   | formail -i "X-Envelope-To: UNKNOWN"
   ```

This will insert an X-Envelope-To header with the original envelope recipient address when the message is delivered the normal way via the virtusertable, and UNKNOWN if for some reason it was sent directly to domuser.

3.30) What do I do when build fails because groff was not found?

Date: September 24, 1998

You can get groff from **ftp://ftp.gnu.org/pub/gnu/**. But it's not a big deal, because:

- ▼ You've already successfully built the sendmail binary to get this far.
- ▲ You can just use the preformatted man pages anyway: % cp *.0 obj*.

3.31) What does "class hash not available" mean?

Date: September 24, 1998

You've built sendmail and/or makemap without NEWDB specified in your DBMDEF configuration, but you specified the class hash in sendmail.cf or on a makemap command. The class hash requires NEWDB support, for which you need the Berkeley database. Please refer to the Database Definitions section of our Compiling sendmail web page.

3.32) How do I configure majordomo with sendmail 8.9 without relaxing the DontBlamesendmail option?

Date: January 26, 1999

We have had some queries about this, as majordomo apparently suggests some configuration values which sendmail 8.9 does not like. Here is what one expert suggests:

The sendmail.cf contains:

```
O AliasFile=/etc/aliases, /etc/majordomo.aliases
O DontBlamesendmail=Safe
```

/etc/aliases contains the general Majordomo aliases:

```
# Majordomo
majordomo: "|/usr/local/lib/majordomo/wrapper majordomo"
owner-majordomo: postmaster
majordomo-owner: postmaster
```

/etc/majordomo.aliases contains the Majordomo lists of the form:

```
wookie: "|/usr/local/lib/majordomo/wrapper resend -l wookie wookie-list"
wookie-list: :include:/usr/local/lib/majordomo/lists/wookie
owner-wookie: head-wookie
wookie-approval: owner-wookie
wookie-request: "|/usr/local/lib/majordomo/wrapper majordomo -l wookie"
```

The various directory owners/groups/permissions:

```
drwxr-xr-x  20 root     root         1024 Dec  1 15:20 /
drwxr-xr-x  25 root     root         3072 Jan 26 01:26 /etc
drwxr-xr-x  20 root     root         1024 Feb  4  1998 /usr
drwxr-xr-x  18 root     root         1024 Jan 16 18:40 /usr/local
```

```
drwxr-xr-x   5 root     root         1024 Feb  6  1996 /usr/local/lib
lrwxrwxrwx   1 root     root    16 Dec  1 10:01 /usr/local/lib/majordomo
 -> majordomo-1.94.4
drwxr-x--x   5 majordom majordom     1024 Jan 25 23:12 /usr/local/lib/
majordomo-1.94.4
drwxr-xr-x   2 majordom majordom    32768 Jan 26 00:49 /usr/local/lib/
majordomo-1.94.4/lists
-rw-rw-r--   1 majordom majordom      655 Nov  3 17:03 /usr/local/lib
majordomo-1.94.4/lists/wookie
-rw-rw----   1 majordom majordom    14588 Jan 19 10:28 /usr/local/lib/
majordomo-1.94.4/lists/wookie.config
-rw-rw-r--   1 majordom majordom       23 Jan 14  1997 /usr/local/lib/
majordomo-1.94.4/lists/wookie.info
```

Now the differences that make this work that may not be the same as instructed by the majordomo instructions:

1. Put the majordomo.aliases file in /etc, not in the Majordomo install directory (/usr/local/lib/majordomo).
2. Make the permissions on /usr/local/lib/majordomo 0751, not 0775.
3. Make the permissions on /usr/local/lib/majordomo/Log 0664, owned by majordom, group majordom.
4. /usr/local/lib/majordomo/lists is mode 0755, owner majordom, group majordom.
5. The permissions/owners for the lists should be as just shown. These permissions/ownership allow majordom to continue to manage the lists.

3.33) How do I configure my system in general with sendmail 8.9?

Date: May 24, 1999

The following is taken directly from the DIRECTORY PERMISSIONS section of the top-level README file in the sendmail distribution.

sendmail often gets blamed for many problems that are actually the result of other problems, such as overly permissive modes on directories. For this reason, sendmail checks the modes on system directories and files to determine if they can be trusted. For sendmail to run without complaining, you MUST execute the following command:

```
chmod go-w / /etc /etc/mail /usr /var /var/spool /var/spool/mqueue
chown root / /etc /etc/mail /usr /var /var/spool /var/spool/mqueue
```

You will probably have to tweak this for your environment (for example, some systems put the spool directory into /usr/spool instead of /var/spool and use /etc/mail for aliases file instead of /etc). If you set the RunAsUser option in your sendmail.cf, the /var/spool/mqueue directory will have to be owned by the RunAsUser user. As a general rule, after you have compiled sendmail, run the command

```
sendmail -v -bi
```

to initialize the alias database. If it gives messages such as

```
WARNING: writable directory /etc
WARNING: writable directory /usr/spool/mqueue
```

then the directories listed have inappropriate write permissions and should be secured to avoid various possible security attacks.

Beginning with sendmail 8.9, these checks have become more strict to prevent users from being able to access files they would normally not be able to read. In particular, .forward and :include: files in unsafe directory paths (directory paths which are group or world writable) will no longer be allowed. This would mean that if user joe's home directory was writable by group staff, sendmail would not use his .forward file. This behavior can be altered, at the expense of system security, by setting the DontBlamesendmail option. For example, to allow .forward files in group writable directories:

```
O DontBlamesendmail=forwardfileingroupwritabledirpath
```

Or to allow them in both group and world writable directories:

```
O DontBlamesendmail=forwardfileinunsafedirpath
```

Items from these unsafe .forward and :include: files will be marked as unsafe addresses—the items cannot be deliveries to files or programs. This behavior can also be altered via DontBlamesendmail:

```
O DontBlamesendmail=forwardfileinunsafedirpath,
forwardfileinunsafedirpathsafe
```

The first flag allows the .forward file to be read, the second allows the items in the file to be marked as safe for file and program delivery.

Other files affected by this strengthened security include class files (i.e. Fw /etc/sendmail.cw), persistent host status files, and the files specified by the ErrorHeader and HelpFile options. Similar DontBlamesendmail flags are available for the class, ErrorHeader, and HelpFile files.

If you have an unsafe configuration of .forward and :include: files, you can make it safe by finding all such files, and doing a "chmod go-w $FILE" on each. Also, do a "chmod go-w $DIR" for each directory in the file's path.

3.34) What does "foo not available for sendmail programs" mean?

Date: September 24, 1999

It means that you are using smrsh, the sendmail restricted shell; see Q2.13 for details on this. To fix this problem, you need to create a sym-link from smrsh's directory for restricted programs to the program foo. The default location of this directory for restricted programs is /usr/adm/sm.bin in the Open Source version, but vendor versions differ. For example, Red Hat Linux 6.0 uses /etc/smrsh, and Solaris 8 uses /var/adm/sm.bin. If you don't know the directory for your OS, first check the smrsh man page, then if that fails, try:

```
% strings /path/to/smrsh | grep ^/
where /path/to/smrsh is the P= argument on the Mprog line in sendmail.cf
.
```

So for example:

```
% cd /usr/adm/sm.bin
% ln -s /usr/bin/vacation
```

would allow the vacation program to be run from a user's .forward file or an alias which uses the "|program" syntax.

Finally, if you want to disable use of smrsh, remove the FEATURE('smrsh') line from the .mc file used to build sendmail.cf; see cf/README for details on this.

4. GENERAL sendmail ISSUES

4.1) Should I use a wildcard MX for my domain?

Date: July 9, 1996
Updated: November 5, 1997

If at all possible, no.

Wildcard MX records have lots of semantic "gotchas". For example, they will match a host "unknown.your.domain"—if you don't explicitly test for unknown hosts in your domain, you will get "MX list for hostname points back to hostname" or "config error: mail loops back to myself."

See RFCs 1535, 1536, and 1912 (updates RFC1537) for more detail and other related (or common) problems. See also _DNS and BIND_ by Albitz and Liu.

They can also cause your system to add your domain to outgoing FQDNs in a desperate attempt to get the mail to where it's supposed to go, but because *.your.domain is valid due to the wildcard MX, delivery to not.real.domain.your.domain will get dumped on you, and you may even find yourself in a loop as the domain keeps getting tacked on time after time after time (the "config error: mail loops back to myself" problem).

Wildcard MX records are just a bad idea, plain and simple. They don't work the way you'd expect, and virtually no one gets them right. Avoid them at all costs.

4.2) How can I set up an auto-responder?

Date: March 23, 1996
Updated: February 16, 1999

This is a local mailer issue, not a sendmail issue. Depending on what you're doing, look at procmail (see Q4.9), ftpmail, or Majordomo.

The latest version of Majordomo can be found at **ftp://ftp.greatcircle.com/pub/majordomo/**. It is written in Perl and requires Perl 4.036, and appears to run with only minor tweaks under 5.001a or later. Make sure to check out the web interface for Majordomo called LWGate at **http://www.netspace.org/users/dwb/lwgate.html**. The latest versions of Perl (both 4.x and 5.x) can be found in **http://www.metronet.com/perlinfo/src/**. More information about Perl can be found at **http://www.metronet.com/perlinfo/perl5.html**

The latest version of ftpmail can be found at **ftp://src.doc.ic.ac.uk/packages/ftpmail** or any **comp.sources.misc** archive (volume 37).

4.3) How can I get sendmail to deliver local mail to $HOME/.mail instead of into /usr/spool/mail (or /usr/mail)?

Date: July 9, 1996
Updated: January 7, 1999

Again, this is a local mailer issue, not a sendmail issue. Either modify your local mailer (source code will be required) or change the program called in the "local" mailer configuration description to be a new program that does this local delivery. One program that is capable of doing this is procmail (see Q4.9), although there are probably many others as well.

4.4) Why does it deliver the mail interactively when I'm trying to get it to go into queue-only mode?

Date: March 23, 1996

Or, I'm trying to use the "don't deliver to ex01pensive mailer" flag, and it delivers the mail interactively anyway. I can see it does it: here's the output of "sendmail -v foo@somehost" (or Mail -v or equivalent).

The -v flag to sendmail (which is implied by the -v flag to Mail and other programs in that family) tells sendmail to watch the transaction. Since you have explicitly asked to see what's going on, it assumes that you do not want to auto-queue, and turns that feature off. Remove the -v flag and use a "tail -f" of the log instead to see what's going on.

If you are trying to use the "don't deliver to expensive mailer" flag (mailer flag "e"), be sure you also turn on global option "c"—otherwise it ignores the mailer flag.

4.5) How can I solve "MX list for hostname points back to hostname" and "config error: mail loops back to myself" messages?

Date: January 17, 1997
Updated: November 5, 1997

I'm getting these error messages:

```
553 MX list for domain.net points back to relay.domain.net
554 <user@domain.net>... Local configuration error
```

How can I solve this problem?

You have asked mail to the domain (e.g., domain.net) to be forwarded to a specific host (in this case, relay.domain.net) by using an MX record, but the relay machine doesn't recognize itself as domain.net. Add domain.net to /etc/sendmail.cw (if you are using FEATURE(use_cw_file)) or add "Cw domain.net" to your configuration file.

IMPORTANT: When making changes to your configuration file, be sure you kill and restart the sendmail daemon (for *any* change in the configuration, not just this one):

```
kill `head -1 /etc/sendmail.pid`
sh -c "`tail -1 /etc/sendmail.pid`"
```

NOTA BENE: kill -1 does not work with versions prior to 8.7.y!

With version 8.8.z sendmail, if the daemon was started up with a full pathname (i.e., "/usr/lib/sendmail -bd -q13m"), then you should be able to send it a HUP signal ("kill -1", or more safely, "kill -HUP") and have it reload itself (version 8.7.y sendmail cannot do this safely, and represents a security risk if it's not replaced with version 8.8.3 or later).

4.6) Why does my sendmail process sometimes hang when connecting over a SLIP/PPP link?

Date: March 23, 1996

I'm connected to the network via a SLIP/PPP link. Sometimes my sendmail process hangs (although it looks like part of the message has been transfered). Everything else works. What's wrong?

Most likely, the problem isn't sendmail at all, but the low level network connection. It's important that the MTU (Maximum Transfer Unit) for the SLIP connection be set properly at both ends. If they disagree, large packets will be trashed and the connection will hang.

4.7) How can I summarize the statistics generated by sendmail in the syslog?

Date: April 9, 1997
Updated: January 4, 1999

This question is addressed on pages 445-449 of _sendmail, 2nd Ed_ (see page 319 of first edition) by Bryan Costales (see entry sendmail-faq//book/ISBN/1-56592-222-0 in 6.1).

An updated version of this syslog-stat.pl script (so that it understands the log format used in version 8 sendmail) is at **ftp://ftp.his.com/pub/brad/sendmail/syslog_stats**. The updated version of ssl has been uploaded to the SMTP Resources Directory (in **ftp://ftp.is.co.za/networking/mail/tools/**), as well as **ftp://ftp.his.com/pub/brad/sendmail/ssl**. There is also another program (written by Bryan Beecher) at **ftp://ftp.his.com/pub/brad/sendmail/smtpstats**.

If you're interested in summarizing POP statistics, there is **ftp://ftp.his.com/pub/brad/sendmail/popstats**, also written by Bryan Beecher, and popstats.pl, written by Ryan Matteson.

To see what else is available today, check the Comprehensive Perl Archive Network **ftp://ftp.funet.fi/pub/languages/perl/CPAN/CPAN** or **ftp://ftp.cis.ufl.edu/pub/perl/CPAN/CPAN** for the site nearest you. For the scripts themselves, look under CPAN/scripts/mailstuff/ at any CPAN site. For more information, see the comp.lang.perl.* FAQs at **ftp://ftp.cis.ufl.edu:/pub/perl/faq/FAQ** or **ftp://rtfm.mit.edu/pub/usenet-by-hierarchy/comp/lang/perl/**.

If you're interested in using these kinds of tools to help you do some near real-time monitoring of your system, you might be interested in MEWS (Mail Early Warning System) from the README.

If you've ever written a Perl script to parse sendmail log files looking for errors, MEWS might be of interest to you. If you've ever thought about writing a Perl script to munge sendmail log files, cringed a little and hurriedly came up with an excuse not to do it, read on.

If you don't have a Solaris 2.5 machine, you can probably stop reading here.

The Mail Early Warning System (MEWS) gives postmasters immediate notification of trouble spots on your mail backbone. It only works with sendmail.

To explain it in a nutshell, whenever sendmail returns a 4xx or 5xx SMTP code, with the MEWS modifications, it also sends the code over UDP to a daemon which then replays the error message to interested parties. The man pages go into a little bit more detail.

If this sounds like something you might be interested in getting more details about, you can find the MEWS archive at **ftp://ftp.qualcomm.com/pub/people/eamonn/mews.tar.Z**.

4.8) How can I check my sendmail.cf to ensure that it's re-writing addresses correctly?

Date: July 9, 1996

The recommended program for this is "checksendmail" by Rob Kolstad. Old versions of this are available on various archive sites, but currently, the only way to get the most recent version (which has been updated to understand version 8.7 long option name syntax, as well as now supporting both Perl 4.x and Perl 5.x) is from Rob himself.

The latest archive will be made publicly available (most likely through the SMTPRD run by Andras Salamon; see 6.5, entry sendmail-faq//online/index/14) as soon as it is received.

4.9) What is procmail, and where can I get it?

Date: April 8, 1997
Updated: February 28, 1999

The program "procmail" is a replacement for the local mailer (variously called /bin/mail, /usr/bin/mail, mail.local, rmail, etc.). It has been ported to run on virtually every UNIX-like OS you're likely to run into, and has a whole host of features. It is typically about 30 percent faster performing the job of the local mailer than programs such as /bin/mail or /usr/bin/mail, it has been hammered on widely to make it extremely secure (much more so than most local mailers) and very robust. Procmail is also capable of helping you put a quota on a user's mailbox through the standard UNIX quota mechanism (see Q4.3).

In short, whatever you've got, you're almost guaranteed that procmail is better (if nothing else, the author has been able to focus lots of time and energy into making it the best and fastest tool available, while most system vendors just throw something together as fast as they can and move on to the whole rest of the OS).

However, this only begins to scratch the surface of what procmail is capable of. It's most important feature is the fact that it gives you a standard way to create rules (procmail calls them "recipes") to process your mail before the messages get put into your mailbox, and for that feature alone, it is one of the most important tools any administrator can have in their repertoire. By filtering out or automatically dealing with 80 percent of your daily craft, it lets you spend more time on the hard 20 percent.

Note that recent releases of version 8 sendmail natively support using procmail as an alternate local mailer (see "FEATURE(local_procmail)" for version 8.7 and above). They also support procmail as an additional local mailer, if you're concerned about flat-out replacing your current local mailer with procmail (see "MAILER(procmail)" in version 8.7 and above).

You can also install procmail as a user and run it out of your .forward file, although this tends to be a bit slower and less efficient.

More information about procmail can be found at **http://www.procmail.org/** and the latest version can be found at **ftp://ftp.procmail.org/pub/procmail/**.

Procmail is also the core to a mailing list management package called "SmartList," so if you've already got procmail, adding SmartList may be a good option. Some list owners prefer Majordomo, Listserv, or one of those other programs, but SmartList has more than a few adherents as well. Your personal tastes will dictate whether you swear by SmartList or at it.

4.10) How can I solve "cannot alias non-local names" errors?

Date: March 24, 1997

I upgraded from my vendor's sendmail to the latest version and now I'm getting these error messages when I run "newaliases":

```
/etc/aliases: line 13: MAILER-DAEMON... cannot alias non-local names
/etc/aliases: line 14: postmaster... cannot alias non-local names
```

How can I solve this problem?

Your local mailer doesn't have the "A" flag specified. Edit the Mlocal line in sendmail.cf and add "A" to the flags listed after "F=".

Better yet, if you're running a recent version of sendmail that uses m4 to generate .cf files from .mc files, regenerate your sendmail.cf and see if that fixes the problem. Remember to install the new sendmail.cf and restart the sendmail daemon.

4.11) Is sendmail year-2000 (Y2K) compliant?

Date: April 24, 1997
Updated: July 7, 1999

Please refer to the sendmail Year 2000 Readiness Disclosure page.

4.12) How can I batch remote mail to be sent using my ISP while delivering local mail immediately?

Date: October 14, 1997
Updated: February 9, 1999

First, you need to get sendmail not to use DNS on your local machine so your host doesn't try to connect to your ISP for a DNS query. See Q3.22 for more information.

You also need to designate a "smart host" or external relay to handle all mail that you can't deliver locally (this would be your ISP's mailhost).

You need to configure it so that the smtp mailer is considered "expensive" by adding the F=e mailer flag and tell sendmail not to connect to expensive mailers by default by setting the HoldExpensive option to True.

You need to add mydomain.com to the sendmail.cw file or the Cw line in the sendmail.cf. See Q4.5.

Finally, you need to run a program periodically to check in with your ISP and get them to deliver any mail they may have queued for you. See Q3.23.

4.13) What does "unknown mailer error 1" mean?

Date: September 24, 1998

In general, sendmail does not perform final delivery of messages, but relies on a local delivery agent instead. Such an agent, mail.local, is provided with the sendmail distribution. Any such agent that sendmail invokes for message delivery, as specified on an M line in sendmail.cf, must exit with code 0 (success), or one of the failure codes noted in src/sysexits.h. These generally run in the range 64 - 78, so 1 would be out of range, and lead to sendmail generating this error.

4.14) How do I queue mail for another domain?

Date: April 28, 1999

Situation: Your system mailserver.my.domain should act as a backup mailserver for mailserver.client.domain. The client wants to receive mail for the address user@client.domain. This requires:

1. MX Records:

   ```
   client.domain.                IN MX 10 mailserver.client.domain.
   client.domain.                IN MX 20 mailserver.my.domain.
   mailserver.client.domain.     IN MX 10 mailserver.client.domain.
   mailserver.client.domain.     IN MX 20 mailserver.my.domain.
   ```

   The last two records are there "just in case" (someone forgot masquerading). Make sure you use the real names of all systems. mailserver.my.domain must know its own name, otherwise you'll get the famous mail loops back to myself error. Instead of using MX records that point to mailserver.client.domain, you can use the FEATURE(mailertable) on mailserver.my.domain as explained in cf/README for routing e-mails.

2. On your system: do nothing unless you have anti-relay rules installed (which you really should have!). In this case, add client.domain to the required files

(8.9) (or for 8.8). Don't add client.domain or mailserver.client.domain to class w on your system!

3. Sendmail on your system will try to deliver mail during queue runs, however, the client may trigger delivery by using the ETRN command.

4.15) How do I create attachments with sendmail?

Date: May 26, 1999

You don't. sendmail is a mail transport agent (MTA). Creating e-mail messages, including adding attachments or signatures, is the function of a mail user agent (MUA). Some popular MUAs include mutt, elm, exmh, Netscape, Eudora and Pine. Some specialized packages (metamail, some Perl modules, etc.) can also be used to create messages with attachments.

4.16) How do I find sendmail's version number?

Date: August 2, 1999

To find out which version is actually running, from without, telnet to the SMTP port (port 25). The daemon usually announces its name and version number, as in

```
thishost% telnet that.host 25
  Trying IP_addr...
  Connected to that.host.
  Escape character is '^]'.
  220 that.host ESMTP sendmail 8.9.3/8.9.3; Mon, 2 Aug 1999 11:39:34
  -0700
  ^]
  telnet> quit
   To query a binary on your local host, the following command should
   display its version number, along with some extra configuration
   information, possibly including the configuration version number:
  % echo \$Z | /usr/sbin/sendmail -bt -d0
  Version 8.9.3
   Compiled with: MAP_REGEX LOG MATCHGECOS MIME7TO8 MIME8TO7 NAMED_BIND
                  NETINET NETISO NETUNIX NEWDB QUEUE SCANF SMTP USERDB
                  XDEBUG
  ============ SYSTEM IDENTITY (after readcf) ============
        (short domain name) $w = knecht
    (canonical domain name) $j = knecht.sendmail.org
```

```
           (subdomain name) $m = sendmail.org
                (node name) $k = knecht.sendmail.org
========================================================
ADDRESS TEST MODE (ruleset 3 NOT automatically invoked)
Enter <ruleset> <address>
> 8.9.3
%
```

Adjust the pathname as needed; /usr/lib and /usr/sbin are the most common locations.

4.17) How do I handle usernames with uppercase characters?

Date: November 18, 1999

You really shouldn't, because uppercase characters in usernames are contrary to the UNIX tradition. If you do, then e-mail addresses will be case sensitive, so that mail to <USER@your.host> will bounce instead of being delivered to <user@your.host>. As this is contrary to the expectations of many, it is not recommended.

But if you insist on doing so anyway, and you have version 8.10, put the following in your .mc file:

```
MODIFY_MAILER_FLAGS(`LOCAL', `+u')dnl
```

If you don't have 8.10, you will need to redefine the LOCAL_MAILER_FLAGS m4 variable, but the initial value varies from OS to OS, so this is yet another reason not to mess with this flag.

5. VENDOR/OS-SPECIFIC sendmail ISSUES

5.1) Sun Microsystems SunOS/Solaris 1.*x*/2.*x*

5.1.1) How can I solve "line 273: replacement $3 out of bounds" errors?

Date: March 23, 1996

When I use sendmail V8 with a Sun config file, I get lines like

```
/etc/sendmail.cf: line 273: replacement $3 out of bounds
```

the line in question reads

```
R$*<@$%y>$*          $1<@$2.LOCAL>$3          user@ether
```

What does this mean? How do I fix it?

V8 doesn't recognize the Sun "$%y" syntax, so as far as it is concerned, there is only a $1 and a $2 (but no $3) in this line. Read Rick McCarty's paper on "Converting Standard Sun Config Files to sendmail Version 8," in the contrib directory (file "converting.sun.configs") in the latest version 8 sendmail distribution, for a full discussion of how to do this.

5.1.2) How can I solve "line 445: bad ruleset 96 (50 max)" errors?

Date: March 23, 1996

When I use sendmail V8 on a Sun, I sometimes get lines like:

```
/etc/sendmail.cf: line 445: bad ruleset 96 (50 max)
```

What does this mean? How do I fix it?

You're somehow trying to start up the old Sun sendmail (or sendmail.mx) with a version 8 sendmail config file, which Sun's sendmail doesn't like. Check your /etc/rc.local, any procedures that have been created to stop and re-start the sendmail processes, etc. Make sure that you've switched everything over to using the new sendmail. To keep this problem from ever happening again, try the following (make sure you're logged in as root):

```
mv /usr/lib/sendmail /usr/lib/sendmail.old
ln -s /usr/local/lib/sendmail.v8 /usr/lib/sendmail
mv /usr/lib/sendmail.mx /usr/lib/sendmail.mx.old
ln -s /usr/local/lib/sendmail.v8 /usr/lib/sendmail.mx
chmod 0000 /usr/lib/sendmail.old
chmod 0000 /usr/lib/sendmail.mx.old
```

Assuming, of course, that you have installed sendmail V8 in /usr/local/ lib/sendmail.v8.

5.1.3) Why does Version 8 sendmail (< 8.7.5) sometimes hang under Solaris 2.5?

Date: May 23, 1996

In moving from Solaris 2.4 to Solaris 2.5, the kernel changed its name and is now in /kernel/genunix instead of /kernel/unix, so _PATH_UNIX in conf.h is pointing to the wrong place. If you can't upgrade to the latest release of sendmail 8.8.z, the next best thing to do is change _PATH_UNIX in conf.h (in the solaris2 part) to point to the generic interface /dev/ksyms, like so:

```
#    define _PATH_UNIX    "/dev/ksyms"
```

5.1.4) Why can't I use SunOS/Solaris to get e-mail to certain large sites?

Date: November 24, 1996

This is most likely a problem in your resolver libraries (DNS, /etc/hosts, NIS, etc.). Older Sun (and Solaris?) resolver libraries allocated enough room for only five IP addresses for each host name, and if any program ever ran across a name with more than five IP addresses for it, the program would crash. For example, this would keep you from getting mail to CompuServe, since (at the time of this writing) they list eleven IP addresses for mx1.compuserve.com (one of the named MXes for compuserve.com). This will affect you even if you use version 8 sendmail, since it's a problem in the resolver libraries, and not in sendmail itself. You should either get patches to the resolver libraries from Sun, or the latest version of BIND (see Q2.12), and install their resolver library routines. Between the two, installing BIND is a bit more work, but it typically gives you much more up-to-date code to help you resist attacks to your systems, more capable programs to be used for serving the DNS (including support for IPv6 and several other features), and some very useful utility programs.

5.1.5) Why do I have trouble compiling on Solaris?

Date: October 20, 1997

Many people have experienced compilation problems on Solaris, with the compiler typically complaining about tm_zone or TopFrame. The Solaris section of our Compiling sendmail page explains these.

5.1.6) How does 8.*x* compare to 8.*x*+Sun?

Date: August 29, 1998

With a Vn/Berkeley config file, they're identical. There are a few minor differences between 8.*x* with a Vn/Berkeley config file and 8.*x* +Sun with the same config file, but the V line changed to Vn/Sun. But most differences are the backwards compatibility hacks needed for 8.*x*+Sun to support old V1/Sun config files.

There are three web pages which discuss these in detail: Berkeley migration (from SMI-8.6 to 8.X), Sun migration (from SMI-8.6 to 8.X+Sun), and Differences (five sections comparing and contrasting config files and binaries).

5.2) IBM AIX

5.2.1) The system resource controller always reports sendmail as "inoperative." What's wrong?

Date: July 5, 1996

When I use version 8 sendmail on an IBM RS/6000 running AIX, the system resource controller always reports sendmail as "inoperative," even though it's actually running. What's wrong?

When running as a daemon, sendmail detaches from its parent process, fooling the SRC into thinking that sendmail has exited. To fix this, issue the commands

```
kill `head -1 /etc/sendmail.pid`
chssys -s sendmail -f 9 -n 15 -S -a "-d99.100"
# use "-d0.1" in sendmail 8.6.x
startsrc -s sendmail -a "-bd -q30m"
# your sendmail args may vary
```

Now the SRC should report the correct status of sendmail. If you are using version 8.6.*x*, use "-d0.1" instead of "-d99.100" (the debug options changed somewhat in version 8.7). In 8.6.*x* a side-effect of the "-d0.1" option is that a few lines of debug output will be printed on the system console every time sendmail starts up. For more information, read up on the System Resource Controller, the lssrc command, and the chssys command in the online AIX documentation.

5.2.2) Why can't I use AIX to get e-mail to some sites?

Date: April 8, 1997

When I use IBM's sendmail on an IBM RS/6000 running AIX trying to get to certain sites, it seems that I can get to some of them and not others. What's wrong?

There are two possible problems here:

1. Your version of sendmail is not configured to recognize MX records in the DNS. Search through your sendmail.*cf* looking for "OK MX" or "OK ALL." Older configurations had this line commented out, and this will cause mail from you to some sites to fail (because those sites have MX records, but no A records in their DNS for the specific Fully Qualified Domain Name you're trying to mail to). For more information, see the comp.unix.aix FAQ, **ftp://rtfm.mit.edu/pub/usenet/news.answers/aix-faq/**.
2. There is a negative caching bug in AIX 3.2.5 with /usr/sbin/named executables that are less than 103000 bytes long. Ask your IBM representative

to give you PMP 3251, or the most recent patch that fixes this problem for your particular configuration and version of the OS.

5.2.3) Why can't I get sendmail 8.7.1 to use MX records with AIX 3.2.5?

Date: July 5, 1996

IBM, in their infinite wisdom, provided a header file that would easily miscompile. This resulted in the struct{} for the DNS query to be mis-allocated, and MX processing would barf.

- **Fix 1** Upgrade to 8.7.5—this has a code fix for this problem.
- **Fix 2** Install the BIND 4.9.4 libraries and include files and tweak the Makefile.AIX to use them—I **think** these Get It Right (if not, at least it'll die during compile rather than failing weirdly at runtime).
- **Fix 3** Hack Makefile.AIX to pass a -DBIT_ZERO_ON_LEFT to cause the headers to use the right #ifdefs.

6. ADDITIONAL INFORMATION SOURCES

Date: April 8, 1997
Updated: April 14, 1999

This probably isn't in strict RFC1807 format, but I'm getting closer. Unfortunately, the format detailed in RFC1807 was never intended to be used in this fashion, so I'm doing a bit of square-peg fitting into round holes.

Note that the publisher IDS that I've assigned should not be misconstrued to imply that I have actually published all these documents, it's just that I need some sort of reasonable entry for the RFC1807 "ID" field, and in lieu of information to the contrary indicating what the actual publishers have registered, I have assigned my own, independent, "third-party" IDs. Hopefully, the following bibliographic entries make it obvious who the real publishers of the various documents are.

6.1) Reference Material Devoted Exclusively to sendmail

BIB-VERSION:: CS-TR-v2.1

ID:: sendmail-faq//online/reference/1

ENTRY:: March 23, 1996

TYPE:: Reference manual, available online in printable format

REVISION:: April 8, 1997; Updated "CONTACT" information

TITLE:: sendmail Installation and Operation Guide

AUTHOR:: Allman, Eric

CONTACT:: Eric Allman **eric@sendmail.ORG**

DATE:: November 19, 1995

PAGES:: 69

RETRIEVAL:: Contents of manual is in doc/op/op.ps of sendmail source archive

KEYWORD:: version 8.7.5 sendmail

LANGUAGE:: English

NOTES:: {g | n}roff "me" macro format version is in doc/op/op.me

See: URL: **http://www.sendmail.org/**

ABSTRACT::

The documentation, written by Eric Allman himself, comes with the sendmail distribution. The file in doc/op/op.me (nroff "me" macro format) may have a different number of pages depending on the type of device it is printed on, etc.

Eric provides his free consulting in the form of continuing development on sendmail, and occasional posts to **comp.mail.sendmail**. Please don't be so rude as to ask him to provide further free consulting directly to you. If you (or your company) are willing to compensate him for his consulting time, he may be willing to listen. At the very least, you should make sure you've exhausted all other courses of action before resorting to adding another message to the thousands he gets per day. Check the sendmail home page at **http://www.sendmail.org/** for late-breaking updates and other useful information.

If you want to be notified regarding future updates to sendmail and other items of potential interest, you may want to subscribe to the sendmail-announce mailing list. Address your subscription requests to **majordomo@lists.sendmail.org** with "subscribe sendmail-announce" as the body of the message.

END:: sendmail-faq//online/reference/1

BIB-VERSION:: CS-TR-v2.1

ID:: sendmail-faq//book/ISBN/1-56592-222-0

ENTRY:: March 23, 1996

REVISION:: April 8, 1997; Updated entire entry re: 2nd Ed.

TYPE:: Reference book, hardcopy

TITLE:: sendmail

AUTHOR:: Costales, Bryan

AUTHOR:: Allman, Eric

CONTACT:: Bryan Costales **bcx@BCX.COM**
O'Reilly & Associates, Inc.
103 Morris Street, Suite A
Sebastapol, CA 95472
Order by phone: 800-998-9938 (US/Canada inquiries)
800-889-8969 (US/Canada credit card orders)
707-829-0515 (local/overseas)

DATE:: January, 1997

PAGES:: 1021

COPYRIGHT:: Copyright (c) 1997 O'Reilly & Associates, Inc. All rights reserved.

LANGUAGE:: English

NOTES:: See: URL: **http://www.ora.com/catalog/sendmail2/**

ABSTRACT::

The definitive reference for version 8 sendmail (specifically, version 8.8). If you can have only one book on the subject of sendmail, this one is it. Bryan provides his consulting to the world in the form of his book, unless you're willing to compensate him for his services as well. Like Eric, you should make sure you've exhausted all other courses of action before you spend any of his valuable time.

END:: sendmail-faq//book/ISBN/1-56592-222-0

BIB-VERSION:: CS-TR-v2.1

ID:: sendmail-faq//book/ISBN/1-55558-127-7

ENTRY:: March 23, 1996

TYPE:: Reference book, hardcopy

REVISION:: Sep 9, 1996; fixed typo

TITLE:: sendmail: Theory and Practice

AUTHOR:: Avolio, Frederick M.

AUTHOR:: Vixie, Paul A.

CONTACT:: Fred Avolio **fma@al.org**, Paul Vixie **vix@al.org**
Digital Press
225 Wildwood Avenue
Woburn, MA 01801, USA
Ordering Info: voice: 1-800-366-2665
fax: 1-800-446-6520

DATE:: 1994

PAGES:: 262

COPYRIGHT:: Copyright (c) by 1995 Butterworth-Heinemann

LANGUAGE:: English

NOTES:: See: URL: **http://www.vix.com/vix/smtap/**

ABSTRACT::

Centers more on IDA sendmail (at least partly because version 8 didn't exist when they began the book). Written more like a college sophomore- or junior-level textbook. While you'll probably never let the Costales book out of your grubby little hands (especially if you do much work with version 8 sendmail), this is a book you'll probably read once or maybe twice, learn some very valuable things, but then likely put on a shelf and not read or reference again (unless you have to write up a bibliographic entry for it). Makes a better introduction to sendmail for management types, especially if you don't want them getting their hands on too much "dangerous" technical information. Also a **lot** smaller and less imposing. If possible, I recommend getting both, but if you can only get one, get Costales—unless you're going to be working exclusively with IDA sendmail, in which case Avolio andVixie will probably be more useful.

Note that Paul Vixie is extremely busy working on further development of BIND, the Internet de facto standard program for serving the DNS, upon which all Internet services depend, mail being only one of them. Like Eric and Bryan, he's also very busy. Unless you're willing to compensate him for his services, please let him get real work done.

END:: sendmail-faq//book/ISBN/1-55558-127-7

BIB-VERSION:: CS-TR-v2.1

ID:: sendmail-faq//book/ISBN/1-56592-278-6

ENTRY:: April 14, 1999

TYPE:: Pocket size reference, hardcopy

TITLE:: sendmail Desktop Reference

AUTHOR:: Costales, Bryan

AUTHOR:: Allman, Eric

CONTACT:: Bryan Costales **bcx@BCX.COM**
O'Reilly & Associates, Inc.
103 Morris Street, Suite A
Sebastapol, CA 95472
Order by phone: 800-998-9938 (US/Canada inquiries)
800-889-8969 (US/Canada credit card orders)
707-829-0515 (local/overseas)

DATE:: June, 1997

PAGES:: 68

COPYRIGHT:: Copyright (c) 1997 O'Reilly & Associates, Inc. All rights reserved.

LANGUAGE:: English

NOTES:: See: URL: **http://www.ora.com/catalog/sendmailqr/**

ABSTRACT::

A companion to the sendmail book. This small guide fits in your pocket and saves you having to carry the thousand page book in your briefcase. For details or tutorial information, see the full sendmail book. There are sections on the config file, databases, and configuring with m4. There are extensive cross-references to the full sendmail book.

END:: sendmail-faq//book/ISBN/1-56592-278-6

6.2) Reference Material with Chapters or Sections on sendmail

BIB-VERSION:: CS-TR-v2.1

ID:: sendmail-faq//book/ISBN/0-13-151051-7

ENTRY:: March 23, 1996

TYPE:: Reference book, hardcopy

REVISION:: May 23, 1996; Updated abstract

TITLE:: Unix System Administration Handbook, Second Edition

AUTHOR:: Nemeth, Evi

AUTHOR:: Snyder, Garth

AUTHOR:: Seebass, Scott

AUTHOR:: Hein, Trent R.

CONTACT:: **sa-book@admin.com**
Prentice-Hall, Inc.
Upper Saddle River, New Jersey 07458

DATE:: January, 1995

PAGES:: 780

COPYRIGHT:: Copyright (c) 1995 by Prentice Hall PTR

LANGUAGE:: English

NOTES:: See: URL: **http://www.admin.com/**

ABSTRACT::

Still the best hands-on UNIX System Administration book around. Covers far more than just sendmail, but the 64 pages (pages 455-518 in the third printing) it does devote are very well written and quite useful. Also provides a version of Rob Kolstad's checksendmail script on the accompanying CD-ROM.

Note that Eric Allman and Marshall Kirk McKusick wrote the Foreword for the Second Edition. This should give you at least an inkling as to how essential this book is, even for experienced UNIX administrators.

END:: sendmail-faq//book/ISBN/0-13-151051-7

BIB-VERSION:: CS-TR-v2.1

ID:: sendmail-faq//book/ISBN/0-201-58629-0

ENTRY:: March 23, 1996

TYPE:: Reference book, hardcopy

REVISION:: March 27, 1996; Changed ID format to include ISBN, moved URL to NOTES field from OTHER_ACCESS field, also updated ABSTRACT

REVISION:: March 29, 1996; Updated ID, PAGES, COPYRIGHT, and ABSTRACT

TITLE:: Practical Internetworking With TCP/IP and UNIX

AUTHOR:: Carl-Mitchell, Smoot

AUTHOR:: Quarterman, John S.

CONTACT:: **tic@tic.com**
Addison-Wesley Publishing Company
Computer Science & Engineering Division
One Jacob Way
Reading, MA 01867
USA
Orders: voice: 800-822-6339 (USA)
fax: 617-942-1117

DATE:: 1993

PAGES:: 476

COPYRIGHT:: Copyright (c) 1993 by Addison-Wesley Publishing Company, Inc.

LANGUAGE:: English

NOTES:: See: URL: **http://heg-school.aw.com/cseng/authors/mitchell/ practical/practical.html**

ABSTRACT::

Devotes 50 pages (most of Chapter 8) to discussion of sendmail. As far as TCP/IP networking books go that also happen to discuss sendmail, it seems well-written and clear (better than I recall Hunt's book being), but rather dated in the face of books devoted to the topic and all the recent development activity in the sendmail community. Forget about the references, though. The newest sendmail-related reference list is dated 1983, ten years before the date on this book and most certainly wildly out-of-date now. There are other books written on the subject of Internetworking with TCP/IP (most notably Comer), but this particular book seems to have a unique mix of theory (if perhaps a bit dated) and practical advice. Other books tend to have lots of one or the other, or split their theory and nitty-gritty details into separate books in a series (like Comer).

Assuming that an update will be coming out soon, it probably deserves a place on the shelf of most System or Network Administrators, right next to *Internetworking with*

TCP/IP by Comer, *Managing Internet Information Services* by Liu, et. al., *DNS and BIND* by Albitz and Liu, *Unix System Administration* by Nemeth, et. al., and last, but certainly not least, *sendmail* by Costales. However, it deserves this place more because of the non-sendmail-related material, as opposed to what sendmail-related material there is.

END:: sendmail-faq//book/ISBN/0-201-58629-0

BIB-VERSION:: CS-TR-v2.1

ID:: sendmail-faq//book/ISBN/1-56592-322-7

ENTRY:: April 14, 1999

TYPE:: Reference book, hardcopy

REVISION:: April 8, 1997; Updated URL in NOTES section

TITLE:: TCP/IP Network Administration 2nd Edition

AUTHOR:: Hunt, Craig

CONTACT:: O'Reilly & Associates, Inc.
103 Morris Street, Suite A
Sebastapol, CA 95472
Order by phone: 800-998-9938 (US/Canada inquiries)
800-889-8969 (US/Canada credit card orders)
707-829-0515 (local/overseas)

DATE:: January, 1998

PAGES:: 630

LANGUAGE:: English

NOTES:: See: URL: **http://www.ora.com/catalog/tcp2/**

ABSTRACT::

Chapter 10 is devoted to sendmail. A very good treatment of sendmail in 50 pages and less daunting than the Costales book. If you only own one, of course make it the Costales book. Appendix E is a 50 page sendmail reference which covers compiling sendmail, sendmail options, sendmail macros and the sendmail K command. The introductory chapters of the book are helpful in understanding the big picture of network services.

END:: sendmail-faq//book/ISBN/1-56592-322-7

6.3) Reference Material on Subjects Related to sendmail

BIB-VERSION:: CS-TR-v2.1

ID:: sendmail-faq//book/ISBN/1-56592-512-2

ENTRY:: April 14, 1999

TYPE:: Reference book, hardcopy

REVISION:: April 14, 1999; Updated entire entry for 3rd Ed.

TITLE:: DNS and BIND 3rd Edition

AUTHOR:: Albitz, Paul

AUTHOR:: Liu, Cricket

CONTACT:: O'Reilly & Associates, Inc.
103 Morris Street, Suite A
Sebastapol, CA 95472
Order by phone: 800-998-9938 (US/Canada inquiries)
800-889-8969 (US/Canada credit card orders)
707-829-0515 (local/overseas)

DATE:: September, 1998

PAGES:: 502

COPYRIGHT:: Copyright (c) 1997 O'Reilly & Associates, Inc. All rights reserved.

LANGUAGE:: English

NOTES:: See: URL: **http://www.ora.com/catalog/dns3/**

ABSTRACT::

As definitive as Costales is on sendmail, this book is on the subject of the Domain Name System (DNS) and the most common server software for the DNS, namely BIND.

The Third Edition deals with the new 8.1.2 version of BIND as well as the older 4.9 versions. Wherever there is a difference in behavior of the versions, the book points out which version does what. Anyone still using the first edition should strongly consider replacing it now since the new features will be the basis for the next generation of name servers.

Since the sending of Internet mail is so very heavily dependent on the DNS, it obviously also belongs on the shelf of any Postmaster or System Administrator whose site does Internet e-mail. That means virtually every administrator of every site on the Internet.

END:: sendmail-faq//book/ISBN/1-56592-512-2

BIB-VERSION:: CS-TR-v2.1

ID:: sendmail-faq//book/ISBN/1-56592-153-4

ENTRY:: April 8, 1997

TYPE:: Reference book, hardcopy

TITLE:: Using & Managing UUCP

AUTHOR:: Ravin, Ed

AUTHOR:: O'Reilly, Tim

AUTHOR:: Dougherty, Dale

AUTHOR:: Todino, Grace

CONTACT:: O'Reilly & Associates, Inc.
103 Morris Street, Suite A
Sepastapol, CA 95472
Order by phone: 800-998-9938 (US/Canada inquiries)
800-889-8969 (US/Canada credit card orders)
707-829-0515 (local/overseas)

DATE:: September, 1996

PAGES:: 424

LANGUAGE:: English

NOTES:: See: URL: **http://www.ora.com/catalog/umuucp/**

ABSTRACT::

Replaces *Managing UUCP and Usenet* by Todino and O'Reilly as the definitive book for using, installing, and managing UUCP. The general assumption with version 8 sendmail is that virtually no one uses UUCP to send e-mail anymore, but if that assumption isn't true for you, then you probably need this book.

END:: sendmail-faq//book/ISBN/1-56592-153-4

6.4) World Wide Web Index/Resource Pages on sendmail

BIB-VERSION:: CS-TR-v2.1

ID:: sendmail-faq//online/index/10

ENTRY:: March 23, 1996

TYPE:: Online sendmail index

REVISION:: April 14, 1999; Updated to sendmail.org address

TITLE:: sendmail FAQ Support Page

AUTHOR:: Beck, John

CONTACT:: John Beck <**sendmail+faq@sendmail.org**>

OTHER_ACCESS:: URL: **http://www.sendmail.org/faq/**

LANGUAGE:: English

ABSTRACT::

Support Page for this FAQ.

END:: sendmail-faq//online/index/10

BIB-VERSION:: CS-TR-v2.1

ID:: sendmail-faq//online/index/17

ENTRY:: March 25, 1996

TYPE:: Online sendmail index

REVISION:: April 14, 1999; Updated to sendmail.org address

TITLE:: comp.mail.sendmail Most Frequently Asked Questions Support Page

AUTHOR:: Assman, Claus

CONTACT:: Claus Assmann **ca@sendmail.org**

OTHER_ACCESS:: URL: **http://www.sendmail.org/~ca/email/english.html**

LANGUAGE:: English

ABSTRACT::

Most Frequently Asked Questions on **comp.mail.sendmail** and their answers. Also has some links to a few other resources.

END:: sendmail-faq//online/index/17

BIB-VERSION:: CS-TR-v2.1

ID:: sendmail-faq//online/resources/22

ENTRY:: November 24, 1996

TITLE:: IICONS sendmail Resources

AUTHOR:: Caloca, Paul

CONTACT:: Paul Caloca **pcaloca@iicons.com**

COPYRIGHT:: Copyright (c) 1996 Paul Caloca. All Rights Reserved.

OTHER_ACCESS:: URL: **http://www.iicons.com/sendmail/index.html**

LANGUAGE:: English

ABSTRACT::

Provides information on how to compile sendmail and the NEWDB db.1.85 for Solaris 2. Also has a section on which Sun patches update Solaris 2 to BIND 4.9.3. Has pointers to some non-Sun/Solaris sendmail resources, especially including CERT Advisories related to sendmail.

END:: sendmail-faq//online/index/22

6.5) World Wide Web Index Pages and Other References on Internet E-Mail in General

BIB-VERSION:: CS-TR-v2.1

ID:: sendmail-faq//online/index/12

ENTRY:: March 23, 1996

TYPE:: Online general Internet e-mail index

REVISION:: March 27, 1996; moved URL from RETRIEVAL field to OTHER_ACCESS field

TITLE:: Internet Mail Consortium web site

CORP-AUTHOR:: Internet Mail Consortium

CONTACT:: **info@imc.org**

OTHER_ACCESS:: URL: **http://www.imc.org/**

LANGUAGE:: English

ABSTRACT::

If it has to do with Internet e-mail, you'll probably find it here, or a link to it from here. They have or have information on e-mail-related Usenet FAQs, RFCs, Internet Drafts (documents that are in the process of becoming RFCs), IETF Working Groups, security standards, and are running a few e-mail-related mailing lists. Tends to be focused on the standards issues. If you care about Internet e-mail, you should make it your duty in life to check this site frequently.

END:: sendmail-faq//online/index/12

BIB-VERSION:: CS-TR-v2.1

ID:: sendmail-faq//online/index/13

ENTRY:: March 23, 1996

TYPE:: Online general Internet e-mail index

REVISION:: August 20, 1996; Updated URL

TITLE:: Email References

AUTHOR:: Wohler, Bill

CONTACT:: Bill Wohler **wohler@worldtalk.com**

OTHER_ACCESS:: URL: **http://www.worldtalk.com/html/msg_resources/email_ref.html**

LANGUAGE:: English

ABSTRACT::

The most exhaustive index site I know of for Internet e-mail-related documents outside of the Internet Mail Consortium. Also has pointers to other organizations that relate to Internet e-mail, such as the Electronic Messaging Association and the European Electronic Messaging Association. Tends to be focused on the server and standards issues.

END:: sendmail-faq//online/index/13

BIB-VERSION:: CS-TR-v2.1

ID:: sendmail-faq//online/index/14

ENTRY:: March 23, 1996

TYPE:: Online general Internet e-mail index

REVISION:: June 28, 1996; added acronym for SMTPRD

TITLE:: SMTP Resources Directory (SMTPRD)

AUTHOR:: Salamon, Andras

AUTHOR:: Knowles, Brad

CONTACT:: Andras Salamon **smtprd@dns.net**

OTHER_ACCESS:: URL: **http://www.dns.net/smtprd/**

LANGUAGE:: English

ABSTRACT::

Another good index site, but still very much in the early phases of gestation. Based very heavily on the DNS Resources Directory, also by Andras Salamon. A well-rounded site, for the amount of material it covers so far.

END:: sendmail-faq//online/index/14

BIB-VERSION:: CS-TR-v2.1

ID:: sendmail-faq//online/index/15

ENTRY:: March 23, 1996

TYPE:: Online general Internet e-mail index

REVISION:: March 27, 1996; moved URL from RETRIEVAL field to OTHER_ACCESS field

TITLE:: E-Mail Web Resources

AUTHOR:: Wall, Matt

CONTACT:: Matt Wall **wall+@cmu.edu**

OTHER_ACCESS:: URL: **http://andrew2.andrew.cmu.edu/cyrus/email/email.html**

LANGUAGE:: English

ABSTRACT::

Another good index site, tends to be more focused on client-side and LAN e-mail packages. Also lists some e-mail services, which no one else that I've seen appears to have taken the time to catalog. Excellent side-by-side feature comparison of various MUAs and their compliance with various Internet protocols.

END:: sendmail-faq//online/index/15

6.6) Online Tutorials for sendmail

BIB-VERSION:: CS-TR-v2.1

ID:: sendmail-faq//online/tutorial/9

ENTRY:: March 23, 1996

TYPE:: Online sendmail tutorial

REVISION:: March 27, 1996; moved URL from RETRIEVAL field to OTHER_ACCESS field

REVISION:: August 29, 1998; Updated URL

TITLE:: sendmail V8: A (Smoother) Engine Powers Network Email

AUTHOR:: Reich, Richard

CONTACT:: Richard Reich **richard@reich.com**

DATE:: February 8, 1996

COPYRIGHT:: Copyright (c) 1995 The McGraw-Hill Companies, Inc. All Rights Reserved.

OTHER_ACCESS:: URL: **http://www.networkcomputing.com/unixworld/tutorial/008/008.txt.html**

LANGUAGE:: English

NOTES:: UnixWorld Online: Tutorial: Article No. 008

ABSTRACT::

Good technical introduction. Some useful references. Notably does not reference this FAQ as a place to get more information.

END:: sendmail-faq//online/article/9

BIB-VERSION:: CS-TR-v2.1

ID:: sendmail-faq//online/tutorial/16

ENTRY:: March 23, 1996

TYPE:: Online sendmail tutorial

REVISION:: March 27, 1996; moved URL from RETRIEVAL field to OTHER_ACCESS field

TITLE:: sendmail—Care and Feeding

AUTHOR:: Quinton, Reg

CONTACT:: Reg Quinton **reggers@julian.uwo.ca**
Computing and Communications Services
The University of Western Ontario
London, Ontario N6A 5B7
Canada

DATE:: March 24, 1992

OTHER_ACCESS:: URL: **ftp://ftp.sterling.com/mail/sendmail/uwo-course/sendmail.txt.Z**

LANGUAGE:: English

NOTES:: Postscript version also available. See **ftp://ftp.sterling.com/mail/ sendmail/uwo-course/sendmail.ps.Z**.

ABSTRACT::

Dated. Only here until I find better.

END:: sendmail-faq//online/tutorial/16

BIB-VERSION:: CS-TR-v2.1

ID:: sendmail-faq//online/tutorial/21

ENTRY:: March 27, 1996

TYPE:: Online sendmail tutorial

REVISION:: August 29, 1998; Updated URL

TITLE:: Explosion in a Punctuation Factory

AUTHOR:: Bryan Costales

CONTACT:: Becca Thomas **editor@unixworld.com**

DATE:: January 1994

COPYRIGHT:: Copyright (c) 1995 The McGraw-Hill Companies, Inc. All Rights Reserved.

OTHER_ACCESS:: URL: **http://www.networkcomputing.com/unixworld/tutorial/01/01.txt.html**

LANGUAGE:: English

ABSTRACT::

Good introduction on how sendmail re-write rules work.

END:: sendmail-faq//online/article/21

6.7) Online Archives of Mailing Lists and Usenet Newsgroups Relating to Internet E-Mail

BIB-VERSION:: CS-TR-v2.1

ID:: sendmail-faq//online/archive/18

ENTRY:: March 25, 1996

TYPE:: Online Usenet newsgroup archive

REVISION:: March 27, 1996; moved URL from RETRIEVAL field to OTHER_ACCESS field

TITLE:: DejaNews

OTHER_ACCESS:: URL: **http://www.dejanews.com**

LANGUAGE:: English

NOTES:: Archives/indexes only Usenet news.

ABSTRACT::

The first, and still most focused, Usenet news archive/index site. Others archive/index news as well as other things, but none that I've seen do it better.

Go to "Power Search" then "Query Filter" if you wish to restrict the newsgroups you search on to something like just **comp.mail.sendmail** and not all newsgroups.

END:: sendmail-faq//online/archive/18

BIB-VERSION:: CS-TR-v2.1

ID:: sendmail-faq//online/archive/19

ENTRY:: March 25, 1996

TYPE:: Online Usenet newsgroup archive

REVISION:: March 27, 1996; moved URL from RETRIEVAL field to OTHER_ACCESS field

TITLE:: AltaVista

OTHER_ACCESS:: URL: **http://www.altavista.digital.com**

LANGUAGE:: English

NOTES:: Archives/indexes Usenet news and World Wide Web pages

ABSTRACT::

One of the leading indexes of World Wide Web pages, and their archive/index of Usenet news is obviously secondary.

END:: sendmail-faq//online/archive/19

BIB-VERSION:: CS-TR-v2.1

ID:: sendmail-faq//online/archive/20

ENTRY:: March 25, 1996

TYPE:: Online Usenet newsgroup archive

REVISION:: April 8, 1997; additional information based on experience

TITLE:: InReference

OTHER_ACCESS:: URL: **http://www.reference.com**

LANGUAGE:: English

ABSTRACT::

Had promised to be the best Usenet news/publicly accessible mailing list index/archive site in the world. The best minds that were working on the project have since left, and the difference is visible. You'll probably be happier with DejaNews instead.

END:: sendmail-faq//online/archive/20

7. THANKS!

Special thanks to:

Eric Allman

The core of the material here comes from his FAQ for version 8.6.9 sendmail. I couldn't even have gotten started were it not for him. And if he hadn't written sendmail, there obviously wouldn't even be a FAQ. Heck, there might not even be an Internet.

Paul Southworth

Provides FAQ posting services, useful comments on various sections, and the mailclient-faq. I couldn't have kept doing this were it not for his help.

Ed Ravin

Virtually all the material regarding the use of sendmail on AIX is his, and most of it has been carried over verbatim.

Thanks also to: Neil Hoggarth, Andras Salamon, Johan Svensson, Christopher X. Candreva, Bill Wohler, Matthew Wall, Henry W. Farkas, Claus Assmann, Curt Sampson, Rebecca Lasher, Jim Davis, David Keegel, Betty Lee, Alain Durand, Walter Schweizer, Christophe Wolfhugel, Al Gilman, Valdis Kletnieks, John Gardiner Myers, Paul DuBois, Adam Bentley, Dave Sill, Dave Wreski, Paul Caloca, Eamonn Coleman, Michael Fuhr, Betty Lee, Derrell Lipman, Era Eriksson, Richard Troxel, and the readers and posters of **comp.mail.sendmail**.

INDEX

Symbols

A

B

C

D

E

F

G

H

I

J

K

L

M

N

O

▼ P

Q

R

S

T

 U

V

W

X

Y

Z

NO POSTAGE
NECESSARY
IF MAILED
IN THE
UNITED STATES

BUSINESS REPLY MAIL

FIRST-CLASS MAIL PERMIT NO 397 OAKLAND CA

POSTAGE WILL BE PAID BY ADDRESSEE

SENDMAIL INC
6603 SHELLMOUND ST
EMERYVILLE CA 94608-9752

ABOUT THE CD...

The CD that accompanies this book contains a variety of tools designed to help you with the Windows 2000 and UNIX integration process for the computers and systems that you manage. Some of these tools are commercial products, others are shareware, and some are freeware:

Directory	**Contents**
Acrobat	PDF file reader
Apache	The UNIX-based Apache web server
ISC	Internet news
Sendmail	Sendmail Port for Windows NT
	User guide and installation instructions
Hummingbird	Various programs and documents

NOTE: As we prepared this book for publication, Microsoft released Windows 2000. Because some of the companies whose products are included on the CD are still developing and testing versions of their products for use with Windows 2000, you may want to contact the individual software vendors to get the most current versions for your use.

WARNING: BEFORE OPENING THE DISC PACKAGE, CAREFULLY READ THE TERMS AND CONDITIONS OF THE FOLLOWING COPYRIGHT STATEMENT AND LIMITED CD-ROM WARRANTY.

Copyright Statement

This software is protected by both United States copyright law and international copyright treaty provision. Except as noted in the contents of the CD-ROM, you must treat this software just like a book. However, you may copy it into a computer to be used and you may make archival copies of the software for the sole purpose of backing up the software and protecting your investment from loss. By saying, "just like a book," The McGraw-Hill Companies, Inc. ("Osborne/McGraw-Hill") means, for example, that this software may be used by any number of people and may be freely moved from one computer location to another, so long as there is no possibility of its being used at one location or on one computer while it is being used at another. Just as a book cannot be read by two different people in two different places at the same time, neither can the software be used by two different people in two different places at the same time.

Limited Warranty

Osborne/McGraw-Hill warrants the physical compact disc enclosed herein to be free of defects in materials and workmanship for a period of sixty days from the purchase date. If the CD included in your book has defects in materials or workmanship, please call McGraw-Hill at 1-800-217-0059, 9am to 5pm, Monday through Friday, Eastern Standard Time, and McGraw-Hill will replace the defective disc.

The entire and exclusive liability and remedy for breach of this Limited Warranty shall be limited to replacement of the defective disc, and shall not include or extend to any claim for or right to cover any other damages, including but not limited to, loss of profit, data, or use of the software, or special incidental, or consequential damages or other similar claims, even if Osborne/McGraw-Hill has been specifically advised of the possibility of such damages. In no event will Osborne/McGraw-Hill's liability for any damages to you or any other person ever exceed the lower of the suggested list price or actual price paid for the license to use the software, regardless of any form of the claim.

OSBORNE/McGRAW-HILL SPECIFICALLY DISCLAIMS ALL OTHER WARRANTIES, EXPRESS OR IMPLIED, INCLUDING BUT NOT LIMITED TO, ANY IMPLIED WARRANTY OF MERCHANTABILITY OR FITNESS FOR A PARTICULAR PURPOSE. Specifically, Osborne/McGraw-Hill makes no representation or warranty that the software is fit for any particular purpose, and any implied warranty of merchantability is limited to the sixty-day duration of the Limited Warranty covering the physical disc only (and not the software), and is otherwise expressly and specifically disclaimed.

This limited warranty gives you specific legal rights; you may have others which may vary from state to state. Some states do not allow the exclusion of incidental or consequential damages, or the limitation on how long an implied warranty lasts, so some of the above may not apply to you.

This agreement constitutes the entire agreement between the parties relating to use of the Product. The terms of any purchase order shall have no effect on the terms of this Agreement. Failure of Osborne/McGraw-Hill to insist at any time on strict compliance with this Agreement shall not constitute a waiver of any rights under this Agreement. This Agreement shall be construed and governed in accordance with the laws of New York. If any provision of this Agreement is held to be contrary to law, that provision will be enforced to the maximum extent permissible, and the remaining provisions will remain in force and effect.

NO TECHNICAL SUPPORT IS PROVIDED WITH THIS CD-ROM.